D0217147

DATE DUE

UPI

PRINTED IN U.S.A.

UNDERSTANDING CONFUCIAN PHILOSOPHY

Classical and Sung-Ming

Shu-hsien Liu

Westport, Connecticut
London

FRAMINGHAM STATE COLLEGE
FRAMINGHAM, MA

The Library of Congress has cataloged the hardcover edition as follows:

Liu, Shu-hsien, 1934–
    Understanding Confucian philosophy : classical and Sung-Ming / Shu-hsien Liu.
        p.   cm.—(Contributions in philosophy, ISSN 0084–926X : no. 61)
    Includes bibliographical references and index.
    ISBN 0–313–30154–9 (alk. paper)
    1. Confucianism.   I. Title.   II. Series.
B127.C65.L59   1998
181'.112—dc21   97–52294

British Library Cataloguing in Publication Data is available.

Copyright © 1998 by Shu-hsien Liu

All rights reserved. No portion of this book may be
reproduced, by any process or technique, without the
express written consent of the publisher.

A hardcover edition of *Understanding Confucian Philosophy* is available from Greenwood
Press, an imprint of Greenwood Publishing Group, Inc. (Contributions in Philosophy,
Number 61; ISBN 0–313–30154–9).

Library of Congress Catalog Card Number: 97–52294
ISBN: 0–275–96317–9

First published in 1998

Praeger Publishers, 88 Post Road West, Westport, CT 06881
An imprint of Greenwood Publishing Group, Inc.

Printed in the United States of America

The paper used in this book complies with the
Permanent Paper Standard issued by the National
Information Standards Organization (Z39.48–1984).

10 9 8 7 6 5 4 3 2 1

B
127
C65
L59
1998

Copyright Acknowledgments

The author and publisher gratefully acknowledge permission for use of the following material:

Liu, Shu-hsien. "The Confucian Approach to the Problem of Transcendence and Immanence." *Philosophy East and West* 22, no. 1 (January 1972): 45–52.

Liu, Shu-hsien. "On the Functional Unity of the Four Dimensions of Thought in the Book of Changes." *Journal of Chinese Philosophy* 17, no. 3 (September 1990): 359–385.

Liu, Shu-hsien. "The Function of the Mind in Chu Hsi's Philosophy." *Journal of Chinese Philosophy* 5, no. 2 (June 1978): 195–208.

Liu, Shu-hsien. "How Idealistic is Wang Yang-ming?" *Journal of Chinese Philosophy* 10, no. 2 (June 1983): 147–168.

Liu, Shu-hsien. "On Chu Hsi as an Important Source for the Development of the Philosophy of Wang Yang-ming." *Journal of Chinese Philosophy* 11, no. 1 (March 1984): 83–107.

Liu, Shu-hsien. "Mencius," prepared for a spiritual encyclopedia edited by Wei-ming Tu, Center for the Study of World Religions, Harvard University.

Liu, Shu-hsien. "The Characteristics and Contemporary Significance of Neo-Confucian Philosophy." *Bulletin of the Chinese Philosophical Association* 3 (1985): 131–150.

Liu, Shu-hsien. "On the Confucian Ideal of 'Sageliness Within and Kingliness Without.' " *Proceedings of the International Symposium on Confucianism and the Modern World* (1988): 401–422.

Liu, Shu-hsien. "Confucius." In *Chinese Thought*, edited by Donald H. Bishop. Delhi, India: Motilal Banarsidass, 1985.

Liu, Shu-hsien. "On Chu Hsi's Search for Equilibrium and Harmony." In *Harmony and Strife: Contemporary Perspectives, East & West* edited by Shu-hsien Liu and Robert E. Allinson. Hong Kong: The Chinese University of Hong Kong, 1988: 249–270. Reprinted with permission of The Chinese University Press.

Liu, Shu-hsien. "Some Reflections on Mencius' Views of Mind-Heart and Human Nature." *Philosophy East & West* 46, no. 2 (April 1996): 143–164.

Liu, Shu-hsien. "The Problem of Orthodoxy in Chu Hsi's Philosophy." In *Chu Hsi and Neo-Confucianism*, edited by Wing-tsit Chan. Honolulu: University of Hawaii Press, 1986.

Liu, Shu-hsien. "The Contemporary Significance of Chinese Philosophy." *Journal of Chinese Philosophy* 13, no. 2 (June 1986).

Liu, Shu-hsien. "The Use of Analogy and Symbolism in Traditional Chinese Philosophy." *Journal of Chinese Philosophy* 1, nos. 3, 4 (June–September 1974): 313–338.

Liu, Shu-hsien. "On Chu Hsi's Understanding of Hsing (Nature)." *Tsing-hua Journal of Chinese Studies*, New Series, 17, nos. 1, 2 (December 1985): 127–148.

Chan, Wing-tsit. *A Source Book in Chinese Philosophy*. Copyright © 1963, 1991 by Princeton University Press. Reprinted by permission of Princeton University Press.

Fung, Yu-lan. *A History of Chinese Philosophy*. Copyright © 1952, 1953 by Princeton University Press. Reprinted by permission of Princeton University Press.

Excerpts from *Instructions for Practical Living*, translated by Wing-tsit Chan. Copyright © 1985 by Columbia University Press. Reprinted with permission of the publisher.

Excerpts from Huang Tsung-hsi in *The Records of Ming Scholars: A Selected Translation*, edited by Julia Ching. Copyright © 1987 by the University of Hawaii Press.

Excerpts from *Chinese Philosophy: Its Spirit and Its Development* by Thomé H. Fang. Copyright © 1981 by Linking Publishing Co.

Contents

Preface

Confucianism certainly has not predominated Chinese thought in the twentieth century. Owing to the impact of the West, in order to survive, China had no choice but to learn from the West. However, the liberal tradition of the West failed to take hold in Chinese soil. Instead, zealous young souls turned to more and more radical forms of thought, finally succumbing to Marxist and Leninist ideologies. The result found its climax in the founding of the People's Republic of China in 1949. During the cultural movement of 1919, anti-traditionalists shouted: "Down with the Confucian shop!" Anti-Confucian sentiment continued during the Cultural Revolution from the mid-1960s to the mid-1970s. During this vigorous anti-Confucian campaign, past traditions were destroyed at will.

However, a handful of refugee scholars scattered in Taiwan, Hong Kong, and overseas refused to give up on Confucianism. After a deep, soul-searching examination of the tradition, they were convinced that even though it needed to transform itself to meet the challenges of the modern world, valuable insights contained in the tradition had to be preserved at all costs. It was largely through their efforts that the spirit of the tradition has survived, and great scholarship has been shown in their works published in the last fifty years.

Recent years, however, have witnessed a dramatic turnaround in the East. In 1986, Mainland China designated Contemporary Neo-Confucians as a concentrated area for national research. Since then, selections and studies of their works have been published at an astonishing speed. In the West, however, no work presently exists that studies the tradition from a contemporary Neo-Confucian perspective. This book, which synthesizes various articles I have written over a twenty-five-year period, and also adds new materials (approximately one-third of the book), fills that gap.

Acknowledgments

First, I would like to pay tribute to my deceased friend Charles Wei-hsun Fu, whose push and encouragement made it possible for me to complete this manuscript. At Greenwood Publishing Group, I would like to acknowledge Alicia S. Merritt, Nina Pearlstein, Frank J. Hoffman, Elisabetta Linton, Marcia Goldstein, Christina Lester, and Susan Badger. I am also grateful to the *Journal of Chinese Philosophy*, edited by Chung-ying Cheng, *Philosophy East and West*, edited by Roger Ames, and the other presses and journals who allowed me to reprint my previously published articles, in part or in whole, in the present volume.

To bring a contemporary Neo-Confucian perspective into focus, not many secondary sources are used. My favorite translator of Chinese philosophy materials is Wing-tsit Chan; most quotations are from his *A Source Book in Chinese Philosophy*. I have also used existing translations by other scholars but unified, to some extent, spelling and the use of terms; where it is not specified, the translations are mine.

I am grateful to The Chinese University of Hong Kong, which granted me sabbatical leave, and to the Institute of Chinese Literature and Philosophy, Academia Sinica, Taipei, which supported the project and provided the right working environment. I also want to thank Mary Evelyn Tucker, Robert Cummings Neville, and John Berthrong, friends who have lent their moral support to the materialization of the project.

And I am grateful for the support of my family. My wife An-yuan Liu has been a lifetime staunch supporter and has provided a valuable critique of my ideas. Dr. James Hou-fu, my elder son, coauthored with me an article entitled

''Modernism, Post-modernism, and Neo-Confucian Thinking: A Critical History of Paradigm Shifts and Values in Psychology.'' The article, which was presented at the Inaugural Conference of the Asian Association of Social Psychology held at The Chinese University of Hong Kong, June 21–23, 1995, is published in *New Ideas in Psychology* 15, no. 2 (1997): 159–177. Jeffrey Chieh-fu (M.F.A.), my younger son, read through Part I of the manuscript. And I am especially grateful to my father, Master Ching-chuang, for initiating me into the world of Confucian philosophy.

Part I

Classical Confucian Philosophy

1

Background for the Emergence of Confucian Philosophy

China has an ancient civilization that may not be as old as the Egyptian and Babylonian civilizations but is certainly older than the Greek civilization, the cradle of Western philosophy. The amazing thing about this civilization is that it has survived many vicissitudes and is still vigorously alive today, while the glories of Greece and Rome have long since become part of the history of the past. As Japan and the so-called four minidragons—Korea, Taiwan, Hong Kong, and Singapore—also share a Confucian background, the current view is that there must be valuable ingredients in this tradition that are worth studying. The present volume proposes to study the meaning and spirit of the Confucian tradition of philosophy that has shaped the ways of thinking of the Chinese people for over 2,000 years and exerted profound influence in East Asia.

The Confucian tradition does not start with Confucius. The term *Confucianism* is misleading, as it seems to suggest that it was Confucius who started the whole tradition. But this was not the case, as the great master himself said in *The Analects*: "I transmit but do not create. I believe in and love the ancients."[1] Even though this statement may be subject to different interpretations, and Confucius may still be regarded as a creative genius of some sort, as we shall see in subsequent discussions, there remains little doubt that Confucius had inherited a rich tradition from the past by "going over the old so as to find out what is new."[2] *Ju-chia* was the Chinese term for Confucianism. According to the traditional account by Liu Hsin (ca. 46 B.C.–A.D. 23) in the Han dynasty:

> The members of the *Ju* school had their origin in the Ministry of Education. . . . This school delighted in the study of the *Liu Yi* [the Six Classics

or six liberal arts] and paid attention to matters concerning human-heartedness and righteousness. They regarded Yao and Shun [two ancient sage-emperors supposed to have lived in the twenty-fourth and twenty-third centuries B.C.] as the ancestors of their school, and King Wen [1120?–1108? B.C., of the Chou dynasty] and King Wu [son of King Wen] as brilliant exemplars. To give authority to their teaching, they honored Chung-ni [Confucius] as an exalted teacher. Their teaching is the highest truth. "That which is admired must be tested." The glory of Yao and Shun, the prosperity of the dynasties of Yin and Chou, and the achievements of Chung-ni are the results discovered by testing their teaching.[3]

Liu Hsin's theory of the origin of Confucianism in the ancient Ministry of Education may be contested, but that Confucianism has to be traced back to sources beyond Confucius is a point that can hardly be disputed.

However, any attempt that ventures to go beyond Confucius in order to recover a true picture of the ancient past seems to be doomed to failure. Even the great master himself keenly felt the difficulty in talking about the past:

I am able to discourse on the rites of the Hsia, but the state of Ch'i does not furnish sufficient supporting evidence; I am able to discourse on the rites of the Yin, but the state of Sung does not furnish sufficient supporting evidence. This is because there are not enough records and men of erudition. Otherwise I would be able to support what I say with evidence.[4]

Since we live about 2,500 years after Confucius, it is easy to see how difficult it would be for us to talk about the ancient dynasties and their civilizations. Moreover, with the progress made in modern archaeological science, we have to face the further difficulty of a vast discrepancy between the legendary account of the ancient past uncritically accepted by tradition and the picture of ancient history reconstructed from the items unearthed by archaeologists.

Let us first give the legendary account of the ancient past, since this account was handed down to us generation after generation without any question until it was challenged by recent historical studies under the impact of Western historiographical studies.

According to the traditional account, P'an Ku created the present universe by separating Heaven and Earth. He was followed successively by the Emperors of Heaven, the Emperors of Earth, and the Emperors of Humanity. Later there appeared the so-called Three Sovereigns and Five Emperors. There are different accounts of who they are. Let us simplify the matter by taking Fu Hsi, Shen Nung, and Huang Ti as the Three Sovereigns; and Chuan Hsiu, K'u, Yao, Shun, and Yü as the Five Emperors.

P'an Ku and the Emperors of Heaven, Earth, and Humanity are purely mythical figures. Fu Hsi and Shen Nung are semimythical figures, sometimes portrayed as having serpent bodies and human heads, whereas Huang Ti, the Yellow

Emperor, is a human ruler, from whom most of the subsequent kings and aristocrats claimed descent. The Three Sovereigns were all regarded as the cultural heroes of the Chinese civilization. Fu Hsi was credited with the creation of a system of natural symbolism that was instrumental to the invention of many important arts and crafts; this system of symbolism was further developed in the Confucian classic *I Ching* (*Book of Changes*). He was also regarded as the patron of hunting and animal husbandry. Shen Nung was believed to have taught people how to farm. He was the patron of agriculture and medicine. Huang Ti was the earliest ruler recognized, by the great historian in the Han dynasty Ssu-ma Ch'ien, who wrote the first general history of China in the first century B.C. Huang Ti was depicted as the founder-hero of the Chinese civilization. Almost all the important cultural inventions as well as institutions were traced back to either him or his associates. These legends about the Three Sovereigns certainly contain idealized pictures of the past.

The legendary stories about the Five Emperors became even more humanized in character. Of the Five Emperors, the two most important figures are Yao and Shun, who as sage-emperors set up the ideal of a ruler for the Confucian tradition. Yao abdicated and gave up his throne to an able and virtuous commoner, Shun, a farmer as well as a filial son. Shun likewise abdicated and passed the empire to Yü, rejecting his own son as unsuitable. Yü merited the choice by solving the problem of floods at the time not by building dams, but by guiding waters into small rivers. Yü also intended to pass on his responsibilities to I, his minister, but the people chose his son Ch'i over I. This was the beginning of the first dynasty, Hsia, as recorded in Chinese history. Apparently, from a Confucian point of view, *shan-jang*, or abdication or nonhereditary selection, is held to be a higher ideal than the dynasty form based upon hereditary succession that was practiced in later times.

The Hsia dynasty lasted about 400 years, until 1557 B.C., under seventeen sovereigns, according to the *Chronology of the Bamboo Books*. The last ruler of the dynasty, Chieh, was a tyrant. He was defeated and dethroned by T'ang, who founded a new dynasty, the Shang, sometimes also called the Yin dynasty. His successors reigned over China for about 600 years until Yin was replaced by the Chou dynasty. The last ruler of the Shang dynasty, Chou Hsin, also a tyrant, was disliked by the people and hence lost the Mandate of Heaven that was passed on to the Chou rulers. The Chou dynasty lasted about 800 years. So ends the succession of Three Dynasties in ancient Chinese history accepted by tradition ever since written accounts began recording history in China.

If the tradition were correct, then China would have more than 5,000 years of cultural history. But some modern scholars in the twentieth century hold a strong skeptical attitude toward the traditional account. The historical documents about the ancient sage-emperors contained in the *Shu Ching* (*Book of History*) were proved to be no earlier than the Chou dynasty. Yü was considered a mythical figure, and he was transformed into a human king only later in the Chou dynasty. The legends about Yao and Shun appeared to be even later fabrications. In short, the more ancient the sage-emperors were supposed to be, the more recently they had entered into the minds of the Chinese people. They were, rather, the idealizations of the later generations. Chou is believed to be the only historical dynasty in the ancient period. This modern view, in opposition to the traditional account, seems to have pushed too far to the other extreme of the spectrum.

Fortunately, at this point, modern archaeological discoveries have come to our aid. The excavations at An Yang, the site of an ancient Shang capital, uncovered a number of oracle bones with inscriptions, bronzes, jades, and other items. These findings have proved that Shang is, beyond a doubt, a historical dynasty. The record of the succession of Shang kings is authentic because their names are mentioned in the archaic inscriptions as deciphered by modern scholars. Even though excavations have thus far failed to identify a historical site for the Hsia dynasty, scholars are optimistic that a breakthrough is near. The atmosphere is now very different from the early twentieth century. Since the Cultural Revolution ended in the mid-1970s, there has been a revival of interest in traditional studies. Much important literature, including the silk scrolls in Han tombs, has been recovered.

Current opinion is that even though the traditional account of the Three Dynasties is not all accurate, the record is basically trustworthy. The Peking Man excavated at Chou K'ou Tian probably lived about 500,000 years ago. The discovery of the Peking Man rendered the postulate that the Chinese people were immigrants from the West unnecessary. After a long cultural gap, the neolithic cultures popped up. The Shang culture that followed the neolithic cultures has not only an advanced system of writing that is properly Chinese but also a brilliant bronze culture. It is simply unimaginable to believe that without any predecessors this culture could have developed to such an advanced stage all by itself. The Hsia legends must not be dismissed offhandedly as mere forgeries. We just have to be patient and wait for the results of future investigations.

Though whether the legendary stories are authentic history is the main concern for historians, the matter has only secondary importance for our purposes. A far more important question for us from a philosophical point of view is what the characteristics are of the tradition that has been inherited and further developed by Confucius and then by the Confucian tradition after him, as this tradition has played an important role in shaping the Chinese psyche as well as Chinese civilization. Some of the characteristics of this tradition may be described as follows:

First, it is an orthodoxy-conscious tradition. Once the orthodox order of succession of the Three Sovereigns, the Five Emperors, and the Three Dynasties (Hsia, Shang, and Chou) is accepted, questions regarding which ethnic group or which geographical area each of the rulers came from are largely ignored as long as the rulers are recognized as the legitimate rulers of the Middle Kingdom (*chung-kuo*). (The term may be of a later origin, however.)

Second, it is a culture-conscious tradition. Clearly, the orthodoxy was not determined by hereditary or racial factors but solely by cultural factors. Those who accepted the Chinese culture were regarded as Chinese; those who refused to accept the Chinese culture were labeled barbarians. Over time, more and more people joined the Chinese culture and became Chinese. The powerful state Ch'u in the South was the most conspicuous example. At first, the Ch'u people regarded themselves as different from the Chinese; but in the late Chou period, they were absorbed into the culture they had fought against for so long. Therefore, China has never been a "nation" in the modern sense of the term. China shows only a cultural unity that supersedes racial as well as geographical differences.

Third, it is a morally conscious tradition. As a rule, the Chinese were more proud of the moral superiority of their culture than of their technological advancement. According to this tradition, there are strong moral obligations between the rulers and the people. The sage-emperors not only have to show great competence in administrative affairs but also have to set moral examples for common people to follow. The Mandate of Heaven is never constant. If a ruler has lost his superior moral qualities, in principle he may be replaced by a better person. For their part, the people have to obey the authority of their leader and are loyal to him as long as he has love and works for their welfare. Ideally, all men must treat each other with human heartedness and righteousness. These ideas will be elaborated on later.

Fourth, it is a socially conscious tradition. The common people, left to their own devices, do not know how to create better living conditions. The rulers are supposed to fulfill this function. Most ancient sage-emperors were seen as cultural heroes credited with creating a number of inventions or establishing institutions that benefited humankind. If a ruler only cared for his own pleasure and interest, he was to be condemned; the evils of a tyrant would be denounced, and in principle, a revolution would be justified. The Chinese have created a human-centered culture; they have never pursued science for science's sake. But as long as science and technology serve to benefit people, the Chinese uphold scientific and technological improvement.

Finally, it is a this-worldly conscious tradition. Scholars have noted that there has never been a separate priest class in China. Historically, some explained this fact by pointing out that since only the emperor, that is, the son of Heaven, has the privilege of making sacrifices to Heaven and Earth, he is to be regarded not only as the secular ruler on Earth but also as the priest-magician who alone can communicate with Heaven. In contemporary times, China has moved beyond such an interpretation because it fails to identify the special characteristics of the Chinese culture. The primary duty of a priest in any civilization is to convey messages about the other world. In China, however, the other-worldly sentiment has never been very strong. Even if traces of belief in a personal God were discernible in ancient times, such belief is toned down in the subsequent development of the Chinese culture. Since Heaven sees according to what people see, and hears according to what people hear, the will of Heaven is known as long as the will of the people is known. Emphasis is put on how to achieve harmony in nature as well as in the human world. The ritual ceremonies are important as rites rather than as magic.

During Confucius's time the tradition was still in the process of becoming, but it was already consolidated to the extent that no one in the late Chou period seriously doubted its authenticity. In some sense, the Taoists, the Moists, and the Confucianists were all traditionists of some sort. But these different schools chose different figures as embodiments of their philosophical ideals. The Taoists revered Huang Ti; the Moists, Yü; and the Confucians, Yao and Shun. Even the iconoclast Legalists did not seriously doubt the general picture of the traditional account of ancient history. For example, Han Fei Tzu said:

> The dominant systems of learning of our time are Confucianism and Moism. . . . Both Confucius and Mo Tzu transmitted the doctrines of (sage-emperors) Yao and Shun. Although they differed in what they accepted or rejected, they each claimed to represent the true teachings of Yao and Shun. Now Yao and Shun cannot come to life again. Who is to determine the truth of Confucianism or Moism? It has been more than seven hundred years from the Yin and Chou times, and more than two thousand years from the times of Yao and Shun. If we are unable to determine the truth of Confucianism or Moism and yet wish to determine the doctrines of Yao and Shun of three thousand years ago, I believe it is impossible to be sure of anything.[5]

Apparently, Han Fei Tzu did not doubt the historical existence of Yao and Shun, but he argued that we know nothing definite about these ancient doctrines, since we are so removed from these ancient periods. The most important difference between the Legalists, on the one hand, and the Confucians and the Moists, on the other hand, lies in that the former held a modernist viewpoint, whereas the latter held a traditionist viewpoint. Again, let us quote from Han Fei Tzu:

> Indeed customs differ between the past and the present. Old and new things are to be applied differently. To try to govern the people of a chaotic age with benevolent and lenient measures is like to drive wild horses without reins or whips. This is the trouble of the lack of wisdom.[6]

Hence, Han Fei Tzu does not really care about knowing things in the past; according to him, the contemporary situation must apply contemporary measures. The faith and the method of the Confucians are entirely different. From the Confucian point of view, the contemporary situation may be different, but the principles employed by Yao and Shun to solve the problems of man are no different now from then. And it is history that provides guidance for our actions. The Way works everywhere, including here and now. Therefore, it is not difficult for us to know the ways of the ancient, even if we do not possess sufficient literature or evidence to talk about the past. Confucius said:

> The Yin built on the rites of the Hsia. What was added and what was omitted can be known. The Chou built on the rites of the Yin. What was added and what was omitted can be known. Should there be a successor to the Chou, even a hundred generations hence can be known.[7]

Thus, the apparently conservative and traditionist outlook of Confucians cannot be discounted as merely an uncritical blind faith in orthodoxy. There are certain rational grounds for them to justify their faith in the tradition. When Ch'in, the dynasty that adopted the Legalist view and strategy to unify China, was quickly overthrown, the Legalist ideology was condemned. Confucianism has been honored as the orthodoxy since the Han dynasty. Even though the Chinese tradition has appropriated many ingredients including the Taoist wisdom, the Yin-yang cosmology, even Legalist practice, the orthodox position of Confucianism has remained unchallenged. The tradition as portrayed by the Confucian scholars was accepted by the posterity without question for over 2,000 years. Thus, no matter whether it points to what actually happened or merely to an idealized picture of the past, there is no doubt that such a perception has become a formative factor of the Chinese civilization and also an important constituent element of the Chinese mentality.

So from this discussion, it is clear that the Confucian tradition did not start with Confucius; however, he was indeed the determining factor in consolidating this tradition. Furthermore, the ancients may be traditionalist, but they are not fundamentalist. Confucius has provided the most important clue to making such a transition. To gain better insight into the matter, it is necessary to examine the social and intellectual backgrounds in Confucius's time.

During the early Chou period, the feudal system was practiced. According to the traditional account, King Wu distributed the land to his brothers, near relatives, those who helped him gain the throne, and the descendants of the earlier dynasties. The people had to pay taxes to their lords, and they in turn had to pay tribute to the Chou emperor. In theory, the emperor had the power to summon the feudal lords to fight the barbarians from outside and to subdue disorder and treachery from within. However, in the late Chou period, the feudal system was in decline, and the emperor was unable to exercise his authority. In the so-called *Ch'un Ch'iu*, that is, the Spring and Autumn period (722–481 B.C.) when Confucius flourished, some feudal lords arose who paid nominal homage to the emperor but became the actual leaders of the Chinese confederation. Such a lord was called a *Pa* (hegemony). A kind of Chinese chivalry was practiced at the time. A *Pa* could summon an allied army to fend off the challenge of the barbarian forces. He could even replace the lord of a feudal state by sheer force or diplomatic maneuvering. But he was obliged to return power to the aristocrats of the state and chose one as the lord in order to continue the lineage. In the Warring States period that followed *Ch'un Ch'iu*, the situation became worse. The stronger states began to annex the weaker states. Finally, there were only seven contending for dominance in China. And it was Ch'in that unified China, destroyed the feudal system, and replaced it with a central bureaucratic government that characterized the Chinese political system for more than 2,000 years.

It was in the *Ch'un Ch'iu* and the Warring States period that the so-called hundred schools of thought contended with one another in China. According to the traditional account, Confucius was probably the first to break up the government's monopoly of knowledge and to begin teaching his own students. Later he was honored as the supreme teacher in Chinese history. In the past, the government had been in total control, written records were kept in the royal library, and the authors were, as a rule, anonymous. Whether Confucius actually wrote the first works of philosophy and history is a point hotly debated among scholars, but it is generally accepted that it was in the Spring and Autumn period that knowledge was allowed to spread to the people. This marked the beginning of a glorious age of philosophy in China. Why it began precisely then is a problem for serious scholarly study. Certainly great social, political, economic, and intellectual changes worked together to bring about the golden age of philosophy. From a philosophical point of view, however, suffice it to say that since this was an unprecedented age of disruption and disorder, talented people with concern were driven to reflect upon the situation, came up with different solutions, and as a result, formed different schools of thought.

Among the so-called hundred schools of thought, only six were philosophically significant: Confucianism, Taoism, Moism, Legalism, the Logical school, and the Yin-yang school.[8] The first three appeared earlier, and the latter three appeared somewhat later. The subsequent development of Chinese philosophy certainly reflected the choice made by the Chinese and, in some ways, revealed the fundamental characteristics and "prejudices" of the Chinese mentality.[9] We shall say a few words about each of these six schools of thought to provide the background to enter into the discussion of the Confucian tradition of philosophy.

The Taoists like Lao Tzu and Chuang Tzu were opposed to all civilizations and human institutions. They preached that we have to return to the primordial unity of nature. The *Tao*, that is, the Way, is beyond oppositions. For example, virtues and vices are relative terms; to elevate virtues, on the one hand, would surely produce vices, on the other hand. One has to learn to transcend all distinctions and to be one with nature. The Taoists would scoff at those Confucians who prize virtues over vices and want to seek employment in civil services. The Taoists much prefer to live their lives as hermits. Although it is impossible to carry out all the Taoist ideals, the Taoist trend has become a permanent ingredient in the Chinese civilization. It functions to counterbalance the overserious and all-too-human attitudes of the Confucians and has been an inexhaustible source of inspiration for the Chinese arts. If Confucianism represents yang, the male, positive, creative aspect, then Taoism represents yin, the female, negative, sustaining aspect in the Chinese civilization.

Both Moism and Legalism appear to be outgrowths of Confucianism. Mo Tzu was said to have studied Confucianism for a time, then decided to initiate his own school of thought. Mo Tzu advocated universal love and nonattack. In a sense, Moism seems to have taught a most traditionist point of view. Society is to be forged into a hierarchical order, with the most virtuous and able man as the ruler who can carry out the will of Heaven, nothing short of a supreme personal God. Moism also sanctified the virtue of self-sacrifice. It condemned rites and music as wasteful luxuries and maintained a strictly puritanic outlook on life. The Moists had a strict organization. Sometimes thousands of followers were sent out to defend a helpless, weak state by sacrificing their own lives. Except for a pragmatic methodology, Moism probably bore more resemblance to Christianity than any other school of Chinese thought. However, it soon became extinct. No trace of the school can be found after the Han dynasty until some of its ideas were revived in the late Ch'ing dynasty. So Chinese religious aspiration took a form notably different from Western development.

As for the Legalist school, the most important figure, Han Fei Tzu, had studied under Hsün Tzu, the Confucian philosopher excluded from the orthodox line by Sung Neo-Confucianism, who taught a naturalistic view of Heaven, insisted that human nature is evil, and maintained that rites are needed to rectify the original evil tendencies of man. Han Fei pushed even further and replaced rites with strict criminal laws. Han Fei was not convinced that any practical problems can be solved by setting up moral examples or by giving constant moral exhortations. The only thing a ruler can rely on is the so-called two handles in punishment and reward. The Legalists worked only for the benefit of the ruler, the one in a position to keep order in the world. The suppression of the aristocrats helped to strengthen the authority of the central government and destroyed the feudal system practiced in the Chou dynasty. The common people were supposed to obey orders from above and avoid contact with knowledge and sophistications. The application of Legalist ideas and strategy helped the Ch'in unify the whole of China, and yet the Legalist ideology fell into disgrace after the cruel Ch'in was rapidly overthrown by the Han. The success of Han rule was based on a shrewd combination of the Confucian system and Legalist practice. The fact that the Legalist practice had to turn underground was most unfortunate for the Chinese, as the condemnation of the Legalist ideology prevented the Chinese from developing the Western concept of law. Most Chinese would rather settle their problems outside a court of law through negotiation and compromise. They have no faith in a life governed by impersonal laws alone.

The Logical school may be better rendered as the school of Dialecticians. While a system of formal logic was never developed in China, a number of parallels may be drawn between the Chinese Dialecticians and the Greek Sophists. There were two main trends among the Chinese Dialecticians. Hui Shih emphasized unity at the expense of difference through sophistry; he declared that Heaven and Earth form one body and showed a tendency to obliterate all differences. Kung-sun Lung, on the contrary, emphasized difference at the expense of unity, as he argued that the white horse is not a horse. Both excelled at sophistry and were condemned by the Confucians and Moists alike, as they were seen as playing with words that confused the minds of the people. Both the condemnation of the Logical school and the identification of logic with sophistry produced most unfortunate effects on the Chinese culture. The development of logical thinking in China was curbed at its early stages of sophistication, and the Chinese have never been able to think in a purely deductive fashion.

The Yin-yang school was hardly an original school. It drew freely from both the Confucian and Taoist schools. It formulated a rather elaborate system of cosmology as well as a philosophy of history. The key figure in this school was Tsou Yen. Some of his ideas were absorbed in Han Confucianism and also in Taoism. From the very beginning, the Yin-yang school was eclectic in character and eventually lost its independent status.

Now we shall return to Confucianism. Confucius put great faith in man's potential, and he believed that the tradition was golden. But during his time, rulers could no longer apply the principles handed down by the sage-emperors that helped people develop their great potentials. Ideally, rulers should set good moral examples and teach rites and music to educate their subjects as civilized human beings. But the system of ruler as example had broken down. While severe punishment could prevent people from committing crimes, the doers would not have a true sense of shame. A sage-emperor would attract people to follow him with his exemplary actions; he would build a strong country by virtue rather than by force. Society under his guidance would be harmonious. People would know how to conduct themselves: the ruler and the subject, the father and the son, the man and the wife, all behaving properly. Only then can a community be seen as a civilized one.

In effect, Confucianism not only offered a way to solve problems at a time of disorder and disruption; it also furnished a faith—different from a religious faith—with a strong other-worldly sentiment. What Confucius committed to was an ultimate concern to settle one's body and soul in this life. As he said, "It is man who can make the Way great, not the Way that can make man great."[10] While such thought can certainly be traced back to a tradition that antedated Confucius, through Confucius it was further strengthened and solidified.

In the *Tso Chuan* (Tso's Commentary on the Spring and Autumn Annals), an anecdote was recorded as follows:

In the spring of the twenty-fourth year (of Duke Hsiang, 546 B.C.) Mu-shu (great officer of Lu) went to Chin. Fan Hsüan Tzu met him, saying, "The ancients had the saying 'Dead but immortal.' What does it mean?"

Before Mu-shu replied, Hsüan Tzu went on to say, "Anciently, the ancestors of our Fan family, from the time Emperor Shun and earlier, were the princes of T'ao and T'ang. In the time of Hsia, their ancestors were the lords of Yü-lung. In the time of Shang, they were the lords of Shih-wei. And in the beginning of Chou, they were the lords of T'ang and Tu. Now Chin has achieved the control of the great alliance and become the lords of Fan. Is this [unbroken heritage] what is meant by immortality?"

Mu-shu said, "According to what I have heard, this is called hereditary rank and emolument, not immortality. There was a former great officer of Lu by the name of Tsang Wen-chung. After his death his words remain established. This is what the ancient saying means. I have heard that the best course is to establish virtue, the next best is to establish achievement, and still the next best is to establish words. When these are not abandoned with time, it may be called immortality. As to the preservation of the family name and bestowment of membership in the clan branch in order to preserve ancestral sacrifices uninterrupted from age to age, no state is without these practices. But even those with great emolument cannot be said to be immortal."[11]

Wing-tsit Chan comments on this paragraph:

Chinese belief in the immortality of influence has not changed since ancient times, and is still the conviction of educated Chinese. It is remarkable that a simple and casual utterance made when Confucius was only a child of three should have remained an unalterable conviction for the Chinese for 2,500 years.[12]

But what makes the message behind such a casual utterance immortal was precisely the work of none other than the great master: Confucius himself.

It is clear that Confucius was molded by the tradition. But what is even more important is that he further molded the tradition. Throughout his life, he tried without success to persuade rulers to adopt his lofty ideals. Finally, he could do nothing but return to his home state Lu to end his career by teaching students, his political career ended. And he would never have dreamed that after his death his ideas would influence more people than any other person in history. Confucian teachings have become not only a legacy for the Chinese but ideas treasured by the whole world.

In closing this chapter, I would like to distinguish between three distinct but related meanings of the term *Confucianism*:[13]

1. *Spiritual Confucianism*. The tradition of great thinkers such as Confucius, Mencius, Ch'eng-Chu, and Lu-Wang that has been revived by contemporary Neo-Confucians as their ultimate commitment.

2. *Politicized Confucianism.* The tradition of Tung Chung-shu, P'an Ku, and others that served as the official ideology of the dynasties and had taken in ingredients from schools of thought such as Taoism, Legalism, and the Yin-yang school.

3. *Popular Confucianism.* Belief at the grassroots level that emphasizes concepts such as family values, diligence, and education and can hardly be separated from other beliefs in popular Buddhism and Taoism, including, for example, various kinds of superstitions.

Many debates on Confucianism are misguided precisely because the meaning of the term itself is unclear. It goes without saying that on the conceptual level the three must be kept distinct, even though in reality the three are intricately related to one another. Here our emphasis will be on the spiritual Confucian tradition. We shall first discuss ancient Confucian philosophy, followed by Sung-Ming Neo-Confucian philosophy.

NOTES

1. Wing-tsit Chan, trans. and comp., *A Source Book in Chinese Philosophy* (Princeton, N.J.: Princeton University Press, 1963), p. 31 (hereafter cited as Chan, *Source Book*).

2. Cf. ibid., p. 23.

3. Quoted from Fung Yu-lan, *A Short History of Chinese Philosophy* ed. Derk Bodde (New York: Free Press, 1948), pp. 32–33 hereafter cited as Fung, *Short History*.

4. D. C. Lau, trans., *Confucius: The Analects* (Hong Kong: Chinese University Press, 1983), p. 21 (hereafter cited as Lau, *Analects*).

5. Chan, *Source Book*, pp. 252–253.

6. Ibid., p. 257.

7. Lau, *Analects*, p. 17.

8. For the six schools of philosophy, cf. Chan, *Source Book*, pp. 14–270.

9. ''Prejudice'' from the perspective of philosophical hermeneutics is not necessarily a bad thing. It only points to the fact that there is always a certain preunderstanding in thinking through a certain tradition. It is impossible for us to get at something that is purely objective. The best we can do is to merge horizons. Cf. Hans Georg Gadamer, *Truth and Method* (London: Sheed & Ward, 1975).

10. Chan, *Source Book*, p. 44, with slight modification.

11. Ibid., p. 13, with slight modification.

12. Ibid.

13. Cf. Shu-hsien Liu, ''Reflections on World Peace through Peace among Religions—A Confucian Perspective,'' *Journal of Chinese Philosophy* 22, no. 2 (June 1995): 197.

2

Confucius

Even though Confucius did not originate Confucianism, he was the key figure in the formation and development of the Confucian tradition. He was born in the small state of Lu, which was located in what is now Shantung province. His family name was K'ung, given name Ch'iu, and Chung-ni was his literary name. *Confucius*, the name widely used in English-speaking countries, is the Latinized form of K'ung Fu-tzu, which means the grand master K'ung. His great-grandparents were immigrants from Sung, the descendant state of the Yin dynasty. His ancestors were aristocrats, but by the time he was born, the family had become poor. We know very little about his formal education; he seemed to be a self-taught man accumulating vast knowledge through all possible sources. As a young teacher not yet thirty years old, he went to the capital of Chou to study rites and ceremonies. He became a renowned teacher. Moral education was the backbone of his educational program; he also taught his disciples how to serve as officials on all levels in the government.

Confucius's primary goal, however, was not just teaching. He kept hoping some ruler might use him to realize his lofty political ideals. But he was disappointed. He only served for a short period in the state of Lu, then wandered thirteen years in various states without much accomplishment. Finally, he returned to Lu in the year 484 B.C. and spent his last years teaching there, dying in the same state where he was born, which happened to be the state of the descendants of the Duke of Chou. Confucius honored the Duke of Chou as his mentor, the man who laid the foundation of the glorious Chou system of rites and ceremonies that Confucius admired and vowed to restore in his own time.[1]

Most scholars today agree that *The Analects*, a collection of the master's sayings and conversations recorded by his disciples, is the best source that can be relied upon to study his ideas. However, *The Analects* is a most difficult book to read. Especially to a Western reader, the book may appear to be just a collection of the master's disconnected aphorisms. Not only does Confucius rarely give a definition of any term, but he also often pronounces his judgments without producing any arguments. At times, it seems that he contradicts himself.

It is here that a most significant difference between Western and Chinese philosophical approaches is found. In a typical Western philosophical treatise, sophisticated logic is used to construct a metaphysical system. In *The Analects*, however, there is neither sophisticated logic nor a grand metaphysical system. And strikingly enough, most traditional Chinese thinkers follow the example of Confucius. Some Western scholars tend to think that no systematic philosophy has ever been developed in the Chinese tradition and that Confucian philosophy is no more than practical ethics. However, if we do not limit ourselves to a narrow Western view of philosophy, which overemphasizes theoretical sophistication and system-building, then we would realize that the Chinese have developed a distinguished philosophical tradition of their own. Their primary concern is an existential, not a theoretical, one. What Confucius teaches is a situational ethics having to do with the ultimate commitment of our lives, an ethics impossible to be reduced to a set of abstract formulas. If there is any unity in Confucius's thought, it is a dynamic unity of life rather than the static unity of a theoretical system.

As rightly pointed out by traditional scholars, the only way to read *The Analects* with any profit is to recite the text over and over again until one can almost relive the life of the master. If one can find out the particular context in which a certain statement is made and, most important of all, can correlate his own moral experience with that of the master, then he may have a chance to be enlightened about the basic principles underlying *The Analects*. And it is only through a proper reading of the messages contained in the text that we can hope to reach an understanding of Confucius's ultimate commitment and philosophy.

Let us start with a paradoxical statement in *The Analects* that has puzzled the minds of scholars throughout the ages:

> Confucius said, "Shen, there is one thread that runs through my doctrines." Tseng Tzu said, "Yes." After Confucius had left, the disciples asked him, "What did he mean?" Tseng Tzu replied, "The Way of our Master is none other than conscientiousness (*chung*) and altruism (*shu*)."[2]

Although Confucius asserts that there is a central thread that runs through all his doctrines, nowhere in *The Analects* does he mention what that thread is; and Tseng Tzu's answer only further confuses us, as *chung* and *shu* are two things instead of one. This apparent paradox cannot be resolved until we have carefully studied the whole text of *The Analects* and grasped the spirit of Confucius's philosophy.

Even a casual reader of *The Analects* cannot fail to notice the central position of the concept of *jen* in Confucius's philosophy. *Jen* has been rendered into English in varied ways such as: *benevolence, man to manness, perfect virtue, human heartedness*, and *humanity*. Not only has *jen* been mentioned more often than any other virtue in the book, but all evidence points to the fact that it has been regarded as *the* virtue in Confucius's thought. Ceremonies and music are the two most important means of education for Confucius, and yet he declares: "If a man is not *jen*, what has he to do with ceremonies (*li*)? If he is not *jen*, what has he to do with music?"[3] Obviously, *jen* is being regarded as none other than the principle underlying the performances of ceremonies and music. Moreover, Confucius said:

> Wealth and honor are what every man desires. But if they have been obtained in violation of moral principles, they must not be kept. Poverty and humble position are what every man dislikes. But if they can be avoided only in violation of moral principles, they must not be avoided. If a superior man [*chün-tzu*] departs from humanity [*jen*], how can he fulfil that name? A superior man never abandons humanity even for the lapse of a single meal. In moments of haste, he acts according to it. In times of difficulty or confusion, he acts according to it.[4]

From this statement it is clear that the principle of *jen* has to be Confucius's ultimate commitment. But what is the exact meaning of *jen?* Here, again, the same difficulty that characterizes the reading of *The Analects* occurs. In the book, Confucius never even makes an attempt to offer a formal definition of *jen*; instead, he gives only various answers to questions about *jen* in different circumstances for students with different temperaments and with varying degrees of understanding. Since it is impractical to list all the statements about *jen* in *The Analects*, only a few key statements from the book are selected and subjected to analysis in order to uncover the layers of meaning contained in Confucius's teachings about *jen*. The five statements selected here are arbitrarily listed with numbers for the sake of convenience in discussion.

1. "Fan Ch'ih asked about humanity. Confucius said, 'It is to love men.' "[5]

2. "Confucius said, 'Only the man of humanity knows how to love people and hate people.' "[6]

3. "Fan Ch'ih asked about humanity. Confucius said, 'Be respectful in private life, be serious (*ching*) in handling affairs, and be loyal in dealing with others. Even if you are living amidst barbarians, these principles may never be forsaken.' "[7]

4. "Yen Yüan asked about humanity. Confucius said, 'To master oneself and return to propriety is humanity. If a man (the ruler) can for one day master himself and return to propriety, all under heaven will return to humanity. To practice humanity depends

on oneself. Does it depend on others?' Yen Yüan said, 'May I ask for the detailed items?' Confucius said, 'Do not look at what is contrary to propriety, do not listen to what is contrary to propriety, do not speak what is contrary to propriety, and do not make any movement which is contrary to propriety.' Yen Yüan said, 'Although I am not intelligent, may I put your saying into practice.' "[8]

5. "Tzu-kung said, 'If a ruler extensively confers benefit on the people and can bring salvation to all, what do you think of him? Would you call him a man of humanity?' Confucius said, 'Why only a man of humanity? He is without any doubt a sage. Even (sage-emperors) Yao and Shun fell short of it. A man of humanity, wishing to establish his own character, also establishes the character of others, and wishing to be prominent himself, also helps others to be prominent. To be able to judge others by what is near to ourselves may be called the method of realizing humanity.' "[9]

The simplest statement that Confucius makes about *jen* is that *jen* is to love men. In this sense, *jen* seems to be the equivalent of benevolence. But to love without a principle means also to spoil. Therefore, on another occasion Confucius points out that only the man of *jen* knows how to love and how to hate people. Although no men are intrinsically worthy of hating, in order to really love men, we have to hate their evildoings so that they may be forced to become educated as better men.

Thus, *jen* is a much more profound kind of love than that of a devoted mother who lavishes all her fondness upon her children. True love in *jen* involves profound wisdom and sound judgment. In the third statement, Confucius goes even further and gives concrete advice about realizing *jen* in life. It is a surprise to find that the first item Confucius lists—"Be respectful in private life"—does not even concern one's attitude toward others but rather his attitude toward himself. *Jen* in this sense cannot be interpreted as merely love or benevolence. It is more like Schweitzer's reverence for life.[10] *Jen* implies a profound reverence for one's own life as well as a concern for others' lives and also for that which transpires in the society. Its meaning is far wider than mere benevolence or even altruism; rather, it is the root of them. Moreover, realizing *jen* is not merely empty talk. The principles involved in *jen* must be practiced even when one lives amid barbarians. They are universal principles not to be renounced simply because one happens to live in a different environment.

This discussion leads to an understanding of the important message conveyed in the fourth statement, which is perhaps one of the most profound statements Confucius makes about *jen*. "To master oneself" is the translation of the Chinese term *k'o-chi*, which may also be interpreted as "to overcome oneself." Although Confucius himself does not specify what is to be overcome in ourselves, it seems that the Sung philosophers are not far wrong in suggesting that we have to overcome the selfish desires within ourselves.[11] If we could discipline ourselves so that we would, under no circumstance, be swayed by unrestrained selfish desires, and hence become masters of ourselves, then our outward behavior would also conform naturally with the rules of propriety. Therefore, the most important thing about *jen* is that we must cultivate the mind-heart (*hsin*) within ourselves so that we can extend it to every aspect of our lives.[12]

Thus, the term "propriety" (*li*) in the text certainly does not mean merely external rules of propriety or just social conventions that have been imposed on our behavior. It is, rather, that in our hearts we have a natural love for, and would like to return to, propriety. Once our selfish desires are under control, the goodwill toward one's own life, as well as toward other lives, flows out without any obstruction. We are then able to recover our normal state of existence, which is none other than a life of propriety. The core of Confucius's teachings is "learning for one's self."[13] As the master said, "What the gentleman [*chün-tzu*] seeks, he seeks within himself; what the small man seeks, he seeks in others."[14]

Here we see clearly that there are parallels between Socrates's and Confucius's thoughts: The excellent moral nature is within himself rather than imposed upon him from an external source. Only the Chinese put emphasis on the existential aspect, whereas the Greeks showed a keen interest in the theoretical aspect of the problem. This difference marks the parting of ways for the two cultures. Although Confucius himself never said that human nature is good,[15] he is convinced that there is great potentiality in man. To develop such potentiality is to follow the natural course of things. Therefore, it becomes the primary duty of a man not to follow animal instincts or selfish desires. As for the detailed items that Confucius lists in his answer to Yen Yüan's further questioning, these are the means to recover our true selves. Since what Confucius refers to as propriety is the spirit underlying it rather than a rigid code of external rules, the chain of negative statements he made should not be interpreted in such a priggish way as would please only the heart of a moral bigot.

Finally, in the fifth statement, Confucius gives his view of the ultimate commitment of a man. A man of *jen* wishes to establish his own character as well as that of other people. The spirit of this statement is similar to that of the Golden Rule, and the formulation of the statement is more detailed than its Western counterpart. Not only should you do unto others what you would like others to do unto you, but you should mold yourself into an ideal character and help others to do the same. Ideally, everyone should find his own way to become a healthy individual, with an ultimate commitment to *jen* and to developing a great concern for society at large and the happiness of fellow human beings.

From the analysis above, we should now have a fairly clear notion of *jen*. It certainly indicates a benevolent attitude toward people, but it is also much more than that. It implies the wisdom to distinguish what is good from what is evil. It is the realization of the intrinsic value of each individual life, and it shows a resolute commitment to an ideal principle in life. The principle of *jen* allows for divergent manifestations. Once a man has grasped the spirit of *jen*, he should be able to find out what he must do in a given situation. Since each concrete situation is somewhat different from another, the best one can do is to give a description of certain concrete situations as manifestations of *jen*. In this way, people may learn from these examples and may realize the dynamic principle of *jen* in their own lives. This is exactly what Confucius does in *The Analects*. If he does not make any attempt to define *jen*, it is not because his mind is unsystematic but because *jen* is itself beyond definition. Moreover, the apparent paradox in Tseng Tzu's answer to the question about the central thread in Confucius's thought can now be resolved. Since *chung* means none other than the full development of the heart of *jen* within the self, and *shu* the extension of this heart to others, they are beyond doubt two sides of the same coin. Therefore, Tseng Tzu's answer did not deviate from Confucius's teaching. There is no paradox because *jen* cannot be neatly defined in any case and because *chung* and *shu* are indeed the two most important aspects of *jen*.

Precisely because the moral discipline of the self and the seeking of the well-being of people cannot be separated, Confucius refuses to draw a sharp line of distinction between moral and political activities. In other words, politics would be an extension of ethics. To establish the character of the self is one's own moral aspiration, and to help to establish the character of others is the aim of political activity. But this aim cannot be achieved by imposing severe punishment upon people. Therefore, Confucius said:

> Lead the people with governmental measures and regulate them by law and punishment, and they will avoid wrongdoing but will have no sense of honor and shame. Lead them with virtue and regulate them by the rules of propriety, and they will have a sense of shame and, moreover, set themselves right.[16]

This statement certainly does not mean that law is altogether useless. It simply points out the fact that law alone is not an adequate means to lead people. How amazingly well Confucius's teaching fits in with the principles of modern educational psychology, which emphasizes love and encouragement rather than hate and coercion. A ruler must set an example for his people, and a father for his son. From a Confucian point of view the highest ideal of a man is what later Confucian scholars phrase "the way of inward sageliness and outward kingliness."

Although what Confucius teaches is a thoroughgoing practical type of philosophy, the realization of it in one's life is by no means easy. Confucius said:

> I have never seen one who really loves humanity or who really hates inhumanity. One who really loves humanity will not place anything above it. One who really hates inhumanity will practice humanity in such a way that inhumanity will have no chance to get at him. Is there anyone who has devoted his strength to humanity for as long as a single day? I have not seen anyone without sufficient strength to do so. Perhaps there is such a case, but I have not seen it.[17]

In other words, although each individual should be able to collect sufficient strength within himself to realize *jen* within his life, very few people are able to do so. Since realizing *jen* is an endless process, not even Confucius himself dares to claim that he is a sage or a man of *jen*.

> The Master said, "How dare I claim to be a sage or a man of *jen*? Perhaps it might be said of me that I learn without flagging and teach without growing weary." Kung-hsi Hua said, "This is precisely where we disciples are unable to learn from your example."[18]

It is instructive to note Confucius's own observation of the educational process he experienced in his life:

> At fifteen my mind was set on learning. At thirty my character had been formed. At forty I had no more perplexities. At fifty I knew the Mandate of Heaven (*T'ien-ming*). At sixty I was at ease with whatever I heard. At seventy I could follow my heart's desire without transgressing moral principles.[19]

It is only after a lifelong discipline of the self that Confucius realizes a deep sense of freedom[20]—not the freedom of being airborne in a plane; not the freedom of being liberated from worldly worries. From Confucius's point of view, humans are always living in a social context, and our behavior is governed by various rules of propriety (*li*), and the ideal of a civilized life is a life of *li*. But we must not see *li* as something imposed on us from an external source; in fact, not only *li* but human civilization as a whole is a natural outgrowth of humanity (*jen*). Only when we can fully develop the great potentiality in each of us will a deep sense of freedom be realized. For example, consider a ballet dancer. It is only through tough discipline that the talent of the individual can be developed fully and a heightened sense of freedom of self-expression, never experienced before, reached. Thus, it must be at the later stages of his life that Confucius was able to declare: "Is humanity far away? As soon as I want it, there it is right by me."[21]

Although Confucius firmly commits himself to the principle of *jen* and has great faith in its application, this does not mean that *jen* will prevail in the world. In fact, great sacrifice is needed for the sake of realizing *jen*; so Confucius vowed: "A resolute scholar and a man of humanity will never seek to live at the expense of injuring humanity. He would rather sacrifice his life in order to realize humanity."[22] His disciple Tseng Tzu further develops his teaching by saying: "A scholar must be great and strong. His burden is heavy and his course is long. He has taken humanity to be his own burden—is that not heavy? Only with death does his course stop—is that not long?"[23]

Confucius has always been pictured as an incurable optimist by temperament.

These quotations should serve as evidence for rejecting such an erroneous opinion. Confucius fully realizes what the actual conditions of life are, that what is contrary to *jen* has always been practiced in real life. Indeed, at times he shows a great despair, but he is unshaken in his ultimate commitment to *jen*. If a man has his ultimate commitment in *jen*, does he still need a religious faith? This question cannot be answered in a simple straight-forward way. We may start by quoting from *The Analects* Confucius's comments on traditional religious beliefs and practices in his day.

> Fan Ch'ih asked about wisdom. Confucius said, "Devote yourself earnestly to the duties due to men, and respect spiritual beings but keep them at a distance. This may be called wisdom."[24]

> Wang-sun Chia asked, "What is meant by the common saying, it is better to be on good terms with the God of the Kitchen [who cooks our food] than with the spirits of the shrine (ancestors) at the southwest corner of the house?" Confucius said, "It is not true. He who commits a sin against Heaven has no god to pray to."[25]

> Confucius was very ill. Tzu-lu asked that prayer be offered. Confucius said, "Is there such a thing?" Tzu-lu replied, "There is. A eulogy says, Pray to the spiritual beings above and below." Confucius said, "My prayer has been for a long time [that is, what counts is the life that one leads]."[26]

> Confucius never discussed strange phenomena, physical exploits, disorder, or spiritual beings.[27]

> Chi-lu (Tzu-lu) asked about serving the spiritual beings. Confucius said, "If we are not yet able to serve man, how can we serve spiritual beings?" "I venture to ask about death." Confucius said, "If we do not know about life, how can we know about death?"[28]

Moreover, Confucius further declared, "It is man who can make the Way great, and not the Way that can make man great."[29]

Because of such passages, many regard Confucius as an irreligious, agnostic, humanistic, moralistic thinker. On the other hand, however, we find that in many instances Confucius acts much like a reactionary traditionalist. He insists upon keeping up the performance of traditional religious rites in a minutely detailed fashion. The following incident was reported: "Tzu-kung wanted to do away with the sacrificing of a lamb at the ceremony in which the beginning of each month is reported to ancestors. Confucius said, 'Tz'u! You love the lamb but I love the ceremony.' "[30] The most puzzling as well as the most important statement Confucius makes about sacrificial rites is the following:

When Confucius offered sacrifice to his ancestors, he felt as if his ancestral spirits were actually present. When he offered sacrifice to other spiritual beings, he felt as if they were actually present. He said, "If I do not participate in the sacrifice, it is as if I did not sacrifice at all."[31]

Is Confucius just a pragmatic make-believer who would like to keep the traditional ritual ceremonies for the sake of invoking a sense of piety in people? And yet Confucius does seem to show a genuine belief in Heaven. On more than one occasion, when he was in great danger, he placed his faith in Heaven. Several times he said something like this: "Heaven produced the virtue that is in me; what can Huan T'ui do to me?"[32] Statements like this induce some scholars to conclude that Confucius still believed in the traditional concept of Heaven as a supreme personal God who has dominant power over the cosmic order as well as the moral order of man. There seems little doubt that Confucius did show a deep sense of mission in his life. Does this mean that, after all, Confucius was a religious man?

Apparently, there are many contradictions involved in these varied interpretations of Confucius's religious philosophy. Is it the case that the old master was such a muddle-headed thinker that he could hardly think anything through? Or is it the case that interpretations by later scholars are questionable? Upon closer examination, one must conclude that Confucius does have a coherent view that is consistent with his ultimate commitment to *jen*. The difficulty, rather, is with the interpreters who have preconceived, one-sided views of what religious belief is and who lose sight of the central thread that runs through his doctrines. Hence, they fail to understand his philosophy as a whole.

These statements concerning religious matters need further analysis. First let us start with an examination of Confucius's attitude toward spiritual beings. It seems clear that Confucius does not care either to assert or to deny the existence of spiritual beings. He simply refuses to talk much about the subject because of an implicit belief that it has nothing to do with the more important aspects of life. Therefore, he is determined to practice an attitude of what phenomenologists call *epoché* (suspension of judgment) against them.[33] At a time when a host of spiritual beings were still firmly believed in and devoutly worshipped on all levels, great insight and courage were required to point out that these do not have any concern with the core of our existence. Indeed, Confucius was introducing something revolutionary in his own day. As a man who lived some 2,500 years prior to our time, and long before the development of modern science, he must be appreciated because it was he who discovered a most intelligent attitude toward the subject matter. This attitude, properly interpreted, could be adopted by a modern man. Do spiritual beings exist?

Paradoxically enough, Confucius's great contribution lies not in his giving an answer to the question, but in his refusal to answer the question. An avowed atheist would be dissatisfied with Confucius's attitude because Confucius was not radical enough to altogether deny the existence of spiritual beings. However, to deny the existence of such beings without inquiry is as irrational as to affirm the existence of them on blind faith. Instead, we should hold an open mind toward the subject. It is no shame to confess our ignorance and to suspend our judgment on the topic until we find more decisive evidence that would enable us to say something definite about the matter. But to be ready to concede the existence of spiritual beings whenever decisive evidence could be produced certainly does not imply that we would do any bargaining with them. The ruling commitment of a man is to live as a man of *jen*. One cannot violate moral principles in order to seek gains through bargaining with spiritual beings. This is why Confucius declares that if one has sinned against Heaven, there is no god to pray to. Sacrifice for Confucius is definitely not a form of bribery, either to appease or to please the spiritual beings. Then what are we sacrificing for? This is a question we must answer in the following discussion.

By reflecting carefully upon the three as-if statements about sacrifice, we have to conclude that for Confucius making sacrifices is an integral part of our lives that has a this-worldly rather than an other-worldly function. There were two main forms of sacrifices: to ancestors and to Heaven. For Confucius it is out of our inner demands that we sacrifice to our ancestors, because they are the origin of our lives; and the emperor has to make sacrifices to Heaven because Heaven is the origin of all things in the world. In fact, it is for the same reason that we must be filial when our parents are still alive. Not only were they the origin of our lives, but they brought us up and took care of us when we were young. Thus, naturally, we have a feeling of filial piety toward them. Once we have realized the intrinsic value of life through an implicit commitment to *jen*, it is only natural for us to appeal to forms of ritual ceremony to express our reverence for life and the world.

And the performance of these ceremonies, in turn, would enhance our feelings of piety toward this life. Moreover, the performance of these sacrifices would have great educational value for the common people. Thus, the real foundation of ritual performances lies deep in the self rather than in the outside world. Confucius seems to take secular as sacred.[34] He seems to imply that there is a profound depth dimension in man, and it is only through the realization of this depth dimension that he is able to develop into a full man.[35]

All the ritual ceremonies thus have the function of helping man to develop this aspect of his life. They do not have much to do with the objective existence of the spiritual beings, and they do not have to presuppose Heaven being a supreme overlord. The crux of the problem lies in whether or not we can extend our heart of *jen* to all lives. It is here that we have to make our existential decision. The apparent riddle of the as-if statements is thus resolved. It should be clear by now that the concept of Heaven is not to be confused with the concept of god in his philosophy. As we have already noticed, although the existence of gods or spiritual beings is not crucial in Confucius's thought, he does show a great faith in Heaven. The only logical conclusion for us to draw is that Heaven is indeed an important aspect of Confucius's philosophy, while god is not. However, many scholars were misled by a statement they found in

The Analects: "Tzu-kung said, 'We can hear our Master's [views] on culture and its manifestation, but we cannot hear his views on human nature and the Way of Heaven.' "[36] On the basis of this statement, they declare that Confucius also holds an agnostic attitude toward Heaven. But to accept such an interpretation would make Confucius's faith in Heaven completely incomprehensible. In fact, the statement only says that the disciples did not hear or understand the master's view of the Way of Heaven. It does not necessarily imply that he does not have a view of the Way of Heaven. It is interesting to note that he does tell us the reasons why he would not say anything on this matter; only scholars fail to notice the connection between this statement and another statement that also recorded a very important conversation between the master and Tzu-kung:

> Confucius said, "I do not wish to say anything." Tzu-kung said, "If you do not say anything, what can we little disciples ever learn to pass on to others?" Confucius said, "Does Heaven (*T'ien*) say anything? The four seasons run their course and all things are produced. Does Heaven say anything?"[37]

The meanings contained in this passage are extremely rich. Precisely because scholars fail to comprehend the implications of the conversation, some even doubt the authenticity of the anecdote, as the passage appeared late in chapter 17 of *The Analects*, and it offers us a rather unique statement in which Confucius talks about Heaven in such a way that we cannot find elsewhere. Seen from a different perspective, however, it is a most valuable document that records a big breakthrough in Confucius's thought totally consistent with his philosophical outlook. I shall try to explicate the meanings of the passage in the following. Confucius seems to imply that Heaven silently communicates with man. The universe as a whole is an orderly and creative universe, and human beings should imitate the example of Heaven, which teaches us by deeds rather than words. Confucius seems to take Heaven to be the transcendent creative power working unceasingly in the universe. It does not show any personal characteristics and does not intervene in the natural state of affairs, and humans should take Heaven as the model to follow.

The document seems to have contradicted the traditional concept of Heaven as the Lord on High, which Confucius still firmly believes, as can be seen in the following quotations:

> When Confucius visited Nan-tzu (the wicked wife of Duke Ling of Wei, r. 533–490 B.C.) [in an attempt to influence her to persuade the duke to effect political reform], Tzu-lu was not pleased. Confucius swore an oath and said, "If I have said or done anything wrong, may Heaven forsake me! May Heaven forsake me!"[38]

> When Confucius was in personal danger in K'uang, he said, "Since the death of King Wen, is not the course of culture (*wen*) in my keeping? If

it had been the will of Heaven to destroy this culture, it would not have been given to a mortal [like me]. But if it is the will of Heaven that this culture should not perish, what can the people of K'uang do to me?''[39]

When Yen Yüan died, Confucius said, "Alas, Heaven is destroying me! Heaven is destroying me!''[40]

From these passages, we find that Confucius never for a moment doubted the existence of Heaven, and he did inherit the traditional faith in Heaven as the Lord on High. On closer scrutiny, however, I do not find any contradiction in his thought, as he made a smooth transition from the traditional belief in Heaven to his own understanding of Heaven. When we carefully read the passages quoted above, we find that Confucius was only making exclamations during moments of distress; he never meant that Heaven would intervene in the natural state of affairs. As humanity has received its endowment from Heaven, it has to shoulder the responsibilities without making any excuses. Another Confucian saying is rather revealing:

Confucius said, "Alas! No one knows me!" Tzu-kung said, "Why is there no one that knows you?" Confucius said, "I do not complain against Heaven. I do not blame men. I study things on the lower level but my understanding penetrates the higher level. It is Heaven that knows me.''[41]

Thus, Heaven for Confucius cannot be identified as the objective order of nature. For Confucius, Heaven is indeed immanent, as it works unceasingly in an unobtrusive manner in the universe, but it is also transcendent, so that Confucius feels a great sense of awe before Heaven:

Confucius said, "The superior man stands in awe of three things. He stands in awe of the Mandate of Heaven [*T'ien-ming*]; he stands in awe of great men, and he stands in awe of the words of the sages. The inferior man is ignorant of the Mandate of Heaven and does not stand in awe of it. He is disrespectful of great men and is contemptuous toward the words of the sages.''[42]

Precisely because the inferior man does not see the silent operation of the Way of Heaven, he feels no sense of awe before the Mandate of Heaven. There are aspects of the decree of Heaven (*T'ien-ming*) that are beyond the understanding of man.

Ssu-ma Niu, worrying, said, "All people have brothers but I have none." Tzu-hsia said, "I have heard [from Confucius] this saying: Life and death are the decree of Heaven (*ming*); wealth and honor depend on Heaven. If a superior man is reverential (or serious) without fail, and is respectful in dealing with others and follows the rules of propriety, then all within the four seas (the world) are brothers. What does the superior man have to worry about having no brothers?''[43]

There are some things in life beyond our control; all we need to do is to accept our fate or decree of Heaven without worrying about them. There are other aspects of the decree of Heaven that can be understood; and even though Heaven says nothing, a man of wisdom can follow the example of Heaven and apply it in this life. The sage-emperors are superb in their achievements in this regard.

The Master said, "Great indeed was Yao as a ruler! How lofty! It is Heaven that is great and it was Yao who modelled himself upon it. He was so boundless that the common people were not able to put a name to his virtues. Lofty was he in his successes and brilliant was he in his accomplishments!''[44]

Confucius said, "To have taken no [unnatural] action and yet have the empire well governed, Shun was the man! What did he do? All he did was to make himself reverent and correctly face south [in his royal seat as the ruler].''[45]

From these two statements, we find in an unexpected way the kind of corroboration we need to support the interpretation of Confucius having faith in Heaven as a transcendent creative power working unceasingly in an unobtrusive fashion in the universe. Yao and Shun are the two sage-emperors greatly admired by Confucius, and he explicitly stated that Yao modeled himself upon Heaven; Shun was said to govern the empire by taking no action. This is exactly how Heaven works in the universe, as it functions in such an unobtrusive fashion that people do not even notice its being there. Yao's achievement was so great that people could not specify anything upon which to heap their praises. Then what did Shun do? He did nothing except sit in his royal seat. Why did Confucius consider their accomplishments unsurpassed by later rulers? The reason is actually very simple: If there is already law and order, how can a ruler be praised for bringing law and order to the state? When people enjoy peace throughout the world under the reign of Yao and Shun, and everything runs smoothly on its course, how can there be any words to characterize their achievements? Therefore, wu-wei (no action) was not an idea monopolized by the Taoists; Confucius had his own idea of wu-wei in his political thought. He said, "A ruler who governs the state by virtue is like the north polar star, which remains in its place while all the other stars revolve around it.''[46] He used a vivid metaphor to illustrate his point of view: "The character of a ruler is like wind and that of the people is like grass. In whatever direction the wind blows, the grass always bends.''[47]

Therefore, by saying that Heaven is not personal is not to downgrade Heaven but to recognize Heaven as a suprapersonal creative power that should serve as the model for humanity. Here we find Heaven and humanity in accord (*T'ien-jen-ho-i*—even if the term was not coined at the time). Because of Confucius's ultimate concern, that ethics and politics form a coherent whole, he also develops his educational program in accordance with his philosophy. He encourages his disciples to develop their own potentiality, teaching them four things: "culture (*wen*), conduct, loyalty, and faithfulness."[48] Each may pursue a different direction. He also teaches them "*liu-yi*" (the six arts), that is, ceremonies, music, archery, carriage driving, writing, and mathematics, so that they can learn skills to serve the community. And Confucius declared: "In education there should be no class distinction."[49] The ideal of education is to become a *chün-tzu*, that is, a superior man or a gentleman, who is no longer defined by birth but rather by virtue. He urges his disciples: "Set your will on the Way. Have a firm grasp on virtue. Rely on humanity. Find recreation in the arts."[50] Each is hoped to develop a wholesome personality.

If this analysis of Confucius's thought is correct, we must caution against the temptation to apply any clichés to his philosophy. The Westerner likes to draw a sharp line between the supernatural and the natural, the sacred and the profane, the world of ideals and the world of facts, the pious and the infidel. But in the Chinese tradition, there are no such sharp dichotomies. A humanist in the West is often an atheist. Such a characterization cannot apply to Confucius. In spite of his mistrust of traditional deities, he did not lose his sense of piety. It is through the demand of our depth dimension that we have faith in realizing the ideals of creativity and harmony in the natural as well as in the human world. Confucius has sown the seeds of a philosophy of union between Heaven and man that was further developed in the *Book of Changes*.[51]

Now we are ready to answer the question, Was Confucius a religious man? If religion is defined in the narrower sense as a belief in a personal god or spiritual beings, then Confucius was not much of a religious man. If, on the other hand, religion is defined in the sense of ultimate commitment that gives satisfaction to the demands of our inner selves, then Confucius was a deeply religious man. He said, "In the morning, hear the Way; in the evening, die content!"[52] I now realize why he needs to get to fifty before he can say that he knows *T'ien-ming*. It is only at such a mature stage that he fully understands the double meaning of the term. On the one hand, he realizes that man's existence is finite, so he accepts the decree of Heaven in the sense of fate. But he is also conscious of his endowment from Heaven; so he also accepts the Mandate of Heaven and develops a heightened sense of duty in his life. As a matter of fact, he has the reputation of being "one who knows a thing cannot be done and still wants to do it."[53] And this is an unmistakable sign of one who commits himself ultimately to the Way. Furthermore, he has been able to find a balance between immanence and transcendence. As he said, "A man has no way of becoming a gentleman [*chün-tzu*] unless he understands Destiny [*ming*]; he has no way of taking his stand unless he understands the rites [*li*]; he has no way of judging men unless he understands words.''[54]

As there is a growing tendency toward secularization in theology, Confucius's religious philosophy merits a reappraisal.[55] The sage of the past may prove to be a prophet for the future. In a way, Confucius's position in Chinese civilization may be compared with that of Jesus Christ in Western civilization. Confucius did not achieve anything great in the practical world, and he must have considered himself a man of failure. And yet he has been honored as the greatest teacher and the only sage without the position of an emperor. And paradoxically, his thought has dominated Chinese civilization ever since. Even today, consciously and subconsciously, most Chinese intellectuals adopt Confucius's philosophy of living: practicing neither unrestrained hedonism, on the one hand, nor rigorous moralism, on the other. He is the one who teaches us the way of the mean.[56]

Confucius has created a personal ideal for later generations. And while he has tremendous respect for the past and a sense of continuity, he is definitely not a reactionary traditionalist. His creativity lies in his ability to put new wines in old bottles; it is through him that the traditional system of rites received new spirit. Confucius said, ''A man who reviews the old so as to find out the new is qualified to teach others.''[57] I do not think we can find a better characterization of him. Practically all of the important ingredients of Confucian thought are present. Now it is for future generations to work out the rich implications therein.[58]

NOTES

1. Ssu-ma Ch'ien (145–86 B.C.?), the great historian who lived about 300 years after Confucius, wrote a complete biography of Confucius in his monumental *Historical Records* (*Shih-chi*). Modern scholars, however, tend to challenge the authenticity of a number of facts as recorded in the biography. For our purpose, however, the only thing we need is just a general picture of his life; accuracy of details is not our concern. He definitely opts for the Chou system, as he said, ''The Chou is resplendent in culture, having before it the example of the two previous dynasties [Hsia and Yin]. I am for the Chou'' (Lau, *Analects*, p. 23). The Duke of Chou was his mentor, as he lamented, ''How I have gone downhill! It has been such a long time since I dreamt of the Duke of Chou'' (ibid., p. 57).

2. Chan, *Source Book*, p. 27. Tseng Tzu was one of Confucius's most important disciples. Shen was his private name.

3. Ibid., p. 24, with slight modification.

4. Ibid., p. 26, with slight modification. ''Humanity'' is Wing-tsit Chan's translation for *jen*, and ''superior man'' for *chün-tzu*, which literally means ''gentleman.'' Before Confucius, a gentleman was determined by his status of birth: Confucius radically changed the meaning of the term by defining a gentleman in terms of his moral and cultural achievement.

5. Ibid., p. 40. Fan Ch'ih was Confucius's pupil.

6. Ibid., p. 25.

7. Ibid., p. 41.

8. Ibid., p. 38. Yen Yüan was Confucius's favorite pupil; unfortunately, he died at an early age.

9. Ibid., p. 31. Tzu-kung was Confucius's pupil. There is also the negative formulation of the Golden Rule in *The Analects*. "Tzu-kung said, 'What I do not want others to do to me, I do not want to do to them.' Confucius said, 'Ah Tz'u! That is beyond you.' " Ibid., p. 28.

10. Cf. Albert Schweitzer, *The Decay and the Restoration of Civilization*, trans. C. T. Champion (London: Unwin, 1961).

11. Man has a natural tendency to seek physical gratification and material gains and hence is tempted to do much evil in this life. But Confucius said, "If you set your mind on humanity, you will be free from evil." See Chan, *Source Book*, p. 25. Also, man tends to cling to his personal biases and prejudices. But Confucius was reported to have been free from four things: "He had no arbitrariness of opinion, no dogmatism, no obstinacy, and no egotism." See ibid., p. 35. It is interesting to note that for Confucian thinking there is an all-important distinction between the self (*chi*) and the ego (*wo*). Self-cultivation and overcoming egotistical desires became a central theme for Sung philosophy. The Sung dynasty existed between A.D. 960–1279, and Neo-Confucian philosophy was the dominant trend during that period.

12. Some scholars thought that Confucius did not have the slightest idea of *jen-hsin* (heart of humanity) as advocated by Mencius. But Confucius said explicitly: "About Hui (Yen Yüan), for three months there would be nothing in his *hsin* (mind-heart) contrary to humanity [jen]. The others could (or can) attain to this for a day or a month at the most." See ibid., p. 29.

13. Cf. William Theodore de Bary, *Learning for One's Self: Essays on the Individual in Neo-Confucian Thought* (New York: Columbia University Press, 1991).

14. Lau, *Analects*, p. 155.

15. The only thing Confucius explicitly said about human nature was: "By nature men are alike. Through practice they have become far apart." Chan, *Source Book*, p. 45.

16. Ibid., p. 22.

17. Ibid., p. 26.

18. Lau, *Analects*, p. 65, with slight modification.

19. Chan, *Source Book*, p. 22.

20. Cf. Shu-hsien Liu, "Individual Freedom from a Confucian Perspective," *Ching Feng* 37, no. 4 (November 1994): 247–254.

21. Chan, *Source Book*, p. 33.

22. Ibid., p. 43.

23. Ibid., p. 33, with slight modification.

24. Ibid., p. 30.

25. Ibid., p. 25. Wang-sun Chia was a great officer and commander in chief in the state of Wei.

26. Ibid., p. 33. Tzu-lu was Confucius's pupil.

27. Ibid., p. 32.

28. Ibid., p. 36.

29. Ibid., p. 44, with slight modification.

30. Ibid., p. 25. "Tz'u" was Tzu-kung's private name.

31. Ibid.

32. Ibid., p. 32. Huan T'ui was a military officer in the state of Sung who attempted to kill Confucius by felling a tree. Confucius was then fifty-nine.

33. Cf. Edmund Husserl, *Ideas: General Introduction to Phenomenology*, trans. W. R. Boyce Gibson (London: George Allen & Unwin Ltd., 1931), Vol. 1, secs. 27–32. Of course, I am not saying that Confucius practiced *epoché* as the phenomenologists do it. I only borrow the idea for the purpose of illustration.

34. Cf. Herbert Fingarette, *Confucius: The Secular as Sacred* (New York: Harper and Row, 1972). The title of the book is illuminating, but I have serious reservations concerning his behaviorist interpretation of Confucian thought.

35. Cf. Paul Tillich, *Systematic Theology*, 3 vols. (Chicago: Chicago University Press, 1951, 1957, 1963) (hereafter cited as Tillich, *Systematic Theology*). Tillich develops the idea of ''depth of reason,'' which I believe would apply even better to the Confucian tradition. See Shu-hsien Liu, ''A Critique of Paul Tillich's Doctrine of God and Christology from an Oriental Perspective,'' in *Religious Issues and Interreligious Dialogues*, ed. Charles Wei-hsun Fu and Gerhard E. Spiegler (Westport, CT: Greenwood Press, 1989), pp. 511–532.

36. Chan, *Source Book*, p. 28.

37. Ibid., p. 47, with slight modification.

38. Ibid., p. 31.

39. Ibid., p. 35.

40. Ibid., p. 36.

41. Ibid., pp. 42–43.

42. Ibid., p. 45.

43. Ibid., p. 39.

44. Lau, *Analects*, p. 73.

45. Chan, *Source Book*, p. 43.

46. Ibid., p. 22.

47. Ibid., p. 40.

48. Ibid., p. 32. In fact, the achievements of some of Confucius's distinguished students were listed under four categories: ''Virtuous conduct: Yen Yüan, Min Tzu-ch'ien, Jan Po-niu, and Chung-kung; speech: Tsai Wo and Tzu-kung; government: Jan Yu and Chi-lu; culture and learning: Tzu-yu and Tzu-hsia.'' Lau, *Analects*, p. 97.

49. Chan, *Source Book*, p. 44.

50. Ibid., p. 31.

51. The *Book of Changes* (*I Ching*) is one of the basic Confucian Classics. It is divided into *Texts* and *Commentaries*. The *Texts* consist of sixty-four hexagrams and judgments on them. These are based on the eight trigrams, each of which consists of three lines, divided or undivided, the divided representing the weak, or yin, and the undivided representing the strong, or yang. These hexagrams symbolize various possible situations. There are seven *Commentaries*, but three of them have two parts, thus constituting the Ten Wings of the book. Tradition has ascribed the eight trigrams to the legendary sage-emperor Fu Hsi, the sixty-four hexagrams to King Wen of Chou (r. 1171–1122 B.C.), and the Ten Wings to Confucius. Most modern scholars have rejected this attribution, but they are not agreed on when and by whom the book was produced. Most probably it is a product of many hands over a long period of time. Current views tend to believe Confucius did make great contributions to the *Commentaries*. There will be another chapter on the classic.

52. Chan, *Source Book*, p. 26.

53. Ibid., p. 43.

54. Lau, *Analects*, p. 205.

55. Cf. Shu-hsien Liu, "The Religious Import of Confucian Philosophy: Its Traditional Outlook and Contemporary Significance," *Philosophy East and West* 21, no. 2 (April 1971): 157–175.

56. Confucius said, "Supreme indeed is the Mean as a moral virtue. It has been rare among the common people for quite a long time." Lau, *Analects*, p. 55. To follow the middle way and to avoid the extremes certainly does not mean not to take a definite stand. Confucius's view of uprightness (*chih*) is instructive. "Someone said, 'What do you think of repaying hatred with virtue?' Confucius said, 'In that case what are you going to repay virtue with? Rather repay hatred with uprightness and repay virtue with virtue.' " Chan, *Source Book*, p. 42. In effect, the middle way is the proper way, and what is proper depends on the situation. There has been much debate concerning Confucius's idea of *chih* (uprightness or straightness). "The Governer of She said to Confucius, 'In our village we have an example of a straight person. When the father stole a sheep, the son gave evidence against him.' Confucius answered, 'In our village those who are straight are quite different. Fathers cover up for their sons, and sons cover up for their fathers. In such behavior is straightness to be found as a matter of course.' " Lau, *Analects*, p. 127. My interpretation is that for a petty theft like this it is not proper for the son to give evidence against his own father; only when loyalty and filial piety cannot both be maintained must drastic measures be taken. The Confucian tradition has been known to have supported the cause of great righteousness (*ta-i*) at the expense of even the lives of the parents.

57. Chan, *Source Book*, p. 23.

58. I do not pretend to discuss all of the important issues in Confucius's thought. For example, problems concerning rectification of names (*cheng-ming*) and righteousness (*i*) and profit (*li*) will be discussed along with other Confucian thinkers. I have not tried to avoid some of the seemingly sticky issues in his thought, either. For example, the following quotations are often cited to prove Confucius's authoritarian attitude: "The common people may be made to follow it (the Way) but may not be made to understand it" (Chan, *Source Book*, p. 33). "In one's household, it is the women and the small men that are difficult to deal with. If you let them get too close, they become insolent. If you keep them at a distance, they complain" (Lau, *Analects*, p. 181). I think he was just making factual observations. What is important, however, is the spirit. From what has been portrayed in *The Analects*, Confucius was never an authoritarian person. In this famous anecdote, Confucius encouraged his disciples to speak their wishes: "Tseng Hsi said, 'In the late spring, when the spring dress is ready, I would like to go with five or six grownups and six or seven young boys to bathe in the I River, enjoy the breeze on the Rain Dance Altar, and then return home singing.' Confucius heaved a sigh and said, 'I agree with Tien.' " Chan, *Source Book*, p. 38. Confucius should not be held responsible for the state authoritarianism that developed since the Han dynasty. In principle, there is no difficulty whatsoever for contemporary Neo-Confucian scholars to vigorously support the practice of democracy and defense of women's rights. Throughout the chapter, the term man was used only for the sake of convenience.

3

Mencius

Mencius (371–289 B.C.?) was a major philosopher in pre-Ch'in Confucianism. His name is the Latinized form of Meng Fu-tzu, meaning Master Meng. He was honored as *Ya-sheng*, a title given to him by the posterity meaning "second only to the sages," and received sacrifices in the Confucian temple. His thought was regarded as representing the orthodox line of Confucian thought by Sung-Ming Neo-Confucian philosophers; and his name was constantly associated with that of Confucius. It is interesting to note that Mencius lived a life very similar to that of the old master. He was also from what is now Shantung province. It is said that he studied under a pupil of Tzu-ssu, Confucius's grandson, then committed himself to the Confucian principle of *jen*. Like the old master, he also wandered among various states looking for opportunities to put his political ideals into practice, without much success. Finally, he had to settle for a teaching career. His thoughts were preserved in a book that records his conversations with his disciples, rivals, kings, and ministers. His ideas have exerted profound influence on the shaping of the Chinese mind. Even during Mencius's own time, Confucianism had already established itself as a prominent school. Consequently, Mencius was able to draw a large number of disciples to follow him and seemed to receive even better treatment from the feudal lords than Confucius did. Otherwise, he was a practical failure like Confucius.

The main source for a study of Mencius's thought is naturally *The Book of Mencius*, which is divided into seven chapters, each with two sections. In style, the book is very different from Confucius's *Analects*. Although the book is presented in dialogue form, it is not a book of laconic moral aphorisms like *The*

Analects. Mencius preferred to talk in a lengthy, argumentative way. He himself was conscious of this fact and gave his reasons:

> Do I like to argue? I cannot help it. The world has been in existence for a long time, with a period of order and a period of chaos succeeding each other. . . . After the death of Yao and Shun, the Way of the sages fell into decay. . . . Sage-emperors have ceased to appear. Feudal lords have become reckless and idle scholars have indulged in unreasonable opinions. The words of Yang Chu and Mo Ti fill the world. If the people in their opinions do not follow Yang Chu, they follow Mo Ti. Yang advocated egoism, which means a denial of the special relationship with the ruler. Mo advocated universal love, which means a denial of the special relationship with the father. To deny the special relationship with the father and the ruler is to become an animal. . . . If the principles of Yang and Mo are not stopped, and if the principles of Confucius are not brought to light, perverse doctrines will delude the people and obstruct the path of humanity and righteousness. When humanity and righteousness are obstructed, beasts will be led on to devour men, and men will devour one another. I am alarmed by these things, and defend the doctrines of the ancient kings and oppose Yang and Mo.[1]

Thus, Mencius defended the Confucian cause with great passion. His performance was judged to be somewhat unbalanced, not to be compared with that of Confucius, who was the embodiment of the ideal of mean. Basically, Mencius's teachings were derived from Confucius. But in many ways he advanced beyond the position of the old master. For example, he put equal emphasis on *i* (righteousness)—the particular principle of differentiation—in addition to *jen*— the universal principle of humanity; he explicitly taught that human nature is good, while Confucius only showed an implicit faith in man's perfectibility. One of his great contributions to the Confucian tradition lies in that he pointed out that human nature is manifested through human feelings, so that the Confucian Way may be approached in a concrete fashion. Mencius loved to use metaphors and analogies to illustrate his points of view. Unfortunately, they were not used properly; hence, they were as enlightening as they were misleading. At any rate, Mencius's colorful way of presentation provoked thought, and it was largely through him that many Confucian presuppositions were put into definitive, explicit forms. Mencius has been regarded by some scholars as a mystic of some sort—an area that needs clarification and elaboration. In the following, I shall give my interpretation of Mencius's philosophical ideas, then discuss the religious, social, and political implications of his thought.

Mencius was the first in the Confucian school to assert that human nature is good. Confucius did not develop a systematic view of human nature; the only thing he explicitly said was, "By nature men are alike. Through practice they have become far apart."[2] The meaning of this statement is not clear and may be subject to different interpretations. Confucius's disciple Tzu-kung testified that "we cannot hear his views on human nature and the Way of Heaven."[3] It was Mencius who contributed a great deal to establish the orthodox version of the Confucian views on human nature and the Way of Heaven that were later commonly accepted by Sung-Ming Neo-Confucian philosophers. Mencius was dissatisfied with the traditional view of human nature that taught that what is inborn is nature. His dissatisfaction may be seen in his debate with Kao Tzu, who seemed to uphold the traditional view.

> Kao Tzu said, "What is inborn is called nature." Mencius said, "When you say that what is inborn is called nature, is that like saying that white is white?" "Yes." "Then is the whiteness of the white feather the same as the whiteness of snow? Or, again, is the whiteness of snow the same as the whiteness of white jade?" "Yes." "Then is the nature of a dog the same as the nature of an ox, and is the nature of an ox the same as the nature of a man?"[4]

On first sight, Mencius's argument appeared to be based on an improper analogy that resulted in sophistry. On deeper reflection, however, Mencius did raise a substantive issue. What he was interested in was the specific human nature, not the generic nature that could be applied to all animals. Further debates between the two showed that this was indeed the case:

> Kao Tzu said, "By nature we desire food and sex. Humanity is internal and not external, whereas righteousness is external and not internal." Mencius said, "Why do you say that humanity is internal and righteousness external?" "When I see an old man and respect him for his age, it is not that the oldness is within me, just as, when something is white and I call it white, I am merely observing its external appearance. I therefore say that righteousness is external." Mencius said, "There is no difference between our considering a white horse to be white and a white man to be white. But is there no difference between acknowledging the age of an old horse and the age of an old man? And what is it that we call righteousness, the fact that a man is old or the fact that we honor his old age?" Kao Tzu said, "I love my own younger brother but do not love the younger brother of, say, a man from the state of Ch'in. This is because I am the one to determine that pleasant feeling. I therefore say that humanity comes from within. On the other hand, I respect the old man of Ch'u as well as my own elders. What determines my pleasant feeling is age itself. Therefore I say that righteousness is external." Mencius said, "We love the roast meat of Ch'in as much as we love our own. This is even so with respect to material things. Then are you going to say that our love of roast meat is also external?"[5]

The desire for food and sex is common to both man and animals. Kao Tzu seemed to argue that humanity, such as love of one's younger brother, is inborn, while righteousness, such as respect for the elders from another state, is acquired and is determined by external causes. This argument would not hold, as even food and sex must involve external factors, while the senses of love and respect in terms of making proper discrimination must have internal sources in man. The message Mencius tried to convey was: External factors provide only the conditions for us to react; the truly determining factor must still lie within.[6] As a matter of fact, only man knows how to make appropriate distinctions in practicing reverence on different occasions.

Thus, it is due to the specific human nature that man knows how to practice humanity and righteousness. Sense perception is common for both man and animals, but the practice of humanity and righteousness is special for man only. It is here that we must look for clues to get hold of the specific nature of humans. Mencius fully realized that "[t]here is only very little difference between man and other animals."[7] If a man knows only to eat and drink, and to satisfy the desires of the senses, he is indeed no different from an animal. Therefore, a gentleman has to devote himself consciously to develop what is properly human in himself. Mencius made a crucial distinction between what he called the greater and the smaller qualities in humans:

> Kung-tu Tzu asked, "We are all human beings. Why is it that some men become great and others become small?" Mencius said, "Those who follow the greater qualities in their nature become great men and those who follow the smaller qualities in their nature become small men." "But we are all human beings. Why is it that some follow their greater qualities and others follow their smaller qualities?" Mencius replied, "When our senses of sight and hearing are used without thought and are thereby obscured by material things, the material things act on the material senses and lead them astray. That is all. The function of the mind [hsin] is to think. If we think, we will get it [the Way]. If we do not think, we will not get it. This is what Heaven has given to us. If we first build up the nobler part of our nature, then the inferior part cannot overcome it. It is simply this that makes a man great."[8]

Obviously for Mencius, what is proper to man lies in his ability to reflect and his capacity to practice humanity and righteousness in actual life. Although the endowments of all men are the same, their existential decisions may make a world of difference. It is the working out of the best of the human endowment that distinguishes the sage from other men. Moral principles are not things aloft that have nothing to do with common men. Every man will experience the function of moral principles if he cares to reflect on his own behaviors; he will find that these principles are inseparable from his immediate feelings. Mencius gave a concrete example to illustrate the point:

When I say that all men have the mind which cannot bear to see the suffering of others, my meaning may be illustrated thus: Now, when men suddenly see a child about to fall into a well, they all have a feeling of alarm and distress, not to gain friendship with the child's parents, nor to seek the praise of their neighbors and friends, nor because they dislike the reputation [of lack of humanity if they did not rescue the child]. From such a case, we see that a man without the feeling of commiseration is not a man; a man without the feeling of shame and dislike is not a man; a man without the feeling of deference and compliance is not a man; and a man without the feeling of right and wrong is not a man. The feeling of commiseration is the beginning of humanity; the feeling of shame and dislike is the beginning of righteousness; the feeling of deference and compliance is the beginning of propriety; and the feeling of right and wrong is the beginning of wisdom. Men have these Four Beginnings just as they have their four limbs. Having these Four Beginnings, but saying that they cannot develop them is to destroy themselves. When they say that their ruler cannot develop them, they are destroying their ruler. If anyone with these Four Beginnings in him knows how to give them the fullest extension and development, the result will be like fire beginning to burn or a spring beginning to shoot forth. When they are fully developed, they will be sufficient to protect all people within the four seas (the world). If they are not developed, they will not be sufficient even to serve one's parents.[9]

Mencius's famous theory of Four Beginnings was purported to give an accurate description of the actual conditions of man as well as the norms of behavior proper to man. Here we find Mencius's unique approach to human nature: Only when we refer to the specific human nature may we pronounce it to be good. Should we include animal nature into the definition of human nature, then it may be said that it is either good or evil, that it is neither good nor evil, or that it is nothing but evil. But all of these approaches fail to capture the unique features that pertain only to the specific human nature that is good without further qualifications from a transcendent perspective. The debates between Kao Tzu and Mencius lend further insights into the issue in question:

Kao Tzu said, "Human nature is like the willow tree, and righteousness is like a cup or a bowl. To turn human nature into humanity and righteousness is like turning the willow into cups and bowls." Mencius said, "Sir, can you follow the nature of the willow tree and make the cups and bowls, or must you violate the nature of the willow tree before you can make the cups and bowls? If you are going to violate the nature of the willow trees in order to make cups and bowls, then must you also violate human nature in order to make it into humanity and righteousness? Your words, alas! would lead all people in the world to consider humanity and righteousness as calamity [because they required the violation of human nature]!''

Kao Tzu said, ''Man's nature is like the whirling water. If a breach in the pool is made to the east it will flow to the east. If a breach is made to the west it will flow to the west. Man's nature is indifferent to good and evil, just as water is indifferent to east and west.'' Mencius said, ''Water, indeed, is indifferent to the east and west, but is it indifferent to high and low? Man's nature is naturally good just as water naturally flows downward. There is no man without this good nature; neither is there water that does not flow downward. Now you can strike water and cause it to splash upward over your forehead, and by damming and leading it, you can force it uphill. Is this the nature of water? It is the forced circumstance that makes it do so. Man can be made to do evil, for his nature can be treated in the same way.''[10]

From the metaphors used by Kao Tzu and Mencius, we can see the different temperaments and ideas of the two philosophers. Kao Tzu was a naturalistic type of empiricist. He inferred from the fact that man actually can be led to do good or evil that human nature is neither good nor evil. But Mencius was an idealist. He believed that the actual evils committed by man are due to adverse environmental influences; if one cares to nurture the specific human nature, then he would naturally do good and also love to do good. Hence, he concluded that human nature is good. In his answer to further queries on the issue, he made clarifications:

Kung-tu Tzu said, ''Kao Tzu said that man's nature is neither good nor evil. Some say that man's nature may be made good or evil, therefore when King Wen and King Wu were in power the people loved virtue, and when King Yu and Li were in power people loved violence. Some say that some men's nature is good and some men's nature is evil. Therefore even under (sage-emperor) Yao there was Hsiang [who daily plotted to kill his brother], and even with a bad father Ku-sou, there was [a most filial] Shun (Hsiang's brother who succeeded Yao), and even with (wicked king) Chou as nephew and ruler, there were Viscount Ch'i of Wei and Prince Pi-kan. Now you say that human nature is good. Then are these people wrong?''

Mencius said, ''If you let your people follow their feelings (original nature), they will be able to do good. This is what is meant by saying that human nature is good. If man does evil, it is not the fault of his natural endowment. The feeling of commiseration is found in all men; the feeling of shame and dislike is found in all men; the feeling of respect and reverence is found in all men; and the feeling of right and wrong is found in all men. The feeling of commiseration is what we call humanity; the feeling of shame and dislike is what we call righteousness; the feeling of respect and reverence is what we call propriety (*li*); and the feeling of right and wrong is what we call wisdom. Humanity, righteousness, propriety, and wisdom are not drilled into us from outside. We originally have them with us. Only we do not think [to find them]. Therefore it is said, 'Seek and you will find it, neglect and you will lose it.' [Men differ in the development of their endowments], some twice as much as others, some five times, and some to an incalculable degree, because no one can develop his original endowment to the fullest extent. *The Book of Odes* says, 'Heaven produces the teeming multitude. As there are things there are their specific principles. When the people keep their normal nature they will love excellent virtue.' Confucius said, 'The writer of this poem indeed knew the Way (Tao). Therefore as there are things, there must be their specific principles, and since people keep to their normal nature, therefore they love excellent virtue.' ''[11]

The key issue is whether virtues are drilled into us from outside. Obviously, there is no point for us to teach a tiger to practice virtues in a conscious fashion because it does not have the kind of natural endowment man has. But there is no reason for us to discriminate against any human being by saying that he cannot be taught to follow his own nature, which is an endowment from Heaven, as well as his own feelings. But Mencius never denied that man actually does evil against his own nature, as he can easily be influenced by his environment and lose his mind-heart. He said, "Humanity is man's mind and righteousness is man's path. Pity the man who abandons the path and does not follow it, and who has lost his heart and does not know how to recover it. When people's dogs and fowls are lost, they go to look for them, and yet, when they have lost their hearts, they do not go to look for them. The way of learning is none other than finding the lost mind."[12] Mencius used a very vivid metaphor to illustrate his point of view:

The trees of the Niu Mountain were once beautiful. But can the mountain be regarded as beautiful since, being in the borders of a big state, the trees have been hewed down with axes and hatchets? Still with the rest given them by the days and nights and the nourishment provided them by the rains and the dew, they were not without buds and sprouts springing forth. But then the cattle and the sheep pastured upon them once and again. That is why the mountain looks so bald. When people see that it is so bald, they think that there was never any timber on the mountain. Is this the true nature of the mountain? Is there not [also] a heart of humanity and righteousness originally existing in man? The way in which he loses his originally good mind is like the way in which the trees are hewed down with axes and hatchets. As trees are cut down day after day, can a mountain retain its beauty? To be sure, the days and nights do the healing, and there is the nourishing air of the calm morning which keeps him normal in his likes and dislikes. But the effect is slight, and is disturbed and destroyed by what he does during the day. When there is repeated disturbance, the restorative influence of the night will not be sufficient to preserve (the proper goodness of the mind). When the influence of the night is not sufficient to preserve it, man becomes not much different from the beast. People see that he acts like an animal, and think that he never had the original endowment (for goodness). But is that his true character? Therefore with proper nourishment and care, everything grows, whereas without proper nourishment and care, everything decays. Confucius said, "Hold it fast and you preserve it. Let it go and you lose it. It comes in and goes out at no definite time and without anyone's knowing its direction." He was talking about the human mind.[13]

To preserve the nourishing air of the night and to recover the lost mind have since become the central concern for discipline of the self in Sung-Ming Neo-Confucianism. The mind must be kept pure and clean throughout the day, as in the calm morning. What is cultivated and developed throughout discipline of the self is, however, none other than drawing out the innate ability and innate knowledge (*liang-chih*) of man. Mencius said:

The ability possessed by man without their having acquired it by learning is innate ability, and the knowledge possessed by them without deliberation is innate knowledge. Children carried in the arms all know to love their parents. As they grow, they all know to respect their elder brothers. To have filial affection for parents is humanity, and to respect elders is righteousness These feelings are universal in the world, that is all.[14]

But to hold on to the principle and to have no more doubt in the mind is, however, an achievement attained only by those who work hard in order to maintain an unperturbed mind. Certainly there are different approaches to maintaining an unperturbed mind. For example, some discipline their minds in such a way that they are unflinching from any challenge put to them in any situation at any time; others discipline their minds so that they can accept any misfortune or disaster with composure; only these may not have much relevance for those who devote themselves to the practice of the sagely way. Mencius quoted Tseng Tzu speaking about Confucius's view of the subject: "If, on self-examination, I find that I am not upright, shall I not be in fear of a poor man in his loose garments of haircloth? If, on self-examination, I find that I am upright, I will go forward against thousands and tens of thousands."[15] Mencius endorsed this view, which seems to imply that if we can find what is upright in our minds, then we should be able to commit ourselves to it to such an extent that we no longer have any perturbed feelings. Mencius further developed his doctrine of an unperturbed mind in his answer to a disciple:

[Kung-sun Ch'ou] asked, ''May I venture to ask, sir, how you maintain an unperturbed mind and how Kao Tzu maintains an unperturbed mind. May I be told?'' Mencius answered, ''Kao tzu said, 'What is not attained in words is not to be sought in the mind, and what is not attained in the mind is not to be sought in the vital force.' It is all right to say that what is not attained in the mind is not to be sought in the vital force, but it is not all right to say that what is not attained in words is not to be sought in the mind. The will is the leader of the vital force, and the vital force pervades and animates the body. The will is the highest; the vital force comes next. Therefore I said, 'Hold the will firm and never do violence to the vital force.' ''

Ch'ou said, ''You said that the will is the highest and that the vital force comes next. But you also say to hold the will firm and never to do any violence to the vital force. Why?''

Mencius said, ''If the will is concentrated, the vital force [will follow it] and become active. If the vital force is concentrated, the will [will follow it] and become active. For instance, here is a case of a man falling or running. It is his vital force that is active, and yet it causes his mind to be active too.''

Ch'ou asked, ''May I venture to ask, sir, in what you are strong?''

Mencius replied, ''I understand words. And I am skillful in nourishing my strong, moving power.''

''May I ask what is meant by the strong, moving power?''

''It is difficult to describe. As power, it is exceedingly great and exceedingly strong. If nourished by uprightness and not injured, it will fill up all between heaven and earth. As power, it is accompanied by righteousness and the Way. Without them, it will be devoid of nourishment. It is produced by the accumulation of righteous deeds but is not obtained by incidental acts of righteousness. When one's conduct is not satisfactory to his own mind, then one will be devoid of nourishment. I therefore said that Kao Tzu never understood righteousness because he made it something external.

''Always be doing something without expectation. Let the mind not forget its objective, but let there be no artificial effort to help it grow. Do not be like the man of Sung. There was a man of Sung who was sorry that his corn was not growing, and so he pulled it up. Having been tired out he went home and said to his people, 'I am all tired. I have helped the corn to grow.' When his son ran to look at it, the corn had already withered.''[16]

This long conversation is extremely rich in content. Kao Tzu appeared to have a naturalistic tendency—he would let natural causes follow their courses. On the other hand, Mencius showed an idealistic tendency; he believed that we can be our own masters and that we have the ability to motivate vital forces for our own use. What is at issue here is never the separation of the internal and the external. There has always been an intimate relationship between the two. The crucial question for Mencius was, Which is taking the leading role, the will or the vital force? Kao Tzu did not seem to care if the external vital force were in control. He thought that the external is the deciding factor, which was why he maintained that righteousness is external. Mencius realized that the relationship between the will and the vital force is that of reciprocal determination. When the will is weak, the vital force takes control; but when the will that follows righteousness and the Way is strong, it can become the master and motivates the vital force for its own use. It is typical of a Chinese philosopher like Mencius not to draw a sharp line of demarcation between the will and the vital force. The crux of the matter lies in whether the will can be kept strong and maintain its autonomy. It is here that one must make his own existential decision. Only a man strongly committed to the sagely Way is capable of becoming the master of himself and maintaining an unperturbed mind.

Mencius claimed that he understood words, as words are the expression of the mind. He also claimed that he was skilled in nourishing his strong, moving power. How should we understand this strong, moving power? This question has intrigued scholars ever since Mencius made his claims. But there is no need to make any wild guesses. For Mencius, man is not to be separated from the universe at large; there is no question that the will can motivate the vital force; likewise, a man can nourish his strong, moving power by the accumulation of righteous deeds. It is a matter of determination and action. There seems to be a correlation between the microcosm and the macrocosm. What is important here is that one must take the initiative and start with the self. When man acts according to the principle of righteousness, he will bring about changes that extend to all aspects of his life, influence others' lives, and even find resonance in the universe at large. If there is any mystery here, it is a mystery that opens to everyone who cares to develop the kind of ability and knowledge that is born with him.

Hence, what appears to be difficult to comprehend at the first mention in his talk of nourishing strong, moving power is in fact thoroughly consistent with his general philosophical position. We find that learning and practicing the Way of the sages are both difficult and easy—difficult because most men cannot hold on to that little difference that distinguishes man from other animals, easy because the Way of the sages does not teach anything esoteric that cannot be shared by common people. A sage has no other secret than developing to the fullest extent those Beginnings that can be, and actually are, experienced by any man in the street. Therefore, it is not a matter of ability but of whether we have the kind of strong commitment to carry it through.

Surely the important question for Mencius was not a purely theoretical problem of epistemology but rather a practical problem: how to exert one's already known mind to its fullest extent. In other words, his teaching implies that ideas and practice cannot be separated.[17] One should always strive to preserve and nurture one's original mind. The structure of the mind permits it to be obscured by the unrestrained desires of the senses and unfavorable environmental forces; but the lost mind can be recovered by following proper discipline of the self, so that the vital force can be motivated by the will, and the strong, moving power can be nourished by the self.

Mencius summarized his philosophy well in the following:

> He who exerts his mind to the utmost knows his nature. He who knows his nature knows Heaven. To preserve one's mind and to nourish one's nature is the way to serve Heaven. Not to allow any double-mindedness regardless of longevity or brevity of life, but to cultivate one's person and wait for [destiny (*ming*, fate, Heaven's decree or Mandate) to take its own course] is the way to fulfill one's destiny.[18]

This is perhaps the most important statement that Mencius made in his career. Not only did he develop a new theory of human nature—in contrast to the traditional theory that regarded what is inborn as nature and hence failed to distinguish the specific human nature from animal nature—but he actually pointed out a way to realize one's nature by developing the feelings one experiences and knows at the moment he is born. Another dimension he opened up in this statement was his understanding of Heaven, also epoch making in his time. There is still some ambiguity in Confucius's thought that leaves some room for interpretation as to whether Heaven is the supreme personal God or an impersonal creative principle that works incessantly in the universe. But there is no longer any ambiguity in Mencius's view of the subject. For Mencius, man is the only being in the world who knows the creative way of Heaven in a conscious fashion. Besides, there is no need to depart from the human way in order to know Heaven. On the contrary, the endowment of man's nature comes from Heaven, so anyone who knows nature would know Heaven. Certainly there is a vast difference between Heaven and man, but Heaven's decree is not totally unknowable to man, even though Heaven does not speak. Mencius's understanding of the political life is highly instructive for us.

> Wan Chang asked, "Is it true that Yao gave the empire to Shun?" Mencius replied, "No. The emperor cannot give the empire to another person." "Yes, but Shun had the empire. Who gave it to him?" Mencius said, "Heaven gave it to him." "By Heaven's giving it to him, do you mean that Heaven gave it to him in so many words?" "No. Heaven does not speak. It simply shows its will by [Shun's] personal character and his conduct of affairs."
>
> "May I ask how Heaven showed its will by [Shun's] character and his conduct of affairs?" Mencius said, "The emperor can recommend a person to Heaven, but he cannot make Heaven give that man the empire. A

feudal lord can recommend a person to the emperor, but he cannot make the emperor make that man a feudal lord. A great officer can recommend a person to a feudal lord, but he cannot make the feudal lord make that man a great officer. In ancient times, Yao recommended Shun to Heaven, and Heaven accepted him. He showed him to the people, and the people accepted him. I therefore say that Heaven did not speak, but that it simply indicated its will by his character and his conduct of affairs.''

"May I ask how it was that Yao recommended him to Heaven and Heaven accepted, and that he showed him to the people and the people accepted him?'' Mencius said, ''He had him preside over the sacrifices, and all the spiritual beings enjoyed them. This means that Heaven accepted him. He had him preside over the conduct of affairs, and the affairs were well managed, and the people felt satisfied. This means that the people accepted him. It was Heaven that gave the empire to him. It was the people that gave the empire to him. Therefore I said, 'The emperor cannot give the empire to another person.' Shun assisted Yao for twenty-eight years. This was more than a man could do; it was Heaven that did it. After the death of Yao, when the three-year mourning was completed, Shun withdrew from the son of Yao to the south of the South River. The feudal lords of the empire, however, going to court, went not to the son of Yao but to Shun, litigants went not to the son of Yao but to Shun, and singers sang not to the son of Yao but to Shun. Therefore I said, 'Heaven [gave the empire to him].' Only then did he go to the Middle Kingdom (China) and take the emperor's seat. If he had occupied the place of Yao and applied pressure to his son, it would have been an act of usurpation, and not a gift of Heaven. The 'Great Declaration' said, 'Heaven sees as my people see; Heaven hears as my people hear.' This is the meaning.''[19]

As Heaven does not speak, there is no sign that Heaven would ever intervene in human history. Nevertheless, Heaven does have a will—only it is manifested through people's likes and dislikes. Mencius has established a unique pattern to link what is transcendent and what is immanent. We do not find any idea or practice like the Sabbath Day in the Chinese culture. There is no gap between the sacred and the profane, the supernatural and the natural, religious and secular activities. It is only man who has the mind-heart that cannot bear to see the suffering of others. The sympathy of man has no limit; it may extend from near to the far, until it pervades the whole vast universe. And through reflection the realization of man's mind-heart has been brought to the conscious level. Our ultimate commitment is to humanity and righteousness within us, and yet the realization of what is proper to man helps him to transcend his own limit so that he can identify with the entire universe. Thus, Mencius said, ''All things are already complete in oneself. There is no greater joy than to examine oneself and be sincere. When in one's conduct one vigorously exercises altruism, humanity is not far to seek, but right by him.''[20] Surely Mencius could not have taught a kind of solipsism here, nor was he teaching a kind of esoteric mysticism. For anyone who cares to develop the great potentiality within himself, he will realize that there is no need to look for any external causes in order to find one's self-realization; yet the realization of the self does not limit him to the small self but makes him in consonance with the whole universe. Paradoxically speaking, one must look up to Heaven in order to find the true realization of man. Mencius said:

> There is nobility of Heaven and there is nobility of man. Humanity, right-eousness, loyalty, faithfulness, and the love of the good without getting tired of it constitute the nobility of Heaven, and to be a grant official, a great official, and a high official—this constitutes the nobility of man. The ancient people cultivated the nobility of Heaven, and the nobility of man naturally came to them. People today cultivate the nobility of Heaven in order to seek for the nobility of man, and once they have obtained the nobility of man, they forsake the nobility of Heaven. Therefore their delusion is extreme. At the end they will surely lose [the nobility of man] also.[21]

It is the realization of what Heaven imparts to man in distinction to other animals that makes man great. Mencius said:

> With Yao and Shun it was their nature. With T'ang and Wu, it was their effort to return [to their nature]. When all movements and expressions are exactly proper according to the rules of propriety, that shows the highest degree of eminent virtue. The sorrow in weeping for the dead is not for the sake of the living. The regular practice of virtue without any deviation is not to seek emolument. And words should always be sincere not because of any conscious desire to do what is right. The superior man practices principle and waits for destiny (*ming*, Mandate of Heaven) to take its own course.[22]

For Mencius, there is just no dichotomy between spirit and matter, the body and the mind; when the spiritual part is in the lead, everything will be in order. The universe as a whole is a creative one with predominant order in it; its operation is not that different from that of the human world. Even though the spiritual part takes the leading role, Mencius does not look down upon the other ingredients in man as well as in the universe. Every ingredient should receive its fullest development according to due measure. Mencius said, "Form and color (our body) are nature endowed by Heaven. It is only the sage who can put his physical form into full use."[23] In other words, a sage must develop an all-round personality in which the potentiality in his life has been realized in its fullest extent. One's commitment to humanity and righteousness must find its manifestation in actual life. A sage must live a rich life both on the spiritual and on the material levels. Mencius said, "What is desirable is good. What one realizes in the self is true. What is full is beautiful. What is full and with splendor is great. What is great and has transforming power is sagely. What is sagely and is beyond the penetration of knowledge is divine."[24] Thus, a fully realized individual is not far from participating in what is divine in the universe. "Whenever the superior man passes through, transforming influence follows. Wherever he abides, spiritual influence remains. This forms the same current above and below with that of Heaven and Earth. Is this a small help?"[25] A sage, realizing his own nature, which is what has been imparted to him from Heaven, is joining forces with Heaven and Earth with their immense task of creation and sustenance in the universe.

Starting from one's existential experience of humanity and righteousness, Mencius moves toward a comprehensive metaphysical and religious outlook. If one looks at the natural world from a spectator's point of view, most probably he would adopt a naturalistic interpretation of Heaven. But man is better characterized as a partaker. In his participation, he apprehends the will of Heaven and, for the first time, truly discovers a creative universe with intrinsic value in it. If this is called mysticism, it is a mystical philosophy that can be taught under the broad sunlight and can be understood by any man in the street, as every person has been endowed with the seed of this profound mystery in himself.[26]

In effect, Heaven is intelligible to those who have realized their nature. It is the source of the cosmic order and does not have to assume the character of a supreme personal God. Man, the noblest creature in the world, should live according to the principles of humanity and righteousness. Sometimes flocks of people may act in deviation from the norms, and this would mean a disaster for all. Mencius said:

> It is useless to talk to those who do violence to their own nature, and it is useless to do anything with those who throw themselves away. To speak what is against propriety and righteousness is to do violence to oneself. To say that one cannot abide by humanity and follow righteousness is to throw oneself away. Humanity is the peaceful abode of men and righteousness is his straight path. What a pity for those who leave the peaceful abode and do not live there, and abandon the straight path and do not follow it![27]

Therefore, the best way to serve Heaven is to preserve one's mind-heart and to nourish one's nature. The way of man is not to be separated from the Way of Heaven; the realization of the way of man is at the same time the realization of the Way of Heaven. It is in this way that Mencius further developed the philosophy of union between Heaven and man implicit in Confucius's thought. According to this trend of thought, there is no need to depart from our ordinary life and to be completely absorbed in the transcendent spiritual source as demanded by certain mystical traditions. Since Heaven has created man, the best way to fulfill the will of Heaven is just to live fully as a man.

If religion is characterized by the belief in a supreme personal God with predominantly other-worldly concerns, then Mencius was not religious. If, however, religion is defined as the ultimate concern of man, then Mencius, like Confucius, is a deeply religious person. Like the old master, he sanctioned the practice of funeral rites and sacrifice to Heaven. But even more specific than Confucius, he openly acknowledged the divine sparks within man and elaborated on the way a man may start from his humble beginning to reach an understanding of the decree of Heaven.

Besides developing a philosophy of human nature and Heaven, Mencius also had something interesting to say about human destiny. He said, "Everything is destiny (*ming*). A man should accept obediently what is correct [in one's destiny]. Therefore, he who knows destiny does not stand beneath a precipitous wall. Death sustained in the course of carrying out the Way to the limit is due to correct destiny. But death under handcuffs and fetters is not due to correct destiny."[28]

Some opponents made charges against the Confucian school, saying that it taught a fatalistic philosophy; such accusations were found groundless, as Mencius made a clear distinction between correct and incorrect destiny. Mencius's understanding of human destiny showed that he accepted the fact that man is a finite being but can still make meaningful choices by following his correct destiny instead of incorrect destiny. Mencius further analyzed the relationship between nature (*hsing*) and destiny (*ming*), as he said:

It is due to our nature that our mouths desire sweet taste, that our eyes desire beautiful colors, that our ears desire pleasant sounds, that our noses desire fragrant odors, and that our four limbs desire ease and comfort. But there is also fate (*ming*) [whether these desires are satisfied or not]. The superior man does not say they are man's nature [and insist on satisfying them]. The virtue of humanity in the relationship between father and son, the virtue of righteousness in the relationship between ruler and minister, the virtue of propriety in the relationship between guest and host, the virtue of wisdom in the worthy, and the sage in regard to the Way of Heaven—these are [endowed in people in various degrees] according to fate. But there is also man's nature. The superior man does not (refrain from practicing them and) say they are matters of fate.[29]

What Mencius tried to tell us was that although it is due to the fact that we are men so that we have sensory desires, we cannot control our fates and should not demand that we have to satisfy these desires; on the other hand, when we fail to practice the virtues of humanity, righteousness, propriety, and wisdom, we should not make the excuse that it is because of our lesser endowments that we cannot help it, as these pertain to the specific human nature found in all men. Mencius actually implied the distinction between man's physical nature and man's moral nature later on specified by the Sung Neo-Confucian philosophers.[30] The distinction between nature and destiny in this particular context seems to mean that nature is something internal, while destiny is something external. Although on the factual level the two may coincide with each other, the meanings of them are quite different. Surely we may say that sensory desires pertain to our nature, but we would rather say that these are matters concerning our fate or destiny that are beyond our control. On the other hand, surely we may also say that the practice of humanity and righteousness pertains to our fate or destiny, but we would rather say that these virtues manifest the specific nature of man. A superior man cannot fail to realize what is endowed in him, that is, his nature, but he is not in a position to control his fate or destiny. Therefore, the most important thing is one's commitment to humanity and righteousness. If one practices according to the Way and leaves the rest to destiny—that is to say, accepts one's correct destiny—then he would be able to gather immense moral courage within himself. Mencius said:

> He who dwells in the wide house of the world, stands in the correct station of the world, walks in the great path of the world; one who practices virtues along with the people when he is successful, and practices the Way alone when he is disappointed; one whose heart cannot be dissipated by the power of wealth and honors, who cannot be influenced by poverty or humble stations, who cannot be subdued by force and might—such a person is a great man.[31]

A man committed to the Way would not even fear death when he has to make a right decision at the crucial moment. Mencius said:

> I like fish and I also like bear's paw. If I cannot have both of them, I shall give up the fish and choose the bear's paw. I like life and I also like righteousness. If I cannot have both of them, I shall give up life and choose righteousness. I love life, but there is something I love more than life, and therefore I will not do anything improper to have it. I also hate death, but there is something I hate more than death, and therefore there are occasions when I will not avoid danger. If there is nothing that man loves more than life, then why should he not employ every means to preserve it? And if there is nothing that man hates more than death, then why does he not do anything to avoid danger? There are cases when a man does not take the course even if by taking it he can preserve his life, and he does not do anything even if by doing it he can avoid danger. Therefore there is something men love more than life and there is something men hate more than death. It is not only the worthies alone who have this

moral sense. All men have it, but only the worthies have been able to preserve it.[32]

Life is not a smooth sail; therefore, a man committed himself to the Way must have firm resolution; very often, he will have a life tougher than most people. Mencius said, "When Heaven is about to confer a great responsibility on any man, it will exercise his mind with suffering, subject his sinews and bones to hard work, expose his body to hunger, put him to poverty, place obstacles in the paths of his deeds, so as to stimulate his mind, harden his nature, and improve wherever he is incompetent."[33] But in the final analysis, for Mencius, "The great man is one who does not lose his [originally good] child's heart."[34] And it is a rare achievement for one to be able to develop what is in him fully.

Politics for Mencius is merely an extension of ethics. The ideal government is one that is built on the mind that cannot bear to see the suffering of others. Mencius said:

All men have the mind which cannot bear to [see the suffering of] others. The ancient kings had this mind and therefore they had a government that could not bear to see the suffering of the people. When a government that cannot bear to see the suffering of the people is conducted from a mind that cannot bear to see the suffering of others, the government of the empire will be as easy as making something go round in the palm.[35]

The foundation of the ideal government is not built on force but on humanity that has a natural attraction for people. Mencius elaborated in the following way:

A ruler who uses force to make a pretense of humanity is a despot. Such a despot requires a large kingdom. A ruler who practices humanity with virtue is a true king. To become a true king does not depend on a large kingdom. T'ang became so with only seventy li, and King Wen with only a hundred. When force is used to overcome people, they do not submit willingly but only because they have not sufficient strength to resist. But when virtue is used to overcome people, they are pleased in their hearts and sincerely submit, as the seventy disciples submitted to Confucius. The Book of Odes says:

From the west, from the east,
From the south, from the north,
None wanted to resist.

This is what is meant.[36]

A government built on inhumanity would certainly fail. According to Mencius:

Confucius said, "There are but two ways to follow, that of humanity and that of inhumanity." A ruler who oppresses his people to the extreme will himself be slain and his kingdom will perish. If he oppresses not to the extreme, even then his life will be in danger and his kingdom will be weakened. They will be called by the names of "King Yu" (meaning an unenlightened king) and "King Li" (meaning a cruel king) and though they may have filial sons and affectionate grandsons, they will not be able in a hundred generations to change these names. *The Book of Odes* says,

> The mirror of the Shang dynasty is not far back,
> It was in the time of the Hsia dynasty [whose last, wicked king was removed by the founder of Shang].

This is what is meant.[37]

Mencius traveled to a number of states to promote his ideal of humane government, when most of the feudal lords were much more interested in military buildup. He counseled King Hui of Liang in the following manner:

> Even with a territory of a hundred *li*, it is possible to become the true king of the empire. If Your Majesty can practice a humane government to the people, reduce punishments and fines, lower taxes and levies, make it possible for the fields to be plowed deep and the weeding well done, men of strong body, in their days of leisure may cultivate their filial piety, brotherly respect, loyalty, and faithfulness, thereby serving their fathers and elder brothers at home and their elders and superiors abroad. Then you can have them prepare sticks to oppose the strong armor and sharp weapons of the states of Ch'in and Ch'u.[38]

When King Hsüan of Ch'i made all kinds of excuses to show that he could not follow Mencius's lofty moral ideals, the way Mencius tried to persuade him was very instructive indeed:

> King Hsüan of Ch'i said, "I have a weakness. I love wealth." Mencius replied, ". . . If Your Majesty love wealth, let your people enjoy the same, and what difficulty will there be for you to become the true king of the empire?" The King said "I have a weakness, I love sex." Mencius replied, ". . . If Your Majesty love sex, let your people enjoy the same, and what difficulty will there be for you to become the true king of the empire?"[39]

In effect, Mencius never asked the kings to give up all their desires; he only counseled them to share and to limit their desires in order to follow the lead of the mind that cannot bear to see the suffering of the people. Although Mencius was an idealist, his counsels were very down-to-earth:

Duke Wen of T'eng asked about the proper way of government. Mencius said, "The business of the people should not be delayed. *The Book of Odes* says,

In the morning go and gather the grass,
In the evening twist your ropes.
Then get up soon on the roof [to do the repair],
For before long the grains have to be sowed.

"The way according to which the people conduct their lives is this: If they have a secure livelihood, they will have a secure mind. And if they have no secure livelihood, they will not have a secure mind. And if they have no secure mind, there is nothing they will not do in the way of self-abandonment, moral deflection, depravity, and wild license. When they fall into crime, to pursue and punish them is to entrap them. How can such a thing as entrapping the people be allowed under the rule of a man of humanity? Therefore a worthy ruler will be gravely complaisant and thrifty, showing a respectful politeness to his subordinates, and taking from the people according to regulations."[40]

After people are well fed, they must receive a decent education in order to develop a more refined culture.

According to the way of man, if they are well fed, warmly clothed, and comfortably lodged but without education, they will become almost like animals. The Sage (emperor Shun) worried about it and he appointed Hsieh to be minister of education and teach people human relations, that between father and son, there should be affection; between ruler and minister, there should be righteousness; between husband and wife, there should be attention to their separate functions; between old and young, there should be a proper order; and between friends, there should be faithfulness. Emperor Yao said, "Encourage them, lead them on, rectify them, straighten them, help them, aid them, so they discover for themselves [their moral nature], and in addition, stimulate them and confer kindness on them." When sages were so much concerned with their people, had they the time for farming?[41]

The sage-emperors taught people *wu-lun* (five relationships). Mencius believed in a hierarchical government, headed by men with the ability and virtue to lead a humane government; he also firmly believed in the principle of division of labor. While there were people who believed that everyone should work in the fields, Mencius rejected this view:

When can the government of the empire alone be done along with farming? There is the work of great men and there is the work of little men. Furthermore, whatever is needed for one single person is supplied by the

FRAMINGHAM STATE COLLEGE
FRAMINGHAM, MA

various artisans. If one must make the things himself before he uses them, this would make the whole empire run about on the road. Therefore it is said, "Some labor with their minds and some labor with their strength. Those who labor with their minds govern others; those who labor with their strength are governed by others." Those who are governed by others support them; those who govern them are supported by them. This is a universal principle.[42]

Not only a ruler is needed; the services of the ministers are also needed. Mencius said, "If a ruler regards his ministers as his hands and feet, then his ministers will regard him as their heart and mind. If a ruler regards his ministers as dogs and horses, his ministers will regard him as any other man. If a ruler regards his ministers as dirt and grass, his ministers will regard him as a bandit and an enemy."[43]

The system of humane government works for the benefit of the people. Mencius declared: "[In a state] the people are the most important; the spirits of the land and grain (guardians of territory) are the next; the ruler is of slight importance."[44] And the difference between a true king and a despot is easy to detect. Mencius said, "Under a despot, the people look brisk and cheerful [only temporarily and superficially, for the despot's kindness is selfishly motivated]. Under a true king, however, the people feel magnificent and at ease with themselves. Though he punishes them by death, they do not complain, and when he benefits them, they do not think of their merit. From day to day they make progress without knowing who makes them do so."[45] Although Mencius taught that subjects must be loyal and obedient to their rulers, it does not mean that they have to be loyal and obedient to despots.

> King Hsüan of Ch'i asked, "Was it a fact that T'ang banished King Chieh and that King Wu punished King Chou?" Mencius replied, "Yes, according to records." The King said, "Is it all right for a minister to murder his king?" Mencius said, "He who injures humanity is a bandit. He who injures righteousness is a destructive person. Such a person is a mere fellow. I have heard of killing a mere fellow Chou, but I have not heard of murdering [him as] the ruler."[46]

Actually, this was the result of Mencius's application of the Confucian doctrine of rectification of names (*cheng-ming*). *The Analects* reported:

> Duke Ching of Ch'i asked Confucius about government. Confucius replied, "Let the ruler *be* a ruler, the minister *be* a minister, the father *be* a father, and the son *be* a son." The duke said, "Excellent! Indeed when the ruler is not a ruler, the minister not a minister, the father not a father, and the son not a son, although I may have all the grain, shall I ever get to eat it?"[47]

Mencius simply spelled out the implications of the doctrine. He unequivocally defended the right to revolt against despots as rulers. But a revolt is justified only under abnormal circumstances—not under the normal and ideal conditions of a state. For Mencius the ideal possibility of a humane government was not just wishful thinking; such a governmental form had been practiced under the reigns of sage-emperors Yao and Shun. In those days, leaders with ability and virtue were chosen as rulers of the state, and Mencius offered an explanation as to how dynasties started in China:

> Wang Chang asked: "People say that when it came to Yü, there was a decline in virtue (from that of Yao and Shun), and that he did not transmit (the empire) to the worthiest but to his own son. Is this true?" Mencius replied: "No, it is not so. When Heaven gave the empire to the worthiest, it was given to the worthiest. When Heaven gave it to a son, it was given to a son. Shun had presented Yü to Heaven. Seventeen years elapsed and Shun died. When the three years' mourning was expired, Yü withdrew from the son of Shun to Yang-ch'eng. The people of the empire followed him, just as after the death of Yao they had not followed Yao's son but had followed Shun. Yü presented Yi (Yü's minister) to Heaven. Seven years elapsed and Yü died. When the three years' mourning had elapsed, Yi withdrew from the son of Yü to the north of Mount Chi. But those who went to Court, and litigants, went not to Yi but went to Ch'i (son of Yü), saying: He is the son of our sovereign. The singers did not sing to Yi but to Ch'i, saying: He is the son of our sovereign.
>
> "That Tan Chu (son of Yao) was not equal to (Yao), and Shun's son also not equal to him; that Shun assisted Yao and Yü assisted Shun over a period of many years, long conferring benefits on the people; that Ch'i (Yü's son) was worthy and capable of respectfully carrying on the way of Yü; that Yi did not assist Yü for a long period and did not long confer benefits on the people, whereas the assistance given by Shun and Yü had been far longer; and that the sons of those rulers were some inferior, and some not inferior; all this was from Heaven, and not something which could have been brought about by man. That which is done without man's doing it, is from Heaven. That which happens without man's causing it to happen, is from Fate (*ming*)."[48]

Mencius also gave an explanation as to why a great man like Confucius did not have a chance to obtain the empire:

> When it is a private individual who obtains the empire, his virtue must be equal to that of Shun and Yü, and in addition to this he must have the Son of Heaven presenting him (to Heaven). This is why Confucius did not obtain the empire.
> When the empire is held through hereditary succession, the Emperor

must be like a Chieh or a Chou to be displaced by Heaven. This is why Yi, Yi Yin, and the Duke of Chou did not obtain the empire.[49]

Mencius was a man of great critical spirit. Although Confucianists were generally characterized as conservative traditionalists, Mencius did not always follow the authority of the Classics handed down to the posterity from the past. He said, "It would be better to have no *Book of History* than to believe all of it. In its 'Completion of War' section [for example], I accept only two or three passages. A man of humanity has no enemy in the world. When a most humane person (King Wu) punished a most inhumane ruler (King Chou), how could the blood (of the people) have flowed till it floated the pestles of the mortars?"[50]

Mencius also made an important distinction between commitment to principle and the practice of expediency.

Shun-yü K'un said, "Is it a rule of propriety that men and women should not touch hands when they give or receive things?" Mencius said, "It is a rule of propriety." "If someone's sister-in-law is drowning, should he rescue her with his hand?" Mencius said, "He who does not rescue his drowning sister-in-law is a wolf. It is a rule of propriety for men and women not to touch hands when giving or receiving things, but it is a matter of expediency to rescue one's drowning sister-in-law with hands." "The whole world is now drowning. Why do you, sir, not rescue it?" Mencius said, "A drowning empire must be rescued with moral principles. Do you wish me to rescue the world with my hand?"[51]

Mencius was firmly committed to moral principles to save the world. Unfortunately, however, most people simply had not heard about the Way and the great doctrine. Mencius said:

From Yao and Shun down to T'ang there were five hundred years and more. As to Yü and Kao Yao, they saw (these earliest Sages) and so knew their doctrines, while T'ang heard their doctrines (as transmitted) and so knew them. From T'ang to King Wen were five hundred years and more. As to Yi Yin and Lai Chu, they saw (T'ang) and knew his doctrines, while King Wen heard them (as transmitted) and so knew them. From King Wen to Confucius there were five hundred years and more. As to T'ai-kung Wang and San-i Sheng, they saw (Wen) and so knew his doctrines, while Confucius heard them (as transmitted) and so knew them. From Confucius downward to today there have been one hundred odd years. Thus I am not yet far from the generation of that Sage, and am extremely close to his residence. Under these circumstances is there no one (to transmit his doctrines)? Yea, is there indeed no one?[52]

Mencius indeed had high hopes. Like Confucius, however, he accomplished very little in the practical world. He also ended up with a teaching career and played an important role in the transmission of the Confucian Way. He further developed Confucius's thought, was honored as representing the orthodoxy by Sung-Ming Neo-Confucianism, and has been regarded as a fountainhead of inspiration by contemporary Neo-Confucian philosophers. Although Hsün Tzu (fl. 298–238 B.C.) attacked him as teaching something loose and obscure, the posterity preferred Mencius to Hsün Tzu, who advocated a naturalistic view of Heaven and taught that human nature is evil and what is good is achieved. As Hsün Tzu opened the gate for Legalism, he was excluded from the Confucian orthodoxy, even though he contributed a great deal to the preservation of the Confucian Classics. There is little doubt that Mencius has been the most influential thinker since ancient times, second only to Confucius himself.[53]

NOTES

1. Chan, *Source Book*, p. 72.
2. Ibid., p. 45.
3. Ibid., p. 28.
4. Ibid., p. 52.
5. Ibid.
6. Cf. Ibid., p. 53.
7. Cf. James Legge, trans., *The Four Books* (New York: Paragon Reprint Corp., 1966), p. 744 (hereafter cited as Legge, *The Four Books*).
8. Chan, *Source Book*, p. 59, with modification. *Hsin* may be rendered as either "mind" or "heart"; there is no distinction between the two in Mencius's thought.
9. Ibid., pp. 65–66.
10. Ibid., pp. 51–52.
11. Ibid., pp. 53–54.
12. Ibid., p. 58.
13. Ibid., pp. 56–57.
14. Ibid., p. 80.
15. Legge, *The Four Books*, p. 526.
16. Chan, *Source Book*, pp. 62–64.
17. In later ages it was especially Wang Yang-ming (1472–1529) who taught the doctrine of the unity of knowledge and action. Cf. ibid., p. 656.
18. Ibid., p. 78.
19. Ibid., pp. 77–78.
20. Ibid., p. 79.
21. Ibid., pp. 59–60.
22. Ibid., p. 83.
23. Ibid., p. 80.
24. Cf. Legge, *The Four Books*, p. 995; translation mine.
25. Chan, *Source Book*, p. 80.
26. Cf. Fung Yu-lan, *A History of Chinese Philosophy*, trans. Derk Bodde, 2 vols. (Princeton, N.J.: Princeton University Press, 1952–1953), 1: 129–131 (hereafter cited as Fung, *History*).

27. Chan, *Source Book*, p. 74.

28. Ibid., p. 79.

29. Ibid., pp. 81–82.

30. These concepts were further developed by Sung Neo-Confucian philosophers such as Chang Tsai (1020–1077), Ch'eng I (1033–1107), and Chu Hsi (1130–1200). Cf. ibid., pp. 511, 552, 612–626.

31. Ibid., p. 72.

32. Ibid., p. 57.

33. Ibid., p. 78.

34. Ibid., p. 76.

35. Ibid., p. 65.

36. Ibid., p. 64; a *li* is approximately one-third of a mile.

37. Ibid., p. 73.

38. Ibid., p. 61.

39. Ibid.

40. Ibid., pp. 66–67.

41. Ibid., pp. 69–70.

42. Ibid., p. 69.

43. Ibid., p. 76.

44. Ibid., p. 81.

45. Ibid., pp. 79–80.

46. Ibid., p. 62. Chan's translation had it: "King Wen punished King Chou"; I made the correction according to the Chinese text.

47. Ibid., p. 39.

48. Fung, *History*, 1:116.

49. Ibid.

50. Chan, *Source Book*, p. 81.

51. Ibid., p. 75.

52. Fung, *History*, 1:107–108.

53. There is no lack of controversy in interpreting Mencius's thought. For some of the issues, cf. Shu-hsien Liu, "Reflections on Mencius' Views of Mind-Heart and Human Nature," trans. Kwong-loi Shun, *Philosophy East and West* 46, no. 2 (April 1996): 143–164. In this chapter, the strategy I employed was to quote as much as possible from *The Book of Mencius* and let the texts speak for themselves. I only added interpretations where necessary to clarify Mencius's system of thought. See also Kwong-loi Shun, *Mencius and Early Chinese Thought* (Stanford, Calif.: Stanford University Press, 1997), pp. 180–231.

4

The Great Learning and The Doctrine of the Mean

The Great Learning (Ta Hsüeh) and *The Doctrine of the Mean (Chung Yung)* are actually two chapters of *The Book of Rites (Li Chi)*. They were extracted from the *Rites* by the Ch'eng brothers, Ch'eng Hao (1032–1085) and Ch'eng I (1033–1107). Chu Hsi (1130–1200) followed them and grouped these two chapters together with *The Analects* and *The Book of Mencius* to form the so-called *Four Books*. He wrote *Commentaries* for them, and they became the basis for civil service examinations from 1313 to 1905. The importance of these two Classics are far greater than their small size would suggest. *The Great Learning* summed up the Confucian educational, moral, and political programs, and *The Doctrine of the Mean* probed Confucian psychology and metaphysics in depth. The former relates the internal to the external, and the latter joins Heaven and man, which is seen by contemporary Neo-Confucian philosophers as having profound religious significance.[1] I shall discuss *The Great Learning* first, then *The Doctrine of the Mean*.

For *The Great Learning*, let us first start with Chu Hsi's remark: "Master Ch'eng I said, '*The Great Learning* is a surviving work of the Confucian school and is the gate through which the beginning student enters into virtue. It is only due to the preservation of this work that the order in which the ancients pursued their learning may be seen at this time. *The Analects* and *The Book of Mencius* are next to it. The student should by all means follow this work in his effort to learn, and then he will probably be free from mistakes.' "[2] According to Chu Hsi, the text is in one chapter. It is the words of Confucius, handed down by Tseng Tzu. The ten sections of commentary that follow are the views of Tseng Tzu and were recorded by his pupils. Modern scholarship doubts that such is the case. But there is no question that thoughts expressed in the document are consistent with the thoughts of Confucius and Tseng Tzu. As the text has included the most important messages in the Classic, I shall quote it in its entirety:

> The Way of the great learning consists in manifesting the illustrious virtue, loving the people, and abiding (*chih*) in the highest good.
>
> Only after knowing what to abide in can one be calm. Only after having been calm can one be tranquil. Only after having achieved tranquillity can one have peaceful repose. Only after having peaceful repose can one begin to deliberate. Only after deliberation can the end be attained. Things have their roots and their branches. To know what is first and what is last will lead one near the Way.
>
> The ancients who wished to manifest their illustrious virtue to the world would first bring order to the states. Those who wished to bring order to their states would first regulate their families. Those who wished to regulate their families would first cultivate their personal lives. Those who wished to cultivate their personal lives would first rectify their minds. Those who wished to rectify their minds would first make their wills sincere. Those who wished to make their wills sincere would first extend their knowledge. The extension of knowledge [*chih-chih*] consists in the investigation of things [*ko-wu*]. When things are investigated, knowledge is extended; when knowledge is extended, the will becomes sincere; when the will is sincere, the mind is rectified; when the mind is rectified, the personal life is cultivated; when the personal life is cultivated, the family will be regulated; when the family is regulated, the state will be in order; and when the state is in order, there will be peace throughout the world. From the Son of Heaven down to the common people, all must regard cultivation of the personal life as the root or foundation. There is never a case when the root is in disorder and yet the branches are in order. There has never been a case when what is treated with great importance becomes a matter of slight importance or what is treated with slight importance becomes a matter of great importance.[3]

The Great Learning teaches us about the so-called three principles and eight items. I will elaborate on them.

The first paragraph lays down the three principles of *The Great Learning*: The first principle addresses the inherent goodness within every individual; it pertains to the ideal of inward sageliness (*nei-sheng*). The second principle has to do with the extension of humanity to others; it pertains to the ideal of outward kingliness (*wai-wang*). When both the inward and outward aspects are taken care of, the supreme good has been achieved. Then the ideal is to maintain it forever. Chu Hsi interpreted the second principle as enlightening the people, an interpretation that is also acceptable. Interestingly enough, the ideal of "sageliness within and kingliness without" (*nei-sheng-wai-wang*) was first mentioned in chapter 33 of *The Chuang Tzu*.[4] But it is even more applicable to the Confucian tradition, as it is, without a doubt, the central theme of *The Great Learning*. One must start with cultivation of the personal life in a conscious fashion; then humanity may be extended to others.

The second paragraph teaches us the discipline of the mind. Some scholars see in this paragraph the influence of Taoism. Actually, so-called transcendental meditation can be practiced in different ways. The Indians taught us Yoga; and they obviously have a strong tradition in transcendental meditation. In China, the Taoists also have such a tradition. It is not clear whether the Confucianists learned it from the Taoists. At any rate, the purposes for practicing transcendental meditation are different in different traditions, and the methods employed are also different. What concerns us here is only that we know from this Classic that in ancient times transcendental meditation had already been employed for the purpose of discipline of the self in the Confucian tradition, and its use is quite consistent with Mencius's nourishment of the night air. In English, terms like *calm, tranquillity*, and *peaceful repose* appear to be synonyms; but in fact they represent different steps in the process of discipline. Being calm has the implication that direction has been set, while tranquillity contrasts with activity, and peaceful repose suggests that the mind is at ease. It is under such conditions that the mind can deliberate. Through the reflection of the mind, principles can be grasped and be put into action. It is in this way that we would know where to start and where to end.

In the third paragraph, *The Great Learning* talks about the eight items. They are the eight steps to be taken to, first, realize Confucian ideals in the individual, then extend those ideals to the society and finally to the world as a whole. The first five items—*ko-wu*, or investigation of things; *chih-chih*, or extension of knowledge; making the wills sincere; rectification of the mind; and cultivation of the personal life—pertain to inward sageliness; the next three items—regulating the family, putting the state in order, and peace throughout the world—pertain to outward kingliness. In the conclusion, it is explicitly stated that from the Son of Heaven, that is, the emperor, to the common people, all must regard cultivation of the personal life as the root or the foundation. Thus to say that Confucian ethics teaches the morality of a scholar-gentry class is clearly false. And it is also not true to say that the Confucian tradition does not value the individual, as everything must start with the individual. What is lacking is the kind of rugged individualism of the West. Everyone is conscious of a strong sense of responsibility to society; there is no dichotomy between the individual and the society, or the internal and the external.

What is problematic is the understanding of *ko-wu* and *chih-chih* as investigation of things and extension of knowledge according to Chu Hsi's interpretation. Furthermore, Chu Hsi believed that the commentary that explains the meaning of the investigation of things and the extension of knowledge is now lost, and he ventured to take the view of Master Ch'eng I, then supplemented it:

The meaning of the expression "The perfection of knowledge depends on the investigation of things (ko-wu)" is this: If we wish to extend our knowledge to the utmost, we must investigate the principles of all things we come into contact with, for the intelligent mind of man is certainly formed to know, and there is not a single thing in which its principles do not inhere. It is only because all principles are not investigated that man's knowledge is incomplete. For this reason, the first step in the great education is to instruct the learner, in regard to all things in the world, to proceed from what knowledge he has of their principles, and investigate further until he reaches the limit. After exerting himself in this way for a long time, he will one day achieve a wide and far-reaching penetration. Then the qualities of all things, whether internal or external, the refined or the coarse, will all be apprehended, and the mind, in its total substance and great functioning, will be perfectly intelligent. This is called the investigation of things. This is called the perfection of knowledge.[5]

Chu Hsi's interpretation carried great authority since his *Commentaries* were adopted as the basis for civil service examinations. Despite his unparalleled achievements, his ideas did not go unchallenged, even in his own day. His friend and younger contemporary Lu Hsiang-shan (1139–1193) felt strongly that the accumulation of empirical knowledge and even the study of Classical texts had little relevance for personal cultivation to form one's moral character. Wang Yang-ming (1472–1529) in the Ming dynasty went even further to give *ko-wu* a totally different interpretation: "*Ko*" for him means "to correct"; as principles are inherent in the mind, it is useless to investigate external things such as the bamboo trees in the courtyard. "*Wu*" means "affairs" and is not limited to just things. *Chih-chih* for him means *chih-liang-chih*, to extend what Mencius called innate knowledge of the good to a myriad of things in the world. And Wang did not believe that any text was lost in *The Great Learning* and urged that the ancient text be restored. In all fairness to Chu Hsi, however, he knew that the investigation of things and the study of Classical texts do not have direct relevance for forming moral character; but he was convinced that all things in the world have principles that are manifestations of the same Principle of Heaven. Thus, conducting the investigation of things to a certain point would bring about enlightenment of the ultimate creative principle that is the origin of all things and values in the world. Despite the longtime rivalry between the so-called Ch'eng-Chu and Lu-Wang schools, both agreed that there is inherent goodness in man, the cultivation of personal lives is the foundation, and peace throughout the world is the ideal to be realized as prescribed by *The Great Learning*.

Now let us examine *The Doctrine of the Mean*, which is the most metaphysical piece in the Confucian Classics. Again, let us start with Chu Hsi's remark:

Master Ch'eng I (Ch'eng I-ch'uan, 1033–1107) said, "By *chung* (central) is meant what is not one-sided, and by *yung* (ordinary) is meant what is unchangeable. *Chung* is the correct path of the world and *yung* is the definite principle of the world." "This work represents the central way in which the doctrines of the Confucian school have been transmitted." Fearing that in time errors should arise, Tzu-ssu wrote it down and transmitted it to Mencius. The book "first speaks of one principle, next it spreads out to cover the ten thousand things, and finally returns and gathers them all under the one principle." Unroll it and it reaches in all directions. Roll it up, and it withdraws and lies hidden in minuteness. "Its meaning and interest are inexhaustible." The whole of it is solid learning. If the skillful reader will explore and brood over it and apprehend it, he may apply it throughout his life, and will find it inexhaustible."⁶

According to *Historical Records*, Tzu-ssu (492–431, B.C.), Confucius's grandson, was the author of the article; Ch'eng-Chu simply accepted the traditional account. But modern scholars have serious reservation about the assertion, as there is no evidence to support the claim. In content, *The Doctrine of the Mean* discussed *ch'eng* (sincerity) in a much more elaborate fashion than Mencius. It could be argued that the article was written after Mencius. But there is no question that the Classic expressed the views of the school of Tzu-ssu and Mencius. For our purposes, we need only to explicate the meanings implicit in the document. The structure of the article is much more complex than *The Great Learning*. It appears that the first part discusses *chung* (centrality), *yung* (universality), *hsing* (nature), and *T'ien-tao* (the Way of Heaven), whereas the second part discusses *ch'eng* (sincerity). But the thoughts expressed in these two parts are certainly consistent with each other. This is why in my presentation of *Chung Yung*'s thought I have not tried to make a distinction between the two.

The opening passage in *Chung Yung* reads as follows:

What Heaven (*T'ien*) imparts [*ming*] to man is called human nature. To follow our nature is called the Way (Tao). Cultivating the Way is called education. The Way cannot be separated from us for a moment. What can be separated from us is not the Way. Therefore the superior man is cautious over what he does not see and apprehensive over what he does not hear. There is nothing more visible than what is hidden and nothing more manifest than what is subtle. Therefore the superior man is watchful over himself when he is alone.⁷

The first three statements here are no less important than the first three statements in *The Great Learning*. The very first sentence declares that human nature is an endowment from Heaven. It will be seen that Heaven no longer shows any characteristics of a personal God; it is a profound metaphysical principle of creativity working incessantly in the universe in an unobtrusive way. There is indeed a union between Heaven and man, even though the term *T'ien-jen-ho-i* (Heaven and man in union) was not yet coined to capture the thrust of the thought, which is totally consistent with Mencius's idea that bringing out the inherent goodness in everyone is the way to serve Heaven. And education is exactly for that purpose. The term *T'ien-ming* appeared in the very first sentence in *Chung Yung*. *T'ien-ming* as a noun is usually rendered into English as the Mandate of Heaven. In more ancient times, Heaven was referred to as a personal God; and the Mandate of Heaven was invoked during the transmission of political powers: Whoever receives the Mandate of Heaven will become the ruler of the people. In *Chung Yung*, however, Heaven is no longer conceived in personal terms, and *T'ien-ming* also no longer refers to something external but to the internal endowment of man.

Let us turn to the last chapter in *Chung Yung*, where there is some elaboration on this new understanding of Heaven. "*The Book of Odes* says, 'I cherish your brilliant virtue, which makes no great display in sound or appearance.' Confucius said, 'In influencing people, the use of sound or appearance is of secondary importance.' *The Book of Odes* says, 'His virtue is as light as hair.' Still, a hair is comparable. 'The operations of Heaven have neither sound nor smell.' "[8] Such an understanding of Heaven is totally consistent with Confucius's teaching that Heaven does not say anything.[9] Such a Heaven will never intervene in the natural course of events. It is far from being a supreme God whose will has been dictating the development of human history. Heaven seems nowhere and hidden, and yet it is everywhere and manifest. Its creative power will never be exhausted. "*The Book of Odes* says, 'The Mandate of Heaven, how beautiful and unceasing.' This is to say, this is what makes Heaven to be Heaven."[10] Thus, even though Heaven's creative power works incessantly in the universe, common people do not even realize its existence. They pay attention only to what can be caught by eyes and ears; only the superior man pays attention to the Way, which cannot be captured by sense perception. This is why the superior man is cautious over what he does not see and apprehensive over what he does not hear. He is the one to follow Heaven's example in a conscious fashion and to make the hidden manifest. For personal cultivation, he has to be watchful when he is alone. The next paragraph gives us more details on such discipline of the self:

> Before the feelings of pleasure, anger, sorrow, and joy are aroused it is called equilibrium (*chung*, centrality, mean). When these feelings are aroused and each and all attain due measure and degree, it is called harmony [*ho*]. Equilibrium is the great foundation of the world, and harmony its universal path. When equilibrium and harmony are realized to the highest degree, heaven and earth will attain their proper order and all things will flourish.[11]

Obviously, *Chung Yung* presupposes a correlation between macrocosm and microcosm. Man modeling after Heaven becomes the agent to bring order in the world. Although Heaven in one sense is none other than the metaphysical principle itself, in another sense it may also be regarded as the first manifestation of this metaphysical principle. Interpreted in the latter sense, Heaven is often mentioned along with Earth. A description of the ways of Heaven and Earth will tell us more about the general characteristics of Heaven.

> The Way of Heaven and Earth may be completely described in one sentence: They are without any doubleness and they produce things in an unfathomable way. The Way of Heaven and Earth is extensive, deep, high, brilliant, infinite and lasting. The heaven now before us is only this bright, shining mass; but when viewed in its unlimited extent, the sun, moon, stars, and constellations are suspended in it and all things are covered by it. The earth before us is but a handful of soil; but in its breadth and depth, it sustains mountains like Hua and Yüeh without feeling their weight, contains the rivers and seas without letting them leak away, and sustains all things.[12]

In this quotation, *Chung Yung* states explicitly that the Heaven and Earth it talks about are not the physical heaven and earth. Heaven creates and earth sustains. These are the two main forces that keep the creative process in the universe going. In this process, a myriad of things in the world receive their natures. That which nourishes its nature will flourish, and that which harms its nature will suffer. "For Heaven, in the production of things, is sure to be bountiful to them, according to their natural capacity. Hence the tree that is well taken care of is nourished and that which is about to fall is overthrown."[13]

Now it is time for us to turn to the problem of man. What is that which Heaven has imparted to man? What is the nature he must develop, and what is the Way he must pursue? Man has the richest endowments of all the animals. He is different from other animals in many ways. He has different physical characteristics. He alone has developed complicated institutional forms. He is the only animal who has civilizations. From a Confucian point of view, however, all these are manifestations of man.

They are indeed important human creations, but man cannot sit on his achievements, however great they are. He must consciously nurture the creative spark within himself so that it will never die out. What is most important is creativity, rather than already-made creations. Creations are manifest, while creativity is hidden. His uniqueness lies in that he alone can read the creative message of Heaven and incorporate it into his own life. Only if one makes a deep commitment to the principle of creativity will he be able to develop a strength to work through all forms of difficulties and adversities without feeling frustrated. It is in this sense that man can consciously develop his nature and pursue the Way.

But self-discipline is a long and hard process; the superior man must not allow the Way to separate from him even for a moment. This is why he needs to be watchful over himself when alone and keeps to the norm of *chung-yung* before the feelings of pleasure, anger, and joy are aroused; and once they come into the open, overt actions are taken to bring them under control—each and all attain due measure and degree. This is indeed a rare achievement. No wonder Confucius always lamented that the Way is not pursued; he is said to have made the observation: "The superior man [exemplifies] the Mean (*chung-yung*). The inferior man acts contrary to the Mean. The superior man [exemplifies] the Mean because, as a superior man, he can maintain the Mean at any time. The inferior man [acts contrary to] the Mean because, as an inferior man, he has no caution."[14] But this does not mean that the Way has nothing to do with common people; but it functions in a hidden fashion in their lives. Even the superior man is not able to manifest the Way except in a limited fashion:

The Way of the superior man functions everywhere and yet is hidden. Men and women of simple intelligence can share its knowledge; and yet in its utmost reaches, there is something even the sage does not know. Men and women of simple intelligence can put it into practice; and yet in its utmost reaches there is something which even the sage is not able to put into practice. Great as heaven and earth are, men can still find something in them with which to be dissatisfied. Thus with [the Way of] the superior man, if one speaks of its greatness, nothing in the world can contain it, and if one speaks of its smallness, nothing in the world can split it. *The Book of Odes* says, "The hawk flies up to heaven; the fishes leap in the deep." This means that [the Way] is clearly seen above and below. The Way of the superior man has its simple beginnings in the relation between man and woman, but in its utmost reaches, it is clearly seen in heaven and on earth.[15]

Thus we find that although the Way operates on every level of human life, only a superior man is seeking to realize the Way in his life fully. According to *Chung Yung*, the key to living a life according to the Way is to achieve *ch'eng* in himself. For lack of a better term, I follow Wing-tsit Chan in rendering *ch'eng* into "sincerity" in English with the understanding, however, that *ch'eng* is more an ontological or metaphysical concept than a psychological or ethical concept. It means none other than Truth or Reality. Let us look at some of the characteristics of *ch'eng*:

Therefore absolute sincerity is ceaseless. Being ceaseless, it is lasting. Being lasting, it is evident. Being evident, it is infinite. Being infinite, it is extensive and deep. Being extensive and deep, it is high and brilliant. It is because it is extensive and deep that it contains all things. It is because it is high and brilliant that it overshadows all things. It is because it is infinite and lasting that it can complete all things. In being extensive and deep, it is a counterpart of Earth. In being high and brilliant, it is a counterpart of Heaven. In being infinite and lasting, it is unlimited. Such being its nature, it becomes prominent without any display, produces changes without motion, and accomplishes its ends without action.[16]

It is clear from this quotation that *ch'eng* is but another name for the all-encompassing metaphysical principle. Not only is man capable of knowing this metaphysical principle, but he also can follow it as his model, which provides guiding lines for his behavior: "Sincerity is the Way of Heaven. To think how to be sincere is the way of man. He who is sincere is one who hits upon what is right without effort and apprehends without thinking. He is naturally and easily in harmony with the Way. Such a man is a sage. He who tries to be sincere is one who chooses the good and holds fast to it."[17] According to *Chung Yung*:

Only those who are absolutely sincere can fully develop their nature. If they can fully develop their nature, they can then fully develop the nature of others. If they can fully develop the nature of others, they can then fully develop the nature of things. If they can fully develop the nature of things, they can then assist in the transforming and nourishing process of Heaven and Earth. If they can assist in the transforming and nourishing process of Heaven and Earth, they can thus form a trinity with Heaven and Earth.[18]

Here we find the Confucian doctrine of trinity. A dialectical relationship holds between Heaven and man. On the one hand, what *Chung Yung* teaches is a complete humanism. All man has to do is to develop his natural capacity, to develop his nature fully. There is absolutely no need for him to depart from his own nature. Yet, on the other hand, whoever can fully develop his nature cannot fail to appreciate the great virtues of Heaven. A sage is a man who takes the Way of Heaven as his model; and like Heaven, he does everything properly in a most natural way. It is true that man is not exactly identical to Heaven. This is why man, however great he is, must look up to Heaven and has great admiration for Heaven, which accomplishes everything in an effortless fashion. This explains why he can cherish a deep sense of piety in his heart. But he does not strive to be other than himself or to be more than himself. In so doing, he will be acting against his nature and hence against the Way of Heaven. But to teach a complete humanism does not mean that man has to cut all his ties with the transcendent. On the contrary, once he realizes the creative source within himself, he can then participate in the creative process of the universe and forget the sorrows that pertain only to his small self. A man who has no other concerns than those of the small self is not a fully developed man. Such a man is caught by a sense of anxiety and never feels free. Only if a man broadens his view and realizes that he is a part of the creative process in the universe will his sense of anxiety be completely overcome. He will then gladly accept his destiny without feeling any regret in his heart. What he achieves is not a kind of personal immortality but a method to live according to the Way and to merge into the transforming and nourishing process of Heaven and Earth that will never cease even if the present form of the universe no longer exists.

Now we can see the Confucian approach to the problem of transcendence and immanence. Heaven is transcendent in the sense that it is an all-encompassing creative power that works incessantly in the universe. It is not a thing, but it is the origin of all things. And it cannot be detected by sense perceptions because its "operations have neither sound nor smell." But Heaven is also immanent in the sense that it penetrates deeply every detail of the natural order, in general, and the moral order of man, in particular. But Heaven in no sense should be regarded as something completely beyond nature; on the contrary, it is that which constitutes the warp and woof of nature. As for man, he is beyond any doubt a creature in the world and hence a part of the natural order.

The Chinese have no love for any dualistic assertions that maintain a sharp dichotomy between the soul and the body, the natural and the supernatural. But man, among all creatures, is indeed unique in that he alone is endowed with the ability to realize the meaning of the creative process in the universe. Because he is a conscious being, he is also endowed with the free will to determine his own existence. He can work with the Way or he can work against the Way. His own choice will make him a superior man or an inferior man. The paradox of life lies in that only he who can transcend his immediate concerns can fully develop the creative potentialities within himself and hence develop his nature. Although every creature in the world is produced by Heaven and sustained by Earth, only man has the spark of the transcendent message in him so that he is driven to transcend his small self in order to bring about his self-realization. He is a being in the boundary situation. Thus, transcendence and immanence are a pair of interdependent concepts for the Confucian philosophers. They are not contradictory to each other.

Now we can appreciate the message of *ch'eng* transmitted in *Chung Yung*:

> Sincerity means the completion of the self, and the Way is self-directing.
> Sincerity is the beginning and end of things. Without sincerity there would
> be nothing. Therefore the superior man values sincerity. Sincerity is not
> only the completion of one's own self, it is that by which all things are
> completed. The completion of the self means humanity. The completion
> of all things means wisdom. These are the character of the nature, and
> they are the Way in which the internal and the external are united.
> Therefore whenever it is employed, everything done is right.[19]

Here we find the messages of *The Doctrine of the Mean* and *The Great Learning* merging. But since it is difficult to develop one's nature fully, *Chung Yung* also allows for other possibilities:

The next in order are those who cultivate to the utmost a particular good-ness [*chih-chü*]. Having done this, they can attain to the possession of sincerity. As there is sincerity, there will be its expression. As it is ex-pressed, it will become conspicuous. As it becomes conspicuous, it will become clear. As it becomes clear, it will move others. As it moves others, it changes them. As it changes them, it transforms them. Only those who are absolutely sincere can transform others.[20]

Chih-chü means to take a roundabout approach; it is inferior to the straight-forward way of the sages. But this is a very important provision, as *nei-sheng-wai-wang* (sageliness within and kingliness without) is an ideal difficult to achieve in the real world. Longtime experience shows that the traditional mon-archy has produced more mediocre rulers and even tyrants than virtuous and able rulers, let alone sage-emperors. Therefore, contemporary Neo-Confucian scholars would rather take the roundabout approach and adopt the Western dem-ocratic system in order to pursue the ideal of a government of humanity. And in a modern pluralistic society, it is better to cultivate citizens with particular goodness than to force conformity on people by exerting political authority.[21] However, humanistic education for individuals should not be ignored. In the family, they should still be taught to honor moral standards and to admire those who achieve. *Chung Yung* urged scholars:

Study it (the way to be sincere) extensively, inquire into it accurately, think over it carefully, sift it clearly, and practice it earnestly. When there is anything not yet studied, or studied but not yet understood, do not give up. When there is any question not yet asked, or asked but its answer not yet known, do not give up. When there is anything not yet thought over, or thought over but not yet apprehended, do not give up. When there is anything not yet sifted, or sifted but not yet clear, do not give up. When there is anything not yet practiced, or practiced but not yet earnestly, do not give up. If another man succeed by one effort, you will use a hundred efforts. If another man succeed by ten efforts, you will use a thousand efforts. If one really follows this course, though stupid, he will surely become intelligent, and though weak, will surely become strong.[22]

Chung Yung contributed a great deal to the Chinese tradition that put emphasis on education. It urged scholars to learn with a critical spirit, not just to follow authority blindly. It also linked learning with practice; there was no gap between knowledge and action. We must have lofty ideals, but we have to lay the bricks one at a time. As *Chung Yung* taught us, "The Way of the superior man may be compared to travelling to a distant place: one must start from the nearest point. It may be compared to ascending a height: one must start from below."[23] Following the Way means to take care of both the high and the low:

Great is the Way of the sage! Overflowing, it produces and nourishes all things and rises up to the height of heaven. How exceedingly great! [It embraces] the three thousand rules of ceremonies and the three thousand rules of conduct. It waits for the proper man before it can be put into practice. Therefore it is said, "Unless there is perfect virtue, the perfect Way cannot be materialized." Therefore the superior man honors the moral nature and follows the path of inquiry and study. He achieves breadth and greatness and pursues the refined and subtle to the limit. He seeks to reach the greatest height and brilliancy and follows the path of the Mean. He goes over the old so as to find out what is new. He is earnest and deep and highly respects all propriety. Therefore when occupying a high position, he is not proud, and when serving in a low position, he is not insubordinate. When the Way prevails in the country, he can rise to official position through his words. When the Way does not prevail in the country, he can preserve himself through silence. *The Book of Odes* says, "Intelligent and wise, he protects his person." This is the meaning.[24]

This paragraph gives us a portrayal of the ideal of the superior man. In the posterity, honoring the moral nature and following the path of inquiry and study were recognized as two possible approaches to follow the Way. The issue was hotly debated and discussed in Sung Neo-Confucian philosophy by Chu Hsi and Lu Hsiang-shan.[25]

After the philosophy of *Chung Yung* is presented, the next problem we must face is: Are these thoughts that were developed 2,000 years ago in China still relevant to us today? To a contemporary thinker who asserts that human knowledge cannot extend beyond empirical, scientific knowledge and that any talk about the transcendent is cognitively meaningless, a Confucian philosopher would retort that such a man pays attention only to what is manifest and not to what is hidden and subtle; consequently, he presupposes the operation of the creative metaphysical principle without acknowledging its existence. And this is not surprising, because a man's world is correlated with his level of understanding. A man who pays attention merely to the existence of particulars and tries to establish the correlation between particulars will not pay attention to the all-encompassing creative metaphysical principle, even if it exists all the time and works incessantly in an unobtrusive fashion. Modern scientific achievements cannot discredit *Chung Yung*'s reflections on Heaven because they do not belong to the same level of *Chung Yung*'s metaphysical understanding. *Chung Yung*'s Heaven cannot be established in terms of empirical generalization; and it has nothing to do with man's superstitious beliefs. It is by realization of the creative spark within himself that he becomes conscious of the subtle operations of Heaven in the universe.

But it is by no means the case that all men will appreciate the work of Heaven. In fact, most people are not even conscious of the existence of Heaven. As a man's world is determined by his understanding of the world, this explains why logical arguments can touch only the surface of the problem. What is more important is man's experience of the world and his view of the world and life. The only way to communicate one's worldview to others is to give a phenomenological description of the world. But whether or not one will succeed in communicating depends on the listener's ability to develop experience analogous to that of the speaker. This is why the Chinese use more assertions or metaphorical expressions than logical arguments.

If one sees the world and human life from the Confucian perspective, then the dichotomy between the transcendent and the immanent becomes no longer necessary. It is only in a distorted relation between the two that a rift is found. The Confucian philosophers have been working hard to find ways to remove such distortions and to restore the normal relation of equilibrium and harmony between the two. When the ideals of *Chung Yung* are fully realized in life, the problem of alienation simply withers away, and the sense of anxiety can no longer trouble the mind. The sages in the past have set examples for all of us, but it depends on the individual's existential commitment and discipline to achieve what has been reached by these sages. During the Fifth East-West Philosophers' Conference held in Hawaii in 1969, the late professor Thomé H. Fang presented a paper on alienation, the theme of the conference, in which he made an interesting observation:

Philosophical anthropology has to align itself with psychology, which may assume three different forms. As a rule, psychology closely coupled up with science is inclined to cast about for an understanding of human mind in the light of clear consciousness. This is analyzed without remainder, first into faculties such as reason, emotion, and will, and then into elements of sensation, perception, and thought, each susceptible of being further reduced to psychical atoms on the plane of natural reason. Every mental fact is clearly seen to the core without mystery. This is the "surface psychology" of the rational type. But men, like children, are lovers of mystery, never too tired to peep through the narrow opening of a kaleidoscope. So nowadays it is the fashion to appeal to "depth psychology" for a systematic apprehension of mental disorders.

As philosophers endowed with speculative reason we cannot shut the door to the mysteriously mysterious mystery disclosed in religion, philosophy, and certain trends of scientific thought. This is the incentive to appeal to a different psychology which I choose to label "height psychology." Instead of laying out the static nature of man over an intellectual flatland, or of apprehending man in the pathetic grimaces of mental disorder, this psychology tries to see into the real man, the dynamics of creative life, and the advancement of cultural order in the light of speculative reason.[26]

There is no need to agree with everything Professor Fang said, but his ideas are highly suggestive. For example, behavioral psychology would fall into the scope of what he called surface psychology, and psychoanalysis, depth psychology. The understanding of the mind in the great traditions of philosophy and religion, East and West, cannot be reduced to either scope. In these traditions, it is believed that the mind can be subject to disciplines, and consciousness can be raised to a higher level. If these phenomena are not to be brushed aside as mere illusions or delusions, then they must fall into the scope of height psychology. As a matter of fact, for decades there has been a wide interest in Yoga and Zen in the West, as the practice of so-called transcendental meditation appears to bring about the effects of psychotherapy. But there is a widespread misconception that Confucianism is merely a secular ethics that has nothing to do with the spiritual transformation of a person. In fact, there is a long tradition, following Confucius and Mencius, of the Confucian discipline of the self that puts emphasis on the discipline of *hsin* (mind-heart). In *The Great Learning* and *The Doctrine of the Mean*, we find the concrete steps to carry out such discipline, which certainly predated the import of Buddhism into China. The Confucian tradition does not have the dichotomy between the body and the mind, and mental hygiene is more emphasized than psychotherapy.

To sum up, the Confucian discipline of *hsin* works on the assumption that the normal state of our mind-heart as endowed from Heaven is creative, humane, and rational. It is quite different from the Freudian assumption that what lies behind is id, which cannot be totally suppressed by external restraints. The Confucian approach may be compared to Emperor Yü's treatment of the Yellow River: allowing the waters to follow their natural course, not building dikes to contain them in an unnatural way. Such an approach steers a middle way that tries to avoid the extremes of dogmatism, on the one hand, and relativism, on the other. The Confucian claim can be partially verified by those who have practiced such a discipline and found that it has manifested a kind of psychotherapeutic function not unlike that of psychiatry. But human beings are not like physical atoms—the approach may work on certain individuals but not on others. It is certainly our wish that some psychiatrists may find a kindred spirit in such an approach and may want to further explore it in order to open up a new path in the field of psychology.[27]

In our own time, some of the Marxist followers have charged the Confucian ideals as being inventions of an elite intelligentsia with a view to protect its class interest. The Confucian philosophers would find that this charge is groundless. They would agree with the Marxists that economic alienation is an important form of alienation. In fact, Confucius and his true followers have never failed to have deep concern over people's lives and to fight for the welfare of the people. But it would be naive to believe that once economic alienation is overcome, other forms of alienation will also be overcome. If man does not experience an inner change of consciousness and transcend beyond his economic concerns, the dissatisfactions in his heart will never come to an end. This is a basic insight shared by all of the three great religious traditions in China: Confucianism, Buddhism, and Taoism. The Confucian philosophers would argue that although the problem of "inward sageliness" (moral and religious concerns) and the problem of "outward kingliness" (political and economic concerns) are closely related, they are not to be confused with one another.

The solution of man's economic problems is not a guarantee for the solution of other human problems. An individual must work hard to overcome his inner sense of alienation. Strangely enough, here the Confucian philosophers teach an uncompromising individualistic philosophy, even if the Confucian position is often interpreted as no more than a system of social and moral codes. It is only through hard discipline of the self that one can realize his freedom and then "can find himself in no situation in which he is not at ease with himself."[28]

Those who overly concern themselves with social problems often neglect this important aspect of human life. They do not seem to realize that mere external social reforms can never rectify all the social evils if the society is made up of people full of greed, ignorance, and prejudices. This is why the Confucian tradition puts so much emphasis on education—not the education of skills but the education of man. If the individuals are educated, the society composed of these individuals will also be improved. The Confucian philosophers are seeking the Way in which the internal and the external are united. They would like to see social reform in its proper perspective.

It is here that we find a most profound practical insight into the Confucian tradition. In recent years, it appears that serious domestic and international problems have forced political authorities all over the world to pay attention to such insight. Since the Cultural Revolution, Mainland China has dramatically reversed its stand; now it expends a good deal of effort to promote spiritual values and seeks to revive Confucian ethics within the Marxist context. In 1993, surprisingly enough, the world parliament of religions endorsed a global ethic and issued a declaration in which the so-called Golden Rule has occupied a prominent place.[29] It is realized that mere emphasis on external human rights is not enough; only a change of inner attitude may bring about peace among religions—a necessary first step to world peace. For people to live together peacefully in a global village, the Confucian tradition certainly has rich resources for us to draw upon.[30]

NOTES

1. Shu-hsien Liu, "The Religious Import of Confucian Philosophy: Its Traditional Outlook and Contemporary Significance," *Philosophy East and West* 21, no. 2 (April 1971): 157–175.

2. Chan, *Source Book*, pp. 85–86.

3. Ibid., pp. 86–87, with modification. Note that Wing-tsit Chan translated *ming-te* as "clear character" instead of "illustrious virtue."

4. Burton Watson, trans., *The Complete Works of Chuang Tzu* (New York: Columbia University Press, 1968), p. 364.

5. Chan, *Source Book*, p. 89, with slight modification.

6. Ibid., p, 97.

7. Ibid., p. 98, with slight modification.

8. Ibid., p. 113.

9. Ibid., p. 47.

10. Ibid., pp. 109–110.

11. Ibid., p. 98.

12. Ibid., p. 109.

13. Ibid., p. 102.

14. Ibid., pp. 98–99.

15. Ibid., p. 100.

16. Ibid., p. 109.

17. Ibid., p. 107.

18. Ibid., pp. 107–108.

19. Ibid., p. 108.

20. Ibid.

21. Shu-hsien Liu, "On the Confucian Ideal of 'Sageliness within and Kingliness Without,' " *Proceedings of the International Symposium on Confucianism and the Modern World* (Taipei: The Chinese Philosophical Association, 1988): 401–422.

22. Chan, *Source Book*, p. 107.

23. Ibid., p. 102.

24. Ibid., p. 110.

25. Ibid., p. 582.

26. Thomé H. Fang, "The Alienation of Man in Religion, Philosophy and Philosophical Anthropology," in *Creativity in Man and Nature* (Taipei: Linking Pub. Co., 1980), pp. 93–94.

27. Shu-hsien Liu, "The Psychotherapeutic Function of the Confucian Discipline of Hsin (Mind-Heart)," in *Psychotherapy for the Chinese*, ed. L. Y. Cheng, F. Cheung, and C. N. Chen (Hong Kong: Department of Psychiatry, Chinese University of Hong Kong, 1993), pp. 1–17. More recently, social psychologists have also shown some interest in Neo-Confucian thinking. See James Hou-fu Liu and Shu-hsien Liu, "Modernism, Postmodernism, and Neo-Confucian Thinking: A Critical History of Paradigm Shifts and Values in Psychology" (paper presented at the Inaugural Conference of the Asian Association of Social Psychology held at The Chinese University of Hong Kong, June 21–23, 1995); the article is published in *New Ideas in Psychology*, 15, no. 2 (1997): 159–177.

28. Chan, *Source Book*, p. 101.

29. Hans Küng and Karl-Josef Kuschel, eds., *A Global Ethic: The Declaration of the Parliament of the World's Religions*, trans. John Bowden (London: SCM Press, 1993).

30. Shu-hsien Liu, "Reflections on World Peace through Peace among Religions—A Confucian Perspective," *Journal of Chinese Philosophy* 22, no. 2 (June 1995): 193–213. Recently, UNESCO (United Nations Educational, Scientific, and Cultural Organization) organized the first meeting of the Universal Ethics Project, which was held on March 26–28, 1997, in Paris. Around twelve philosophers representing different theories and traditions participated in the meeting to discuss problems of definition, content, approach, justification, and diversity. I was invited to speak and engage in the interchange of ideas from a Confucian perspective. Then about thirty philosophers participated in the second meeting of the Universal Ethics Project, which was held between December 1–4, 1997 in Naples, Italy. I presented a paper entitled "Reflections on Approaches to Universal Ethics from a Contemporary Neo-Confucian Perspective."

5

Book of Changes

The *I Ching* (*Book of Changes*) is a great Chinese Classic that has been regarded as a fountainhead of Chinese wisdom. It has not only exerted profound influence over the Chinese mind for over 2,000 years but still enjoys great popularity in the present world. It is divided into *Texts* and *Commentaries*. Modern scholars believe that they were compiled in different times. The *Texts* were probably compiled in the early Chou dynasty, around 1000 B.C., while the *Commentaries* were much later products, probably the works of Confucius and several generations of his followers. Some of the *Commentaries* were completed during the Warring States period (403–222 B.C.).

There is little doubt that originally the *I Ching* was just a book of divination. This explains why it was not burned along with other classics by the cruel Ch'in: It was not honored as a classic at the time. It was in the *Commentaries*—the so-called Ten Wings supposedly authored by Confucius—that a philosophy of creativity was developed. In the posterity, it has constantly been associated with *Chung Yung*, together regarded as the two metaphysical works of the Confucian school. The fortunes of the *I Ching* changed rapidly in the Han dynasty. Not only was it included among the classics, but it was honored as the first of the six Classics, because it was seen as laying the foundation of Confucian philosophy. I am convinced that unless we take a developmental point of view, it would be impossible for us to work out a comprehensive understanding of the rich implications of this classic.

Since the Cultural Revolution, there have been exciting archaeological discoveries in China that might have a bearing on tracing the origins of the *Book of Changes*. In addition, new ideas have emerged in the interpretation of its philosophy. I think it is an erroneous approach to try to locate one central theme in the classic and reduce everything else to the theme. Not only is it impossible to achieve this goal, but it would create unnecessary controversies that would never be settled. Therefore, a different approach is suggested. At least four layers of meaning can be identified in the *Book of Changes*, each one succeeding the other and yet also interpenetrating the other; this explains why it is so difficult to have a comprehensive understanding of the implications of this classic. The four layers of meaning are:

1. A system of mystical symbolism
2. A system of rational/natural symbolism
3. A system of cosmological symbolism
4. A system of ethical/metaphysical symbolism

Only after the four kinds of symbolism are carefully studied can a functional unity be found, even though we have to give up the hope of finding a substantial unity among them.[1] In the following, I shall examine them one by one, in that order.

MYSTICAL SYMBOLISM

Today most scholars would agree that the *Book of Changes* was originally a book of divination. The symbols involved were saturated with mystical implications; they were supposed to help us foretell the future. Now I would like to trace the origins of this mystical symbolism.[2] It is well known that the book in its present form contains a system of symbolism—the so-called Eight Trigrams: *ch'ien* (Heaven), ☰, is heaven; *k'un* (Earth), ☷, is earth; *chen* (activity), ☳, is thunder; *sun* (bending), ☴, is wind; *k'an* (pit), ☵, is water; *li* (brightness), ☲, is fire; *ken* (to stop), ☶, is mountain; and *tui* (pleasure), ☱, is a marsh. Each trigram is combined with another, one upon the other, thus making sixty-four hexagrams.[3] There is also a definite procedure to conduct divination. Those who believe in such practice obviously presuppose that there is a mystical correlation between the system of symbolism and natural and human events in the world; hence, the system of symbolism may be regarded as a kind of mystical symbolism.

According to traditional accounts, ultimately the system can be reduced to two basic symbols, that is, the yin and the yang, represented by a divided line (▬ ▬) and an undivided line (▬▬▬), respectively. One may then develop the whole system by way of one (*T'ai-chi*, the Great Ultimate), two (modes—yin and yang), four (forms—younger and elder yin and yang), and eight (trigrams); or by way of one, three (trigrams), and six (hexagrams). There has been a lot of speculation about the origin of the symbols of the yin and the yang. One prevalent theory takes them to be symbols derived from the procreative organs of the female and the male. Recently, however, archaeological discoveries have unearthed the so-called *shu-tzu-kua* (numerical-grams); it is beyond doubt that they belong to the early Chou period.[4] At first, scholars had trouble understanding these symbols; they were thought to be emblems for tribes.[5] Then larger numbers of these numerical-grams turned up; scholars made attempts to formulate new ideas about them and finally have been able to identify them as numerical-grams. Surprisingly enough, the number of hexagrams found is far greater than the number of trigrams; hence, scholars today are not certain that the hexagrams are derived from trigrams.[6] One thing seems certain, however: These symbols do contain ancient numbers, long before forms or images are found. The implication seems to be, contrary to prevalent opinion, that the use of numbers might have preceded forms or images. If this understanding is correct, then many traditional accounts have to be revised. If in ancient times there were only odd and even numbers such as 1, 5, 6, 7, and 8, and these even antedate the symbols of the yin and the yang, then we are forced to come up with better interpretations than, for example, being symbols derived from procreative organs.

Recent studies seem to have opened up entirely new vistas. Anthropologist Wang Ning-sheng has made a very interesting suggestion: He finds that even today minorities in Southwest China still practice divination by numbers. Such a fact may shed light on the formation of the so-called trigrams in the *Book of Changes*.[7] The Miaos simply break a piece of wood into two halves; when they are dropped on the ground, there are three possibilities: one piece faces up and the other faces down, or both face up, or both face down. The result would be interpreted as neither good nor bad, good, and bad. Such combinations are much too simple to help with making decisions in response to the demands of a more complicated social life. The Yis at Liangshan, Sichuan, however, have a much more complex type of practice called *lei-fu-zi*: The witch doctor (*pi-mo*) holds some stalks in his left hand and takes away some by his right hand; what is left is either in odd numbers or even numbers. This procedure must be repeated three times. Then there are eight possibilities: even-even-even, middle flat; odd-odd-odd, middle flat; even-odd-odd, bad; odd-even-even, very bad; even-odd-even, middle flat; even-even-odd, good; odd-odd-even, flat; odd-even-odd, good. *Lei-fu-zi* is often used to help make decisions on matters such as whether to have a fight with other tribes. One cannot fail to see the parallel between such a practice among minorities and the practice of divination according to the system of the *Book of Changes*. Wang wrote his article with a view to discredit the classic, which from his point of view was based on primitive superstitions. There is no need for us to agree with his conclusions, however, as a humble origin would not be accepted as a sufficient reason to prevent the development of a creative philosophy in the future. Nevertheless, I do think Wang has shown great insight in his attempt to answer the question of the origin of the trigrams.

And surprisingly enough, his seemingly novel suggestion actually confirms the traditional account handed down to us through the *Commentaries* of the Classic since the ancient times. According to this account, it was the sage-emperor Fu Hsi who first invented the eight trigrams.[8] At first sight, this account may appear to be sheer speculation that cannot be substantiated by factual evidence, as Fu Hsi was only a legendary figure, and we cannot be sure that such a person actually existed. Approached from another perspective, however, the account may appear under a completely different light. It happens that Fu Hsi was a god worshipped by minorities in Southwest China, and his legends were widely circulated among these minorities.[9] To be sure, legends never tell us real history as it was, but in the East as well as in the West, they must not be simply dismissed as pure fantasies; very often, they can tell us a great deal about the remote past if we are ready to receive the messages conveyed to us through proper interpretations. In this case, Fu Hsi may be understood as the symbol of the ancient minority cultures in Southwest China; it is plausible that this method of divination by numbers was indeed first originated in that area, then later adopted by the Chinese people, becoming a part of their commonly accepted tradition. The date could be very ancient—certainly much earlier than Shang and Chou dynasties; that is why the origin of the eight trigrams is pushed further back to the days of the legendary sage-emperors. And we should also not forget that Fu Hsi is regarded as the symbol representing a civilization raising herds, which predates the period of legendary sage-emperor Shen Nung (the divine farmer), who is taken to be the symbol of farming.

When we explore this line of thinking, we realize that when eight possibilities are not enough, it is quite natural that trigrams may be doubled up to form hexagrams. This interpretation also conforms with the traditional account of the development of the *Book of Changes*.[10] It is said that Fu Hsi invented the eight trigrams; then King Wen (r. 1171–1122 B.C.) developed the sixty-four hexagrams and also wrote the *kua-tz'u*, or the explanation of the text of the whole hexagram, and the *yao-tz'u*, or the explanation of the component lines. Another version ascribed the *yao-tz'u* to the Duke of Chou (d. 1094 B.C.). And the Ten Wings were said to be the work of Confucius. Most modern scholars have rejected this account, thinking it impossible for King Wen and Duke Chou to be knowledgeable about things after their times; it is also impossible for a single person to have completed the Ten Wings. But the traditional account, though inaccurate, is not without merit. The book probably evolved during the transitional period from the Yin dynasty to the Chou dynasty at a time of great distress, and its main text was completed in the early Chou; both King Wen and Duke Chou might have had a great deal to do with it. And even though Confucius could not have been the author of the Ten Wings, they were undoubtedly the work of his followers. It was in the hands of these Confucian scholars that a book of divination was gradually transformed into a book of philosophy.

A strange phenomenon that has received no satisfactory explanation was that since the early Chou for several hundred years there were virtually no traces of the development of the book. Then suddenly in the late Chou period we find in historical works such as *Tso Chuan* and *Kuo Yü* that a number of divinations were recorded. These divinations were not the same as those practiced in later ages, but there were citations of the explanations of the hexagrams and their component lines. Suddenly, the interest in such matters seemed to have gained momentum. And it was during the Warring States period that yin and yang were singled out as the two basic forces working in the universe; this theory was further combined with the doctrine of the Five Agents—that is, metal, wood, water, fire, and earth—and the key figure developing such ideas was Tsou Yen (305–240 B.C.?).[11]

Tsou combined a cyclic philosophy with a cosmology to form a comprehensive system of philosophy with serious political implications. His ideas were tremendously influential in his time. Strangely enough, however, even though his influence persisted throughout the Han dynasty (206 B.C.–A.D. 220), very few scholars had acknowledged his achievements; perhaps they simply did not want to have any association with the bizarre character of his grand philosophical system. His basic idea is that there is a mysterious correlation between natural phenomena and human phenomena. The Five Agents must take their turns, and each dynasty is characterized by an agent; later on, it will be replaced by another dynasty characterized by the next agent in turn. Tsou appeared to have some connections with the Confucian school, as he urged the rulers to practice virtues according to their station and duties. Anyhow, we find that Tsou Yen's ideas were gradually blended with the ideas of the followers of Confucius and Mencius. But even though the Ten Wings might have taken in some of Tsou's ideas, they had developed a creative philosophy in the main that put emphasis upon moral commitment and had very little to do with Tsou's deterministic philosophy. Unfortunately, however, most Han scholars, including the great Tung Chung-shu (c. 179–c. 104 B.C.) who helped to establish Confucianism as the state orthodoxy, endorsed Tsou's cyclic philosophy of history and believed in a strict correlation between natural phenomena and human phenomena. This twist in the history of Chinese thought certainly left its imprint on the way of thinking of the Chinese for years to come. Even the great Chu Hsi partially endorsed this approach to the *Book of Changes*. Now the question may be asked: Is correlative thinking a thing of the past in an age of science such as ours? This is hardly the case, as A. C. Graham argues:

> [W]hile thinking causally, attention is diverted from the correlating of concepts in the background; whenever there is nothing to put in front, correlative thinking is necessarily in the foreground. In the conduct of ordinary affairs, whenever circumstances are too complex and move too fast for analysis, there is likewise nothing in front of the instantaneous act of assimilation and differentiation.[12]

RATIONAL/NATURAL SYMBOLISM

Mystical symbolism is, however, gradually superseded by a system of natural symbolism. Each trigram would then stand for a certain natural phenomenon in the universe. For example, in Appendix V, it is said,

(The trigram) *Ch'ien* ☰ is Heaven, round, and is the father. . . . (The trigram) *K'un* ☷ is Earth and is the mother. . . . (The trigram) *Chen* ☳ is thunder. . . . (The trigram) *Sun* ☴ is wood and wind. . . . (The trigram) *K'an* ☵ is water . . . and is the moon. . . . (The trigram) *Li* ☲ is fire and the sun. . . . (The trigram) *Ken* ☶ is mountain. . . . (The trigram) *Tui* ☱ is marsh.[13]

In fact, we find that even in seemingly fantastic mythological references there are already certain natural elements in them. For example, in the very first hexagram *Ch'ien*, dragons are constantly referred to in phrases such as "hidden dragon," "dragon appearing in the field," and "flying dragon in the heavens."[14] From a modern viewpoint, dragons do not actually exist; hence, these are only figurative speeches. But in *Tso Chuen*, it was recorded when a dragon was sighted; historians in those days told stories of the past when dragons were fed by dragon tamers in the service of their rulers; a rational explanation was provided as to why dragons were rarely seen in later ages.[15] So in ancient times, dragons were regarded as real; some scholars even speculate that they belong to a species of crocodiles.[16] But what really matters here is not even whether dragons actually exist but, rather, that dragons were treated as if they were real. Hence, there must be certain empirical elements even in seemingly fanciful mythological tales handed down to us from the past. Through the studies of modern scholars such as Ku Chi-kang,[17] Li Ching-chi,[18] and Kao Heng,[19] we now know that many lines in the *Book of Changes* refer to events that actually happened in the past. From this perspective, the book may be regarded as a valuable source to study the conditions of ancient civilizations.

When symbols are believed to be in some way correlated with natural phenomena, they may be further employed to invent utensils and institutions. Hu Shih put it this way:

> Thus it is the ideas which have been responsible for the creation or invention of our utensils and institutions. The history of civilization, according to Confucius, has been a long series of successive attempts to realize the "ideas" or perfect heavenly ideals into human instruments, customs, and institutions. Some of Confucius' explanations of the beginning of human institutions are extremely interesting, if not entirely true from the anthropological point of view. The invention of the plowshare, for example, which marked the beginning of agriculture, is held to have been suggested by the idea of increase or growth represented by ☴ (wood) over ☳ (thunder; hence motion). The institution of a midday market for the exchange of wares and goods among the people is said to have originated in the idea of friction represented by ☲ (fire; hence lightning) and ☳ (thunder).[20]

Hu Shih further pointed out, "The same view pervades the whole of the Confucian Appendices. All the '*hsiang*'-remarks (Appendix III) separately appended to the sixty-four *kwas* are illustrations of the doctrine that our mechanical inventions, religious rites, moral codes, traditional customs, etc., have had their 'former causes' in the ideas.''[21] Modern scholars such as Joseph Needham would seriously doubt that such an interpretation actually reflects the development of Chinese science in ancient times.[22] But possibilities of institutions and inventions originating from ideas should not be totally precluded. It is odd that Needham should give high praise for the Yin-yang school while criticizing the *Book of Changes*. In fact, they are very similar to each other in function: Both, may have helped the development of science to some extent, on the one hand, and precluded it from further development, on the other hand. Benjamin Schwartz says:

> I . . . question his [Needham's] contrast between the correlative cosmology of Tsou Yen and the system of the *Changes*. Did the five elements and two force theories in themselves generate natural observation, experiment, or technical invention? Were they not also rather used as categories for classifying and filing? Above all, did not the dominant preoccupations of the correlative cosmologists, like those of the fashioners of the *Book of Changes*, also lie elsewhere? The preoccupation which led to the canonization of the *Book of Changes* as a Confucian classic was based, it would appear, on the continued preoccupation with human destiny and normative behavior in a precarious world full of contingency.[23]

I cannot but agree with Schwartz's criticism of Needham's one-sided view of the *Book of Changes*.

Here I would like to expand my thesis a little. Instead of talking only about natural symbolism, I propose to discuss rational/natural symbolism, as the *Book of Changes* has a whole system of numbers and forms that are closely related to its understanding of nature. Ancient people had a profound mystical feeling about numbers, especially those within ten. The Pythagoreans provide one such example; the *hsiang-shu* (forms and numbers) school of the *Book of Changes* provides another example. When numbers are arranged in a certain way, they exhibit certain dazzling characteristics; hence, it is not surprising that they are believed to have had a divine origin—a rational element is inextricably intertwined with a mystical element. As an example, the nine rooms of the so-called *Ming-t'ang* (the bright hall) were built according to the numerial system developed from the *Book of Changes*. The shape of the hall is round on top and square at the bottom; it symbolizes that Heaven is round, while the Earth is square. Heaven covers, while the earth sustains. The numbers involved may be diagramed as in Figure 1.[24]

The image of the diagram is that of a tortoise. The saying goes, ''To have nine overhead and one to tread on; three is on the left and seven is on the right; two and four are shoulders; six and eight are feet; five occupies the middle.'' The sum of each line from whatever direction would come to fifteen. The numbers from one to nine were arranged in such a way that they were called ''the

Figure 1

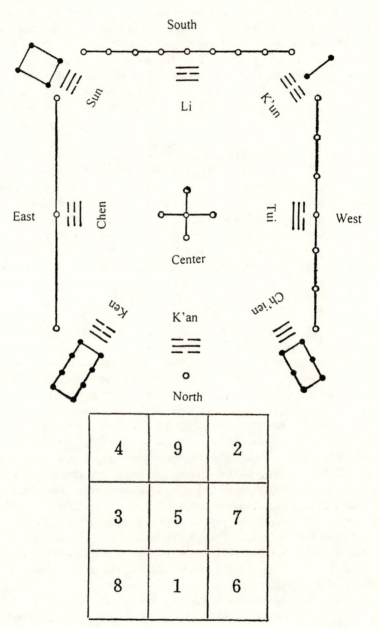

forty-five points of the *Lo-shu* (the Book of Lo).'' They were supposedly the lucky signs obtained from the back of the tortoise of the river Lo. The diagram is actually none other than the magical square in mathematics. Obviously, there is a logic in the operation of numbers. Emphasis may be put either on mathematical calculation or on making use of such mathematical knowledge to design a comprehensive scheme to frame celestial phenomena and human events and determine their beneficial or harmful results in fortune-telling. Most Han scholars were inclined toward the latter approach to the *Book of Changes*.

By the same token, the sixty-four hexagrams can be rendered into a binary arithmetic system. Leibniz acknowledged that some 3,000 years ago Fu Hsi had already figured out the key to this approach:[25] If we substitute ''0'' for ▬ ▬ and ''1'' for ▬▬▬, then the hexagram *k'un* ☷ can be rendered into ''000000'' and *ch'ien* ☰ into ''111111.'' The further development of such a binary arithmetic laid the foundation for the invention of modern computers. Surely, the Chinese should take pride in the achievements of their ancestors, but they should not delude themselves into thinking that the ancient arithmetic system implicit in the *Book of Changes* was exactly the same as the binary arithmetic worked out by Leibniz and his successors, as a subtle difference may be found among the two approaches. Because the Chinese have always refused to separate form from content, they have never developed the kind of pure mathematics or symbolic logic found in the West.

Through the efforts of Needham and his corroborators, there remains little doubt that the Chinese indeed contributed a great deal to the development of science and civilization. There seems to be a limit to their progress, however. They appear to have worked on rather different paradigms; for example, they favored the organic model over the mechanical model.[26] This approach seems to discourage the development of a purely quantitative approach to things, the secret behind the success of modern science and technology. Not only have they missed out on some of the West's achievements, but evidence suggests that they never could have reached the same results independently. On the other hand, they have surpassed Western achievement in various areas such as the mind-body connection, where Chinese acupuncture and medicine work on quite different premises and principles.

To sum up, side by side with the mystical aspect of the *Book of Changes*, there is also a rational/natural aspect inextricably interwoven with it. The classic may be used as a source to study ancient history and society, it may offer some insights on the development of science in China, and it contains a symbolic system that has a certain affinity with the so-called binary arithmetic as developed by Leibniz and his successors. From the scientific perspective, the *Book of Changes* has shown clearly both its merits and its limitations.

COSMOLOGICAL SYMBOLISM

As was stated in the last section, Han studies of the *Book of Changes* were dominated by the *hsiang-shu* (forms and numbers) approach. But this is not the only possible approach, and magic and science certainly do not exhaust the meaning of the classic. During the Wei-Chin period, Wang Pi (226–249) was the first to brush the whole thing aside and concentrated on *i-li* (meanings and principles) alone. Wang took the *Book of Changes* primarily as a philosophical work. Still limited by his time, his interpretation of the classic was based on his understanding of the Taoist philosophy. Then Ch'eng I (1033–1107) of the Sung dynasty continued the *i-li* approach, but he reinterpreted the classic in terms of his Neo-Confucian philosophy. From this perspective, Confucius was seen as the author of the Ten Wings that gave expression to a creative philosophy with profound wisdom, and it was unfortunate that the Han scholars had totally failed to truly understand the significance of the classic.

We have already pointed out that from a historical perspective this view is untenable, as Confucius could not have been the author of the Ten Wings. But it is indeed possible to reconstruct a creative philosophy from the Ten Wings that must have been the work of Confucian followers. And it is not without justification that some ideas may be traced back to the old master himself.[27] Recently, the silk scroll version of the *Book of Changes* was unearthed from certain Han tombs, and it sheds much light on this problem.[28] Modern scholars have expressed doubt that Confucius had anything to do with the book at all, as *The Analects* made only one questionable reference to it and quoted only once from it, even though the *Historical Records* reported that Confucius loved to study the *Book of Changes* in his old age and authored the so-called Ten Wings.

The silk scroll version included materials that could shed light on these questions; it not only arranged the sixty-four hexagrams in a different order but carried several *Commentaries* hitherto unknown in place of part of the Ten Wings familiar to us. One such commentary with the title of *Yao* is especially important for our purposes. *Yao* probably means "summaries," as it contains several sections unrelated to one another. One section reported a long conversation on the *Book of Changes* between Confucius and his disciple Tzu-kung. It was said that Confucius loved the book so much in his old age that Tzu-kung questioned his wisdom to change his course as to believe in divination against his earlier teachings. Confucius patiently explained to Tzu-kung that such was never the case. He valued the book because it was important literature that included materials on ancient civilizations even more useful than the books of old. And even though he did practice divination, this was never where he put his emphasis. Even more important was the message of *te-i* (virtue-righteousness) included in it. Of course, there is no way for us to find out if this conversation actually took place or if it was just an imaginary conversation. At any rate, what was recorded in the document certainly does not contradict the Confucius and Tzu-kung we know through *The Analects* and other sources. We must conclude that the message conveyed through the conversation is authentic. Now we can safely say that there is strong evidence to support the account of the *Historical Records*—that Confucius loved to study the *Book of Changes* in his old age.

Apparently, he taught a different group of disciples—men such as Shang Chü (b. 522 B.C.), whose name did not even appear in *The Analects*; and for ten generations the line of transmission was unbroken. Thus, even though Confucius could not have been the author of the Ten Wings, they must have been the work of generations of Confucian scholars; and it is customary for them to ascribe their own words to the old master in order to lend authority to such commentaries. Since many ideas were handed down from generation to generation, it should be no great surprise that some may be traced back to Confucius, as the spirit seems to be consistent with the teachings of Confucius and his followers.

Professor Thomé H. Fang finds a very interesting parallel between the interpretations of *The Book of Odes* and the *Book of Changes*.

> In the major Preface to the *Book of Odes*, it is asserted that there are three different styles of writing poems, i.e., (1) in the language of (factual) depiction [*fu*], (2) in the language of matched simile or concealed parable [*pi*], and (3) in the language of exhilarated symbolization [*hsin*]. The first is prevalent in epic; the second, in allegories; and the third, in lyrics. It may be said that the first is employed to state the facts; the second, to conceal the meaning of implicit signification; and third, to add beauty to creative imagination. For a similar reason, the language developed to interpret the formal logical scheme in the *Book of Change* may be diversified into three different kinds, i.e., the language of factual depiction, the language of implicitly concealed signification, and the language of creative imagination in virtue of explicitly significant symbolization.[29]

Confucius's main effort to interpret classics lay in the third category, which explains how he could put new wine into old bottles. He did this to *The Book of Odes* as well as to the *Book of Changes*. Fang says, "Thenceforward the *Book of Change* as a treatise of historical depiction was turned over into a systematic philosophy of change."[30] Or to use our own terminology, a system of natural symbolism has been transformed into a system of cosmological symbolism. Professor Fang proceeds to describe the process of transformation as follows:

> And this new philosophy of change initiated by Confucius himself and, upon the evidences of Ssu-ma Tan and Ssu-ma Ch'ien, continued in further elaboration from Shang Chü onward, was to be diversified into four different forms.
>
> 1. There came into view a new philosophy of enlivened Nature which, unlike the mechanic order of material elements and physical processes as conceived a little later by the Yin-yang school of materialism, was permeated with the dynamical confluence or consanguinity of life. . . . Nature is power or vital impetus creative in advance and conducive to the fulfilment and consummation of life partaken by all beings. The cardinal doctrine of the vital impetus in the process of harmonious fulfilment was set forth by Confucius in the *Tuan*

Chuan—the *Compendiums*, in the *Hsi-ts'u-chuan*—the *Conspectus*, and in the early sections of the *Shuo-kua-chuan*—the scholia on the Hexagrams. . . .

2. There emerged, on the basis of an appreciated enlivened Nature, achievement of intrinsic moral goodness in human life, adorned with beauty. . . . Such a conception of moral-aesthetic perfection constitutive of the unique human personality was first set forth by Confucius in the *Ch'ien-K'un Wen-yen-chuan*—corollaries to *Ch'ien* and *K'un* and more systematically in the *Shang-chuan*—the *Symbolics* emphasizing the moral achievements of great men.

3. Upon the completion of a systematic philosophy of Nature and an all-round philosophy of moral-aesthetic perfection of human personality, there was developed a general theory of value in the form of the Supreme Good or absolute worth assimilating into it all the relative ranks of values prevalent in the entire universe. This is the cardinal idea in the *Hsi-ts'u-chuan*—the important *Conspectus* of the whole book.

4. On the foundation of individual creative nature emerging into the perfection of humanity, and of consummations in the achievement of the Supreme Good on a cosmic scale, Confucius finally formulated a general ontology of the fulness of Being in its entirety which is all through invested with value. It is really a value-centric ontology which we should take for the highest achievement of Confucianism as is found in the *Book of Change*.[31]

It may be questionable that Professor Fang ascribed everything to Confucius, but it is certainly not unreasonable to ascribe the above-mentioned insights to Confucius and his followers. Fang further elaborated on a set of four principles that are at work in this philosophy of change:

1. Principle of Life.
2. Principle of Extensive Connection.
3. Principle of Creative Creativity.
4. Principle of Creative Life as a Process of Value-realization.[32]

And he had summarized their interrelationship as follows:

Metaphysically, the philosophy of change is a system of dynamic ontology based upon the process of creative creativity as exhibited in the incessant change of time as well as a system of general axiology wherein the origin and development of the idea of the Supreme Good is shown in the light of comprehensive harmony. Thus the principle of extensive connection asserts at the same time that the confluence of life, permeating all beings under heaven and on earth, partakes of the creative process of time, and achieves, as a natural consequence, the form of the Supreme Good. From the view-point of organicism, no set of fundamental principles formulated in a system of metaphysics can be cut and thrust into an air-tight compartment without interpenetration. And, therefore, the principle of extensive connection serves as a prelude to the principle of creative creativity which, in turn, furnishes a keynote to the principle of life in the process of value-realization.[33]

Professor Fang may be said to have given a phenomenological description of the philosophy of change. He has highly prized this philosophy, as man is seen as an integral part of nature. It is in sharp contrast to the kind of scientific materialism developed in the West that has as its consequence the bifurcation of nature. Professor Fang comments:

For they [the majority of modern European savants], much influenced by physical science, cannot but assume that the universe consists of a system of inert matter. The universe, in their opinion, is made up of the ultimate units of matter and energy, distributed and redistributed in all sorts of ways in observance of rigid mechanical laws. It is true that this habit of thought, as exhibited in the procedure of scientific investigations, has worked successfully, giving rise to a system of laws which are abstract and accurate.

But if scientific materialism of this type is made use of in the very attempt to account for human life, then it will be overwhelmed with insurmountable difficulties. And, therefore, modern European philosophers, for the sake of formulating tenable theories concerning the meaning and value of human life, must start anew with different sets of assumptions. The trouble is that they are always making a great divide between matter and spirit. It is rather hard for them to bring things together which have been rashly severed. All through history they have been imposing on themselves an arduous task of developing a system of philosophy in which Weltanschauung and Lebensanschauung will work harmoniously together. But this effort of theirs, I am afraid, will eventually result in contradiction, if not in failure.

With regard to this problem, the Chinese philosophers have worked out a theory which is quite satisfactory. The universe, considered from our viewpoint, is fundamentally the confluence and concrescence of Universal Life in which the material conditions and the spiritual phenomena are so coalesced and interpenetrated that there can be no breach between them. And, therefore, as we live in the world, we find no difficulty in infusing the spirit into matter and immersing the matter in spirit. Matter manifests the significance of what is spiritual and spirit permeates the core of what is material. In a word, matter and spirit ooze together in a state of osmosis concurrently sustaining life, cosmic as well as human.[34]

One may agree or disagree with Fang's appraisal of Chinese philosophy, but it is true that the *Commentaries* of the *Book of Changes* have given expression to a universal philosophy of life that has dominated the Chinese types of cosmology throughout the ages.

ETHICAL/METAPHYSICAL SYMBOLISM

After the philosophy of change was shaped up in the *Commentaries*, it was speculated as to how Fu Hsi invented the Eight Trigrams:

> Of old, when Pao Hsi [Fu Hsi] ruled all beneath Heaven, looking up, he contemplated the emblems (i.e., sun, moon, stars, etc.) exhibited in Heaven, and looking down, surveyed the patterns shown on Earth. He contemplated the markings of birds and beasts and the suitabilities of the ground. Near at hand, in his own person, he found things for consideration, and the same at a distance, in things in general. Thereupon he first devised the eight trigrams to show fully the attributes of spirit-like intelligence (in its operations), and to classify the qualities of myriads of things.[35]

Obviously, this was the result of rationalization in a later age. But one thing seems certain: Whoever invented the eight trigrams first started with reading the mysteries of Heaven, then found applications in human affairs. For the followers of the philosophy of change, there is indeed an intimate relationship between Heaven and man, and man has always taken Heaven as his model.

> The character of the great man is identical with that of Heaven and Earth; his brilliance is identical with that of the sun and the moon; his order is identical with that of the four seasons; and his good and evil fortunes are identical with those of spiritual beings. He may precede Heaven and Heaven will not act in opposition to him. He may follow Heaven, but will act only as Heaven at the time will do.[36]

Such thought is thoroughly consistent with the sentiment of Confucius as reported in *The Analects*:

> Confucius said, "I do not wish to say anything." Tzu-kung said, "If you do not say anything, what can we little disciples ever learn to pass on to others?" Confucius said, "Does Heaven say anything? The four seasons run their course and all things are produced. Does Heaven say anything?"[37]

Clearly, Confucius was taking Heaven as his model. But if Heaven does not speak, then the emphasis would naturally be shifted to man, who is consciously working hard to carry out the mission bestowed on him by following the example of Heaven. Hence, Confucius said, "It is man who can make the Way great, and not the Way that can make man great.''[38] Confucius's humanism should not be understood as one that is totally cut off from Heaven; rather, the actualization of the Way of Heaven depends on the work of man. Subsequent development of Confucian thought through Mencius, *The Doctrine of the Mean*, and the *Commentaries* of the *Book of Changes* shows that cosmological symbolism is gradually superseded by ethical symbolism with profound metaphyscial implications.

It is no accident that Mencius was honored by the posterity as representing the orthodox line of Confucian thought, as he struck a perfect balance between transcendence and immanence in the fulcrum of man. He said:

He who exerts his mind to the utmost knows his nature. He who knows his nature knows Heaven. To preserve one's mind and to nourish one's nature is the way to serve Heaven. Not to allow any double-mindedness regardless of longevity or brevity of life, but to cultivate one's person and wait for [destiny (*ming*, fate, Heaven's decree or mandate) to take its own course] is the way to fulfil one's destiny.[39]

Wing-tsit Chan comments on the Confucian theory of waiting for destiny:

According to this doctrine, man should exert his utmost in moral endeavor and leave whatever is beyond our control to fate. It frankly admits that there are things beyond our control but there is no reason why one should relax in his moral endeavor. The tendency was definitely one of moralism and humanism. The Confucian theory represents the conviction of enlightened Chinese in general.[40]

This explains why Mencius never discussed the *Book of Changes*; apparently, he would not have anything to do with divination. Mencius's rival Hsün Tzu went even further to say that "those who are well-versed in the *Book of Changes* would not practice divination,"[41] even though he often quoted from the hexagrams to support his position. Thus, these two major Confucian philosophers after Confucius developed philosophies that had nothing to do with those ideas popularized by the Yin-yang school. Perhaps Hsün Tzu went a bit too far, as he adopted a totally naturalistic interpretation of Heaven and cut man off from the transcendent source.

Both *The Great Learning* and *The Doctrine of the Mean*, however, gave expression to thoughts that are consistent with Mencius's ideas. The opening statement in *The Great Learning* says: "The Way of the great learning consists in manifesting the illustrious virtue, loving the people, and abiding in the highest good."[42] The opening statement of *The Doctrine of the Mean* reads: "What Heaven imparts to man is called human nature. To follow our nature is called the Way. Cultivating the Way is called education."[43] It is not difficult to find that some statements in the *Commentaries* of the *Book of Changes* were thoroughly consistent with this line of thought. For example, in chapter 5 of *The Appended Remarks*, part 1:

> The successive movement of yin and yang constitutes the Way (Tao). What issues from the way is good, and that which realizes it is the individual nature. The man of humanity (*jen*) sees it and calls it humanity. The man of wisdom sees it and calls it wisdom. And the common people act according to it daily without knowing it. In this way the Way of the superior man is fully realized. It [spirit] is manifested in humanity but is concealed in the functioning. It promotes all things without sharing the anxiety of the sage. How perfect is its eminent virtue and great achievement! Its achievement is great because it possesses everything, and its virtue is abundant because it renovates things every day.
>
> Changes mean creative creativity. *Ch'ien* means the completion of forms and *k'un* means to model after them. Divination means to go to the utmost of the natural course of events in order to know the future. Affairs mean to adapt and accommodate accordingly. And that which is unfathomable in the operation of yin and yang is called spirit.[44]

The key transformation here is that in the cosmic process the transcendent Way of Heaven is internalized in man and becomes his nature, and what is realized is exuberant with values. This position is unmistakably Confucian, even though certain Taoist and yin-yang ideas had been absorbed into its philosophy. Divination here was given a totally rational interpretation, and a creative philosophy has emerged from primitive beliefs in supernatural powers. Moreover, the relation between Heaven and man was turned around. Although man has received his endowment from Heaven, it is through man that the Way of Heaven is manifested.

Now we can see why Sung Neo-Confucian philosophers especially honored the *Commentaries* of the *Book of Changes* as well as the *Four Books*. And it is interesting to note that a similar process of development from an emphasis on Heaven to one on man can be found in the early Sung period. Chou Tun-i (1017–1073) was honored as the pioneer of Neo-Confucianism. His essay "An Explanation of the Diagram of the Great Ultimate" exerted profound influence on subsequent Neo-Confucian philosophies.[45] Chou had further developed what he had learned from the *Book of Changes* into a comprehensive scheme of cosmological philosophy with man as the center of the universe. Later scholars pointed out that the Diagram appeared to emerge from a Taoist source, but the philosophy Chou developed in his explanation of the Diagram was clearly a Confucian one.[46] He was not so much interested in following the Diagram to carry out the Taoist discipline to return to the root as he was in the construction of a creative philosophy abounding in cosmological symbolisms. Chang Tsai (1020–1077), another leading Neo-Confucian philosopher in the same period, showed an even stronger interest in cosmological speculations. It was with the Ch'eng brothers, Ch'eng Hao (1032–1085) and Ch'eng I (1033–1107), who studied under Chou when they were young scholars, that we find the decisive turn from the emphasis on cosmological speculation to ethical/metaphysical realization. The following anecdote illustrates the case in point:

> Master Yang [Yang Hsiung (53 B.C.–A.D. 18)] said, "To observe Heaven and Earth, then one would get a vision of the sage." I-Chuan [Ch'eng I] said, "That is not correct. To observe the sage, then one would get a vision of Heaven and Earth."[47]

The Ch'eng brothers had not shown much interest in cosmological speculation; their efforts had been to realize the metaphysical depth in every human being through their moral endeavor based on their endowment from Heaven. The proper direction is not from Heaven to man, but the other way around: One must start from what is near at hand, then reach as far as the entire universe.

This line of thought was picked up again by contemporary Neo-Confucian philosophers. Professor T'ang Chün-i (1909–1978) reported a real-life story on his progress in appreciating the deeper insights implied in the *Book of Changes*.[48] When he first published his essay "On Chinese Cultural Spirit," most teachers and friends complimented his work; only Professor Hsiung Shih-li (1885–1968) did not. He pointed out that Professor T'ang was wrong in thinking that the philosophy of change did not have a *t'i* (literally, "a substance," meaning an ultimate metaphysical principle), based on the saying, "What is divine has no rules and changes have no substance." At first, Professor T'ang did not accept Professor Hsiung's criticism; but later on, he realized that it is not true that there is not an ultimate metaphysical principle amid changes in the philosophy of change. After all, Professor Hsiung was the one with deeper insight, as he had been able to grasp the most important message of *Changes*.

Professor Hsiung is now commonly regarded as the founder of Contemporary Neo-Confucianism in the narrow sense. Among his disciples we find such eminent scholars as T'ang Chün-i and Mou Tsung-san (1909–1995), whose efforts helped the movement gain international recognition. Professor Hsiung first engaged in revolutionary activities to overthrow the Ch'ing dynasty, then he studied Buddhist philosophy, and finally he was converted to Confucianism. Following his conversion, he worked hard throughout his life, trying to expound his insight into the mystery of life through his understanding of the *Changes*,[49] and he exerted a profound influence on his disciples even though none accepted his system of philosophy. They went beyond his position and developed philosophies of their own.

Especially noteworthy is Professor Mou Tsung-san.[50] He studied Kant and took him as the point of departure in order to show the limitations of traditional Western philosophies and the insights of Chinese philosophies. According to Mou, although the Chinese must learn science and democracy from the West, there is no need for them to give up their own philosophical tradition. Metaphysics must be distinguished as two kinds: the so-called *shih-yu* metaphysics (metaphysics of reality) and *ching-jie* metaphysics (metaphysics of realization). The first kind is a metaphysics of substance that was developed in the West from Aristotle to the Rationalists. This kind of metaphysics takes ultimate reality as something external and objective. It has lost its appeal, owing to the criticisms of Hume and Kant. But Kant reopened the door to a new kind of metaphysics through the postulates of Practical Reason. It is here that Professor Mou finds the limitations of traditional Western philosophy. As Kant was limited by his Christian background, it was impossible for him to establish a moral metaphysics. The best he could do was to develop a metaphysics of morals and a moral theology. There is still an unbridgeable gap between God, on the one hand, and the world of nature and man, on the other hand. But in the Chinese tradition, the finite (man) has always had access to the infinite (Heaven). Therefore, Professor Mou claims that the three major traditions in China—Confucianism, Taoism, and Buddhism—all assert that man has intellectual intuition in the sense that man even though finite can achieve the realization of the Way, and that there is no gap between transcendence and immanence. Therefore, for the Chinese philosophers, the ultimate is not just a postulate, as the Way as presence is manifested in reality, and there is interpenetration of phenomenon and reality.

Professor Mou has traced his insight back to Sung-Ming Neo-Confucian philosophies. He pays special tribute to Ch'eng Hao's interpretation of *Changes*, distinct from his brother's interpretation, and then gives Neo-Confucian insight a contemporary reinterpretation through contrast with Western philosophies. From this perspective, the most profound message of the *Book of Changes* is the realization of the most simple and the changeless amidst changes. And again, the insight can be traced back to Confucius, as he said, "In the morning, hear the Way, at night, die content!"[51] It is by realizing the spiritual fountain within the self that one can become a person with ultimate commitment, who knows that it is impossible to achieve his goals but keeps trying and making himself a creative person.[52]

SIGNIFICANCE IN THE CONTEMPORARY WORLD

I have outlined the four dimensions of thought expressed through the four different kinds of symbolism we find in the *Book of Changes*. The descriptions may be sketchy, but the four different directions are unmistakable. All four approaches are still thriving today. For example, *fung-shui* (geomancy) is still a way of life for common Chinese people; acupuncture and Chinese medicine have attracted the attention of, and are being studied by, Western medical doctors; contemporary philosophers are still busy trying to recapture the messages of the *Book of Changes* through efforts to reinterpret the cosmological, ethical, and metaphysical symbolisms in the classic. As early as the beginning of the Ch'ing dynasty, when the royal libraries were compiled, there were already more than 3,000 pieces written on the classic. Even today, enthusiasm for the classic has not died; every year more books and articles are published that give new interpretations of the classic. However, their accounts are often contradictory. If studying the *Book of Changes* is like entering a labyrinth, how is it possible to find the clue of Ariadne to lead us out of the maze?

We could, of course, do it by way of elimination. Many Mainland Chinese scholars still continue what had been started by the May Fourth movement in 1919; they have made attempts to discredit the classic by adopting a strategy of demystification. They have tried to show that many statements in the *Book of Changes* really do not have any profound messages: Some were merely recording events of the ancient past; others were superstitions of a very primitive kind that ought to be discarded by more civilized people; and the best among them could offer us no more than rational thinking and dialectics in its first stages. In this approach, the *Book of Changes* would be studied as merely a document of historical significance but not much else. The interpretations of later Confucian scholars were regarded as fabrications with the purpose of supporting a kind of feudal morality in the interests of the ruling classes. This approach ignores the fact that all the classics in the world have a perennial attraction for the future. A. N. Whitehead declared that subsequent European philosophies consisted of a series of footnotes to Plato.[53] Naturally, what had been written thousands or hundreds of years ago cannot be applied today without making massive modifications; therefore, some sort of demythologization is inevitable. But I would agree with Paul Tillich that complete demythologization is neither possible nor desirable.[54] If the symbols of the Christian tradition can still be meaningful today, messages conveyed through the *Book of Changes* concerning the union between Heaven and man can also be meaningful—only they need to be given totally new interpretations. Symbols live and die; they cannot be manufactured artificially. In a way, for centuries the *Book of Changes* has dominated the traditional ways of thinking in China like the Bible in the West.

When scholars exaggerate the contributions of the *Book of Changes* to the development of science, they should be reminded that whatever it has accomplished, it has not yet passed the threshold of modern science. Needham is certainly right to urge us not to overestimate the impact of this classic on science. But his attempt to dismiss it as merely providing a vast filing system without making any positive contributions to science seems to go to the other extreme. For example, the *Book of Changes* with its yin-yang, Five Agents model did provide a framework that enabled traditional Chinese medicine to develop into a distinct system of its own. The only thing we now know is that Chinese medicine did operate on a different paradigm, and it produces effects that must not be ignored by Western medicine. What needs to be done is to find an even more comprehensive framework that includes the accomplishments of Chinese medicine in its system.

Because the Chinese refuse to separate form from content, they have had to pay a dear price in the development of their civilization. Hence, we find that the Chinese have failed to develop a formal logic as well as a mechanical model of physics like that found in the West. It is quite true that the Chinese have a great deal to learn from the West if they want to survive and to catch up with the West in science and technology. Ironically, however, in moving toward the so-called postmodern era, we now find that Western science and technology could also create serious problems for the world. Certainly, they have not brought us all blessings, as believed by the eighteenth-century Enlightenment thinkers. Today they could also bring about dehumanization, upset ecology, and inflict other harmful consequences if they are allowed to expand without limit. Professor Fang has already pointed out the merits of a Chinese cosmology based on the model of the *Book of Changes*. Perhaps for certain practical purposes, the abstractions needed for the development of Western science and technology are a necessity, but they must be put into proper perspective.

The holistic view of man and nature must not be totally forgotten and discarded. We have to reconstruct some of the traditional insights and give them contemporary reinterpretations. It is not difficult for modern scholars to see that there is indeed a certain affinity between the philosophy of Whitehead and the *Book of Changes*. It is perhaps possible for us to develop a new cosmology by looking for a synthesis between tradition and modernity, between East and West. Northrop has already pointed out a general direction,[55] but progress requires more scholars and greater efforts to work together to overcome the difficulties we face today.

Whether a new organic model will work in the world of science is not for us to tell; it has to produce concrete results before it can be regarded as a new paradigm for another age to come. But no speculation is needed when we turn to the ethical and metaphysical dimensions of man. Kant has shown decisively that we cannot establish a metaphysics by way of scientific generalization. There is no way to prove that we have freedom of will which is why Kant was forced to treat it as a postulate of Practical Reason. But Kant's approach is not the only possible approach. If we start with pure reason, it appears inevitable that we will come up with a theory like Kant's. But if we start from Practical Reason at the very beginning, then the problem will be seen under a totally different light. This is exactly why we need to review the Chinese approach to the problem. One can never establish that life is meaningful either by logical deduction or by empirical generalization. It is by way of the realization of humanity (*jen*) and creativity (*sheng*) within ourselves that the problem is naturally dissolved.

Now that we have examined each of the four dimensions of thought expressed by the four different kinds of symbolism found in the *Book of Changes*, one wonders how they are related to one another. Is it possible to find a unity among them? So far, we have combined a historical approach with a structural approach. We find that from a historical perspective mystical symbolism comes first, followed by rational/natural symbolism, cosmological symbolism, and ethical/metaphysical symbolism. The genetic order of them cannot be reversed. But once these symbolisms have been developed, they exist side by side, and there could be backslides; we cannot assume that they developed according to a linear progressive sequence. Each symbolism has shown distinct characteristics, and it cannot be reduced to another symbolism; further, we can give a phenomenological description of these characteristics. Hence, the structural, phenomenological approach must not be confused with the genetical, historical approach.[56] As the subject matters are different, it seems impossible to find a common denominator for all of them. But Ernst Cassirer's philosophy of culture has helped to point toward a new direction:

> Here we are under no obligation to prove the substantial unity of man. Man is no longer considered as a simple substance which exists in itself and is to be known by itself. His unity is conceived as a functional unity. Such a unity does not presuppose a homogeneity of the various elements of which it consists. Not merely does it admit of, it even requires, a multiplicity and multiformity of its constituent parts. For this is a dialectical unity, a coexistence of contraries.
>
> "Men do not understand," said Heraclitus, "how that which is torn in different directions comes into accord with itself—harmony in contrariety, as in the case of the bow and the lyre." In order to demonstrate such a harmony we need not prove the identity or similarity of the different forces by which it is produced. The various forms of human culture are not held together by an identity in their nature but by a conformity in their fundamental task. If there is an equipoise in human culture it can only be described as a dynamic, not as a static equilibrium; it is the result of a struggle between opposing forces. This struggle does not exclude that "hidden harmony" which, according to Heraclitus, "is better than that which is obvious."[57]

As the *Book of Changes* encompasses the whole realm of human culture, Cassirer's reflection has important bearing on our study of the classic. The Neo-Confucian dictum *li-i-fen-shu* (One principle, many manifestations)[58] provides a clue for us to solve our problems by moving along the same direction Cassirer took. As creativity must be manifested in various diverse forms, its central theme *T'ien-jen-ho-i* (Heaven and man in union) finds its various expressions in the four different kinds of symbolism, as in the music of a symphony.

In mystical symbolism we find that there appears to be a mysterious union between man and Heaven. Although such a primordial unity was long broken when civilization reached a certain stage, the process of demystification and demythologization cannot be carried to the extreme without producing harmful results. At the extreme, modern man is totally cut off from nature and becomes a stranger in the universe; anxiety is the inescapable result, as has been amply described by contemporary existentialist writers. As Kant pointed out, we can never prove that there is any purpose in the world of nature, but we must still feel awed by the stars in Heaven and the moral laws of man. There is still something sacred about life; it is in this sense that a little myth is needed even for a man living in the twentieth century.

In rational/natural symbolism, we find that "Heaven and man in union" is expressed in a totally different fashion. We must formulate hypotheses and design experiments in order to find verification by empirical evidence. It is untenable to maintain a dualism between formal sciences and empirical sciences like the logical positivists;[59] it would become totally unexplainable as to why mathematics finds such ample use in empirical sciences unless there is a certain relationship between the mathematical order and the physical order. Northrop's idea of epistemic correlation has pointed toward the right direction to solve the problem.[60]

In cosmological symbolism, we find that "Heaven and man in union" is expressed through a philosophy of comprehensive harmony formulated by Chinese philosophers throughout the ages, and the *Book of Changes* remains a source of inspiration to give new expression to this philosophy. It is true that cosmological speculation is not in vogue today. But it is not impossible for us to form certain world hypotheses, as suggested by S. C. Pepper.[61] The adventure of ideas is somewhat beyond the scope of normal science as portrayed by Kuhn.[62] One insight offered by Chinese philosophers is that value must have an ontological basis; it cannot be adequately explained through emotive responses or subjective preferences. True, *Is* and *Ought* pertain to two different realms; but while they should be kept distinct, they must not be separated from each other. The Chinese view is somewhat congruent to Whitehead's attempt to find values in the structure of being.[63] And man should be seen as a being with an intimate relationship with nature. Future explorations along this line should be encouraged.

In ethical/metaphysical symbolism, we find that "Heaven and man in union" is expressed through the establishment of an ultimate concern through the realization of a depth dimension within the self. Creative manifestations must find their root in creativity. This is perhaps the most profound insight offered by the Chinese philosophers. For those who deny that there is a depth dimension in the self, Wang Yang-ming has this to say: "Their behavior resembles that of descendents of the rich clan, who have been careless in their management of the inherited property, gradually forgetting and losing it till they themselves become poor beggars."[64]

By his endowment, man is able to be united with Heaven, which is not just the totality of nature but a transcendent, creative, ontological principle that works incessantly in the universe. Such searches do not pertain to the realm of science but to the realm of moral metaphysics; only those who make their ultimate commitment to the Way and go through proper discipline may find union with the source.

For Sung-Ming Neo-Confucian philosophers, principle is one, while manifestations are many. It seems that the West has paid too much attention to the manifestations and neglected the principle, whereas the East has adhered too much to the principle itself and somewhat neglected to find novel and creative ways to manifest the principle. Now it is high time for us to seek a golden mean in order to realize the wisdom we have inherited from the *Book of Changes*. The classic is no longer understood to give us a closed system. It is pointing to a direction. The principle of creativity is seeking ever new expressions. It is here that we find the meeting point between tradition and modernity, East and West. Inadequate as it may be, this introduction is offered to illustrate the possibility of revitalization and reconstruction of the Chinese philosophy.

NOTES

1. This chapter is based on my presidential address delivered at the Fifth International Conference of Chinese Philosophy of the International Society for Chinese Philosophy in San Diego, California, on July 13, 1987. A somewhat abridged version of the address "On the Functional Unity of the Four Dimensions of Thought in the *Book of Changes*" was published in the *Journal of Chinese Philosophy* 17, no. 3 (September 1990): 359–385. The unabridged version was published in Yugoslavia in the now-defunct *Synthesis Philosophica* 7 (January 1989): 323–345. The methodology was based on an earlier article of mine, "The Use of Analogy in Traditional Chinese Philosophy," *Journal of Chinese Philosophy* 1, nos. 3–4 (June–September 1974): 313–338.

2. Cf. my article "On Mystical Symbolism in the *Book of Changes*" (in Chinese), published as No. 9 in *Occasional Paper and Monograph Series* (The Institute of East Asian Philosophies, Singapore, 1987).

3. Chan, *Source Book*, p. 262.

4. Cf. Hsü Hsi-tai and Lou Yü-tung, "Hsi-Chou kua-hua shih-shuo" (An attempt to give explanations of diagrams of hexagrams of West Chou), *Chung-kuo Che-hsüeh* (Chinese Philosophy) 3 (August 1980): 13–19.

5. Famous scholars such as Kuo Mu-jo and Tang Lan had maintained such a viewpoint.

6. Cf. Chang Wu, "New Results, Characteristics, and Directions in Research on the *Book of Changes*," in *Chou-i tsung-heng lu* (Essays on the *Book of Changes*) (Hupei: People's Publications, 1986), pp. 611–612.

7. Wang Ning-sheng, "Pa-kua chi-yüan" (The origins of trigrams), *Kao-ku* (Archaeology), no. 145 (1976): 242–245.

8. This account was handed down to us since Ssu-ma Ch'ien's *Historical Records*.

9. Cf. Yüan Ko, *Chung-kuo ku-tai shen-hua* (Ancient Chinese mythology) (Beijing: Chung-hua shu-chü, 1985), pp. 41–51.

10. The *Commentaries* in the present version of the *I Ching* are called the Ten Wings. There are sixty-four hexagrams. Each hexagram is followed by two texts: (1) the *kua-tz'u*, or the explanation of the text of the whole hexagram: and (2) the *yao-tz'u*, or the explanation of the component lines. There are seven *Commentaries*: (3) the *tuan-chuan*, or the commentary on (1); (4) the *hsiang*, or the explanation of images of (1) and (2); (5) the *wen-yen*, or commentary of the first two hexagrams—*ch'ien* and *k'un*—to stress their philosophical or ethical meaning. Following these sixty-four hexagrams and their discussions, there are (6) the *hsi-tz'u*, or the appended remarks, (7) the *shuo-kua*, or the remarks on certain trigrams, (8) the *hsü-kua*, or the remarks on the order of the hexagrams, and (9) the *tsa-kua*, or the random remarks on the hexagrams. Numbers 3, 4, and

6, each in two parts, and numbers 5, 7, 8, and 9 form the Ten Wings of the book. Cf. Chan, *Source Book*, p. 262.

11. Cf. ibid., pp. 244–250.

12. A. C. Graham, "Yin-Yang and the Nature of Correlative Thinking," *Institute of East Asian Philosophies Occasional Paper and Monograph Series*, no. 6, p. 8.

13. Fung, *Short History*, p. 141

14. These are taken from the *yao-tz'u*, or the explanation of the component lines of the hexagrams.

15. The discussions were recorded in the twenty-ninth year of Duke Chao of Lu.

16. For example, Ho Hsin, formerly of the Institute of Literature, Chinese Academy of Social sciences, maintains that dragons were actually a species of crocodiles: *Crocodilus porosus*.

17. Ku Chi-kang first started the trend. See his contributions in *Ku-shih-pien* (Discussions in ancient Chinese history) (Shanghai: Ku-chi Publications, 1982), Vol. 3, pt. 1.

18. Li Ching-chi, *Chou-i t'an-yüan* (An exploration of the origins of the *Book of Changes*) (Beijing: Chung-hua shu-chü, 1978).

19. Kao Heng, *Chou-i ku-ching ching-chu* (A contemporary commentary on the ancient text of the *Book of Changes*) (Hong Kong: Chung-hua shu-chü, 1980).

20. Hu Shih, *The Development of the Logical Method in Ancient China* (Shanghai: Oriental Book Co., 1928), p. 37.

21. Ibid., p. 38.

22. Joseph Needham, *Science and Civilization in China* (Cambridge: Cambridge University Press, 1956), 2: 326–327.

23. Benjamin I. Schwartz, *The World of Thought in Ancient China* (Cambridge, Mass.: Harvard University Press, 1985), p. 400.

24. Cf. Jen Chi-yü, *Chung-kuo che-hsüeh fa-chen-shih (Ch'in-Han)* (The developmental history of Chinese philosophy: Ch'in-Han) (Beijing: People's Publications, 1985), p. 452.

25. Chu Ch'ien-chih, *Chung-kuo che-hsüeh tui Ou-chou ti yin-hsiang* (The influence of Chinese philosophy on Europe) (Fu-chou: Fu-chien People's Publications, 1983), pp. 229–233.

26. Cf. Thomé H. Fang, *The Chinese View of Life* (Hong Kong: The Union Press, 1957), pp. 44–86 (hereafter cited as Fang, *The Chinese View of Life*).

27. Cf. Thomé H. Fang, *Chinese Philosophy: Its Spirit and Its Development* (Taipei: Linking Pub. Co., 1981), pp. 102–104 (hereafter cited as Fang, *Chinese Philosophy*).

28. Cf. Liao Ming-ch'un, "Po-shu shih-yao" (An interpretation of the silk scroll document: "Summaries") *Chung-kuo Wen-hua* (Chinese Culture), no. 10 (1994): 63–76.

29. Fang, *Chinese Philosophy*, p. 99, with slight modification.

30. Ibid., p. 103.

31. Ibid., pp. 103–104.

32. Ibid., pp. 106–112.

33. Ibid., p. 109.

34. Fang, *The Chinese View of Life*, pp. 51–52.

35. Fung, *History*, 1: 393–394.

36. Chan, *Source Book*, p. 264.

37. Ibid., p. 47, with slight modification.

38. Ibid., p. 44, with slight modification.

39. Ibid., p. 78.

40. Ibid., p. 79.

41. *The Hsün-tzu*, ch. 27, *Ta Lue* (Scattered Sayings), translation mine. Cf. Homer H. Dubs, *Hsüntze* (London: Arthur Probsthain, 1927), p. 45.

42. Chan, *Source Book*, p. 86, with modification.

43. Ibid., p. 98, with slight modification.

44. Ibid., p. 266, with modification.

45. Ibid., pp. 463–464.

46. Fung, *History*, 2: 442.

47. *Wai-shu* (Additional works), 11:3b, in the *Erh-Ch'eng ch'uan-shu* (Complete works of the two Ch'engs) (SPPY ed.), translation mine.

48. T'ang Chün-i, *Chung-kuo wen-hua chih ching-shen chia-chih* (The spiritual values of Chinese culture) (Taipei: Cheng-chung shu-chü, 1953), preface, p. 2.

49. For an introduction to Professor Hsiung's ideas, see Shu-hsien Liu, "The Contemporary Development of a Neo-Confucian Epistemology," *Inquiry* 14 (1971): 19–27. The article was republished as a chapter in *Invitation to Chinese Philosophy*, ed. Arne Naess and Alastair Hannay (Oslo-Bergen-Tromsö: Universitetsforlaget, 1972), pp. 19–44.

50. For an introduction to Professor Mou's ideas, see ibid., pp. 27–40.

51. Chan, *Source Book*, p. 26.

52. Cf. ibid., p. 43. Confucius himself was regarded as the embodiment of such an ideal of man by the posterity.

53. A. N. Whitehead, *Process and Reality* (New York: Free Press, 1969), p. 53 (hereafter cited as Whitehead, *Process and Reality*).

54. Cf. Tillich, *Systematic Theology*, 2: 29.

55. F.S.C. Northrop, *The Meeting of East and West* (New York: Macmillan Co., 1945).

56. Cf. Ernst Cassirer, *An Essay on Man* (New Haven, Conn.: Yale University Press, 1944), pp. 30–31.

57. Ibid., pp. 222–223.

58. Chan, *Source Book*, pp. 499–500.

59. Dewey's pragmatic approach to logic would also reject the view of logical positivism. Cf. John Dewey, *Logic: The Theory of Inquiry* (New York: H. Holt & Co., 1938), pp. 519–520.

60. Cf. F.S.C. Northrop, *The Logic of the Sciences and the Humanities* (New York: Macmillan Co., 1947).

61. Cf. S. C. Pepper, *World Hypotheses* (Berkeley: University of California Press, 1970).

62. Cf. Thomas S. Kuhn, *The Structure of Scientific Revolution* (Chicago: University of Chicago Press, 1962).

63. Whitehead, *Process and Reality*.

64. Julia Ching, *To Acquire Wisdom: The Way of Wang Yang-ming* (New York: Columbia University Press, 1976), p. 214 (hereafter cited as Ching, *To Acquire Wisdom*).

6

The Transformation of Confucianism since the Han Dynasty

According to contemporary Neo-Confucian philosophers, the evolution of Confucian philosophy in ancient times culminates in the development of a moral metaphysics. But the actual development of Confucianism took a twist in the Han dynasty. Even though in name it had been honored, since 136 B.C. under the reign of Emperor Han Wu, as the sole state doctrine at the expense of hundreds of schools, in fact it was eclectic in nature, taking in ingredients from Taoism, Legalism, and especially the Yin-yang school. It was not able to keep up the spirit of the moral metaphysics developed by Mencius; instead, it formulated a cosmology of two forces—yin and yang—and Five Agents—metal, wood, water, fire, and earth—which presupposed a strict correlation between celestial phenomena and human events. In the understanding of human nature, the transcendent approach of Mencius was also not appreciated; instead, attention was on the physical nature of man, which could not be seen as all good. Finally, the application of the theory of Five Agents to human history formed a deterministic philosophy of history with serious political implications.

Strangely enough, we can find no traces of yin-yang and the Five Agents in the *Four Books*, even though Hsün Tzu made charges against the school of Tzu-ssu and Mencius of teaching an untenable theory of the Five Agents that confused the minds of people. Now with the unearthing of the silk scroll Mencian work from a Han tomb, we realize that Hsün Tzu's criticism was unfounded, because even though the author of this work associated the virtues of *jen* (humanity), *i* (righteousness), *li* (propriety), *chih* (wisdom), and *sheng* (sageliness) with *ch'i* (material or vital forces), so that they were identified as the Five Agents, the implications are quite different from the teachings of the Yin-yang

school.[1] From the contemporary Neo-Confucian perspective the correlative cosmology developed in the Ch'in-Han period was certainly a degeneration of the
moral metaphysics of Confucius and Mencius. But there is no denial that such
thought had been adopted as the state ideology since the Han dynasty and was
promoted by political authorities for over 2,000 years. It could not but exert
profound influence on the shaping of the Chinese mentality, and it became the
origin of so-called politicized Confucianism and popular Confucianism. We simply cannot afford to ignore this aspect of the problem; hence, in this chapter I
shall give a sketch of the transformation of Confucianism in the Ch'in-Han
period.

In the last chapter, I proposed taking a developmental approach to studying
the *I Ching*. I shall continue to do so in studying the transformation of Confucianism since the Ch'in-Han period. When we go back to the ancient texts, we
find that yin-yang and the Five Agents came from separate sources. Let us start
with an examination of yin and yang. At first, the two concepts probably did
not have any philosophical implications. *Yang* simply means ''the side that faces
the sun,'' whereas *yin* means ''the other side.'' Not only did the *Four Books*
say nothing about them, but even in the text of the *I Ching*, the character of
yang never appears, and the character of yin appears only once, where it meant
just ''shades.''[2] It was in history books such as *Tso Chuan* that they were
regarded as two of the six forces (*ch'i*).[3] Finally, they were probably lifted out
by Tsou Yen as two basic forces working in the universe, and the *Commentaries*
of the *I Ching* simply took for granted that such is the case.

The understanding of the Five Agents had undergone similar processes. When
they first appeared in ''The Great Norm'' of the *Book of History*, they did not
seem to have much philosophical significance. As the text said:

> Heaven gave him (Great Yü) with its Nine Categories. And the various
> virtues and their relations were regulated. . . .
>
> The first category is the Five Agents; namely, Water, Fire, Wood, Metal,
> and Earth. The nature of Water is to moisten and descend; of Fire, to burn
> and ascend; of Wood, to be crooked and straight; of Metal, to yield and
> to be modified; of Earth, to provide for sowing and reaping. That which
> moistens and descends produces saltiness; that which burns and ascends
> produces bitterness; that which is crooked and straight produces sourness;
> that which yields and is modified produces acridity; that which provides
> for sowing and reaping produces sweetness.[4]

These seem to have been based on empirical observations. Again, it was also
probably through Tsou Yen that the Five Agents were transformed into vital
forces, along with yin and yang: Through a combination of them, natural phenomena and human events were being formed. Unfortunately, however, we do
not have any of Tsou Yen's works today; the only thing left about him is a
biography in *Historical Records*.[5] Some of his ideas may survive in the works

of the so-called *Tsa Chia* (the miscellaneous school). In a work compiled under the sponsorship of Lü Pu-wei, a prime minister of Ch'in, we find the application of the theory of Five Agents to political events in history characteristic of Tsou Yen's thought:

> Whenever an emperor or king is about to rise, Heaven will always first manifest some good omen to the common people. In the time of the Yellow Emperor, Heaven made a large number of earthworms and mole crickets appear. The Yellow Emperor said, "The force of Earth is dominant." As the force of Earth was dominant, he chose yellow as his color and Earth as the model for his activities.
>
> When it came to the time of Yü, Heaven first made grass and trees appear which did not die in the autumn and winter. Yü said, "The force of Wood is dominant." As the force of Wood was dominant, he chose green as his color and Wood as the model for his activities.
>
> When it came to the time of T'ang (r. 1751–1739 B.C.?), Heaven first made some metal blades appear in the water. T'ang said, "The force of Metal is dominant." As the force of Metal was dominant, he chose white as his color and Metal as the model for his activities.
>
> When it came to the time of King Wen, Heaven first made fire appear, while red birds holding a red book in their bills gathered on the altar of the soil of the House of Chou. King Wen said, "The force of Fire is dominant." As the force of Fire was dominant, he chose red as his color and Fire as the model for his activities.
>
> Water will inevitably replace Fire. Now Heaven will first make the dominance of Water manifest. As the force of water is dominant, black will be chosen as the color and Water the model for activities. The force of Water reaches its limit without people realizing it. The course is now completed, and the process will revert to Earth (*Lü-shih ch'un-ch'iu*, ch. 13, sec. 2, sppy, 13:4a).[6]

Such a fanciful interpretation of the past was no more than just a theory. Only the First Emperor of Ch'in firmly believed in the theory under the influence of Lü and designated water as the virtue of Ch'in. The Han inherited the theory from Ch'in. There was a hot debate on which virtue was proper for the new dynasty. One theory assigned fire to Han, as this dynasty was the successor to Ch'in; the other theory assigned water to Han, as the Ch'in dynasty's reign was considered too short to merit a turn; so the Han dynasty was the real successor to Chou. Finally, Han settled for water as the virtue of the dynasty. At any rate, these ideas of the Yin-yang school were completely absorbed by Han Confucianism.

As is well known, Confucianism was established as the state doctrine under the reign of Emperor Han Wu (the Martial Emperor). Perhaps there were needs of the time that made it necessary to make such a move. The feudal system of

Chou was destroyed. The cruel Ch'in used legalist practices to bring about the unification of China but was quickly overthrown; naturally, Legalism also fell into disgrace. As the founder of the Han dynasty, Emperor Han Kao was a commoner. Those who fought with him were men in the street, including butchers and others with lowly professions who did not know how to behave properly in court. Hence, a Confucianist, Shu-Sun Tung, was summoned to draw up a court ceremonial. It was then that the emperor could really enjoy the nobility of being the Son of Heaven.[7] Here we find the other face of Confucianism—a face that undisputably serves the interests of the rulers. This is what I call politicized Confucianism; its characteristics 100m in sharp contrast to the critical spirit of Mencius's spiritual Confucianism.

In the early Han, after years of war and violence, people yearned for peace and stability. Under the reign of Emperors Han Wen and Han Ching, the guiding principles were Huang-Lao (the Yellow Emperor and Lao Tzu), a kind of politicized Taoism, which taught the doctrine of *wu-wei* (taking no action) and allowed the people to be restful. But under the reign of Han Wu, the empire had accumulated sufficient wealth and needed something more positive to guide its actions; naturally, it turned to Confucianism. Emperor Han Wu accepted the advice of Tung Chung-shu and designated Confucianism as the state doctrine. Tung Chung-shu further developed a comprehensive philosophy to give justification to the empire. Finally, in the Eastern (later) Han (25–220) under the reign of Emperor Han Chang, scholars were summoned to hold a meeting at Po-hu-kuan (the White Tiger Temple) to produce a document to provide the guidance for state ideology. The principles of the Three Bonds (*san-kang*)—between ruler and minister, father and son, and man and wife—were further solidified. The program of politicized Confucianism was basically complete.

Obviously, Tung Chung-shu (c. 179–104 B.C.) played a key role in the transformation of Confucianism in the Han period. His magnum opus was *Ch'un-ch'iu fan-lu* (Luxuriant gems of the *Spring and Autumn Annals*). Let us quote several key passages from the work in order to show the directions in which his thought moved:

Heaven possesses yin and yang and man also possesses yin and yang. When the universe's material force of yin arises, man's material force of yin arises in response. Conversely, when man's material force of yin arises, that of the universe should also arise in response. The principle is the same. He who understands this, when he wishes to bring forth rain, will activate the yin in man in order to arouse the yin of the universe. When he wishes to stop rain, he will activate the yang in man in order to arouse the yang of the universe. Therefore the bringing forth of rain is nothing supernatural. People suspect that it is supernatural because its principle is subtle and wonderful. It is not only the material forces of yin and yang that can advance or withdraw according to their kind. Even the way misfortunes, calamities, and blessings are produced follows the same

principle. In all cases one starts something himself and other things become active in response according to their kind.[8]

There is a strict correlation between natural and human phenomena; the relationship between them is one of mutual influence. Not only yin and yang but
also the Five Agents played important roles in his thought:

> Heaven has Five agents (i.e., Elements): the first is Wood, the second,
> Fire; the third, Earth; the fourth, Metal; and the fifth, Water. Wood is the
> beginning of the cycle of the Five Agents, Water is its end, and Earth is
> its center. Such is their natural sequence. Wood produces Fire, Fire pro-
> duces Earth, Earth produces Metal, Metal produces Water, and Water pro-
> duces Wood. Such is their father-and-son relationship. Wood occupies the
> left, Metal occupies the right, Fire occupies the front, Water occupies the
> rear, and Earth occupies the center. Such is their order as that of father
> and son, and the way in which they receive from each other and spread
> out. Therefore Wood received from Water, Fire from Wood, Earth from
> Fire, Metal from Earth, and Water from Metal. Those that give are fathers
> and those that receive are sons. It is the Way of Heaven that the son
> always serves his father. Therefore when Wood is produced, Fire should
> nourish it, and after Metal perishes, Water should store it. Fire enjoys
> Wood and nourishes it with yang, but Water overcomes Metal and buries
> it with yin. Earth serves Heaven with the utmost loyalty. Therefore the
> Five Agents are the actions of filial sons and loyal ministers. The Five
> Agents are so called because they are tantamount to five actions. That is
> how the term was derived. The sage knows this and therefore he shows
> much love and little sternness, and is generous in supporting the living
> and serious in burying the dead. This is to follow the system of Heaven.
> It is the function of the son to receive and to fulfill. For him to support
> is like Fire enjoying Wood, to bury one's father is like Water overcoming
> Metal, and serving the ruler is like Earth showing respect to Heaven.
> People like these may be said to be good in their actions.[9]

Notice that the sequence of the Five Agents is not the same as that in the "Great
Norm" and that there is the relation of production and the relation of overcoming between the Agents. Tung also believed that man truly occupies a special position in the universe:

> Heaven is characterized by the power to create and spread things, Earth
> is characterized by its power to transform, and man is characterized by
> moral principles. The material force of Heaven is above, that of Earth
> below, and that of man in between. Spring produces and summer grows,
> and all things flourish. Autumn destroys and winter stores, and all things
> are preserved. Therefore there is nothing more refined than material force,

richer than Earth, or more spiritual than Heaven. Of the creatures born from the refined essence of Heaven and Earth, none is more noble than man. Man receives the mandate from Heaven and is therefore superior to other creatures. Other creatures suffer troubles and defects and cannot practice humanity and righteousness; man alone can practice them. Other creatures suffer troubles and defects and cannot match Heaven and Earth; man alone can match them. Man has 360 joints, which match the number of Heaven (the round number of days in a year). His body with its bones and flesh matches the thickness of Earth. He has ears and eyes above, with their keen sense of hearing and seeing, which resemble the sun and moon. His body has its orifices and veins, which resemble rivers and valleys. His heart has feelings of sorrow, joy, pleasure, and anger, which are analogous to the spiritual feelings (of Heaven). As we look at man's body, how much superior it is to that of other creatures and how similar to Heaven! Other creatures derive their life from the yin and yang of Heaven in a non-erect way, but man brilliantly shows his patterns and order. Therefore with respect to the physical form of other creatures, they all move about in a non-erect and incumbent position. Man alone stands erect, looks straight forward, and assumes a correct posture. Thus those who receive little from Heaven and Earth take the non-erect posture, while those receiving much from them take the correct posture. From this we can see that man is distinct from other creatures and forms a trinity with Heaven and Earth.[10]

As can be seen, Tung carried the correlation between Heaven and man to an extreme. For the same reason, he rejected Mencius's theory that human nature is good, as both good and evil can be found in Heaven and man.

That the person possesses nature and feelings is similar to the fact that Heaven has yin and yang. To say that there is no feeling in man's basic substance is like saying that there is yang in Heaven but no yin. Such absurd ideas are never acceptable. What we call nature does not refer to the highest type of man nor to the lowest, but to the average. The nature of man is like a silk cocoon or an egg. An egg has to be hatched to become a chicken, and a silk cocoon has to be unravelled to make silk. It is the true character of Heaven that nature needs to be trained before becoming good. Since Heaven has produced the nature of man which has the basic substance for good but which is unable to be good [by itself], therefore it sets up the king to make it good. This is the will of Heaven. The people receive from Heaven a nature which cannot be good [by itself], and they turn to the king to receive the training which completes their nature. It is the duty of the king to obey the will of Heaven and to complete the nature of the people.[11]

From this passage, we can see that the origin of evil is yin. Tung believed that there are three grades of man. Clearly, nature for him is constituted by the material forces yin and yang; it is a mixture of good and evil. He did not go to the extreme and declare that human nature is evil, as Hsün Tzu did, but he, like Hsün Tzu, put emphasis on education and culture. Ordinary people have the potential to be good, but they need the guidance of a king, and this is the will of Heaven. Here we find the basis of the authority of a king, and his duty is to lead people to develop the good part in their nature. Tung also applied his ideas to political history and believed that there were historical cycles. His version, however, was somewhat different from that of the Yin-yang school:

One becomes a king only after he has received the Mandate of Heaven. As the king, he will determine which day is to be the first day of the year for his dynasty, change the color of clothes worn at court, institute systems of ceremonies and music, and unify the whole empire. All this is to show that the dynasty has changed and that he is not succeeding any human being, and to make it very clear that he has received the mandate from Heaven. . . . Therefore T'ang received the mandate and became king. In response to Heaven he abolished the Hsia dynasty [whose system was symbolized by red]. He called his dynasty Yin (Shang). The system was corrected to be that symbolized by white. . . . King Wu received the mandate. . . . Therefore [in the beginning of] the *Ch'un-ch'iu* period [of the Chou dynasty], in response to Heaven, he undertook the business of a new king. The system was corrected to be that symbolized by black.[12]

Tung's grand theory provided the justification for the newly founded dynasty. A ruler who had received the Mandate of Heaven could justify the exercise of imperial authority. In the meantime, he had to be watchful for manifestations of Heaven's pleasure or displeasure and to act accordingly. Abnormal natural phenomena would give him cause to be uneasy. Tung's theory of the succession of the reigns also set a limit to the tenure of a given dynasty. When the end comes, it must give way to another dynasty.

According to Tung, neither the Ch'in nor the Han was the true successor of the Chou dynasty. He believed that it was Confucius who received the Mandate of Heaven to succeed the Chou and to represent the Black Reign. But Confucius did not get the position; he was the uncrowned king. Tung also believed that the *Ch'un Ch'iu* (*Spring and Autumn Annals*), originally a chronicle of Confucius's native state of Lu, was an important political work in which Confucius exercised his right as the new king. This was why Tung quoted the *Ch'un Ch'iu* as the main source of his authority. According to him, Confucius used differing words or phrases to record the events of the period. It is by carefully studying the way in which these words or phrases are used that one may discover the esoteric meaning of the *Ch'un Ch'iu*.[13]

There have been three important commentaries written on the *Ch'un Ch'iu*, and since the Han dynasty these have become classics themselves. They are the *Tso Chuan* (the *Tso Commentary*), the *Kung Yang*, and *Ku Liang Commentaries*. All three were named after the authors who composed them. The *Kung Yang Commentary*, in particular, interprets the *Ch'un Ch'iu* in agreement with the views of Tung Chung-shu. In the latter part of Han, Ho Hsiu (129–182) wrote a commentary on the *Kung Yang Commentary*, in which he elaborated on the theory of the "three ages" as taught by the *Commentary* and Tung Chung-shu. According to him, the *Ch'un Ch'iu* is a record of the process through which Confucius ideally transformed the age of "decay and disorder" into that of "approaching peace" and finally into that of "universal peace," in which the whole world, far and near, great and small, would become like one. This was, of course, merely an ideal construction, as Confucius did not actually have the power and authority to accomplish this goal.[14] But this fantastic theory did exert important influence on Confucian scholars in later ages, as K'ang Yu-wei (1858–1927) belonged in the Kung Yang school and made attempts to carry out political reform in the late Ch'ing dynasty (1644–1912).[15]

In this connection, I would like to mention the controversy between the New and the Old Text schools. Because the Classics were burned in the "fires of Ch'in" in 213 B.C., scholars were invited to restore the Classics by memory, and they were written in the form of script current in the Han dynasty—hence, the origin of the New Text school. Then some Classics that were claimed to have been hidden behind walls were discovered; they were written in the form of script that had already become archaic by the time of their recovery—hence, the origin of the Old Text school. As the Han measure decreed that persons who wished to be candidates for official positions should study the Six Classics and Confucianim, they became the foundation for China's famed examination system that was used to recruit government officials. Naturally, there was competition between the two schools, as they vied for recognition of their particular version of the Classics. The Old Text school arose as a reaction against the New Text school. At the end of the Former Han dynasty, eminent scholar Liu Hsin (ca. 46 B.C.–A.D. 23) enthusiastically backed the Old Text school and was wrongly accused of having forged all the Classics written in the Old script.[16] The controversy between the two schools lasted for many, many generations until the end of the Ch'ing dynasty. The New Text school believed that Confucius was the uncrowned king, while the Old Text school believed that Confucius was the greatest teacher of all times. Kang Yu-wei spread the esoteric meaning of the *Ch'un Ch'iu* of the Kung Yang school and believed that Confucius was merely borrowing the authority of the ancient past in order to carry out reform of the institutions in the present. His thought exerted great influence before the fall of the Ch'ing dynasty.

There is no question that Tung Chung-shu was a great Confucianist. He did not care much for profit and showed moral integrity by serving only a brief time in the court. It was through him that the examination system was established.

He urged the rulers to cultivate virtues and pay attention to abnormal natural phenomena; hence was formed a de facto check-balance system to limit the power of the monarch. As a result, Confucian institutions were consolidated and Confucian ethics were internalized by the Chinese; the basic program of politicized Confucianism was completed so as to produce a so-called superstable system. As dynasties came and went, the structure of the system remained unchanged until it was totally destroyed after the fall of the last dynasty under the impact of the West. Many characteristics of so-called popular Confucianism were also formed following the Han dynasty, as the Chinese revered such values as loyalty, filial piety, obedience to authority, family connections, diligence, and education.

In spite of Tung Chung-shu's achievement, however, we find that the characteristics of Han Confucianism as represented by his thought are quite different from Pre-Ch'in Confucianism as represented by the thought of Confucius and Mencius, or even *The Doctrine of the Mean*, and the mainstream thought as expressed in the *Commentaries* of the *Book of Changes*. Let us examine the problem from three perspectives: metaphysics, theory of human nature, and ethics and politics.

Metaphysically, we have noted that no traces of yin-yang and the Five Agents can be found in the so-called *Four Books*. Even in the *Appended Remarks* of the *Book of Changes*, we can find passages in which yin and yang are taken to be two basic forces in operation to form the cosmic order. They are quite compatible with the idea of a creative metaphysics. For example, Confucius was reported to have said, "*Ch'ien* and *k'un* are indeed the gate of Change! *Ch'ien* is yang and *k'un* is yin. When yin and yang are united in their character, the weak and strong attain their substance. In this way the products of Heaven and Earth are given substance and the character of spiritual intelligence can be penetrated."[17] Then there was the famous statement: "The successive movement of yin and yang constitutes the Way (Tao). What issues from the Way is good, and that which realizes it is the individual nature."[18] These ideas could be later products formulated after Confucian scholars were impacted by the Yin-yang school, but they did add an important dimension to Confucian metaphysics: The one creative principle needs the two, that is, yin and yang, in order to manifest its creative power in creations in the universe. And this is indeed the line of thought inherited by Sung-Ming Neo-Confucian philosophers.

But we do not find a correlative cosmology with great details as developed by Tung Chung-shu. It seems that Tung had shifted his emphasis to ch'i (material or vital force) and paid much more attention to the physical ingredients that made up the universe. When he applied his cosmology to human affairs, he further developed his deterministic philosophy of history as governed by the Five Agents, traces of which we could not even find in the *Commentaries* of the *I Ching*. What he had accomplished was actually none other than a kind of proto-science that could reflect the level of scientific studies in his day. Thus, we find in Chinese philosophy a situation not unlike that found in Christianity today. Contemporary Protestant theologians such as Rudolf Bultmann urged that we have to demythologize the Christian faith so as to liberate the message of Christ from an obsolete cosmology developed in the medieval ages.[19] By the same token, we have to liberate the message of a creative metaphysics in the Confucian tradition from an obsolete correlative cosmology developed by Han Confucianists such as Tung Chung-shu.

On the theory of human nature, Tung Chung-shu again paid exclusive attention to the physical ingredients that make up the human nature in material forces. He rejected Mencius's theory because he lost sight of the transcendent perspective proposed by Mencius. In a way, he reverted back to Kao Tzu, who believed that what is born is nature. Throughout the Han dynasty and the Wei-Chin dynasties, the attention was put on what Sung-Ming philosophers called the physical nature; hence, they advanced theories along the lines proposed by Tung Chung-shu, who saw human nature as a mixture of both good and evil and identified three grades in human nature. This explains why Mencius was not particularly honored in the Han dynasty. But Sung Neo-Confucian philosophers changed their perspective and honored Mencius as representing the orthodoxy in the Confucian tradition. They simply dismissed Tung Chung-shu as failing to realize the true nature of man, which refers to his moral nature rather than his physical nature.

Thus, even though it was in the Han dynasty that Confucianism was established as the state doctrine, and in the Han and T'ang dynasties that China created great civilizations, Sung-Ming Neo-Confucian philosophers believed that the Way did not really prevail in these periods, as the governments were not based on the mind-heart of humanity and the rulers merely used humanity and righteousness as means to further their selfish interests. Therefore, the production of a great civilization does not necessarily mean the realization of philosophical ideals. The situation is not unlike Rome, which produced great civilizations but failed to impress the philosophers. Sung-Ming Neo-Confucian philosophers did not hold Tung Chung-shu in high regard, as he was thought to have failed to hold tight to the core of Confucian teachings.

Finally, from the perspective of ethics and politics, there was also a big twist in Han Confucianism. Tung Chung-shu promoted the so-called *san-kang* (the Three Bonds), that is, the authority of the ruler over the minister, the father over the son, and the husband over the wife. Ironically, we cannot find anything about the doctrine of the Three Bonds in Confucius's or Mencius's thought. They taught only *cheng-ming*, that is, the rectification of names, which prescribes that the king has to act like a king, so that there is a correlation between name and reality. Likewise, the father and the husband are also obliged to perform certain duties. In other words, the mutuality between the ruler and the minister, the father and the son, and the husband and the wife is being stressed. There is undeniably a critical spirit underlying the doctrine of rectification of names as manifested by Mencius's denunciation of King Chou of the Shang dynasty as merely a fellow. Such a critical spirit seems to have disappeared under the doctrine of the Three Bonds, which emphasizes only a one-way relationship by putting emphasis on loyalty, filial piety, and subservience. Interestingly enough, the idea can be traced back to the *Han Fei Tzu*, the Legalist classic: "The minister serves the king, the son serves the father, and the wife serves the husband. If the three are followed, the world will be in peace; if the three are violated, the world will be in chaos."[20] Obviously, the Three Bonds, based on dominance/subservience, underscore the hierarchical relationship as an inviolable principle for maintaining social order. Tu Wei-ming observed: "The value of obedience, specifically practiced by the son, the minister, and the wife looms large in the ideology of the three bonds. The politicization of Confucian ethics fundamentally restructures the five relationships, making them the 'legalist' mechanism of symbolic control rather than the interpersonal base for the realization of the Mencian idea of a fiduciary community."[21] Thus, the doctrine of the Three Bonds became a double-edged sword; on the one hand, it was instrumental to maintaining the superstable order of the dynasties, and on the other hand, it was condemned as the backbone of the "man-eating system of rites" in modern days.

From this discussion, we can see that the three aspects of Confucianism—spiritual, politicized, and popular—are intertwined with one another and that the heritage and the burden of our tradition are also inseparable from one another.

NOTES

1. For a discussion of the problem, see Shu-hsien Liu, "Some Reflections on Mencius' Views of Mind-Heart and Human Nature," *Philosophy East and West* 46, no. 2 (April 1996): 158–159.

2. See the hexagram *chung-fu*, the explanation of the component lines, the second line. I am indebted to Professor Hsü Fu-kuan, who took a developmental approach to study the formation of the concepts of yin-yang and the Five Agents. See his *Chung-kuo jen-hsing-lun shih: Hsien-ch'in-pien* (A history of Chinese theories of human nature: Pre-Ch'in period) (Taipei: Commercial Press, 1969).

3. See the first year, Duke Chao of Lu. The six vital forces are yin, yang, wind, rain, darkness, and brightness.

4. Chan, *Source Book*, p. 249. These were supposedly the words of Viscount Chi given to Emperor Wu of Chou in the year 1121 B.C. Some scholars were of the opinion that this work was actually completed in the Warring States period. Nowadays, most scholars believe that the document may contain some ancient ideas. In any event, taking the Five Agents to be five kinds of materials seems to predate taking them to be five kinds of material or vital forces.

5. Ibid., pp. 246–248.

6. Ibid., p. 250.

7. See *Historical Records*, ch. 8.

8. Chan, *Source Book*, pp. 283–284.

9. Ibid., p. 279.

10. Ibid., pp. 280–281.

11. Ibid., pp. 275–276.

12. Ibid., p. 287.

13. Fung, *Short History*, pp. 200–201.

14. Ibid.

15. Chan, *Source Book*, pp. 723–736.

16. Fung, *Short History*, pp. 207–208.

17. Chan, *Source Book*, pp. 248–249.

18. Ibid., p. 266.

19. For a brief introduction to Bultmann's thought, see John Cobb, Jr., *Living Options in Protestant Theology* (Philadelphia: Westminster Press, 1962), pp. 227–258.

20. See the *"Chung-hsiao"* (loyalty and filial piety) chapter of the *Han Fei Tzu*.

21. Tu Wei-ming, "Confucianism," in *Our Religions*, ed. Arvind Sharma (New York: HarperCollins Publishers, 1993), p. 194.

Part II

Sung-Ming Neo-Confucian Philosophy

7

The Characteristics and Contemporary Significance of Sung-Ming Neo-Confucian Philosophy

The so-called Confucian State lasted until the twentieth century when the last dynasty was overthrown in 1911. But politicized Confucianism as a state ideology had lost its appeal for many intellectuals since the late Han period. In Wei and Chin periods, the mainstream was Neo-Taoism; and in Sui and T'ang periods, creative talents were attracted by Buddhism, Hua-yen, T'ien-t'ai, and especially Ch'an (Zen), developed by Mahayana Buddhism with unmistakable Chinese characteristics. After the fall of T'ang, the political situation in China was very unstable, and the moral standards of the people plunged. It was to answer such challenges both in theory and in practice that Neo-Confucian philosophy as a movement started in the Northern Sung (960–1126) period.

Naturally, this movement did not start spontaneously; we can find factors that helped the movement take shape. In the T'ang dynasty, Han Yü (768–824) made fierce attacks on Buddhism and Taoism; he was the first to comment on the transmission of the Way from ancient sage-emperors to Confucius and Mencius. According to him, after Mencius, the Way was no longer transmitted, and he wanted to undertake the task. But Han Yü attacked monks and nuns on cultural grounds, charging them as not participating in the productive forces and hence making no contributions to society. His ideas lacked philosophical depth.[1] His friend and disciple Li Ao (fl. 798) shared his concerns and wrote an essay entitled ''The Recovery of the Nature'' that seemed to have anticipated some of the Neo-Confucian ideas.[2]

Ironically, the most important stimulation for the movement actually came from Buddhism and Taoism, as most Neo-Confucian thinkers drifted along for years before they returned to the Confucian Way. In fact, the most important concept in Sung-Ming Neo-Confucian philosophy—*li* (principle)—was barely mentioned in ancient Confucian philosophy. As Hua-yen first developed *li* as a philosophical concept,[3] it was probable that Neo-Confucian thinkers took over the concept from Hua-yen and instilled new meanings into it. Neo-Confucian philosophers never made an attempt to conceal the fact that they were much indebted to Buddhism and Taoism for the introduction of new ideas; they supplied their own interpretations and in spirit were against the negativism they saw in Buddhism and Taoism. Thus, they developed sophisticated theories of metaphysics and cosmology and human nature in competition with Buddhism and Taoism, but in spirit they believed their theories were true to the teachings of Confucius and Mencius.

As they undertook the transmission of the Confucian Way as the goal of their lives, the movement was labeled *Tao-hsüeh* (Learning of the Way) by *Sung-shih* (History of the Sung dynasty). Again, one of the key concepts of the movement was *li* (principle). It is even more common to address the movement as Sung-(Yüan)-Ming *Li-hsüeh* (Learning of *li*). Finally, the term *Neo-Confucianism* was a newly coined Western equivalent for *Tao-hsüeh*, which has become popular since the middle of the century. For practical purposes, I also follow the popular usage of the term.[4]

Before we can say anything about the general characteristics of Neo-Confucian philosophy, it is advisable to examine the representative ideas of the important thinkers in this period. According to Professor Mou Tsung-san,[5] the most important Neo-Confucian philosophers in the Sung-Ming period were the following nine thinkers: Chou Tun-i (Lien-hsi, 1017–1073),[6] Chang Tsai (Heng-ch'u, 1020–1077),[7] Ch'eng Hao (Ming-tao, 1032–1085),[8] Ch'eng I (I-ch'uan, 1033–1107),[9] Hu Hung (Wu-feng, 1100–1155),[10] Chu Hsi (Yüan-hui, 1130–1200),[11] Lu Chiu-yüan (Hsiang-shan, 1139–1193),[12] Wang Shou-jen (Yang-ming, 1472–1529),[13] and Liu Tsung-chou (Chi-shan, 1578–1645).[14] A brief review of their teachings and relationships may give us some insights.

Owing to the recognition given by Chu Hsi, commonly regarded as the great synthesizer of the movement, Chou Tun-i was honored as the first to start the trend, as he was the teacher of the young Ch'eng brothers. His originality lay in that he was the first Sung scholar to put emphasis on *The Doctrine of the Mean* and the *Book of Changes*; he instilled them with a new interpretation, developed a philosophy of creativity, and gave expression to insights that could be traced back to Confucius and Mencius.[15] Following the line of thought in *Mencius*[16] and *The Doctrine of the Mean*,[17] he explicitly took *ch'eng* (sincerity) to be the ultimate metaphysical principle. In the very first chapter of his work *Penetrating the Book of Changes*, he said:

Sincerity (*ch'eng*) is the foundation of the sage. "Great is the *ch'ien*, the originator! All things obtain their beginning from it." It is the source of sincerity. "The way of *ch'ien* is to change and transform so that everything will obtain its correct nature and destiny." In this way sincerity is established. It is pure and perfectly good. Therefore "the successive movement of yin and yang constitute the Way (Tao). What issues from the Way is good, and that which realizes it is the individual nature." Origination and flourish characterize the penetration of sincerity, and advantage and firmness are its completion (or recovery). Great is the Change, the source of nature and destiny.[18]

Sincerity in this context should not be understood as merely a psychological or even a moral virtue. It means something that is forever true and without deceit; it stands for the Way of Heaven, which is the ultimate source of creativity for all things. When it is embodied in man, it is the virtue that characterizes the sage who is in perfect union with the Way of Heaven. Chu Hsi, especially, paid tribute to Chou Tun-i's essay "An Explanation of the Diagram of the Great Ultimate." In it, he incorporated the ideas of yin and yang and the Five Agents, that is, water, fire, wood, metal, and earth, from Han philosophy and developed a comprehensive cosmological philosophy based on the idea of creativity without falling into the kind of determinism of Han philosophies that advocated a strict correlation between natural phenomena and human phenomena. His mind was broad. He took over the Diagram of the Great Ultimate from the Taoists. Its original purpose was to serve as a guide for the practice of Taoist transcendental meditation to induce the vital forces to return to the root, and it made use of the Diagram to give expression to a Neo-Confucian philosophy of creativity with an evolutionary perspective based on the insights of the *Book of Changes*.[19] In self-discipline, he regarded tranquillity as fundamental, while tranquillity and activity were seen to form an unceasing circular movement. Such thoughts profoundly influenced subsequent Sung-Ming Neo-Confucian philosophies.

Chang Tsai's approach was really extraordinary. He took the idea of *hsü* (vacuity) from the Taoists but transformed it into the ultimate creative ontological principle of Neo-Confucian philosophy. He also put a great deal of emphasis on *ch'i* (material force), that which transforms into the myriad things in the world. For Chang Tsai, only that which is devoid of form but functions as spirit can be the origin of all things: *hsü* and *ch'i* are a pair of complementary concepts that are indispensable for the understanding of change. They work together to form the Great Harmony that characterizes the Way. He said:

The Great Harmony is called the Way (Tao). It embraces the nature which underlies all counter processes of floating and sinking, rising and falling, and motion and rest. It is the origin of the process of fusion and intermingling, of overcoming and being overcome, and of expansion and contraction. At the commencement, these processes are incipient, subtle, obscure, easy, and simple, but at the end they are extensive, great, strong, and firm. It is *ch'ien* (Heaven) that begins with the knowledge of Change, and *k'un* (Earth) that models after simplicity. That which is dispersed, differentiated and can be expressed in form is material force (*ch'i*), and that which is pure, penetrating, and cannot be expressed in form is spirit. Unless the whole universe is in the process of fusion and intermingling like fleeting forces moving in all directions, it may not be called Great Harmony. When those who talk about the Way know this, then they really know the Way, and when those who study Change (or the *Book of Changes*) understand this, then they really understand Change. Otherwise, even though they possess the admirable talents of Duke Chou, their wisdom is not praiseworthy.[20]

Chang Tsai also made other important contributions such as his distinctions between original nature and physical nature,[21] moral (ontological) knowledge and empirical knowledge (from seeing and hearing);[22] these became the common heritage of the Neo-Confucian tradition. But sometimes his expressions were not mature, and his ideas were easily subject to misunderstanding. Therefore, the Ch'eng brothers had rather mixed feelings concerning his larger work *Cheng-meng* (Correcting youthful ignorance). His short essay ''Western Inscription,'' however, earned the highest praise from Ch'eng I. As Wing-tsit Chan said:

Just as Chou Tun-i's short essay on the diagram of the Great Ultimate has become the basis of Neo-Confucian metaphysics, so Chang's ''Western Inscription'' has become the basis of Neo-Confucian ethics. Ch'eng I was not exaggerating when he said that there was nothing like it since Mencius. It is important because, as Ch'eng said, it deals with the substance of humanity (*jen*). Its primary purpose, as Yang Shih (Yang Kuei-shan, 1053–1135) pointed out, was to urge students to seek *jen*.[23]

Wing-tsit Chan further pointed out:

[A]s Ch'eng I explained to him [Yang Shih], it is precisely in harmonizing substance and function that the ''Western Inscription'' is of great significance to Confucian ethics. Underlying the essay, according to Ch'eng, is Chang's epoch-shaking theory that ''Principle is one but its manifestations are many [*li-i-fen-shu*].''[24]

Chang Tsai himself never formulated the theory in his essay, even though the idea was implicit there. However Ch'eng I made it explicit in his explanation, and the theory has since exerted profound influence on Neo-Confucian thought.

Although Chang Tsai was the uncle of the Ch'eng brothers, he himself admitted that he heard the Way later than his nephews. And although Chou Tun-i was once the teacher of Ch'eng Hao and Ch'eng I, they did not agree with Chou and developed philosophies of their own. Moreover, Chou was an obscure figure when he was alive; hence, it was really through the efforts of the Ch'eng brothers that Neo-Confucian philosophy became a prominent movement following the Sung dynasty. As is well known, the two brothers showed utterly different temperaments; Ch'eng Hao was warm and easygoing, while his younger brother Ch'eng I was austere and strict. Ch'eng I survived his elder brother by more than twenty years; he had a big following, but he also made a number of powerful enemies and caused many controversies in his lifetime. Ch'eng I followed his brother's lead when he was young; and although he so highly regarded his brother's opinion that he would have liked to have thought their ideas were in total agreement, such was not the case. In appearance, they seemed to have taught the same things; on closer scrutiny, however, they actually taught quite different things. Many of the sayings in the *I-shu* (Surviving works) and *Wai-shu* (Additional works) of the *Erh-Ch'eng ch'üan-shu* (Complete works of the two Ch'engs) are assigned to both, as in most cases scholars do not agree as to which brother they should be ascribed. In the following, I shall follow Professor Mou Tsung-san's suggestion to draw a clear distinction between the different patterns of thought of the two brothers.[25]

The Ch'eng brothers elevated *li* (principle) into a metaphysical principle; since that time Sung-Ming Neo-Confucian philosophy has been known as Sung-Ming *li-hsüeh* (study of principle). Ch'eng Hao was reported to have said, "Although I have learned some of my doctrines from others, the idea of *t'ien-li* (heavenly principle), however, has been realized by myself."[26] Obviously, for Ch'eng Hao, *li* is not something that can be acquired through empirical generalization; but, rather, the ultimate metaphysical principle of the universe can only be captured through personal realization. The concrete manifestation of *li* in man is none other than the Confucian *jen*. He wrote the famous essay "On Understanding the Nature of *Jen* (Humanity)" which may be quoted as follows:

The student must first of all understand the nature of *jen*. The man of *jen* forms one body with all things without any differentiation. Righteousness, propriety, wisdom, and faithfulness are all [expressions of] *jen*.

[One's duty] is to understand this principle (*li*) and preserve *jen* with sincerity and seriousness (*ching*), that is all. There is no need for caution and control. Nor is there any need for exhaustive search. Caution is necessary when one is mentally negligent, but if one is not negligent, what is the necessity for caution? Exhaustive search is necessary when one has not understood principle, but if one preserves *jen* long enough, it will automatically dawn on him. Why should he have to depend on exhaustive search?

Nothing can be equal to this Way (Tao, that is, *jen*). It is so vast that nothing can adequately explain it. All operations of the universe are our operations. Mencius said that "all things are already complete in oneself" and that one must "examine oneself and be sincere (or absolutely real)" and only then will there be great joy. If one examines himself and finds himself not yet sincere, it means there is still an opposition between the two (the self and the non-self). Even if one tries to identify the self with the non-self, one still does not achieve unity. How can one have joy?

The purpose of (Chang Tsai's) "Western Inscription" is to explain this substance (of complete unity) fully. If one preserves it (jen) with this idea, what more is to be done? "Always be doing something without expectation. Let the mind not forget its objective, but let there be no artificial effort to help it grow." Not the slightest effort is exerted! This is the way to preserve jen. As jen is preserved, the self and the other are then identified.

For our innate knowledge of good and innate ability to do good are originally not lost. However, because we have not gotten rid of the mind dominated by habits, we must preserve and exercise our original mind, and in time old habits will be overcome. This principle is extremely simple; the only danger is that people will not be able to hold on to it. But if we practice it and enjoy it, there need be no worry of our being unable to hold to it.[27]

In this essay, we find that Ch'eng Hao took all his quotations from *The Book of Mencius*. He was consciously trying to revive the thread of thought transmitted by Confucius and Mencius as he saw it, which became obscure after Mencius passed away. While Ch'eng Hao was short in analytical skills, he excelled in personal realization of *jen* in his life. Only one who has had firsthand experience practicing *jen* could write an essay like this. For him, *jen, li,* and *Tao* are but different names for the same thing; in effect, even righteousness, propriety, wisdom, and faithfulness are nothing but the manifestations of *jen*. He had strong faith in man's ability to realize *jen* in his life. There is no cleavage between Heaven and man, and there is no gap between knowledge and action. Professor Mou listed five quotations that best characterized Ch'eng Hao's understanding of *jen*:[28]

1. "The man of *jen* forms one body with all things without any differentiation."[29]

2. "A book on medicine describes paralysis of the four limbs as absence of *jen*. This is an excellent description."[30]

3. "A student should understand the substance of *jen* and make it concretely part of his own self. Then all that is necessary is to nourish it with moral principles."[31]

4. "Feeling the pulse is the best way to embody *jen*."[32] "Observe the chicks. (One can see *jen* in this way.)"[33] "Observe the way that Heaven and Earth produce all things."[34]

5. "The most impressive aspect of things is their spirit of life. This is what is meant by origination being the chief quality of goodness. This is *jen*."[35]

Ch'eng Hao loved to use all kinds of illustrations to help us to realize *jen*; but these illustrations should never be taken to mean anything more. For Ch'eng Hao, personal realization is the only way to embody *jen* in one's life; it is impossible to establish *jen* in terms of empirical generalization, as surely we can find as many people who act against *jen* as those who practice *jen*. Personal commitment is the only way to help us realize the great potentiality and full meaning of our existence.

It is true that Ch'eng I also showed a strong commitment to *jen* and to *li*, just like his elder brother, and he himself could not find any serious disagreements with his brother. It cannot be denied that there was basic agreement between the two, as both were devoted to the promotion of the Confucian cause in the world. However, there were subtle and essential differences in their thoughts that escaped their own notice. In effect, Ch'eng I opened up a new direction in Neo-Confucian thought that was further developed by, and found its mature expression in, Chu Hsi's works. According to Professor Mou Tsung-san,[36] Ch'eng I's understanding of *jen* is best characterized by the following statements:

1. "But love is feeling whereas humanity is the nature."[37]

2. "Essentially speaking, the way of *jen* may be expressed in one word, namely, impartiality. However, impartiality is but the principle of *jen*; it should not be equated with *jen* itself. When one makes impartiality the substance of his person, that is *jen*."[38]

3. "For humanity is nature, while filial piety and brotherly respect are its function. There are in our nature only humanity, righteousness, propriety, and wisdom. Where do filial piety and brotherly respect come in?"[39]

4. "The mind is the principle of production. As there is the mind, a body must be provided for it so it can produce. The feeling of commiseration is the principle of production in man."[40]

5. "The mind is comparable to seeds of grain. The nature of growth is *jen*."[41]

From these statements, we find that Ch'eng I, like his brother, also took *jen* to be the principle of production (creativity). On closer scrutiny, however, his understanding of *jen* was quite different from Ch'eng Hao's. Unlike his brother, Ch'eng I was highly analytical in his thought. He was not satisfied with regarding *jen* as the ultimate source of all values; rather, he had to draw a sharp distinction between the substance and the function of *jen*. For him, *jen* pertains to nature, while love, the manifestation of *jen*, pertains only to feeling: they should not be treated as the same thing. To be more specific, nature is principle (*li*), which is universal and eternal, while feeling is material force (*ch'i*), which is concrete and subject to change. Principle and material force are inseparable, but they must be kept distinct from each other and should not be confused with each other. True, for Ch'eng Hao, there is also the distinction between what is metaphysical and what is concrete, but they are taken to be the two sides of the same coin: One is in the other, and the other is in the one. For Ch'eng I, however, what is metaphysical must be embodied in what is concrete, but the two have completely different characteristics and should never be confused with each other.

Professor Mou Tsung-san finds that for Ch'eng Hao *li* is both existing and also dynamic—it is the unitary source of all beings; while for Ch'eng I and later for Chu Hsi, although *li* exists and it is the metaphysical principle behind change, it is itself eternal and beyond change.[42] Hence, there must be a material basis for change; *ch'i* is that which actually changes according to *li*. For Ch'eng Hao, there is no *ch'i* apart from *li*, and there is no *li* apart from *ch'i*; there is only one foundation for all changes. In the final analysis, *li* is the *li* of *ch'i*, while *ch'i* is the *ch'i* of *li*; the two are not to be distinguished from each other except in abstract conceptual thinking. While for Ch'eng I, *li* is metaphysical and *ch'i* is concrete, the two work intimately together to form the universe, but they must be kept distinct from each other and should never be confused with each other.

In effect, a dualism surreptitiously replaces the monism of Ch'eng Hao, which Professor Mou Tsung-san believes characterizes the orthodox way of Confucian thinking from Confucius and Mencius to Chou Tun-i and Chang Tsai. Ironically, however, Chu Hsi, following the lead of Ch'eng I, developed a grand system of thought, honored as the orthodoxy of Confucian thought since the Yüan dynasty. This is a most remarkable phenomenon, and it has been studied extensively in Professor Mou's monumental work on Neo-Confucian philosophy: *Hsin-t'i yü hsing-t'i*.[43]

Hu Hung was an important philosopher in the Hunan school. Unfortunately, however, his disciples were not able to defend and to develop his ideas further. His most famous disciple, Chang Shih (Nan-hsien, 1133–1180), was a good friend of Chu Hsi's, but he did not study under Hu Hung for long; eventually, he changed some of his ideas and often went along with Chu Hsi. Because of Chu Hsi's severe criticisms of the ideas of Hu Hung and his followers, the Hunan school declined quickly and did not receive much attention by later scholars. But Chu Hsi failed to grasp the spirit of Hu Hung's thought, which was a further development from Ch'eng Hao and his disciple Hsieh Liang-tso (Shang-ts'ai, 1050–1103). Hu Hung's understanding of *hsing* (nature) and *hsin* (mind) is particularly interesting and suggested a unique approach to the problem. For him, nature is something transcendental that allows no opposite, while the mind is the principle of manifestation. Nature is the absolute beyond good and evil that must await the mind to manifest its function in the world. Hence, what is important is that one must extend his mind to the utmost to manifest the Way of Heaven, and only a man of *jen* can extend his mind to the utmost. The enlightenment of the mind cannot be reached by any external means; it depends on self-realization. Thus, for Hu Hung, nature is what is hidden, and the mind is what is manifest. But the two are actually one; there is no gap between the two. Chu Hsi thought, on the other hand, that the mind must have the ability to penetrate into what is hidden. He was launching a different way of thought, and his criticisms of Hu Hung were external rather than internal.[44]

Chu Hsi was undoubtedly the greatest philosopher in the Southern Sung period. He was diligent in pursuing the Way but did not reach his mature thought until he was in his late thirties.[45] At one time, he thought that his ideas closely resembled those taught by the Hunan school, as he believed that the function of the mind could only deal with what had become manifest, while nature referred to what had not become manifest. But he changed his mind, then believing that if the discipline of the mind could not reach what had not become manifest, then the ideal state of equilibrium and harmony as portrayed in *The Doctrine of the Mean* could not be attained. After puzzling for a number of years, he finally found the answer by turning to Ch'eng I's instruction: "Self-cultivation requires seriousness; the pursuit of learning depends on the extension of knowledge."[46] Thus, Chu Hsi accused the Hunan school of having totally neglected the state before feelings are aroused and hence become somewhat superficial and lacking in depth. But he did not realize that his understanding of the examination of the mind meant something quite different from what had been taught in the Hunan school; the Hunan school employed examination as a means not to extend (empirical) knowledge but to recover the original mind as taught by Mencius. On the other hand, he also did not go back to the approach of his teacher Li Tung (1093–1163), who transmitted the method handed down from Ch'eng Hao and his disciple Yang Shih (Kuei-shan, 1053–1135), which emphasized sitting in meditation in order to realize equilibrium in the mind and to correlate it with the creative metaphysical principle that works incessantly in the universe,[47] as Chu Hsi mistook equilibrium to be merely a psychological state. Thus, Chu Hsi parted ways with the two major approaches that can be traced back to Ch'eng Hao. Instead, he chose to follow the lead of Ch'eng I and believed that by practicing self-cultivation before feelings were aroused and examination after feelings were aroused, he had been able to accomplish a synthesis of the two approaches, taking up their strengths and avoiding their weaknesses.

Chu Hsi started from his existential concern to calm his mind-heart: once he reached his mature views, he further developed them into a comprehensive system of philosophy. He upheld the tripartite division of mind (*hsin*), nature (*hsing*), and feelings (*ch'ing*). And he developed a metaphysics of principle (*li*) and material forces (*ch'i*) to analyze the content of these concepts. Nature pertains to *li* and is transcendent, while feelings pertain to *ch'i* and are immanent; the mind is made of the most subtle kind of *ch'i*, so that it has the ability to get hold of *li* and give guidance to *ch'i*.[48] A more complicated theory of nature was further developed as he inherited Chang Tsai's views and made a distinction between the moral nature and the physical nature.[49] The moral nature is transcendent and essentially good, while the physical nature refers to what is made of *ch'i* and shows a tendency to fall into evil ways. Chu Hsi showed both an idealistic perspective and a realistic perspective. As an idealist, he belongs in the Mencian tradition by upholding that the essential-nature of man is good, whereas as a realist, he explains actual human evils by means of the physical nature of man. As a Neo-Confucian philosopher, he firmly believes in the possibility of transforming man's physical temperaments as long as one works hard and commits himself to following the Confucian Way.

Chu Hsi also took the decisive step to identify *jen* (humanity) with *sheng* (creativity). *Jen* was understood by him as "the character of the mind and the principle of love."[50] Chu Hsi was the one who helped to establish the Confucian orthodoxy that was accepted by the posterity.[51] Since his commentaries on the *Four Books* had been adopted as the basis for civil service examinations since the Yüan dynasty, he was regarded as the most important Confucian thinker after Confucius and Mencius.

Despite Chu Hsi's achievements, even in his own time he was challenged by his friend and rival Lu Hsiang-shan. Although Lu agreed with Chu in thinking that the primary purpose of Confucian studies was not for a career in the government but rather for the realization of the Way, Lu did not believe Chu's gradual approach, which emphasized that the study of Classics and conformity with the moral codes would lead to the Way. He said:

> Chu Yüan-hui (Chu Hsi) once wrote to one of his students saying, "Lu Tze-ching (Lu Hsiang-shan) taught people only the doctrine of 'honoring the moral nature.' Therefore those who have studied under him are mostly scholars who put their beliefs into practice. But he neglected to follow the path of study and inquiry. In my teaching is it not true that I have put somewhat more emphasis on 'following the path of study and inquiry'? As a consequence, my pupils often do not approach his in putting beliefs into practice." From this it is clear that Yüan-hui wanted to avoid two defects (failure to honor the moral nature and failure to practice) and combine the two merits (following the path of study and inquiry and practicing one's beliefs). I do not believe this to be possible. If one does not know how to honor his moral nature, how can he talk about following the path of study and inquiry?[52]

For Lu, the key lies in the realization of what is within everyone's own mind. Before building up the nobler part of one's nature as taught by Mencius, study and inquiry are irrelevant to forming one's moral character. In the understanding of the relation between the mind and nature, Lu and Chu also had irreconcilable differences. While Chu Hsi could only assert that the mind comprises the principle, Lu declared that the mind and the principle are one.

As Chu Hsi's thought was becoming the main stream in the posterity, Lu's thought was being suppressed until the spirit of his philosophy was revived by Wang Yang-ming in the Ming dynasty. Wang was dissatisfied with Chu's interpretation of *ko-wu* and *chih-chih* in the text of *The Great Learning* to mean "investigation of things" and "extension of knowledge," respectively, as these could not be relied upon to establish the moral principle as well as the moral character. He reinterpreted *ko-wu* to mean "the elimination of selfish material desires," and *chih-chih* to mean "the extension of the innate knowledge of the good (*liang-chih*)."[53] In his answer to a student, he declared, "The mind is principle. Is there any affair in the world outside of the mind? Is there any principle outside of the mind?"[54] Wang went even further to advocate the unity of knowledge and action. If one truly has the knowledge of the good, he cannot fail to put it into practice. Seen from this perspective, Wang drew the conclusion that "knowledge is the direction for action and action the effort of knowledge, and that knowledge is the beginning of action and action the completion of knowledge. If this is understood, then when only knowledge is mentioned, action is included, and when only action is mentioned, knowledge is included."[55]

Wang's philosophy became very popular for some time; then people began to misunderstand and misinterpret his ideas, and undesirable effects resulted. Because Wang emphasized the fact that each of us has *liang-chih* within himself, some of his followers twisted his teachings to mean that all the people walking on the street are sages. Liu Tsung-chou reacted to this and gave another new interpretation to *The Great Learning*. He put the emphasis on *cheng-i* (making the will sincere) and *shen-tu* (being cautious when one is alone). One must do strict discipline in order for the mind to manifest its nature. It is only in the enlightened state that mind and nature are one.[56]

Now that we know something about the representative ideas of the Neo-Confucian philosophers and what concerned them most, we may venture to make some general remarks about this trend. First, I would like to discuss some of the labels we commonly use to describe the trend. The term *Neo-Confucianism* used in a technical sense to designate the trend was actually a relatively new term coined in the West in the mid-twentieth century; later on, it was widely accepted by both Western and Chinese scholars. In the official history of the Sung dynasty, the term *Tao-hsüeh* had been used. It is true that this trend of Confucianism had devoted itself to the study of Tao, and this preoccupation with the Way can certainly be traced back to Confucius. But Confucianism does not have a monopoly on the term *Tao*. In fact, Taoism as a school is named after the term, and it understands the Way quite differently. Hence, there are problems with this term. *Li-hsüeh* has been an even more widely accepted term by scholars for good reasons. *Li* (principle, reason) is not only a major concept in Sung-Ming Confucianism but a new concept as well. The term itself is old, but it receives completely new and rich meanings after the impact of Buddhism. Especially as the term applies to the most prominent school of thought established by Chu Hsi, which had been honored as the orthodoxy since the Yüan dynasty for more than 700 years, it is quite natural to extend the name to cover the whole of Sung-Ming Confucianism as Sung-Ming *li-hsüeh*. The only drawback is, the term has a broader and a narrower meaning. Used in the latter sense, it refers only to the so-called Ch'eng-Chu *li-hsüeh* (school of principle) in contrast to the so-called Lu-Wang *hsin-hsüeh* (school of mind). It seems inconvenient to include both *li-hsüeh* in a narrower sense and *hsin-hsüeh* within the scope of *li-hsüeh* in a broader sense. If it is possible, certainly it would be better for us to find another name for Sung-Ming Confucianism as a whole. As a result, I accept the term *Neo-Confucianism* for the movement.[57]

According to Professor Mou Tsung-san, for Chou Tun-i, Chang Tsai, and Ch'eng Hao, *li* (principle) both exists and acts. But for Ch'eng I and Chu Hsi, *li* exists only and cannot act; it has to depend on *ch'i* (material force) for actualization. In other words, *li* is static, while *ch'i* is dynamic. Thus, the so-called Ch'eng-Chu *li-hsüeh* could only refer to Ch'eng I, whose thought is quite different from his brother's; only it escapes the notice of scholars because of the close relationship between the two brothers.[58] Lu-Wang's monistic thought is certainly in sharp contrast to Ch'eng-Chu's dualistic thought—hence, the traditional opposition between the two schools.

But Professor Mou proposed an interesting thesis: He pointed out that there was actually a third school represented by Hu Hung and Liu Tsung-chou. This line of thought went back to Chou, Chang, and Ch'eng Hao's approach. Unlike Lu-Wang, who relied heavily on Mencius and simply declared that mind is principle, they would rather take a roundabout approach and rely instead on *The Doctrine of the Mean* and the *Book of Changes*. For them, even though mind and nature are one, nature is hidden, while the mind is manifest. This line of thought became obscure because of the decline of the Hunan school. Professor Mou admitted that Liu Tsung-chou did not develop his thought from Hu Hung, but he noticed that there are striking similarities in their approaches. Thus, he advanced the novel thesis of the three schools: Adding Hu-Liu to the traditional Ch'eng-Chu and Lu-Wang opposition, he pointed out that Hu-Liu and Lu-Wang are variations of the same thought, which took *li* to be a dynamic metaphysical principle; only Ch'eng-Chu deviated from the insight. Ironically, however, it was the Ch'eng-Chu school that was honored by the posterity as representing the orthodoxy—hence, the intriguing phenomenon of the side branch taking over the position of orthodoxy. Admittedly, from a philosophical point of view, Professor Mou's thesis has its ground, but from the perspective of the history of thought, it is difficult to accept Professor Mou's theory. Not only did Hu and Liu not have any connections in the lineage of thought, but their views on nature also showed serious differences; Hu Hung thought that nature is beyond the characterization of good and evil, while Liu insisted that nature is good without any qualification.[59] Regardless of whether or not we accept Professor Mou's suggestion, from the discussion we can clearly see the main concerns of the Sung-Ming Neo-Confucian philosophers. In the following, I shall try to identify certain common characteristics of Neo-Confucian philosophy in general.

1. As far as literature is concerned, the Neo-Confucian philosophers saw special importance in the two works *The Great Learning* and *The Doctrine of the Mean*; so they were lifted out of the text of *The Book of Rites* and placed with

The Analects and *The Book of Mencius* to form the so-called *Four Books*. Their importance superseded that of the traditional *Five Classics*. Another favorite source for them was the *Commentaries* to the *Book of Changes*.

2. Besides *jen* (humanity) and *sheng* (creativity), the Neo-Confucian philosophers were very much interested in problems concerning *hsin* (the mind), *hsing* (the nature), and the Way of Heaven about which Confucius said very little. Obviously, Neo-Confucian philosophy had added a new dimension to Confucian thought.

3. The reason why there was this new emphasis must be attributed to the stimulation received from Buddhism and Neo-Taoism. Buddhism introduced a sophisticated new philosophy that included a new cosmology as well as psychology. Confucianism had to develop something new in response to such challenges. Naturally, they adopted many concepts and terminologies from Buddhism and Neo-Taoism. But it would be wrong to say that Neo-Confucian philosophies were teaching nothing but Buddhist and Neo-Taoist ideas in disguise, as the guiding spirit for them was *jen* and *sheng*; the ultimate commitment to them would surely contradict the Buddhist *kung* (*shunya*, void) and the Taoist *wu* (nothingness).[60]

4. The Neo-Confucian philosophers broke new grounds by giving new interpretations to concepts such as *li* (principle) and *ch'i* (material force). And they made important distinctions between the so-called moral nature and physical nature, and also moral knowledge and empirical knowledge (through eyes and ears).

5. In metaphysics the Neo-Confucian philosophers believed that Heaven is the ultimate source of creativity in the universe and that there is a depth dimension in man that enables him to have direct access to Heaven. It is by discipline of the mind and the realization of nature that each of us can find the creativity functioning within the self and in the universe at large.

6. In cosmology, the Neo-Confucian philosophers believed in an evolutionary theory of the world. So long as there were no obstructions, the natural as well as the human world would function in harmony. Man happens to have received the best endowment from Heaven; hence, he has the capacity to realize the message of creativity from Heaven and to participate in the creative process along with Heaven and Earth.

7. In actuality, however, it is fairly easy for man to deviate from the norms and fall into undesirable states of affairs; this applies to the individual as well as to the whole state. Hence, it is the duty of the educated man to recover the essentially good nature and to propagate the Way so that peace may be brought to the world. Sophisticated ways of self-discipline were developed along different lines. The Neo-Confucian philosophers turned inward and found a broad world as well as a profound mystery within the self. In contrast to depth psychology, Professor Thomé Fang coined the term ''height psychology,'' which studies how man can discipline himself to go through various psychological

states in following the ways of the sages and worthies.[61] This is a virgin soil that needs to be explored. The Neo-Confucian philosophers had made great contributions to open up the field.

8. The Neo-Confucian philosophers were not only interested in individual selves. They believed that whatever one does would have profound effects on others and the world. Hence, they urged the rulers to have strict self-discipline, to make their wills sincere, and to run a government of humanity with a view to bringing about peace in the whole world.

As we have reviewed the general characteristics of Neo-Confucian philosophy, now we are in a position to discuss its contemporary significance. Were the ideas of the Neo-Confucian philosophers dated, or are some of them still very meaningful for us today? I propose to discuss the problem from five different perspectives: metaphysical, ethical, cosmological, scientific, and political.[62] Within our limited scope, naturally we can only discuss the problems in broad outlines.

At one time, *metaphysics* was regarded as conceptual poetry devoid of cognitive meanings by the logical positivists. But now it is found that even the principle of verifiability itself is not verifiable. Furthermore, if the metaphysical quest is understood to be the quest for one's ultimate concern or absolute presupposition, then the metaphysical problem cannot be avoided by anyone. The Confucian faith in the ultimate metaphysical principle of creativity working incessantly in the universe is not falsified by any known empirical evidence. The personal realization of creativity within the self is most vivid and immediate for the enlightened, and such experience is not denied to any man in the street. It is certainly not unreasonable to identify this creativity with the creativity of Heaven, the source of creativity, as the self cannot be the originator of such creativity. Furthermore, the commitment to creativity truly makes a whole world of difference to the self, as it has the power to completely change one's personality and the outlook for the whole life. The kind of metaphysics established here is not an objective one through any external means such as empirical generalization or intellectual conjecture. The metaphysical depth can only be realized through personal commitment and appropriation. Such faith does not contradict science; the only thing it contradicts is the erroneous faith in scientism, as no science can claim to provide the foundation for ultimate meaning in life. It is only through a quest for wisdom that we may find an answer for the metaphysical question and rest in our innermost minds.

From the *ethical* perspective, contemporary ethical theories show us that there is no way for us to establish any transcendent universal moral principles in an objective fashion. And yet we would not want to fall into a reckless moral relativism, either. Moral behaviors are possible only if the moral agent enjoys moral autonomy and has the ability to understand and make judgments in a moral situation. The Confucian tradition simply asserts that man has the endowment to do good. As long as we could overcome our selfish desires, then the main obsruction would be removed, and we would be able to form right judgments and do good things. The Confucian philosophers realize that there is no gap between knowledge and action as far as morality is concerned. They put a good deal of emphasis on self-discipline: Be cautious when one is alone; otherwise, it would be too late when overt actions are taken. The Neo-Confucian philosophers probably made the greatest contributions to find ways to help us overcome existential anxieties that shake the whole being of man. An enlightened person can calmly face the problem of death without losing his composure. Its teachings would be a very effective antidote to the modern existential way of thinking. The principle is one, while the manifestations are many. The ultimate commitment to *jen* is absolute, but the application of this principle to concrete states of affairs is situational. It would be entirely wrong to identify Confucian ethics with the moral codes practiced in the past, which are subject to change. The Neo-Confucian philosophers have tried to steer a middle course between absolutism and relativism. A lot may be learned by reviewing the whole tradition.

From the *cosmological* perspective, although many cosmological speculations by Sung-Ming Neo-Confucian philosophers were obviously dated, there are still certain insights behind these speculations that should not be overlooked by us even today. China never went through a stage of scientific, mechanical materialism; it has kept an organic view of the universe in which the relationship between values and existence is not completely cut off. It has not committed what Whitehead called the "fallacy of misplaced concreteness," which takes abstractions as concrete reality.[63] A new cosmological philosophy based on contemporary data consistent with the insights of Neo-Confucian philosophies can be worked out that may provide certain stimulation to those who are interested in working along the lines of a Whiteheadean type of process philosophy.

From a *scientific* perspective, there is no denial that China has lagged behind in science and technology in the last several hundred years. Scholars have had different interpretations to explain why this should be the case. One possible reason may be that the Chinese were dominated by Neo-Confucian thinking, which refused to separate form from content; hence, formal, deductive reasoning as well as pure mathematics was not highly developed in China. As a result, one important link is missing; in addition, moral knowledge was overemphasized at the expense of empirical knowledge. Professor Liang Sou-ming certainly had a point when he said that Chinese thinking was somewhat premature so that it bypassed certain vital stages of development, which proved to be disastrous for the Chinese culture.[64] Surely the Chinese have a lot to learn from the West concerning matters of science and technology. But Japan has already showed us one example of how a nation with a Confucian ingredient in the past could outperform the West in certain areas after it became an ardent student of the West. There is no need to denounce one's own tradition in order to carry out its modernization program. In fact, modernization must be implemented according to the needs of each nation. We simply cannot cut ourselves off from our own tradition; the only thing we can do is to draw strength from our traditional resources while trying to minimize the undesirable effects of our traditional burdens. Moreover, it should be pointed out that, after all, science and technology are not all there is to life; they should be kept in their proper places.

From a *political* perspective, there are also bottlenecks that traditional Neo-Confucian thinking has failed to break. From the very beginning, the Confucian scholars advocated a government for the people but never went so far as to endorse the ideal of a government by the people. The only check-balance mechanism the Confucians relied upon was an educational program for would-be rulers, which was usually not very effective. Now the dynasty days were over; with the educational level of the people raised in the contemporary era, the practice of democracy and law should be the future. Naturally, democracy cannot be implemented overnight, nor is it a panacea that can solve all the problems. In fact, it could add many problems when power is distributed to different authorities. But it can avoid the evil of letting the power become concentrated in the hands of a despot, and it succesfully solves the problem of succession. But because democracy is too easily combined with commercialism, it can also produce a lot of undesirable consequences. The Confucian emphasis on the value of education and culture should not be given up. In fact, only educated people with a strong sense of integrity can make democracy really work. A government by law should be combined with the traditional ideal of a government by man.

I have tried to point out where the Neo-Confucian insights may have significance for us today and where the tradition shows its serious limitations. The relationship between the past and the present is a dialectical one. We could use the contemporary perspective to broaden the horizon of the past, but we can also use the traditional perspective to reveal the onesidedness of contemporary development. However, a successful synthesis of the past and the present would still have to depend on the efforts of the present and future generations to come.

NOTES

1. Chan, *Source Book*, pp. 450–456.
2. Ibid., pp. 456–459.
3. Ibid., pp. 406–424.
4. For ''Neo-Confucianism'' as a newly coined term in the West, I found direct evidence in Fung, *Short History*. As he said: ''The term Neo-Confucianism is a newly coined western equivalent for *Tao-hsüeh*'' (p. 268). Derk Bodde, translator of Fung's *A History of Chinese Philosophy*, and famous scholars in the field such as Carsun Chang, Wing-tsit Chan, and William Theodore de Bary all adopted the term, which later on was accepted by Chinese scholars as well. But this term is not without its problems. Hoyt Tillman thinks that the notion is ambiguous and virtually useless in historical description. See his ''A New Direction in Confucian Scholarship: Approaches to Examining the Differences between Neo-Confucianism and *Tao-hsüeh?*'' *Philosophy East and West* 42, no. 4 (October 1992). Jo-shui Chen, in the introduction of his book *Liu Tsung-yüan and Intellectual Change in T'ang China* (Cambridge: Cambridge University Press, 1992), discussed the problem and still opted to use the term *Neo-Confucianism* for practical

purposes, as it is difficult to avoid using a general term such as this one. My position is somewhat similar to Chen's; only I would like to limit the use of the term to Sung-Ming Confucian philosophy from Chou Tun-i to Liu Tsung-chou and his disciple Huang Tsung-hsi and exclude early Ch'ing philosophers such as Yen Yüan (1635–1704) and Tai Chen (1723–1777) from the trend, as they started from totally different presuppositions. My characterization of Sung-Ming Neo-Confucian philosophy would not apply to these thinkers.

5. Mou Tsung-san, *Hsin-t'i yü hsing-t'i* (The metaphysical principle of the mind and nature), 3 vols. (Taipei: Cheng-chung-shu-chü 1968–1969), 1: 414–415 (hereafter cited as Mou, *Hsin-t'i*).

6. Chan, *Source Book*, pp. 460–480.

7. Ibid., pp. 495–517.

8. Ibid., pp. 518–543.

9. Ibid., pp. 544–571.

10. Mou, *Hsin-t'i*, 2: 429–545.

11. Chan, *Source Book*, pp. 588–653.

12. Ibid., pp. 572–587.

13. Ibid., pp. 654–691.

14. Mou Tsung-san, *Ts'ung Lu Hsiang-shan tao Liu Ch'i-shan* (From Lu Hsiang-shan to Liu Ch'i-shan) (Taipei: Hsüeh-sheng-shu-chü, 1979), pp. 451–541 (hereafter cited as Mou, *Ts'ung Lu tao Liu*). This book may be considered the fourth volume of *Hsin-t'i yü hsing-t'i*.

15. Mou, *Hsin-t'i*, 1: 322.

16. Chan, *Source Book*, p. 74: *Mencius*, 4A:12.

17. Chan, *Source Book*, pp. 107–108; *The Doctrine of the Mean*, chs. 20–22.

18. Chan, *Source Book*, pp. 465–466.

19. Ibid., pp. 463–464. Also see Fung, *History*, 2: 442.

20. Chan, *Source Book*, pp. 500–501, with slight modification.

21. Ibid., p. 511.

22. Ibid., p. 515.

23. Ibid., p. 498.

24. Ibid., p. 499.

25. Mou, *Hsin-t'i*, 2: 1–20, 251–259.

26. Chan, *Source Book*, p. 520, with slight modification.

27. Ibid., pp. 523–524.

28. Mou, *Hsin-t'i*, 3: 231.

29. Chan, *Source Book*, p. 523.

30. Ibid., p. 530.

31. Ibid., p. 531, with slight modification.

32. Ibid., p. 535.

33. Ibid.

34. Ibid., p. 536. Please note that my translation is different from Chan's. His translation was: "Observe the disposition of all living things within heaven and earth."

35. Ibid., p. 539.

36. Mou, *Hsin-t'i*, 3: 232.

37. Chan, *Source Book*, p. 559.

38. Ibid., p. 556.

39. Ibid., pp. 559–560.

40. Ibid., p. 569.

41. Ibid., p. 560.

42. Mou, *Hsin-t'i*, 1: 44–45.

43. Ibid., pp. 19–60.

44. Ibid., 2: 429–545.

45. Shu-hsien Liu, *Chu-tzu che-hsüeh ssu-hsiang ti fan-chen yü wan-ch'eng* (The development and completion of Chu Hsi's philosophical thought) (Taipei: Hsüeh-sheng-shu-chü, 1982), pp. 87–89 (hereafter cited as Liu, *Chu-tzu*).

46. Chan, *Source Book*, p. 562.

47. For a detailed analysis of the case, see Liu, *Chu-tzu*, pp. 71–138.

48. Shu-hsien Liu, "The Function of the Mind in Chu Hsi's Philosophy," *Journal of Chinese Philosophy* 5 no. 2 (June, 1978): 195–208.

49. Chan, *Source Book*, pp. 623–624.

50. Ibid., p. 597.

51. Wing-tsit Chan, "Chu Hsi's Completion of Neo-Confucianism," in *Études Song-Sung Studies in Memorian Étienne Balaz*, ed. Françoise Aubin, Series 2, No. 1 (Paris: 1973), p. 75.

52. Chan, *Source Book*, p. 582.

53. Ibid., p. 656.

54. Ibid., p. 667.

55. Ibid., pp. 669–670.

56. Mou, *Ts'ung Lu tao Liu*, p. 457; also see Mou, *Hsin-t'i*, 1: 45–46.

57. Shu-hsien Liu, "Some Reflections on the Sung-Ming Understanding of Mind, Nature, and Reason," *Journal of the Institute of Chinese Studies of The Chinese University of Hong Kong* 21 (1990): 331–343 (hereafter cited as Liu, "Some Reflections").

58. Although Fung Yu-lan said in his autobiography that one of his contributions was to make a sharp distinction between the thoughts of the Ch'eng brothers, his observations remained on the surface level; only Professor Mou Tsung-san worked out in great detail the differences in their thought in the second volume of his *Hsin-t'i yü hsing-t'i*.

59. Liu, "Some Reflections."

60. Liu, *Chu-tzu*, pp. 397–413.

61. Thomé H. Fang, *Creativity in Man and Nature* (Taipei: Linking, 1980), p. 93.

62. Liu, *Chu-tzu*, pp. 521–552.

63. A. N. Whitehead, *Science and the Modern World* (New York: Free Press, 1967; first published by Macmillan, 1925), p. 51.

64. While Liang Sou-ming was an insightful thinker, his ideas were not always precise. I only borrow his expression to advance my own thought; there is no need for me to agree with his ideas. Cf. Liang Sou-ming, *Chung-kuo wen-hua yao-i* (Essentials of the Chinese culture) (Taipei: Cheng-chung, 1963), pp. 251–303.

8

On Chu Hsi's Search for Equilibrium and Harmony

According to Thomas Metzger, Max Weber's interpretation of Chinese culture as characterized by a lack of moral tension is not quite correct, and he has tried to develop a new model in his book *Escape from Predicament*.[1] I myself am not ready to accept any models, but Metzger's idea of predicament is quite illuminating. I feel traditional Chinese philosophers did aspire toward the ideal of harmony that was supposed to transcend all strife, but it is open to question whether they were successful in realizing such a lofty ideal. Both inwardly and outwardly they had experienced profound crises parallel to their experiences of equilibrium and harmony. Perhaps we need to study more before we can draw any definite conclusions. Chu Hsi's (1130–1200) striving after a way to realize equilibrium and harmony appears to be a paradigmatic case. I propose to study the case in depth, as it would shed light on a typical Neo-Confucian approach to the problem of harmony and strife.

The text of *The Doctrine of the Mean* says:

> Before the feelings of pleasure, anger, sorrow, and joy are aroused it is called equilibrium (*chung*, centrality, mean). When these feelings are aroused and each and all attain due measure and degree, it is called harmony [*ho*]. Equilibrium is the great foundation of the world, and harmony its universal path. When equilibrium and harmony are realized to the highest degree, heaven and earth will attain their proper order and all things will flourish.[2]

In retrospect, Chu Hsi reported his own quest for equilibrium and harmony in his "Preface to *My Old Views of Equilibrium and Harmony*" as follows:

In my early years I studied with Master Li Yen-ping (Li T'ung, 1093–1163); he taught me the *Doctrine of the Mean*. I tried to understand the meaning implied in the statement: "Before the feelings of pleasure, anger, sorrow, and joy are aroused, . . ." But he died before I had been able to do so. I lamented the fact that I lacked a superior intelligence, and I felt like a poor man without a home to return. . . . Recently I found some time to reexamine my correspondence, and found several letters on the subject. Hence I put them together with the title: *My Old Views of Equilibrium and Harmony* and wrote a preface for the volume. My purpose was to expose my past mistakes thoroughly, to allow scholars who wanted to pursue the subject to learn from my mistakes. My only regret was that I had no chance to confirm my understanding with Master Li. But by inferring from what he already said we might learn something about what he did not say; hopefully, my understanding may not deviate too far from what he might have taught.[3]

According to Wang Mou-hung (1668–1741), the early Ch'ing author of the standard biography of Chu Hsi, this preface was written in 1172 when Chu Hsi was forty-three years old after his thought had matured on the subject. Unfortunately, however, even in Wang's time the text of Chu Hsi's *My Old Views of Equilibrium and Harmony* was no longer available. What we have today are two letters from his *Collection of Literary Works* that definitely belong in this group of correspondence, plus two other letters Wang Mou-hung judged also to belong in the same group. Wang dated these letters to 1166, when Chu Hsi was thirty-seven years old.[4] Although Wang's opinions were usually quite reliable, he still made certain incorrect inferences. Professor Ch'ien Mu tried to correct Wang's mistakes in his monumental work on Chu Hsi, dating these letters to 1168.[5] His views appear to be plausible. But Professor Ch'ien failed to provide a correct interpretation of Chu Hsi's thought from a philosophical point of view, while Professor Mou Tsung-san developed penetrating insights into Chu Hsi's philosophical ideas.[6] However, Professor Mou placed too much trust in Wang Mou-hung and was unable to pinpoint possible mistakes Wang made from the point of view of historical development, as Professor Ch'ien Mu did. The present effort attempts to give the available materials a coherent interpretation and provide a full account of Chu Hsi's search for equilibrium and harmony.[7]

From Chu Hsi's own testimony quoted above we learn that his understanding of equilibrium and harmony underwent at least three stages: (1) the stage before the formulation of what he called his old views of equilibrium and harmony; (2) the stage when he expounded his old views; and (3) the stage of mature thought after he had discarded his old views. In the following, I shall examine these three stages and Chu Hsi's reflections on equilibrium and harmony.

According to Wang Mou-hung, Chu Hsi wrote the following letter to Ho Shu-ching when he was thirty-seven years old:

When Master Li taught his students, he usually instructed them that in tranquility one must realize in a distinct fashion the prevailing spirit even before the great foundation becomes manifest; so that when one deals with affairs and responds to things, he can attain due measure and degree naturally. This was the key formula transmitted by the followers of Yang Kuei-shan (Yang Shih, 1053–1135). However, when I studied with Master Li, I loved to listen to lectures and discussions, and also loved to study texts from a philological point of view, so I did not devote myself to this issue. Now the insight seems to be there and yet nowhere; indeed I did not have true understanding and wasted my teacher's efforts to teach me. When I thought about it, I always felt ashamed, and my clothes were permeated by sweat.[8]

As Professor Mou Tsung-san pointed out, at this stage Chu Hsi indeed had a very superficial understanding of the problem, as he said, "[B]efore the great foundation becomes manifest."[9] The text of *The Doctrine of the Mean* only said that "the feelings are not aroused" (*wei-fa*) but never said anything like "the great foundation is not manifest" (*wei-fa*). In Chu Hsu's biography of his teacher, he put it much better: "Master Li meditated the whole day, examined the prevailing spirit before the feelings of pleasure, anger, sorrow, and joy were aroused in order to seek equilibrium."[10] The reason why Chu Hsi made the mistake can be traced to ambiguity in the word *wei-fa*, which means an undifferentiated state as well as a state of equilibrium, which implies a correlation with the operation of the Way as taught by his teacher Li T'ung. Although Chu Hsi did not comprehend the message of Li T'ung's teachings, he was now trying very hard to solve the problem. Here is another letter to Ho Shu-ching from the same period:

Although I did not dare to neglect the practice of realization and preservation, yet I failed to go ahead and find ease in myself. However, compared with the past, there has been some progress. What I miss is help from my friends. All day long I try to reflect and elevate myself, but the only result I achieve is to avoid the dullness of my mind. When I just relax a bit, then I feel lost again. This was a moment of struggle between heavenly principle and human desires, so I had little choice but to work hard on this. I do not know how much progress you had made recently. Have you overcome your doubts yet? If you truly grasped the insight, then you would have realized [the truth about] nature and the mind, whether before or after the feelings are aroused, all are united, leaving nothing to be worried about. From thus, one overcomes the self and maintains seriousness, so as to accomplish what one sets out to do. Then in daily life there is nothing but the realization of this. *The Doctrine of the Mean* must have made this its central issue. Scholars' interpretations of the document were hardly satisfactory. Recently I read it again, and found many dubious points. Thus even disciples' recording of Master Ch'eng's sayings could not but miss the point occasionally. Perhaps this is the fault of the person who recorded it, yet we still must be cautious in making our choice.[11]

Apparently, Chu Hsi was struggling with the problem and had some ideas of his own. At that time he was trying to exercise critical thinking and did not even trust the authority of Master Ch'eng's words as recorded by his immediate disciples. In still another letter to Ho Shu-ching in the same period, he wrote:

In the past I learned from my teacher that one should achieve realization and corroboration at moments when the feelings are not aroused and yet are about to be aroused. Only then can meanings of the texts and principles of things be understood by tracing them to the same origin. As everything is but a manifestation of the same principle, there is no need to seek any further by making a philological study of the texts. Although I received my teacher's instructions, yet I did not know their justification. Now I finally realize that this was indeed his most important and correct teaching, but it was not easy to leap to his level of achievement.[12]

Chu Hsi seemed to have realized the Way as manifested in the whole universe in a rather vague fashion. He wrote a poem to illustrate his understanding of the Way:

The square half-*mou* pond opens up like a mirror;
Heavenly light and the shadows of cloud wander together.
Why is the water as clear as this?
Because fresh water always flows from the fountainhead.[13]

Chu Hsi suggested that there is a creative ontological principle working ceaselessly in the whole universe. If one appreciates this message, one can realize the vitality of the self and the whole universe.

At this stage Chu Hsi was corresponding with Chang Shih (Ching-fu, Nan-hsien, 1133–1180), who told him about what he had learned from his teacher Hu Hung (1100–1155). Greatly inspired, Chu Hsi decided to meet with Chang Shih to obtain a deeper understanding of the Hunan school, where it was taught that "one must first examine and reflect before one can practice self-cultivation."[14]

According to Professer Mou Tsung-san, Li T'ung and Hu Hung's approaches were two possible ways of realizing equilibrium developed from teachings taught by the two major disciples of the Ch'eng brothers, Yang Kuei-shan and Hsieh Shang-ts'ai (Liang-tso, 1050–1103), who based their understanding on *The Book of Mencius* and *The Doctrine of the Mean*. Chu Hsi, however, had problems with both approaches and failed to appreciate the true depth of their teachings.[15]

According to Professor Mou Tsung-san, Li's approach was "to realize equilibrium through temporary separation from daily activities." Li put a strong emphasis on practicing meditation until one had achieved equilibrium that would resist all interference by selfish desires. Once this was accomplished, one could easily realize equilibrium in daily life and achieve an ultimate sense of unity, like ice melting in water and leaving no visible traces. But Chu Hsi disliked this approach because he was the kind of person who diligently studied classical texts and carried out all of his duties in life and would hardly care to divorce himself from the world, as his teacher did. But for Li, sitting still actually meant much more than calming the mind; it was a way for him to make a correlation with the ultimate creative ontological principle, which manifested itself in an equilibrium realizable through discipline of the mind. This explains why Chu Hsi chose not to follow Li T'ung and probe deeply into the matter while his teacher was still alive.[16] But after Master Li died, Chu Hsi found serious problems in his own experience of discipline of the mind and lamented the fact that he had missed the opportunity of learning from his teacher; he tried to reconstruct what his teacher taught him but without much success. Though he was compelled to seek other ways, his respect for his teacher inspired him to search for a way to realize equilibrium in his formative years.

After Li died, Chu began to experience certain doubts, and this problem seemed to have become more urgent for him. In a letter to his friend Lo, he reported that he had just read Hu Jen-chung's (Hu Hung) *Knowing the Words* and had been corresponding fruitfully with his disciple Chang Ching-fu:

> In sum, the Heng-shan [Hunan] school teaches that one should exercise and preserve [the mind], discern and investigate [principles] in daily life activities; as the beginning and the end coincide, hence it is easy to obtain results. Recently I felt that this was the case. But not until I had a chance to discuss this with him [Chang] in person. I could not be sure.[17]

This approach apparently greatly appealed to him, as it seemed to accord well with his temperament. But Professor Mou pointed out that Chu Hsi's understanding of this approach is equally superficial. The Hunan approach was a development of Ch'eng Hao's quest for *shih-jen* (understanding humanity), a form of understanding on a different level from our empirical investigation of things. It was a perception of the ontological principle at work.

Chu visited Chang Shih at the age of thirty-eight. They lived together for two months and climbed Mt. Heng-shan together. Unfortunately, we have no record of what they discussed during this period. Surely they talked about a number of things including humanity. One entry in the biography of Chu Hsi is of special interest for us: "Fan Nien-te accompanied him, and reported that the two masters discussed the problem of equilibrium and harmony. They debated for three days and nights but could not reach an agreement.''[18] Some scholars doubt they ever had such a debate, but as several biographies include this entry, there seems to be little reason to doubt its authenticity. It is up to us to find a reasonable account for this entry. One of Chu Hsi's poems composed when he bid farewell to Chang Shih begins with, "In the past I was holding both ice and coal; I was following you to understand the meaning of *ch'ien* and *k'un*.''[19] Surely this poem was referring directly to the Great Ultimate, but these issues are related and should not be cited as evidence to quash the debate over the problem of equilibrium and harmony taking place between the two scholars. A plausible explanation is that Chu Hsi told Chang Shih what he learned from his teacher Li T'ung, and Chang Shih told Chu Hsi about what he had learned from Hu Hung. But as the two approaches were quite different, they were naturally unable to agree when they first got together to discuss the issues. But when they parted, they seemed to be able to agree on a number of things. Chu Hsi praised his friend Chang Shih highly, and they vowed to practice the principles outlined in an engraved inscription by Chang Shih, "*Ken-chai-ming*," in which Chang wrote:

> There are endless ways that things may move people; as a man is enticed
> by things, his desires will arise. If a man fails to reflect on himself, then
> the heavenly principle will be lost. Sagely enlightenment lies in knowing
> where to abide. The heavenly mind is pure with all the ontological and
> moral principles contained in it. This is the supreme good, and the origin
> of all changes. If this is what a man has preserved in himself, why would
> he act against it? If one searches according to the Way, will it be discov-
> ered so far away? We must examine the manifestations of the so-called
> four beginnings [humanity, righteousness, propriety and wisdom]; and not
> only must we think, but we must act accordingly. When we discipline
> ourselves to a certain extent, then we will be able to understand the broad
> principle. This is not imposed on us from without; it is like a spring which
> flows on its own accord. Understanding is the beginning of realizing the
> ultimate. Under adverse conditions I am restraining my wandering
> thoughts, and holding on to principles with a sense of trembling. Although
> there are a myriad of things in the world, each follows its own principle.
> There is nothing else but to follow the essentials of my nature. I move
> and rest according to time; there is light and there is substance. It is here
> that I realize the wonder of abiding in *ken* [a hexagram]. Our duties are
> heavy, but the distance is long while time is short. Therefore colleagues
> like us should encourage each other constantly. We must remind ourselves
> that we are afraid that we cannot establish ourselves. All colleagues must
> arise and help one another out.[20]

Clearly Chang was following the guidance of Mencius's thought. The understanding he refers to is the understanding of what is implicit in our nature

through the manifestations of the beginnings of our mind. Chu Hsi may not have a thorough understanding of the implicit message in the document, but he was greatly impressed by the Hunan approach, as evidenced by his letters to friends after he returned from his visit there.

In his letter to Ch'eng Yun-fu, Chu Hsi said:

When I went to Hunan last winter, the discussions were beneficial. But what is important is to practice self-discipline in such daily activities as walking, standing, sitting and sleeping, from which true insights may be gained. Following this procedure, one exercises and preserves the mind to the utmost extent, whereupon it is truly appropriated by the self. Ching-fu's understanding is on a very high level. His achievement cannot be matched. . . . His essay ''*Ken-chai-ming*'' describes the steps we should take to discipline ourselves. Recently we worked together to examine what has been transmitted by the ancient sages, and to establish a principle for us to commit ourselves to.[21]

In another letter to Ho Shu-ching from the same period, he wrote:

I used to talk about maintaining seriousness but took an incorrect attitude; now I cannot even remember the details. But one can follow the subtle manifestations of the mind and pull himself up, so that the mind will not lose its brightness. This is the way to practice self-discipline. When self-discipline is practiced, we naturally start from below and later attain a higher level. If one does not examine the manifestations of the mind, I am afraid that we will get lost in a vacuum and will not know where to start. . . . You said that we must study as much as possible words and actions of the past; these are indeed important undertakings. I agreed with you in the past. But recently when I have tried to return to the self, I have not been able to find a place to abide, whereupon I have realized that in the past my search was deviating and scattered. If we follow recent masters in order to go back to the Ch'eng brothers' teachings, and then follow the Ch'eng brothers to return to the sages, this is a rather roundabout way. A better approach would be to establish a foundation by self-realization in one's own mind. Then we would be able to find a criterion for judging what words are right or wrong. Ching-fu's achievement in learning stands high above the crowd. He can feel at ease with himself, is not fettered by words, and his approach is very close to the self. His sayings are sound, even though they are not absolutely right, and his achievement cannot be matched by us. Just study closely and you will find that this indeed is the case.[22]

The interesting thing was that Wang Yang-ming quoted this letter in the book he edited, *Chu Hsi's Final Conclusions Arrived at Late in Life*, and took it as representative of Chu Hsi's later thought, perhaps because of the fact that the thought expressed in this letter was close to his own. But he failed to notice that this letter was written when Chu Hsi was still searching for a way.[23] At this early stage he was still following Chang Shih, and there was still a long way to go before he was able to formulate his mature views on the subject.

At about this stage, Chu Hsi experienced a breakthrough of some sort and worked out his so-called old views of equilibrium and harmony. It appeared that after his visit to Hunan, Chu Hsi kept up his correspondence with Chang Shih and discussed the issue further in their letters. As mentioned above, the book Chu Hsi edited on his old views is no longer extant, and Chang Shih's letters to Chu Hsi were all lost. Yet we do have two of Chu Hsi's letters that not only discussed the issues but included his own footnotes to them, which we can use to study his old views. Furthermore, Chu Hsi biographer Wang Mou-hung found two other letters written about the same time that also shed further light on Chu Hsi's views. In the first letter, Chu Hsi said:

When a person is born, he possesses certain knowledge and perceptions. Things come and go to which we are constantly responding. Thoughts and ideas change accordingly until the moment of death. There is not a moment of rest; this applies to everyone in the world. And yet the sages and worthies tell us that there is a so-called equilibrium before the feelings are aroused, and that it is tranquil and inactive. Do our daily activities refer to the state after the feelings are aroused, while the state before the feelings are aroused refers to the moment of temporary rest when there is no contact with things? I have followed this line of thought to discover that at the moment of unconsciousness there is only that which is perverse, dark, pent up and lacking an outlet, and not that which is vacuous, bright and ready to respond to things. When we gain a certain inkling of consciousness, then we have already entered the moment when feelings have been aroused; this is not to be characterized as tranquil. The more I search, the more remote the truth seems to me. Then I have to retreat and examine my daily activities. Ironically I find openness in feelings and consciousness in contact, there seems to be an undifferentiated whole which responds to things and cannot be exhausted. This is indeed where the mandate of Heaven flows and creativity functions incessantly; even though in a whole day there are thousands of arisings and perishings, the substance of tranquility has maintained its tranquility. Therefore I realized that the state when the feelings are not aroused should be understood in this way. Is there an equilibrium separate from other things, limited to one time and one place? The heavenly principle is always true, it can be discovered everywhere. As its substance and function are like this, it will not stop and perish because of the overflow of selfish material desires. Hence if the mind is hemmed in by material desires, is it not true that the discovery of its first manifestations may also begin with daily events? Thus if a scholar devotes himself to examining and preserving the mind, he can gain a comprehensive understanding of the Way and recover his original nature. If he fails to examine and preserve the mind, then the mind will remain fettered and wavering and be unable to preserve the so-called restorative influence of the night. He will thus degenerate into an animal. Let us ask whose fault this is? Master Chou said, "The five agents are but yin and yang, and yin and yang are but the great ultimate, and the great ultimate is fundamentally the limitless." He also talked about Sincerity and described it as follows: "When tranquil, it is in the state of non-being, and when active, it is in the state of being." Master Ch'eng asked, "How can we seek anything before the feelings are aroused? All you need to do is to practice self-cultivation in daily life." He also said, "Those who know how to observe [the operation of the Way] can do so only after the feelings are aroused." As these two masters taught us in this fashion, it is clear that the great foundation is everywhere, and that the mind has always been aroused.[24]

When Chu Hsi wrote this letter, he was obviously under the spell of Chang Shih. His position was drifting away from his teacher's approach since he no longer put emphasis on practicing transcendental meditation. But later on, he encountered difficulties with this approach and changed his mind. He left the following note attached to this letter: "What has been said in this letter is not correct. I am only preserving it as a record of the details of our discussions. The same is true for the next letter."[25]

It appears that Chang Shih had written to Chu Hsi to discuss the issue, but since his letters have been lost, we can only proceed by studying what is implied in Chu Hsi's letters to Chang Shih.

In his second letter, Chu Hsi wrote:

The reason I sent you the last letter was because I was afraid that I did not have a proper understanding and I wanted to ask you to correct me. I received your letter and realized that I made the mistake of taking it as two things. This is exactly why I wanted to hear from you, and it is fortunate for me to have your response. The problem is that when I suddenly realized what the principle was, I feared that I could not characterize it intimately or clearly, hence I had wavered from east to west, anxious about not being able to hold on to the essentials. Now I see the point: there is substance and function within a moment of thought. The moment when what has been aroused goes, what is not yet aroused comes; there is no interruption or separation. How can there be another thing that can be pointed to by another name? However, the heavenly principle is infinite, and man's understanding is varied. There is difference between far and near, deep and shallow. If I take it in this way, can I avoid making errors? I hope that you will send me a word to enlighten me. You feel that Yang Kuei-shan's interpretation of the *Doctrine of the Mean* is doubtful. Recently I have felt the same way. Again, it is said that, "If a scholar uses his mind to examine things the moment before the feelings of pleasure, anger, sorrow, and joy are aroused, then the substance of equilibrium can manifest itself naturally." I do not think that this is quite right. In sum, this thing is completely beyond distinctions of time sequence and order. When we discuss this from such perspectives, faults become apparent. What if there was only the substance that is tranquil and without any activity? I have doubts about Ch'eng I-chuan's [Ch'eng I] recorded conversations, in which he said that "One should preserve [the mind] before the feelings are aroused." Questions were asked about the moment of realizing equilibrium when even the eyes do not see and the ears do not hear, but his answers did not seem to drive straight to the point. I wonder if you have similar doubts, and I hope that you will give me your instructions. I have read your work "On Equilibrium" in which you said, "Before the feelings are aroused, the mind correlates with the nature in a wonderful fashion, and after the feelings are aroused, the nature manifests itself in the functioning of the mind." But I have doubts on this point. Although the nature manifests itself constantly in the functioning of the mind, yet there may be nature which has not yet been manifest in functioning. You use the word "before." It seems that there may be a slight interruption between what is before and what is after. What do you think about this point? When you study the *Doctrine of the Mean* intimately, the term "not yet" suggests that it [the Way] is so lively that there can be no moment of arrest. When something comes infinitely, there is invariably something which is not yet aroused. If there is no such thing, then the mandate of Heaven can cease, the creation of things can come to an end, and the everchanging activity of material force will be interrupted and come to an end. In this case, all that remains would be ancient times and nothing of the present to talk about. It is here that we have realized the great foundation of all things. If there is a lack of true insight, there will be no way even to make conjectures about it.[26]

Chu Hsi was obviously still in the midst of his search, and Chang was still leading the way. But Chu Hsi was able to give certain feedback to Chang Shih. It appears that Chang Shih told him that substance and function are one and that they should not be regarded as two things. Chu Hsi took these instructions to heart and admitted that his own formulation of the problem could be improved. But Chu Hsi did not understand the background of Chang Shih's expressions, as these were most likely based on Hu Hung's teachings, which take nature as the ultimate ontological principle and the mind as the principle of manifestation, though the two are essentially one. Furthermore, Chu Hsi seems to have made the mistake of shifting his ground, for when *The Doctrine of the Mean* was referring to self-discipline, Chu Hsi drifted into a discussion of the unceasing cosmic process instead. Again, Chu Hsi attached a footnote to this second letter, which said, "What is discussed in this letter is even more erroneous. It is wrong of me to cast doubts on the recorded conversations. Later on I shall give a detailed analysis of the issue."[27] Unfortunately, we do not have Chu Hsi's comments on the problem. But his later writings provide enough materials to reconsruct the development of Chu Hsi's thought.

Wang Mou-hung identified two more letters that he judged to belong in the same group, designating them as letters three and four. In the third letter, Chu Hsi wrote:

You gave me instructions on the discursiveness of the issue, and I could not but have doubts in the beginning. When I thought about them, I doubted some of them and I believed others, but they did not make a coherent whole. Recently I probed deeper and found that I missed only one point, and then found obstacles all over the place. I have spotted the reasons and would like to set them forth. I hope you will give me your opinion as to whether I am on the right track. Perhaps what I realized in the last few days, which I set forth in my letters to you, only gave a vague impression of the great foundation and the universal path. I thought then that I had gotten hold of the right thing, but in fact I had not thought through the implications of "how to attend equilibrium and harmony" [as taught in *The Doctrine of the Mean*]. Therefore you wrote me several times, telling me that it is urgent to seek humanity, but I felt that I did not have a solid ground under my feet to practice self-discipline. The problem was that I only saw the origin itself. The atmosphere resembled the violent torrents of the sea, and I felt everyday that I was driven by a great transforming process, as if I was under huge waves, and did not get a moment of rest. As my understanding was always like this, when I responded to things, I felt even twice as coarse and brave as I felt before, and there was a total lack of magnanimous sentiment. Although I worried about it, I could not identify the source. From then on I realized that in the great transforming process, every family has its own safe residence, where one establishes one's life, becomes the master of one's consciousness, holds on to the essentials such as resting on the great foundation and follows the universal path. It is here that one finds that "substance and function are of one source, and there is no gap between what is manifest and what is hidden." In my last letter I talked about what comes and goes. This shows that I did not know where to put my hands and feet and could not find a proper place to settle. The Way is near, but I was looking for it in a far-off place. This is really a laughable matter! . . . Regarding the doctrine that we can see the mind of Heaven and Earth in *fu* [the hexagram return], my view is that the mind of Heaven and Earth is that which creates the myriad things in the world. Material forces may close or open, fullness and emptiness may alternate, but the mind of

Heaven and Earth persists through ancient and modern times without one moment of interruption. Hence when Yang exhausts without, Return grows within. The sage felt that here we may see the mind of Heaven and Earth, for what returns is material force while what causes the return has its own resources. If the mind of Heaven and Earth did not create incessantly, then when Yang was exhausted and came to an end, how would it be possible for Return to grow within and manifest itself in the infinite process of closing and opening? Therefore when we refer to the Beginning of Yang, we mean that which causes Yang to move and not to the past actions of Yang. Therefore, even though we cannot say that the restorative air of the night is the mind of Heaven and Earth, yet it is the moment when the material force returns. If we try to trace its origin we will be able to see the mind of Heaven and Earth.[28]

There is no doubt that this letter belongs in the same group, as the issues it discusses display continuity with the content of the last two letters. Chu Hsi's critique of his own thought was basically sound. What is interesting here is that Chu Hsi made a sharp distinction between what actually moves, that is, material force, and the origin of such activities, which seems to belong to a different level. Chu Hsi's thought was moving away from where Chang Shih meant to lead him. Later Chu Hsi found his mentor in Ch'eng I of the Northern Sung, bypassing both Li T'ung and Hu Hung of the Southern Sung dynasty.

There is a fourth letter that relates to the issues discussed in the last three letters:

In my last letter when I talked about what is tranquil before the feelings are aroused and the beginning of the manifestation of the mind, I felt my understanding was somewhat different from my past views, which were rather one-sided. And there were a number of errors in my writing, which was not to the point exactly. After I sent my letter, I studied for several more days and gained a clearer understanding of the substance. I read the works of the sages and worthies, and more recent works by masters of our age; they all confirmed what I had found. My doubts and misunderstanding seemed to fall away, and there was no need for me to artificially look for a way to act naturally. Now I began to have self-confidence. I believe that all the principles in the world rest on this, and I shall find a way to practice how to extend knowledge, investigate things, abide in seriousness and refine meanings. How could the documents handed down by the sages and worthies possibly deceive me? In the universe there is but one creative principle which flows and functions without a moment of rest. From what had been aroused we can trace back to what is not yet aroused. Then we may say that what is aroused is the mind, while what is not yet aroused is the nature. Nothing is left out. How is it possible to have another thing, limited to one place and one time, which needs another name? The undifferentiated whole works in daily activities like a flowing stream, demonstrating the inexhaustible workings of Heaven. This is how substance and function, the subtle and the coarse, motion and rest, the root and the branches, all become clear. There is an instant realization of the atmosphere, like hawks flying up to the sky and fish leaping in the deep [as in *The Book of Odes* and *The Doctrine of the Mean*]. To preserve means only to preserve this principle, and to cultivate means only to cultivate this principle. "Always be doing something without expectations. Let the mind not lose sight of its objective, but let there be no artificial effort to help it grow." In the past I tried to make many arrangements without finding a place to settle. Now I feel as if there is enough water for the boat to float; lift the anchor and it will go up or down the stream with great ease. It is as simple as that. Now I believe that Master Ming-tao's saying, "there is no need to exert the slightest amount of effort," is not just idle talk. Only the immediate disciple [of Ming-tao] Master Hsieh Shan-ts'ai realized this point thoroughly without any gaps. As for the others, even if I dare not criticize them, when I study their words, I know their intentions. Recently Fan Po-ch'ung came from Shao-wu and discussed this issue with me in detail. I had to exclaim that this had never been done before, and realized that in the past I had very much been on the wrong track. I also feel that even though those who attained enlightenment left words illustrating the Way in an intimate fashion, yet I was still drifting along and could not find the right clues. Had you not pointed out the key to me, helped me to identify my problems, gave me instructions constantly and stuck with me despite my dull wit, I do not think I could have achieved anything like this. I am extremely grateful to you, though my pen is inadequate to express my thanks. I just wonder how would you react to this [realization] from your lofty perspective?[29]

Professor Mou Tsung-san points out that this letter does not seem to be a reply to a letter from Chang Shih. Judging by its contents, it could have been written after Chu Hsi sent Chang Shih his first letter, had some further deliberations, and hurriedly sent a follow-up to that letter.[30] The important point here is that, in this letter, Chu Hsi identified for the first time what is not aroused as the nature and what is aroused as the mind. He apparently received a reply from Chang Shih, who pointed out that it was wrong to view these as two things. After sending his second letter and receiving further replies from Chang Shih, Chu Hsi's newly acquired self-confidence seemed to waver. Then in his third letter, he took a new direction that finally led him to his mature thought. This was indeed the end of a long quest.

Wang Mou-hung dated these letters to 1166 when Chu Hsi was thirty-seven years old and before he had visited Chang Shih in Hunan. Professor Ch'ien Mu has pointed out Wang Mou-hung's mistakes.[31] The best evidence for this is Chu Hsi's own preface to his *My Old Views of Equilibrium and Harmony*:

I have heard that Chang Ching-fu mastered what had been taught by Master Hu of Heng-shan, so I visited him and asked him about it. Ching-fu told me what he had learned from Master Hu, but I could not grasp its meaning. I deliberated on the issue, neither sleeping nor eating. One day I lamented: a person lives through infancy and old age and finally dies. Even though there is a difference between speaking and silence and motion and rest, on the whole these refer to the state after the feelings are aroused, and what is not aroused is simply not aroused. Since I realized that, I had no more doubts. I believe the teachings of the *Doctrine of the Mean* refer to nothing but this realization. Later on I got hold of the works of Master Hu, and read his letter to Tseng Chi-fu in which he discussed the meaning of what is not yet aroused. His ideas happen to coincide with my own, and thus my self-confidence was further enhanced. Even when I found that some of Master Ch'eng's ideas were not consistent with my own, I thought that these were his early works and did not set much store by them. However, when I talked to others about my realization, very few appreciated my views. In the spring of 1169, I held a discussion with my friend Ts'ai Chi-t'ung. As we argued back and forth, I suddenly began to have doubts. Surely nothing should prevent me from conveying this principle to others. Why, then, when I tried to analyze it, did it become so complicated and hard to comprehend, and when others heard my explanations, they felt that my ideas were obscure and difficult to accept? I always believed that the principle underlying *ch'ien* and *k'un* must be easy to understand by all people. Why it is not like this? Furthermore, since Master Ch'eng's words were recorded by his able disciples, they should not be as erroneous as they are. Could it be that I actually held mistaken views with which I misled myself? So I took Master Ch'eng's works and reread them. After only a few lines, like ice melting, I realized what the original state of nature and the feelings was like, and the subtle teachings of the sages and worthies were balanced, straightforward and clear. It was I who did not read carefully, and created problems where there were none. What I toiled on led only to my own errors. As to bringing the consequences to their logical conclusions, I examined them myself and found that the harm was indeed great, for it involved more than just mistakes in language and expression. Therefore I became agitated, and hurriedly wrote a letter to Ching-fu and the others who shared my view. Only Ching-fu replied in the affirmative, while the others only agreed to some extent. This dragged on until the present. It has been years already, and no definitive results have been achieved. Here we see the fault of seeking from afar and neglecting what is nearby, hating what is common and loving what is novel. Should not we be warned by this situation?[32]

According to Wang Mou-hung, this preface was written in 1172, when Chu Hsi was forty-three years old. There are no good reasons to doubt Chu Hsi's own authority regarding what had happened only a few years ago.

We can now reconstruct the entire episode. After Li T'ung died, Chu Hsi was disturbed by the problem of equilibrium and harmony and tried to no avail to recall what he had learned from his teacher. He sought the help of Chang Shih, who taught him what he learned from Hu Hung. At first Chu Hsi had difficulties with what Chang Shih taught him because the teachings of the Hunan school were so different from what he had learned from Li T'ung. Gradually, however, he was more and more influenced by the Hunan approach, as his own temperament was not suited to the transcendental meditation transmitted by his teacher. After experiencing an enlightenment of some sort, he formulated what he called his old views, which on the surface appeared very close to the teachings of the Hunan school: The mind is regarded as what is manifested, while the nature is regarded as what is hidden. But the two views only coincide in a very superficial way. For Hu Hung, both the mind and the nature are transcendent: When the mind manifests the nature, they are not two different things. But Chu Hsi regarded what is not yet aroused as the nature and what is aroused as the mind, and thus for him they became two successive stages. Moreover, for those who hold such a view no self-discipline can be practiced when the feelings are not aroused. When Chu Hsi identified the problem, he immediately denounced his old views, along with the teachings of the Hunan school, and had serious debates with followers of the Hunan school. Unfortunately, however, the latter only stuck to their traditional views and could not effectively defend the teachings of their school, while the most famous member of the Hunan school, Chang Shih, though not always in agreement with Chu Hsi, nevertheless accepted many of his suggested revisions. As a result the Hunan school nearly became extinct after Chu Hsi's time. Not until recently did Professor Mou Tsung-san resurrect their teachings and place them beside the two mainstream schools of Ch'eng-Chu and Lu-Wang. Although Chu Hsi misunderstood the teachings of the Hunan school, he found his own path by following Ch'eng I, in whose teachings he saw a synthesis of what had been taught by Li T'ung and Hu Hung; however, this synthesis did not achieve its purpose, as Chu Hsi failed to appreciate the essentials of both approaches. Chu Hsi finally formulated an independent viewpoint of his own and succeeded in persuading later scholars to follow him and regard his philosophy as the orthodox transmission of the teachings of the sages.[33]

After traveling down a long and bumpy road, Chu Hsi finally formulated a mature conception in his "First Letter to the Gentlemen of Hunan on Equilibrium and Harmony." His letter will be cited in its entirety because of the importance of its content.

Concerning the meaning in the *Doctrine of the Mean* that equilibrium (*chung*, centrality, the Mean) is the state before the feelings of pleasure, anger, sorrow, and joy are aroused and that harmony [*ho*] is that state after they are aroused, because formerly I realized the substance of the operation of the mind, and, furthermore, because Master Ch'eng I had said that "whenever we talk about the mind, we refer to the state after the feelings are aroused,'' I looked upon the mind as the state after the feelings are aroused and upon nature as the state before the feelings are aroused. However, I have observed that there are many inconsistencies in Master Ch'eng's works, I have therefore thought the matter over, and consequently realized that in my previous theory not only are the [contrasting] terms ''mind'' and ''nature'' improper but the efforts in my daily task also completely lack a great foundation. Therefore the loss has not been confined to the meanings of words.

The various theories in Master Ch'eng's *Wen-chi* (Collection of literary works) and *I-shu* (Surviving works) seem to hold that before there is any sign of thought or deliberation and prior to the arrival of [stimulus] of external things, there is the state before the feelings of pleasure, anger, sorrow, and joy are aroused. At this time, the state is identical with the substance of the mind, which is absolutely tranquil and inactive, and the nature endowed by Heaven should be completely embodied in it. Because it is neither excessive nor insufficient, and is neither unbalanced nor one-sided, it is called equilibrium. When it is acted upon and immediately penetrates all things, the feelings are then aroused. In this state the functioning of the mind can be seen. Because it never fails to attain the proper measure and degree and has nowhere deviated from the right, it is called harmony. This is true because of the correctness of the human mind and the moral character of the feelings and nature.

However, the state before the feelings are aroused cannot be sought and the state after they are aroused permits no manipulation. So long as in one's daily life the effort at seriousness and cultivation is fully extended and there are no selfish desires to disturb it, then before the feelings are aroused it will be as clear as a mirror and as calm as still water, and after the feelings are aroused it will attain due measure and degree without exception. This is the essential task in everyday life. As to examination when things occur and seeking understanding through inference when we come into contact with things, this must also serve as the foundation. If we observe the state after the feelings are aroused, what is contained in the state before the feelings are aroused can surely be understood in silence. This is why in his answers to Su Chi-ming, Master Ch'eng discussed and argued back and forth in the greatest detail and with extreme care, but in the final analysis what he said was no more than the word ''seriousness'' (*ching*). This is the reason why he said, ''Seriousness without fail is the way to attain equilibrium,'' and ''For entering the Way there is nothing better than seriousness. No one can ever extend knowledge to the utmost without depending on seriousness,'' and again, ''Self-cultivation requires seriousness, the pursuit of learning depends on the extension of knowledge.''

All along in my discussions and thinking I have simply considered the mind to be the state after the feelings are aroused, and in my daily affairs

I have also merely considered examining and recognizing the clues [of activity of feelings] as the starting points. Consequently I have neglected daily self-cultivation, so that my mind is disturbed in many ways and lacks depth and purity. Also, when it is expressed in speech or action, it is always characterized by a sense of urgency and lacking in reserve; and there is no longer any disposition toward ease or profundity. For a single mistake in one's viewpoint can lead to as much harm as this. This is something we must not overlook.

When Master Ch'eng said, "Whenever we talk about the mind, we refer to the state after the feelings are aroused," he referred [only] to the mind of an infant [whose feelings have already been aroused]. When he said, "Whenever we talk about the mind . . ." he expressed it mistakenly and therefore admitted this and corrected himself [by saying, "This is of course incorrect, for the mind is one. Sometimes we refer to its substance (namely, the state of absolute tranquillity and inactivity) and sometimes we refer to its function (namely, its being acted on and immediately penetrating all things). It depends on one's point of view"]. We should not hold on to something which he had already corrected and on that basis doubt the correctness of his various theories, nor simply dismiss it as incorrect without examining the fact that he was referring to something else. What do you gentlemen think about this?[34]

In this letter, Chu Hsi pinpointed his problem. If the mind is taken as the state after the feelings are aroused, then it is impossible to practice self-discipline before the feelings are aroused, and the lack of such a discipline has caused many problems. Here he was admitting that he had been misled by one of Ch'eng I's incorrect sayings, and only later was he able to follow the correct way as expressed by Ch'eng I in some of his most important writings. The mind encompasses both the state before and after the feelings are aroused. Self-cultivation by maintaining seriousness is required before the feelings are aroused, and the extension of knowledge through the examination of things is required after the feelings are aroused. Chu Hsi believed that by emphasizing the practice of self-cultivation, he could accomplish what Li T'ung had taught him but what he in his early years and the followers of the Hunan school had neglected. He now worked out a synthesis that balanced the two approaches. He compared them to the two wings of a bird or the two wheels of a cart. This was his mature view; once he formulated it, he never changed his course again.

As this was only his first letter, there must have been other letters, but none to our knowledge are extant. Chu Hsi, however, wrote an essay entitled "On the Problem concerning the States before and after the Feelings Are Aroused," the contents of which are virtually identical with what he wrote in the letter—the only difference being that in this essay he quoted Ch'eng I's works in order to support his thesis. Apparently, most of the followers of the Hunan school stuck close to their own tradition and rejected Chu Hsi's new views. Only Chang

Shih showed some sympathy for his viewpoint. Hence, Chu Hsi wrote another long letter to him, further discussing the issue:

> I am indeed happy that you have confirmed my views, and that you did not take issue with my most important thesis on the state before the feelings are aroused. Compared to my old views, my expressions seemed to lack a systematic presentation. Hence I examined them and reflected upon them again, and found that in realizing this principle we must rely on the mind as the master. When we proceed to this sort of discussion, the virtues of nature and the feelings, and the wonder of equilibrium and harmony appear in good order and never in disarray. As a man's body and the functioning of perceptions must invariably depend on action of the mind, the mind has to be the master of the body, regardless of the difference between motion and rest, speaking and silence. When it is tranquil, things have not yet come into contact [with the mind], thoughts have not yet begun, and nature remains undifferentiated with all principles embodied in it. Here we find a form of equilibrium which demonstrates that the mind is the substance which is tranquil and inactive. When there is activity, things crowd together, thoughts begin to emerge, and the seven emotions alternate with one another, each following its own guidance. Then there is a form of harmony which demonstrates the functioning of the mind: when acted upon, it immediately penetrates all things. Although nature in itself is tranquil, activities cannot but ensue, and there must be a way of regulating the activity of feelings. This is how the mind becomes tranquil and inactive, and when acted upon, immediately penetrates all things. As it circulates, substance and function never separate from each other. However, even though every man has this mind, yet they can act against humanity and fail to manifest the wonder of this mind. If a man wishes to practice humanity, yet fails to maintain seriousness, it is because he fails to follow the way of extending humanity. The mind is the master of the body, regardless of the difference between motion and rest or speaking and silence. Therefore when a superior man practices seriousness, he exerts the effort regardless of the distinction between motion and rest or speaking and silence. There is a form of seriousness before the feelings are aroused, as preservation and cultivation have already established the foundation, while there is also seriousness after the feelings are aroused, as function is manifested in reflection and examination. When it is preserved before thoughts emerge and consciousness is nevertheless bright, this is activity in tranquillity. This is apparent in *fu* (return) where the mind of Heaven and Earth can be seen. When the mind examines all sorts of things crowding together, yet order is maintained without any deviation, this is tranquillity in activity, which can be seen in *ken* (abide), where the body cannot be spotted and the person cannot be seen at court. As there is mastering of activity in tranquillity, even though it is tranquil it has

always been acted on. As there is an examination of tranquillity in activity, hence even though it is acted upon, it has always been tranquil. Precisely because when it is tranquil and being acted upon, and is acted upon and being tranquil, the mind is circulating everywhere, and there is no moment in which it is not inspired with humanity. Here we find the principle by which a superior man attains equilibrium and harmony, by which Heaven and Earth will attain their proper order, and by which all things will flourish. That which is the master of the body regardless of motion and rest, speaking and silence, is the mind. Humanity is the Way of the mind, seriousness is its firmness. This is the Way which encompasses both the transcendent and the immanent, indicating the fundamental teachings of the sages. Once this is understood, only one word is needed to uncover the virtues of nature and the feelings, and the wonder of equilibrium and harmony.[35]

This is the first half of the long letter in which Chu Hsi gave a systematic and elegant presentation of his mature views. In the second half Chu Hsi disagreed with Chang Shih, who still insisted that one should reflect and examine before one can practice self-cultivation. Thus, even though Chang Shih showed sympathy for Chu Hsi's views, he did not subscribe to all of his views without qualification, as Chang's philosophical basis was quite different from Chu Hsi's. From then on, Chu Hsi began to formulate his grand system of philosophy, which will be discussed in the next chapter.

From the above, we can see that Chu Hsi's striving after a way to realize equilibrium and harmony is indeed a paradigmatic case. Contrary to the popular notion that traditional Chinese scholars had a tendency to obey authority and conform to accepted social norms, the great Chinese thinkers in the Neo-Confucian tradition, like Chu Hsi, were fiercely independent men who engaged in personal quests for the truth and obtained satisfaction by raising issues on a conscious level. The purpose of learning was self-realization. On this score Chu Hsi was not much different from his rival Lu Hsiang-shan (1139–1193), who declared that "the Six Classics are my footnotes."[36]

The Neo-Confucian philosophers maintained the faith that equilibrium and harmony could be attained and that fundamental truths were embodied in the Classics. They also believed that all sages taught essentially the same thing—only their expressions and emphases were different. These truths had to be apprehended by the self; otherwise, they were meaningless. The search for one's own way could be long and arduous, but realizing the truth is an experience similar to what is admirably expressed in the following lines:

> You have tried to find him hundreds and thousands of
> times;
> Suddenly you turned around.
> He was right there under the dim light.[37]

The Neo-Confucian philosophers claimed that knowledge and action are one in the sense that once an ultimate commitment is made, one's behavior has to change accordingly; otherwise, the knowledge attained cannot be said to be true knowledge. But the discipline of becoming a sage is an endless process, and no one can proclaim himself as a sage. Although a sage can usually achieve inner and outer harmony, it is by no means true that he can solve all problems. Chu Hsi was no doubt an idealist, but he was a realist, too. He often said, "Material force is strong while principles are weak; as the symbol which stands for yang is an undivided line (▬▬▬), and that which stands for yin is a divided line (▬ ▬), evil things are naturally more numerous than good things in the world."[38] Who can claim that traditional Chinese thinkers are incurable optimists?

Another aspect is missed with a one-sided interpretation of Neo-Confucian teachings. There is a strong sense of quandary in these thinkers, as they believe that the transmission of the mind does not stand on a very steady foundation: "The human mind is precarious, the mind of Tao is subtle; aspire only to the refined and the one, hold firm to the ultimate commitment to equilibrium."[39] In principle, inner tension may be resolved after a lifetime of self-discipline, but that does not mean that every problem can be solved, even if in principle all problems are solvable if the Way is followed. Unfortunately, however, very few people can follow the Way in a conscious fashion, as history shows us. Actually, Confucius was the last in a long line of recognized sages and a great teacher, yet he was a failure in politics. Furthermore, even though one may find his commitment, his approach may not be accepted by other scholars. Though there may be points of agreement among varied approaches, there are also irreconcilable differences.

While faith has failed to remove all tensions from the mind, traditional Confucian thought has never been able to solve the problem of "outward kingliness." The advice Confucian philosophers gave to the rulers was invariably to rectify the mind, make the wills sincere, follow good people, and avoid evil people. If a ruler chose to disregard such advice, the only alternative was to start a revolution and establish a new dynasty, though the same problems would recur in the future. Actually, revolutions were rare, and most rulers were mediocre; hence, the ideal of great unity forever remained a dream. Confucian philosophers could only laud the so-called Government of the Three Dynasties (Hsia, Shang, and Chou); the actual existence of ideals remains in doubt.

While this discussion has shed some light on the limitations of traditional thought, its study is not rendered meaningless. The ideal of "a unity of the inner and the outer" is a principle difficult to surpass. Furthermore, we must reinterpret the traditional insight "Principle is one while manifestations are many" in a radically new sense if it is to be relevant in the postmodern era. But it depends on present and future scholars to help us achieve the ideal of harmony and turning strife into a necessary condition for creativity.

NOTES

1. Thomas A. Metzger, *Escape from Predicament* (New York: Columbia University Press, 1977), pp. 4, 15.

2. Chan, *Source Book*, p. 98.

3. *Chu-tzu wen-chi* (Collection of literary works by Chu Hsi), 75:22a–23b. SPPY. Unless otherwise indicated, the translations are mine.

4. Wang Mou-hung, *Chu-tzu nien-p'u* (Chronological biography of Master Chu) (Taipei: Shih-chieh shu-chü, 1973), pp. 23–26, 254–256 (hereafter cited as Wang, *Biography*).

5. Ch'ien Mu, *Chu-tzu hsin-hsüeh-an* (A new study of Chu Hsi), 5 vols. (Taipei: San-min shu-chü, 1971), 2: 130–140, 160–168 (hereafter cited as Ch'ien, *Chu-tzu*). The date is only probable; scholars still have different opinions over this matter.

6. Mou, *Hsin-t'i*, 3: 71–175.

7. Liu, *Chu-tzu*, pp. 71–138.

8. *Chu-tzu wen-chi*, 40:8a.

9. Mou, *Hsin-t'i*, 3: 100–103.

10. *Chu-tzu wen-chi*, 97:27b.

11. Ibid., 40:9a.

12. Ibid., 40:10b.

13. Ibid., 2:10b. A *mou* is about one-sixth of an acre.

14. See his letter to his friend Lo in *Chu-tzu wen-chi hsü-chi* (Collection of literary works by Chu Hsi, a supplement), 5:12a. SPPY.

15. Mou, *Hsin-t'i*, 2:501–512; 3:139–146.

16. Ibid., 3: 4–9, 100–107.

17. See *Chu-tzu wen-chi hsü-chi*, 5:12a.

18. Wang, *Biography*, p. 29.

19. Ibid., p. 30.

20. *Chang Nan-hsien hsien-sheng wen-chi* (Collection of literary works of Master Chang Nan-hsien) (Shanghai: Commercial Press, 1937), pp. 111–112.

21. *Chu-tzu wen-chi*, 41:17a–b.

22. Ibid., 40:23b–24a.

23. Cf. Wing-tsit Chan, trans., *Instructions for Practical living and Other Neo-Confucian Works*, by Wang Yang-ming (New York: Columbia University Press, 1963), p. 263 hereafter cited as Wang, *Instructions*.

24. *Chu-tzu wen-chi*, 30:19a–b.

25. Ibid., 30:19a.

26. Ibid., 30:19b–20b.

27. Ibid., 30:19b.

28. Ibid., 32:4a–5a.

29. *Ibid.*, 32:5a–6a.

30. Cf. Mou, *Hsin-t'i*, 3: 93–94.

31. See Ch'ien, *Chu-tzu*, 2:130–140, 160–168.

32. See *Chu-tzu wen-chi*, 75: 22a–23b.

33. Cf. Mou, *Hsin-t'i*, 1: 41–60; and Shu-hsien Liu, "The Problem of Orthodoxy in Chu Hsi's Philosophy," in *Chu Hsi and Neo-Confucianism*, ed. Wing-tsit Chan (Honolulu: University of Hawaii Press, 1986), pp. 437–460.

34. *Chu-tzu wen-chi*, 64:28b–29b. See Chan, *Source Book*, pp. 600–602, with slight modification.

35. *Chu-tzu wen-chi*, 32:24b–25b.

36. *Hsiang-shan ch'üan-chi* (Complete works of Hsiang-shan), 34:1b. SPPY. See Chan, *Source Book*, p. 580.

37. From a poem by the Southern Sung poet Hsin Ch'i-chi.

38. *Chu-tzu yü-lei* (Classified conversations of Master Chu) (Taipei: Cheng-chung shu-chü, 1970), 4:13b, 21a (Vol. 1, pp. 114, 129).

39. "Counsels of Great Yü" in *The Book of History*.

9

Chu Hsi's Understanding of the Mind, Nature, and Feelings

Chu Hsi's philosophy was labeled as *li-hsüeh* in contrast to Lu Hsiang-shan's *hsin-hsüeh*, but that does not mean that he did not put any emphasis on *hsin* (the mind-heart). The difference between the two approaches lies in the relationship between *hsin* and *li* (principle), as Lu maintained that the mind is principle, while Chu Hsi maintained that the mind comprises principle. The mind as the active agent does play a pivotal part in his thought. In his letter to the gentlemen of Hunan on equilibrium and harmony (*chung-ho*), it was still the mind that occupied the foreground; nature was kept in the background. The relationship between the two is that nature is transcendent, while mind is immanent. There is a correlation between the two. Nature provides a solid foundation for mind to act, so it will not go astray and get lost, while mind is the ability to put the principles implicit in nature to work in life.

What is remarkable is that Chu Hsi started with an existential concern, but the concern had forced him to develop a comprehensive philosophy of mind and nature. And his mentor was clearly Ch'eng I, not Ch'eng Hao. Ch'u Hsi's mentality was highly analytical like Ch'eng I's. It was by no means an accident that Chu Hsi had such great admiration for Ch'eng I. Not only did Chu Hsi follow Ch'eng I's lead to solve the problem of equilibrium and harmony; he also followed Ch'eng I to make a sharp distinction between *hsing* (nature) and *ch'ing* (feeling). He fully endorsed Ch'eng I's view that "love is feeling whereas humanity is the nature."[1] This statement actually became the guideline for him to approach the problem of *jen*, the most fundamental virtue in Confucian teachings. In his famous essay "A Treatise on *Jen*," Chu Hsi said,

"The mind of Heaven and Earth is to produce things." In the production of man and things, they receive the mind of Heaven and Earth as their mind. Therefore, with reference to the character of the mind, although it embraces and penetrates all and leaves nothing to be desired, nevertheless, one word will cover all of it, namely, *jen* (humanity).[2]

Here Chu Hsi explicitly stated that *jen* is the character of the mind and that the human mind is essentially the same as the creative mind of Heaven and Earth. He further elaborated:

For *jen* as constituting the Way (Tao) consists of the fact that the mind of Heaven and Earth to produce things is present in everything. Before feelings are aroused, this substance is already existent in its completeness. After feelings are aroused, its function is infinite. If we can truly practice love and preserve it, then we have in it the spring of all virtues and the root of all good deeds. This is why in the teachings of the Confucian school, the student is always urged to exert anxious and unceasing efforts in the pursuit of *jen*.[3]

Such thought was thoroughly consistent with his understanding of *chung ho*. What intrigues us is that there was a set of questions and answers on *jen* and love included in this essay.

Someone said: According to our explanation, is it not wrong for Master Ch'eng to say that love is feeling while *jen* is nature and that love should not be regarded as *jen?*

Answer: Not so. What Master Ch'eng criticized was the application of the term to the expression of love. What I maintain is that the term should be applied to the principle of love. For although the spheres of man's nature and feelings are different, their mutual penetration is like the blood system in which each part has its own relationship. When have they become sharply separated and been made to have nothing to do with each other? I was just now worrying about students' reciting Master Ch'eng's words without inquiring into their meaning, and thereby coming to talk about *jen* as clearly apart from love. I have therefore purposely talked about this to reveal the hidden meaning of Master Ch'eng's words, and you regard my ideas as different from his. Are you not mistaken?[4]

In Chu Hsi's answer, *jen* was clearly understood to be the principle of love, which is itself not a principle but a feeling. The relation between the two is that they are not to be mixed up with each other and at the same time are not separable from each other. It was in this way that Chu Hsi defined *jen* as "the character of the mind and the principle of love,'' a formula he was happy with throughout his life.

Now we have three important ingredients: mind, nature, and feelings. Chu Hsi summed up his views in the following statement:

> Some time ago I read statements by Wu-feng (Hu Hung) in which he spoke of the mind only in contrast to nature, leaving the feelings unaccounted for. Later when I read Heng-chü's (Chang Tsai's) doctrine that ''the mind commands [unites] man's nature and feelings,'' I realized that it was a great contribution. Only then did I find a satisfactory account of the feelings. His doctrine agrees with that of Mencius. In the words of Mencius, ''the feeling of commiseration is the beginning of humanity.'' Now humanity is nature, and commiseration is feeling. In this, the mind can be seen through the feelings. He further said, ''Humanity, righteousness, propriety, and wisdom are rooted in the mind.'' In this, the mind is seen through nature. For the mind embraces both nature and the feelings. Nature is substance and feelings are function.[5]

What is interesting here is that Mencius himself never made a sharp distinction between *hsin* (mind-heart) and *ch'ing* (feelings), and the term *ch'ing* used by Mencius means only *ch'ing-shih* (as is the case), which has nothing to do with feelings,[6] even though commiseration can be understood as a feeling through interpretation. Likewise, mind and nature were not sharply differentiated in Mencius's thought; the essential goodness of nature is seen through the essential goodness of mind-heart. For Chu Hsi, however, only the transcendent nature (principle) is good; the empirical mind can be either good by following principles or evil by acting against the principles.[7] The tripartite division of mind, nature, and feelings was actually something new and quite original developed by Chu Hsi. In fact, he further developed a comprehensive metaphysics of *li* (principle) and *ch'i* (material force) that he heavily relied upon to give an exact analysis of the ontological status of mind, nature, and feelings.

In Chu Hsi's philosophy, principle is understood to be ''incorporeal, one, eternal and unchanging, uniform, constituting the essence of things, always good, but it does not contain a dichotomy of good and evil, does not create things.''[8] In contrast, material force is understood to be ''physical, many, transitory and changeable, unequal in things, constituting their physical substance, involving both good and evil (depending on whether its endowment in things is balanced or partial), and is the agent of creation.''[9] The relation between the two is that they are not separable from each other and yet they must not be mixed up with each other. Wherever there are things, there must be principles of these things. In other words, without the principles, it is impossible to conceive even the existence of things. And yet principles are devoid of matter; it is material force that enables principles to become actualized in the world. Although principles are many, they are but manifestations of one single principle, namely, the Great Ultimate. It is the interplay of principle and material force that produces the world order.

> Throughout the universe there are both principle and material force. Principle refers to the Way, which exists before physical form [and is without it] and is the root from which all things are produced. Material force refers to material objects, which exists after physical form [and is with it]; it is the instrument by which things are produced. Therefore in the production of man and things, they must be endowed with principle before they have their nature, and they must be endowed with material force before they have physical form.[10]

In a sense, principle is without any doubt ontologically prior. And it is only because this principle is a principle of creativity that things in the world, including material force, would come into being. But the world of principle or principles is a pure, clean, vast but vacuous world. It is the indispensable ground for the present world order to emerge. But left in itself, it cannot do anything. Principle must attach to material force in order to be realized in the world. It is in this sense that Chu Hsi feels that material force is strong, while principle is weak. Not only is material force needed for principle to be actualized; it also imposes its character on things in the process of creation and transformation. The origin of evils and limitations, for Chu Hsi, certainly lies in material force, not in principle itself. In the process of creation and transformation, myriad things are created and values are achieved, but principle in its purity cannot be fully realized in an actual world order—hence, evils and limitations become the results. And to conform or not to conform with principle has become an important problem for beings with a high level of consciousness. It is here that we must encounter the problem of the discipline of the mind.

With the background understanding of principle and material force, we are now ready to return to the discussion of the mind, the nature, and feelings. It is clear that by following this line of thought Chu Hsi could not have taken the mind to be principle that is static in nature, as the mind is obviously an active agent. In fact, Chu Hsi does maintain that the mind is made of the most refined and subtle kind of material force, and it has the ability to penetrate into principles. Chu Hsi says:

> The mind embraces all principles and all principles are complete in this single entity, the mind. If one is not able to preserve the mind, he will be unable to investigate principle to the utmost. If he is unable to investigate principle to the utmost, he will be unable to exert his mind to the utmost.[11]

The meanings implied in this paragraph are extremely complicated. If we fail to understand them in a proper way, we shall completely miss what Chu Hsi has intended to say. I would venture to analyze them in the following fashion:

1. By maintaining that all principles are complete in the mind, Chu Hsi does not mean that the mind is a creative ontological principle that is the source of all principles, a view upheld by his rival Lu Hsiang-shan. Otherwise, Chu Hsi would contradict his own contention that *li* and *ch'i* must not be mixed up even though they are not separable from each other.

2. But the mind and principle do have a very close relation between them, even though it falls short of identity. Chu Hsi maintains that the mind embraces all principles. He says, "Without the mind, principle would have nothing in which to inhere."[12] Thus, *hsin* and *li* are two, but the relation between them is that of inherence. It is in this sense that from the very start they pervade each other.

3. The essence of the mind is that it can know principles and it can be the master of itself, but in actuality, it is often obstructed by selfish material desires endowed by material force. Therefore, efforts must be made to preserve the mind. The mind is where the principle of consciousness comes into union with material force so as to make consciousness possible. As consciousness is always consciousness of something, the way to preserve the mind is not just to contemplate on the mind alone but to investigate principle. When principle is investigated to the utmost, the mind will also be exerted to the utmost.

4. It is here that we find the distinction between the so-called moral mind and the human mind. Moral mind is that which thoroughly conforms to principle, while human mind is that which mixes with physical endowment and human desires. The moral mind is originally good, while the human mind is precarious and liable to make mistakes. In fact, the whole purpose of man's moral cultivation lies exactly in how to transform the human mind into the originally good moral mind.

Finally, does the universe have a mind? Chu Hsi, typical of the Neo-Confucian tradition, has provided us with a highly dialectical answer, as is illustrated by the following quotation:

> Heaven and Earth have no other business except to have the mind to produce things. The material force of one origin . . . revolves and circulates without a moment of rest, doing nothing except creating the myriad things.

> *Question*: Master Ch'eng I said, "Heaven and Earth create and transform without having any mind of their own. The sage has a mind of his own but does not take any [unnatural] action."

> *Answer*: This shows where Heaven and Earth have no mind of their own. It is like this: The four seasons run their course and the various things flourish. When do Heaven and Earth entertain any mind of their own? As to the sage, he only follows principle. What action does he need to take? This is the reason why Ming-tao (Ch'eng Hao) said, "The constant principle of Heaven and Earth is that their mind is in all things and yet they have no mind of their own. The constant principle

of the sage is that his feelings are in accord with all creation, and yet he has no feelings of his own.'' This is extremely well said.

Question: Does having their mind in all things not mean to pervade all things with their mind without any selfishness?

Answer: Heaven and Earth reach all things with this mind. When man receives it, it then becomes the human mind. When things receive it, it becomes the mind of things (in general). And when grass, trees, birds, animals receive it, it becomes the mind of grass, trees, birds, and animals (in particular). All of these are simply the one mind of Heaven and Earth. Thus we must understand in what sense Heaven and Earth have mind and in what sense they have no mind. We cannot be inflexible.[13]

Thus, the human mind has its origin and its model in the mind of Heaven and Earth, which is a mind that has no mind of its own. And only when the human mind completely overcomes its selfishness does it become united with the mind of Heaven; then mind and principles are coalesced like water and milk mixed together.

As feelings could run wild and become rampant, the mind has to govern them according to principles inherent in nature. Again, following the guidance of Ch'eng I, Chu Hsi explicitly stated that nature is principle and further developed his ideas in the following way: "The nature is the same as principle. In relation to the mind, it is called the nature. In relation to events, it is called principle."[14] Such being the case, nature and principle are actually two sides of the same coin—principles inherent in a person constitute the nature of the person. Other quotations may tell us more about the relation between the two. "The principle of life is called the nature."[15] "The nature consists of innumerable principles created by Heaven."[16] "The nature consists of concrete principle, complete with humanity, righteousness, propriety, and wisdom."[17] His ideas were succinctly expressed in the following conversation with his student Ch'en Ch'un (1153–1217):

The teacher asked how the nature is concrete embodiment of the Way. Ch'un replied: The Way is principle inherent in the nature. The teacher said: The term Way is used with reference to a universal order, whereas the term nature is used with reference to an individual self. How do we know that the Way operates in the world? Simply by putting it into operation in one's own experience. Wherever nature is, there is the Way. The Way is the principle inherent in things, whereas nature is the principle inherent in the self. But the principle in all things is also in the principle inherent in the self. One's nature is the framework of the Way.[18]

Once nature is understood as principle, we may also gain better insight into the relation between nature and mind. Chu Hsi said, "Nature consists of principles embraced in the mind, and the mind is where these principles are united.''[19] He further gave a vivid metaphor to illustrate the relation between the two, as he said, "Nature is principle. The mind is its embracement and reservoir, and issues it forth into operation.''[20] Chu Hsi particularly appreciated one of the sayings by Shao Yung and interpreted it in such a way to illustrate his own point of view:

Shao Yao-fu (Shao Yung, 1011–1077) said that "nature is the concrete embodiment of the Way and the mind is the enclosure of the nature." This theory is very good. For the Way itself has no physical form or body; it finds it only in man's nature. But if there were no mind, where could nature be? There must be mind before nature can be gotten hold of and put forth into operation, for the principles contained in man's nature are humanity, righteousness, propriety, and wisdom, and these are concrete principles. We Confucians regard nature as real, whereas Buddhists regard it as unreal. However, it is incorrect to equate mind with nature.[21]

For Chu Hsi, the relation between nature and mind is exactly parallel to that between principle and material force; they are not to be mixed up with each other, and yet they are not to be separated from each other. He gave us an explanation of the situation in the following manner:

The nature is comparable to the Great Ultimate, and the mind to yin and yang. The Great Ultimate exists only in the yin and yang, and cannot be separated from them. In the final analysis, however, the Great Ultimate is the Great Ultimate and yin and yang are yin and yang. So it is with nature and mind. They are one and yet two, two and yet one, so to speak.[22]

These words appear to be vague and mysterious, but if you understand Chu Hsi's way of thinking, they are anything but vague and mysterious. The Great Ultimate is principle, and yin and yang are material forces; they are not to be equated with each other. But you cannot find principle without material force, and material force without principle; hence, they are inseparable from each other. The same applies to the relation between nature and mind. They are one, because when you find one of them, you also find the other; yet one pertains to principle, and the other pertains to material force; hence, they must also be said to be two. While they should never be equated with each other and must be regarded as two from an ontological point of view, in actuality they always work together and can never be separated from each other from a functional point of view; in this sense, then, they may also be said to be one. Other seemingly enigmatic statements can be understood as well. For example, Chu Hsi said:

Although nature is a vacuity, it consists of concrete principles. Although the mind is a distinct entity, it is vacuous, and therefore embraces all principles. This truth will be apprehended only when people examine it for themselves.[23]

For Chu Hsi, nature is a vacuity because it is not made of material force, but it should never be understood as *shunya* in the Buddhist sense, as it consists of concrete principles that are real even though they are not actually existent. The mind is also vacuous, but it cannot be vacuous in the same sense that nature is a vacuity. Only when the mind is rid of selfish desires will it become vacuous and will it be able to correlate with principles. It is like when a mirror is rid of the dust covering its face and becomes clear—the true state of things will find their reflections in the mirror. Furthermore, when the mind has been able to embrace principles, then it can function as a master. As Chu Hsi said:

> The mind means master. It is master whether in the state of activity or in the state of tranquillity. It is not true that in the state of tranquillity there is no need of a master and there is a master only when the state becomes one of activity. By master is meant an all-pervading control and command existing in the mind by itself. The mind unites and apprehends nature and feelings, but it is not united with them as a vague entity without any distinction.[24]

Chu Hsi summarized his views as follows:

> Nature is the state before activity begins, the feelings are the state when activity has started, and the mind includes both of these states. For nature is the mind before it is aroused, while feelings are the mind after it is aroused, as is expressed in [Chang Tsai's] saying, "The mind commands man's nature and feelings." Desire emanates from feelings. The mind is comparable to water, nature is comparable to the tranquillity of still water, feeling is comparable to the flow of water, and desire is comparable to its waves. Just as there are good and bad waves, so there are good desires, such as "I want humanity," and bad desires which rush out like wild and violent waves. When bad desires are substantial, they will destroy the Principle of Heaven, as water bursts a dam and damages everything. When Mencius said that "feelings enable people to do good," he meant that the correct feelings flowing from our nature are originally all good.[25]

It is clear by now that Chu Hsi started with an existential concern and ended up with a comprehensive metaphysics of principle and material force. Heaven is the creative source of all things. In the evolutionary process there emerges the human species. The human mind has the ability to comprehend the heavenly mind because it correlates with the same principle or principles inherent in it. There are disruptions in the great nature as there are disruptions in the human world. Evils in the world are a matter of fact due to malfunctioning of material force, as principle or principles are always good. The crux of the matter lies in whether material force can be induced to work according to principles. On the human level, it is the decision and understanding of the conscious human mind that could make a whole world of difference. As nature is principle, so Chu Hsi could say with Mencius that nature is good. But Mencius did not have a comprehensive metaphysics of principle and material force to back his theory of human nature; he did not have to face the further complications that Chu Hsi had to face in the formulation of his theory of human nature.

Chu Hsi followed the lead of Chang Tsai and Ch'eng I, and he believed by endorsing the distinction between moral nature and physical nature that problems concerning nature could be solved without the need for further debates. He elaborated on his own ideas in a discussion on the problem with his disciples:

Question: With whom originated the theory regarding the material force?

Answer: It began with Chang (Tsai) and the Ch'eng (brothers). I regard them as having enormously helped the School of the Sages, and as having done great service to the scholars who have come after. A reading of them fills one with a strong realization that, before their time, no one had touched on this point. Han Yü, for example, in his *On the Origin of the Nature*, propounded the theory of three grades (of the nature). Yet though what he said is true, he failed to state clearly that what he was speaking about is only the nature as found in the material force. For how, in the nature (as originally constituted) could there be these ''three grades''?

When Mencius says that the nature is good, he speaks of it only with respect to its origin, and says nothing about it as found in the material force. Thus he, too, fails to make a clear distinction. Other philosophers have asserted that the nature is evil, or that in it both good and evil are intermingled. But if the doctrines of Chang and the Ch'engs had appeared earlier, there would have been no need for all this discussion and controversy, If, therefore, the doctrines of Chang and the Ch'engs are admitted, those of the other philosophers go into discard. . . .

Moreover, if we are to say that humanity, righteousness, propriety, and wisdom alone constitute the nature, how is it that there are some people born unruly in the world? It is only owing to the physical endowment that this is so. If one does not take this physical element into account, the theory will not be well rounded, and therefore will be incomplete. But if, on the contrary, one takes only the physical endowment into account, some of which may be good and some bad, while disregarding the fact that in the first place there were only these Principles, then one will fall into obscurity.

Since the time when Confucius, Master Tseng, Tzu-ssu and Mencius understood these ideas, no one has propounded them (until Chang and the Ch'engs).[26]

For Chu Hsi the physical nature in itself is not evil; nevertheless, the origin of evils still lies in material force, as there is no room for evil in principles that are embodied in the original nature. For this reason, in an earlier view he did not even like the idea of the physical nature: if nature is truly principle, then we may only say that the good nature has fallen into material force and undesirable consequences are the result, there does not seem the need to talk about nature being physical. But in later years Chu Hsi tended to put more and more emphasis on material force, as principle and material force are inseparable; so he accepted the distinction and was convinced that the two-nature theory could help him to give answers to many puzzling problems.[27] His views were summarized in the following statement:

> Nature is principle only. However, without the material force and concrete stuff of the universe, principle would have nothing in which to inhere. When material force is received in its state of clearness, there will be no obscurity or obstruction and principle will express itself freely. If there is obscurity or obstruction, then in its operation of principle, the Principle of Heaven will dominate if the obstruction is small and human selfish desire will dominate if the obstruction is great. From this we know that the original nature is perfectly good. This is the nature described by Mencius as "good," by Master Chou Tun-i as "pure and perfectly good," and by Master Ch'eng I as "the fundamental character of our nature" and "the nature traced to the source of our being." However, it will be obstructed if physical nature contains impurity. Hence, [as Chang Tsai said] "In physical nature there is that which the superior man denies to be his original nature," and "If one learns to return to the original nature endowed by Heaven and Earth, then it will be preserved." In our discussion of nature, we must include physical nature before the discussion can be complete.[28]

Thus, for Chu Hsi, principle or nature is without any qualification good, but nature must be embodied in material force to make the principles inherent in it manifest. When material force is received in its state of clearness, there will be no obscurity or obstruction, and principle will express itself freely. But this is not always the case: If the obstruction is great, human selfish desire will dominate. Chu Hsi believed that everyone has the same original nature but receives different material force. Through proper discipline, everyone's original nature may shine through different material force, although the difficulties one encounters may be greater or smaller. Those who are able to make principles embodied in nature eminently manifest are sages and worthies; they are the models for common people to follow. In other words, the original nature endowed by Heaven is the same in everybody, but material force received is not the same, and the effort to recover one's original nature is not the same. It is here we find the difference between sages and worthies, on the one hand, and common people, on the other, even though in principle everyone can be sage, as each has received the same endowment of the original nature as the sages.

For Chu Hsi, between nature and mind there is a relation of correspondence. And as there are two natures in man, there are also two minds in correlation with them.

> For example, wherever there is the nature as endowed by Heaven, there is also the physical nature. If we regard the nature endowed by Heaven as rooted in the mind, then where will you place the physical nature? When, for example, it is said that "the human mind is precarious (liable to make mistakes), the moral mind is subtle (the mind that follows Tao)," the word "mind" is used in both cases. It is incorrect to say that the mind following Tao is mind whereas the mind of the natural man is not mind.[29]

In the above we have concentrated our discussion on Chu Hsi's theory of human nature. In fact, Chu Hsi had stretched his theory to apply to the nature of things in the whole world. For Chu Hsi, principle or nature is not different in man and other living species in the world. The only difference lies in that in other living species the material force received is turbid, so that they are not in a position to manifest principles in a conscious fashion. He said:

> Nature is like water. If it flows in a clean channel, it is clear, if it flows in a dirty channel, it becomes turbid. When physical nature that is clear and balanced is received, it will be preserved in its completeness. This is true of man. When physical nature that is turbid and unbalanced is received, it will be obscured. This is true of animals. Material force may be clear or turbid. That received by men is clear and that received by animals is turbid. Men mostly have clear material force; hence the difference between them and animals. However, there are some whose material force is turbid, and they are not far removed from animals.[30]

Chu Hsi further elaborated on his case as follows:

> Although nature is the same in all men, it is inevitable that [in most cases] the various elements in their material endowment are unbalanced. In some men the material force of Wood predominates. In such cases, the feeling of commiseration is generally uppermost, but the feeling of shame, of deference and compliance, and of right and wrong are impeded by the predominating force and do not emanate into action. In others, the material force of Metal predominates. In such cases, the feeling of shame is generally uppermost, but the other feelings are impeded and do not emanate into action. So with the material force of Water and Fire. It is only when

yin and yang are harmonized and the five moral natures (of humanity, righteousness, propriety, wisdom, and good faith) are all complete that a man has the qualities of the Mean and correctness and becomes a sage.[31]

Clearly, there was a strong empirical tendency in Chu Hsi's thought. Chu Hsi came up with an explanation as to why some men are sages, while others are not. The sage has manifested the right combination between nature and material force. But still the emphasis must be put on man's effort to develop what is endowed in man, instead of relegating everything to fate by putting all the blame on physical endowment. Chu Hsi answered a disciple's questioning in the following way:

On being asked about (Chang Tsai's) section on moral character failing to overcome material force, (Chu Hsi) said: Master Chang Tsai merely said that both man's nature and material force flow down from above. If my moral character is not adequate to overcome material force, then there is nothing to do but to submit to material force as endowed by Heaven. If my moral character is adequate to overcome material force, however, then what I receive from the endowment is all moral character. Therefore if I investigate principle to the utmost and fully develop my nature, then what I have received is wholly Heaven's moral character, and what Heaven has endowed in me is wholly Heaven's principle. The cases in which material force cannot be altered are life, death, longevity and brevity of life, for these, and poverty and wealth, and honor and humble station, all depend on material force. On the other hand, the practice of righteousness between the ruler and his ministers and the exercise of humanity between father and son, are what we call matters of fate. But there is also man's nature. The superior man does not say they are matters of fate. They must proceed from myself, not from fate.[32]

What Chu Hsi meant was that some people have extremely weak moral character; that must be due to material force. Certain matters such as longevity and brevity of life, and poverty and wealth, are not within our control, and they are also due to material force. But righteousness and humanity are our moral duties; most people can fulfill these duties if they try hard enough to overcome the difficulties involved, however formidable they are; so we cannot say they are matters of fate. When what is endowed in nature is fully manifested in material force, then one's whole being transforms into a moral character that is the embodiment of heavenly principle.

By adding material force in his conceptual framework, Chu Hsi was able to provide rational explanations for many seemingly puzzling phenomena. Under his guidance, a student of his worked out a very sophisticated theory concerning the nature of man and the nature of things. It is worthwhile to quote the lengthy discussion as it provides a rather comprehensive picture of Chu Hsi's understanding.

Chi [Ch'en Chi] submitted to the Teacher the following statement concerning a problem in which he was still in doubt: The nature of man and the nature of things are in some respects the same and in other respects different. Only after we know wherein they are similar and wherein they are different can we discuss nature. Now, as the Great Ultimate begins its activity, the two material forces (yin and yang, passive and active cosmic forces) assume physical form, and as they assume physical form, the myriad transformations of things are produced. Both man and things have their origin here. This is where they are similar. But the two material forces and the Five Agents, in their fusion and intermingling, and in their interaction and mutual influence, produce innumerable changes and inequalities. This is where they are different. They are similar in regard to principle, but different in respect to material force. There must be principle before there can be that which constitutes the nature of man and things. Consequently, what makes them similar cannot make them different. There must be material force before there can be that which constitutes their physical form. Consequently, what makes them different cannot make them similar. For this reason, in your *Ta-hsüeh huo-wen* (*Questions and Answers on the Great Learning*), you said, "From the point of view of principle, all things have one source, and of course man and things cannot be distinguished as higher and lower creatures. From the point of view of material force, that which receives it in its perfection and is unimpeded becomes man, while those that receive it partially and are obstructed become things. Because of this, they cannot be equal, but some are higher and others are lower." However, while in respect to material force they are unequal, they both possess it as the stuff of life, and while in respect of principle they are similar, in receiving it to constitute his nature, man alone differs from other things. This consciousness and movement proceed from material force while humanity, righteousness, propriety, and wisdom proceed from principle. Both man and things are capable of consciousness and movement, but though things possess humanity, righteousness, propriety, and wisdom, they cannot have them completely. Now Kao Tzu (c. 420–c. 350 B.C.) pointed to material force and neglected principle. He was confined to what is similar and ignorant of what is different, and was therefore attacked by Mencius. In your [*Meng Tzu*] *chi-chu* (Collected Commentaries on the *Book of Mencius*) you maintain that "in respect to material force, man and things do not seem to differ in consciousness and movement, but in respect to principle, the endowment of humanity, righteousness, propriety, and wisdom are necessarily imperfect in things." Here you say that men and things are similar in respect to material force but different in respect to principle, in order to show that man is higher and cannot be equaled by things. In the *Ta-hsüeh huo-wen*, you say that man and things are similar in respect to principle but different in respect to material force, in order to show that the Great Ultimate is not deficient in anything and cannot be interfered with by any individual. Looked at that way, there should not be any question. When someone was puzzled by the discrepancies in the *Ta-hsüeh huo-wen* and the *chi-chu*, I explained it in this way. Is this correct?

The teacher commented: On this subject you have discussed very clearly. It happened that last evening a friend talked about this matter and I briefly explained to him, but not as systematically as you have done in this statement.[33]

Chu Hsi's ideas were well thought out. There is only one metaphysical principle in the whole universe, and it is a creative principle. It is owing to this principle that material force may transform into a myriad things in the world. Before there are things, there must be this principle—hence, ontologically, principle is prior to material force, but in reality, principle and material force are inseparable. As all things come from the same origin, principle is the same, and they are made of different material forces, which must be understood as the source of differentiation. But if we look at the problem from a different perspective, as principle is one while manifestations are many, the manifestations of the one principle may be loosely said to be composed of many principles. For example, although humanity in the primary sense is the perfect virtue that is the root of all virtues, it may be manifested in humanity, righteousness, propriety, and wisdom; yet each may be said to have a different principle. Humanity in the secondary sense is only one of the manifestations of humanity in the primary sense. By the same token, since all things are made of material force, they are similar in this respect, while they are different because they have embodied different principles—hence, principles become the source of differentiation. A comprehensive picture of nature can only be brought out by combining these two perspectives.

Once Chu Hsi developed a comprehensive theory of nature, other related problems also popped up. He was engaged in a rather interesting debate on whether dry and withered things also have nature.[34] His views may be seen in the following discussion:

Question: How is it that dry and withered things also possess the nature?

Answer: Because from the very beginning they possess this nature. This is why we say so. There is not a single thing in the universe that is without nature.

Thereupon the Teacher walked up the step and said: The bricks of these steps have in them the principle of bricks. Then he sat down and said: A bamboo chair has in it the principle of the bamboo chair. It is correct to say that dry and withered things have no spirit of life, but it is incorrect to say that they have no principle of life. For example, rotten wood is useless except as fuel—there is in it no spirit of life. But when a particular wood is burned, a particular kind of force is produced, each different from the other. This is so because of the principle originally inherent in it.[35]

As Chu Hsi identified nature with principle, he had to say that dry and withered things also possess nature. From his viewpoint, not only is the Great Ultimate in everything, but each and everything has a specific principle embodied in it. Chu Hsi also made some very interesting remarks on the problem of consciousness:

Question: Man and birds and animals all have consciousness, although with varying degrees of penetration or impediment. Do plants also have consciousness?

Answer: Yes, they also have. Take a pot of flowers, for example. When watered, they flourish gloriously, but if broken off, they will wither and droop. Can they be said to be without consciousness? Chou Mou-shu (Chou Tun-i) did not cut the grass growing outside his window and said that he felt toward the grass as he felt toward himself. This shows that plants have consciousness [insofar as it has the spirit of life]. But the consciousness of animals is inferior to that of man, and that of plants is inferior to that of animals. Take also the example of the drug rhubarb, which, when taken, acts as a purgative, and the drug aconite, which, when taken, produces heat (vitality and strength). In these cases, the consciousness acts in one direction only.

When asked further whether decayed things also have consciousness, the Teacher said: They also have, as when burned into ashes, made into broth, and drunk, they will be caustic or bitter.[36]

Not only may these ideas be compared to Leibniz's; they are even closer to Whitehead's ideas. A whole cosmology may be constructed out of Chu Hsi's speculations.

In sum, Chu Hsi started with an existential concern and developed a comprehensive system of philosophy. He established the tripartite division of the mind, the nature, and feelings and analyzed them in terms of a metaphysics of principle and material force. The mind indeed owns an important place in Chu Hsi's philosophy, as it is the bridge between nature and feelings. When the mind is alienated from nature and principle, feelings and desires will overflow and become totally out of control; evils will ensue as the inevitable consequences. Thus, it is no exaggeration to say that for Chu Hsi moral discipline is none other than the discipline of the mind so that the mind will become one or united with principle and good feelings. A man will do good only when his mind follows the lead of principle; hence, seeking knowledge of principle becomes a most crucial issue in Chu Hsi's philosophy. It is clear that in this sense Chu Hsi's approach is intellectual in character, even though he believes that knowledge and action always go together and cannot be separated from each other.

> To investigate principle to the utmost means to seek to know the reason for which things and affairs are as they are and the reason according to which they should be, that is all. If we know why they are as they are, our will will not be perplexed, and if we know what they should be, our action will not be wrong. It does not mean to take the principle of something and put it in another.[37]

It appears that Chu Hsi does not see a sharp distinction between moral knowledge and natural knowledge, or knowledge of the "ought" and knowledge of the "is." On this point I shall elaborate later. Indeed, it seems that Chu Hsi does believe that there is a correlation between the universe at large and the human mind. And the way to accumulate knowledge and to discipline the mind is a long and gradual process. He says:

> The meaning of the expression "The perfection of knowledge depends on the investigation of things (ko-wu)" is this: If we wish to extend our knowledge to the utmost, we must investigate the principles of all things we come into contact with, for the intelligent mind of man is certainly formed to know, and there is not a single thing in which its principles do not inhere. It is only because all principles are not investigated that man's knowledge is incomplete. For this reason, the first step in the Great Learning is to instruct the learner, in regard to all things in the world, to proceed from what knowledge he has of their principles, and investigate further until he reaches the limit. After exerting himself in this way for a long time, he will one day achieve a wide and far-reaching penetration. Then the qualities of all things, whether internal or external, the refined or the coarse, will all be apprehended, and the mind, in its total substance and great functioning, will be perfectly intelligent. This is called the investigation of things. This is called the perfection of knowledge.[38]

There are a number of problems involved in this famous paragraph quoted from his *Commentaries on The Great Learning*. First, Chu Hsi seems to believe, as there are (material) things and human affairs in the world, they must have principles that can be examined one after another. And here, like elsewhere, Chu Hsi does not seem to see the need to make a distinction between seeking for natural knowledge and seeking for moral knowledge. Second, Chu Hsi seems to imply also that by thoroughgoing investigation of principles one can achieve what he calls "perfection of knowledge." Does that mean that the human mind can know the principles of all things and in that sense becomes omniscient?

Both of these interpretations of Chu Hsi's thought without qualifications are at best highly questionable, however. Let me quote another statement from Chu Hsi in order to show the complexity of the issue we are facing at the present moment:

> The mind is not like a side door which can be enlarged by force. We must eliminate the obstructions of selfish desires, and then it will be pure and clear and able to know all. When the principles of things and events are investigated to the utmost, penetration will come as a sudden release. Heng-ch'u (Chang Tsai) said, "Do not allow what is seen or heard to fetter the mind." "By enlarging one's mind one can enter into all things in the world." This means that if penetration is achieved through moral principles, there will be penetration like a sudden release. If we confine (the mind) to what is heard and what is seen, naturally our understanding will be narrow.[39]

In this statement, by following Chang Tsai, contrary to our expectation Chu Hsi does seem to have made a rather clear distinction between knowledge from the senses and knowledge from moral enlightenment. From "what is heard and what is seen" we may accumulate information about the actual world, but feelings and desires may also be aroused, and the mind may henceforth become a slave to them. In order for the mind to be the master, obstructions of selfish desires must be removed, and then penetration will be achieved through moral principles. Therefore, Chu Hsi does seem to admit that there are two different kinds of knowledge, the qualities of which are totally different from each other. By naively following what is heard and what is seen, not only will enlightenment not be achieved, but it will be blocked by our pursuit of external things. There must be a leap before we can experience the kind of sudden release of the mind where penetration is achieved through moral principles.

Does this view contradict the other view also seemed to be held by Chu Hsi that there is no need to make a distinction between natural knowledge and moral knowledge? Not if we see along with Chu Hsi from a dialectical point of view. In the first stages, there is indeed no need to make a distinction between the two, as there are principles in both material things and human affairs, and investigation of things and extension of knowledge can start from any point in one's life. But pursuit of external things alone may lead to undesirable consequences, as the mind may be fettered by what is heard and what is seen; so Chu Hsi also emphasizes self-cultivation as a measure of safeguard other than extension of knowledge. He wholeheartedly endorses Ch'eng I's dictum "Self-cultivation requires seriousness; the pursuit of learning depends on the extension of knowledge."[40] And seriousness for Chu Hsi "merely means the mind being its own master."[41] These two aspects are like the two wings of a bird. When both aspects are emphasized, they corroborate each other. "If one succeeds in preserving seriousness, his mind will be tranquil and the heavenly principle will be perfectly clear to him."[42] Finally, there is the breakthrough; then "the qualities of all things, whether internal or external, the refined or the coarse, will all be apprehended, and the mind, in its total substance and great functioning, will be perfectly intelligent.''[43] Paradoxically, from Chu Hsi's point of view, only those who have gone through strict moral discipline can achieve a systematic knowledge of nature, as only their minds are pure and clear and can penetrate into the profound mystery of nature. Moral knowledge and discipline certainly take the leading role in Chu Hsi's philosophy, but in the final stages, both moral knowledge and natural knowledge are achieved at the same stroke. Hence, moral knowledge and natural knowledge are not separable from each other, and they must not be mixed up. The case is parallel to the relation between principle and material force.

When perfection of knowledge is achieved, does Chu Hsi mean that the mind actually possesses empirical knowledge of all things? This is an absurd position, as Chu Hsi freely admits that there are things even the sage does not know. Hence, what Chu Hsi means is that when the mind is pure and clear and without the obstructions of selfish desires, it cannot fail to grasp the principles of things and respond freely to things as concrete situations call for; and as the human mind is united with the mind of Heaven, it does not exclude anything from its scope and is in that sense all-inclusive. Moreover, since the principles are none other than manifestations of one single principle, the realization of the substance and function of the principle will enable the mind to unfold the rich content of the principle without any hindrances. Chu Hsi said:

> Fundamentally there is only one Great Ultimate, yet each of the myriad things has been endowed with it and each in itself possesses the Great Ultimate in its entirety. This is similar to the fact that there is only one moon in the sky but when its light is scattered upon rivers and lakes, it can be seen everywhere. It cannot be said that the moon has been split.[44]

Perfection of knowledge means only that each in his own way can manifest the Great Ultimate fully without any obstuctions; it by no means implies that an individual mind can exhaust all the manifestations of the Great Ultimate without any residue. Therefore, Chu Hsi's "perfection of knowledge" should never be understood as omniscience enjoyed by God in the Christian sense.

Thus, Chu Hsi's view is definitely not as absurd as it first appears to be, but his position is also not without its difficulties. If the accumulation of natural knowledge does not automatically lead to the establishment of moral knowledge, and if indeed these two kinds of knowledge pertain to two different orders, then Lu-Wang's criticisms of Chu Hsi are not without reason, as they maintain that Chu Hsi's gradual approach is devious and completely misses the distinct nature of moral knowledge, because Chu Hsi has failed to distinguish it adequately from natural knowledge of external things. Such controversies would also affect the problem of orthodoxy, which we will consider in the next chapter.

It is extremely difficult to attempt a reconstruction of Chu Hsi's thought. First, Chu Hsi's thought has gone through several stages, and his earlier thought may not agree with his later and more mature thought; second, the scope of his thought covers a wide range, so his comments on one subject may be scattered throughout his writing; third, his thought is highly dialectical in nature, his answers to different disciples on different occasions may vary from time to time, and they may even appear contradictory to one another, even if in fact they are not and help to shed light on the many facets of a problem; fourth, and worst of all, many of Chu Hsi's important writings appear in the form of commentaries; his thought is built upon his interpretations of the Classics, but a great many times, he is only making use of the traditional texts and terminologies to express his own thought even when he sincerely believes that he is following traditional thought. In sum, it is by no means easy to work out a coherent picture of his thought.

In this chapter, I have tried to provide a coherent account of what I believe to be his mature thought by working out the implications of a metaphysics of principle and material force and his understanding of the tripartite division of the mind, nature, and feelings.

NOTES

1. Chan, *Source Book*, p. 559.
2. Ibid., pp. 593–594.
3. Ibid., p. 594.
4. Ibid., p. 595.
5. Ibid., p. 631, with slight modification.
6. Mou, *Hsin-t'i*, 3: 417–418.
7. Liu, *Chu-tzu*, pp. 239–240.
8. Chan, *Source Book*, p. 590.
9. Ibid.
10. Ibid., p. 636.
11. Ibid., p. 606.
12. Ibid., p. 628.
13. Ibid., pp. 642–643.
14. Ibid., p. 614.
15. Ibid.
16. Ibid.
17. Ibid.
18. Ibid., p. 616.
19. Ibid., p. 631.
20. Ibid.
21. Ibid., pp. 615–616.
22. Ibid., p. 630.
23. Ibid.
24. Ibid., p. 631.

25. Ibid.
26. Fung, *History*, 2: 554–555, with slight modification.
27. Liu, *Chu-tzu*, pp. 198–199.
28. Chan, *Source Book*, pp. 623–624.
29. Ibid., p. 616, with slight modification.
30. Ibid., p. 625.
31. Ibid.
32. Ibid., pp. 612–613.
33. Ibid., pp. 621–622.
34. Cf. Liu, *Chu-tzu*, pp. 212–216.
35. Chan, *Source Book*, p. 623, with slight modification.
36. Ibid.
37. Ibid., p. 611.
38. Ibid., p. 89, with slight modification.
39. Ibid., p. 630.
40. Ibid., p. 601.
41. Ibid., p. 606.
42. Ibid., with slight modification.
43. Ibid., p. 89; see n. 38.
44. Ibid., p. 638.

10

The Problem of Orthodoxy in Neo-Confucian Philosophy

It is a well-known fact that Chu Hsi was the person mainly responsible for the establishment of the orthodox line of transmission of the Way, the so-called *Tao-tung*, in the Confucian tradition. Wing-tsit Chan has reported that "the line, with minor variations, is this: Fu-hsi . . . Shen-nung . . . the Yellow Emperor . . . Yao . . . Shun . . . Yü . . . T'ang . . . Wen . . . Wu . . . Duke of Chou . . . Confucius . . . Tseng Tzu . . . Tzu-ssu . . . Mencius . . . Chou . . . Ch'engs . . . Chu Hsi."[1] In a very influential essay, *Chung-yung chang-chu hsü* (Preface to the *Commentary on the Doctrine of the Mean*), Chu Hsi said:

> The orthodox line of transmission of the Way had a long history. It was reported in the Classics: Yao taught Shun that you must hold fast to the Mean, and Shun taught Yü that the human mind is precarious, and the moral mind is subtle; have absolute refinement and singleness of mind, hold fast to the Mean. . . . From then on, such insights were passed on from one sage to another. . . . Even though our Master Confucius [551–479 B.C.] did not have the position [of a king], yet he had succeeded the sages in the past, and opened up new courses for students in the future; his achievement was greater even than that of Yao or Shun. But in his time there were only Yen Yüan [521–490 B.C.?] and Tseng Shen [505–436 B.C.?] who had learned about the Way and transmitted the line. Then in the second generation of Master Tseng's disciples there was Confucius' grandson Tzu-ssu [492–421 B.C.?]. . . . Still another two generations, there was Mencius. . . . After Mencius (372–289 B.C.?) died, the line of transmission was broken. . . . It was not until the Ch'eng brothers [Ch'eng Hao,

1032–1088, and Ch'eng I, 1033–1107], who studied and regained the insight, that the line of transmission which was discontinued for a thousand years was revived.[2]

Professor Chan has noted that although the idea of *Tao-tung* may be traced back to Mencius, Han Yü (768–824), Li Ao (fl. 798), and then Ch'eng I, Chu Hsi was the first Neo-Confucian philosopher to use the term *Tao-tung*,[3] and this idea was taken seriously by his disciples. Chan said:

> According to Chu Hsi's pupil Huang Kan [1152–1221], ''the transmission of the correct orthodox tradition of the Way required the proper men. From the Chou dynasty [1111–249 B.C.] on, there have been only several people capable of inheriting the correct tradition and transmitting the Way, and only one or two could enable the Way to become prominent. After Confucius, Tseng Tzu and Tzu-ssu perpetuated it in its subtlety, but it was not prominent until Mencius. After Mencius, Chou Tun-i [1037–1073], the two Ch'engs, and Chang Tsai [1020–1077] continued the interrupted tradition, but only with our Master did it become prominent.'' This view was accepted in the *History of Sung* and by practically all Neo-Confucianists.[4]

Professor Chan further pointed out that Chu Hsi excluded the Han (206 B.C.–A.D. 220) and T'ang (618–907) Confucianists including Han Yü, Li Ao, and also Shao Yung (1011–1077), Ssu-ma Kuang (1019–1086), and others of the Sung dynasty (910–1279) from the line of transmission for philosophical reasons.[5] His points are very well taken.

The questions I would like to raise are on a different level. We know that Chu Hsi taught something quite different from Confucius, from Mencius, and even from Ch'eng I, his own mentor to whom he was greatly indebted. His contemporary and rival Lu Hsiang-shan (Lu Chiu-yüan, 1137–1193) even charged that he had smuggled certain Taoist and Buddhist ideas into his philosophy.[6] My question is, then, Are there any real philosophical grounds for him to claim that his thoughts may be traced back to pre-Ch'in (221–206 B.C.) Confucian philosophers such as Confucius and Mencius? Or was he merely borrowing their names to promote ideas that were radically different from what they had taught? Especially in view of the fact that the statement Chu Hsi quoted in his essay—''The human mind is precarious, and the moral mind is subtle; have absolute refinement and singleness of mind, hold fast to the Mean''[7]—is now known to have been taken from a fabricated document, we must have serious doubts. Furthermore, if Chu Hsi is to be regarded as the representative of Sung Neo-Confucian philosophy, an even more serious question would arise: Is the so-called Neo-Confucian philosophy truly a Confucian philosophy, or is it rather a radically new philosophy based on Taoist and Buddhist ideas with only a Confucian cloak? Indeed, it is not uncommon for Confucian scholars themselves to attack their own colleagues as being Confucian on the surface but Buddhist in essence. All these issues need to be clarified; otherwise, there is no way for us to come up with a clear picture of Sung-Ming (1368–1644) Neo-Confucianism. Finally, when all the smoke is cleared, I would like to reevaluate Chu Hsi's position in that tradition, especially with regard to the orthodox line of transmission he himself helped to establish and since then has dominated Chinese thought for several hundred years.

In other words, the problems at issue are: Is there truly any continuity between Neo-Confucianism in the Sung and Ming dynasties and classical Confucianism in the late Chou period represented by Confucius and Mencius, whom the Neo-Confucianists claimed to have followed closely? And are there truly essential differences between Neo-Confucian philosophies, on the one hand, and Buddhist and Taoist philosophies, on the other? These are important questions that must be answered by any serious student of intellectual history of Sung and Ming thought. As Chu Hsi had always been in the thick of things, it would be most instructive to study his thought to find clues to answer these questions.

First, let us examine Chu Hsi's attitude toward Buddhism. As is well known, Chu Hsi was fascinated by Buddhism when he was young, but he renounced Buddhism in favor of Confucianism after he studied under Li T'ung (1093–1163).[8] From then on, he made strong criticisms against Buddhism, and yet even in his later years, he still held a high opinion of Buddhism. For example, he said:

> The Buddhists simply do not concern themselves with many things. Their only concern is the self. Although their teachings are incorrect, yet their intention is to take care of the problem of the self. That is why they attracted a number of talents, while we do not have followers. Today's Confucianists who can still hold fast to the Classics merely know how to read and discuss the texts, and when they study history, they know only how to calculate about what is profitable or harmful. But the Buddhists want really to take care of the self and to begin their discipline with the self. If the self is not being taken care of, what is the use to talk about others' strength or shortcomings?[9]

Chu also recognized that "the Buddhists spend a lot of efforts to discipline the mind."[10] What is especially interesting is that Chu Hsi never denied that Confucianists may learn from the Buddhists. For example, he said:

> At first Buddhism had only words; there was not the discipline of preservation and cultivation. It was not until the Sixth Patriarch [of Ch'an, Zen] in the T'ang dynasty that discipline of preservation and cultivation was being taught. At first, Confucian scholars also only had words; they

did not practice discipline of the self. It was not until Ch'eng I-ch'uan [Ch'eng I] that discipline of the self was being taught. Therefore it is said that Ch'eng I-ch'uan had stolen from Buddhism for his own use.[11]

It appears that vulgar scholars had as their only goal the seeking of profit. Buddhists, however, turned their attention away from thinking about how to make a profit or to advance their careers in the world. Therefore, Buddhism had a great deal of attraction for Neo-Confucian philosophers, as the primary goal of theirs was none other than to find a way of self-liberation. No wonder so many Neo-Confucian philosophers drifted along the paths of Buddhism and Taoism for many years before they returned to the Classics and found that the Confucian way was self-sufficient. It is for this reason that we can easily find a number of similarities between Neo-Confucianism, on the one hand, and Buddhism and Taoism, on the other.

But once a Neo-Confucian philosopher declared that he had rediscovered the Confucian way, then more often than not, he would have some very strong words against Buddhism. Chu Hsi seems to have followed this pattern. Having been once attracted by Buddhism, he realized even more deeply the dangers of Buddhist teachings, as they appeared to be ''very close to the principles and yet they produced a good deal of confusion about learning of truths.''[12] When we examine the grounds for Chu Hsi's opposition to Buddhism, we have to conclude that there are indeed essential differences between Neo-Confucianism and Buddhism. Even though many of Chu Hsi's criticisms of Buddhism were unfair and not supported by good evidence, they were true reflections of Chu Hsi's feelings toward Buddhism.[13] We may say that Chu Hsi had only a rather superficial understanding of Buddhism and that he was merely instinctively reacting to something that posed a serious threat to the very things that he had tried hard to defend. If such is the case, then surely it is impossible to see Chu Hsi as a disguised Buddhist thinker with only a Confucian cloak. As he did not even know much about Buddhism, how could he be able to sell its messages under a different cover? What remains for us to do, then, is to locate the differences between these two different lines of thought.

Let us start with the most obvious. The Confucianists highly value the function of human institutions, while the Buddhists hold a negative, or at best a passive, attitude toward them. Chu Hsi said:

It is not necessary to examine the doctrines of Buddhism and Taoism deeply to understand them. The mere fact that they discard the Three Bonds [between ruler and minister, father and son, and husband and wife] and the Five Constant Virtues [righteousness on the part of the father, deep love on the part of the mother, friendliness on the part of the elder brother, respect on the part of the younger brother, and filial piety on the part of the son] is already a crime of the greatest magnitude. Nothing more need be said about the rest.[14]

And these differences are manifestations of profound ontological differences between the two schools. Both schools take problems of the mind and of human nature to be of crucial importance, and yet they have reached completely different conclusions.

> Ts'ao asked how to tell the difference between Confucianism and Buddhism. The teacher said: Just take the doctrine "What Heaven imparts to man is called human nature." The Buddhists simply do not understand this, and dogmatically say that nature is empty consciousness. What we Confucianists talk about are concrete principles, and from our point of view they are wrong. They say, "We will not be affected by a single speck of dust [such as distinction of right and wrong or subject and object] ... and will not discard a single element of existence (dharma) [such as the minister's loyalty to the ruler or the son's filial piety to the father]." If one is not affected by any speck of dust, how is it possible for him not to discard a single element of existence? When he arrives at what is called the realm of Emptiness, he does not find any solution. Take the human mind, for example. There is necessarily in it the Five Relations between the father and son, ruler and minister, old and young, husband and wife, and friends. When the Buddhists are thorough in their action, they will show no affection in these relationships, whereas when we Confucianists are thoroughgoing in our action, there is affection between father and son, righteousness between ruler and minister, order between old and young, attention to their separate functions between husband and wife, and faithfulness between friends. We Confucianists recognize only the moral principles of sincerity and genuineness. Sincerity is the essence of all good deeds.[15]

Regardless of whether Chu Hsi's interpretation of Buddhist teachings is correct or his criticisms sound, the difference between the two positions cannot be overlooked. Chu Hsi sees the contrast between these two positions as follows: "The Buddhists are characterized by vacuity, whereas we Confucianists are characterized by concreteness. The Buddhists are characterized by duality (of Absolute Emptiness and the illusory world), whereas we Confucianists are characterized by unity (one principle governing all). The Buddhists consider facts and principles as unimportant and pay no attention to them."[16] Even though the Buddhists may evaluate the differences between the two positions differently, they must also recognize that there are essential differences between the two approaches. While the ultimate commitment for the Confucianists is *jen* (humanity),[17] the Buddhists' ultimate commitment is *k'ung* (*shunya* or emptiness). While the principle the Confucianists realize is *hsing-li* (principle inherent in human nature), that understood by the Buddhists is *k'ung-li* (principle as emptiness). While the function of the mind for the Confucianists is to realize in itself the principles of what is ontologically real, that for the Buddhists is to provide the basis for an illusory phenomenal world through the transformation of the consciousnesses. While the primary goal of the Confucianists is realization to the fullest extent of the intrinsic value in life, that for the Buddhists is to transcend the bitter sea of life and death. In short, the basic orientations of the two approaches are different, and such differences are recognized by both sides. Surely the Confucianists may learn or even borrow something from the Buddhists, and the Buddhists have made adjustment to the Confucian traditions, but the guiding principles of the two schools are different. This fact should never be obscured by apparent similarities that can easily be found in these two schools.

Now, as we have established that Neo-Confucianism is not to be taken as a disguised form of Buddhism, we must go one step further to examine the claim that Neo-Confucianism is the true heir of the classical Confucianism of Confucius and Mencius, the origin of which may even be traced back to ancient sage-emperors. Our investigation shows that the historical grounds for Chu Hsi to make such a claim are extremely weak. Still lacking sufficient evidence to substantiate the claim of the historical existence of Hsia dynasty (2183–1752 B.C.?), scholars currently can only say that authentic history begins with the Shang dynasty (1751–1112 B.C.?); beyond this point is the age of legends, the authenticity of which cannot be taken for granted.

But Chu Hsi's line of transmission of the orthodoxy is based precisely on such legendary stories. Not only did Chu Hsi and other Neo-Confucian philosophers use apocryphal sources; they had a tendency to read their own thoughts into the Classics. For example, in *The Book of Odes* were the two lines "The Mandate of Heaven,/How beautiful unceasing!"[18] Chu Hsi remarked that the Mandate of Heaven means the "Way" or the moral order of Heaven; however, in early Chou (1111–249 B.C.) the belief in an anthropomorphic God was still quite strong. Again, in *The Analects*, it was reported that "Confucius, standing by a stream, said, 'It passes on like this; never ceasing day or night!' "[19] What was Confucius thinking about? Was he thinking of the unceasing operation of the universe as suggested by Chu Hsi and Ch'eng I? It seems far-fetched to think that Confucius's remark was meant to be a characterization of the Way itself (*Tao-t'i*).[20] Therefore, from a strictly historical perspective we may easily dismiss the story about the line of transmission of the orthodoxy as a big chunk of nonsense. But for scholars of a more sophisticated mind, the investigation of the problem cannot stop here. In fact, the real search has not yet begun, because the problem at issue is not a historical one. The crux of the matter actually lies in one's existential decision over one's ultimate commitment or philosophical faith. And the ultimate concern of Sung learning, in contrast to Han learning, is beyond any doubt a philosophical one, not a historical one.

Paul Tillich's distinction between Christology and Jesusology is highly instructive for our purposes.[21] Christology concerns the religious faith in Christ, whose message is that the end of this life is the beginning of another life, much richer than this life, while Jesusology studies the historical Jesus by trying to collect more or less probable evidence concerning the man. Tillich says:

> The search for the historical Jesus was an attempt to discover a minimum of reliable facts about the man Jesus of Nazareth, in order to provide a safe foundation for the Christian faith. This attempt was a failure. Historical research provided probabilities about Jesus of a higher or lower degree. On the basis of these probabilities, it sketched "Lives of Jesus." But they were more like novels than biographies; they certainly could not provide a safe foundation for the Christian faith. Christianity is not based on the acceptance of a historical novel; it is based on the witness to the messianic character of Jesus by people who were not interested at all in a biography of the Messiah.[22]

By the same token, Confucianism is not based on the acceptance of a historical legend; it is based on the witness to the clear character of the sagely mind that found its manifestations among the ancient sage-emperors and that is inherent in everybody. Hence, accuracy of historical details is not that important for those who had faith in the manifestation of the sagely mind in the human world. Surely I do not mean that the problems of Confucianists are exactly the same as those of Christians, as the messages they try to convey are different. But without any doubt, their problems are parallel to one another. The Confucian message must be traced back to Confucius, as the Christian message must be traced back to Jesus as the Christ. It is through a study of the ideals Confucius embodied that we may hope to find the continuity between Neo-Confucianism and classical Confucianism.

When we go back to the time of Confucius, we find that Confucius himself already complained about the lack of evidence to substantiate his claim of knowledge of the spirit and practice of propriety (*li*) in the Hsia and Shang dynasties, but he never wavered in his faith in the function of propriety as a means to educate people.[23] This shows that even though Confucius showed a genuine love of history, what he cared for most were the ideals embodied in the historical legends as he saw them. The same attitude was adopted by Neo-Confucian philosophers. In establishing the line of transmission of the orthodoxy, Chu Hsi made it clear that he was following in Confucius's steps, and he explicitly stated that Confucius's achievements were even more important than those of the ancient sage-emperors, as the Confucian ideals were most clearly embodied in the person of Confucius. Now the problem lies in whether these Confucian ideals defended by Neo-Confucian scholars are truly the ideals represented by Confucius himself. The Neo-Confucian philosophers firmly believed that they could understand the sagely mind even though their time was behind the time of the Sage by more than a thousand years. Although there were a variety of opinions among Neo-Confucian philosophers, it is not difficult to find some common characteristics. For the sake of convenience, I shall mention only two. They all believed that man's moral nature is good[24] and that it is an endowment from Heaven; they also believed that Heaven is the ultimate creative principle, which works incessantly in the universe and can be grasped by the mind. Now, our burden is to show, if we can find it, the foundation of such thoughts in Confucius himself.

On the surface, it seems that we can only give a negative answer. It was reported in *The Analects* that Tzu-kung said, "We can hear our Master's [views] on culture and its manifestation, but we cannot hear his views on human nature and the Way of Heaven [because these subjects are beyond the comprehension of most people]."[25] But the main interests of the Neo-Confucian philosophers lay exactly in what Confucius talked about least before his students—human nature and the Way of Heaven. If we look into the matter more deeply, however, we shall find that there are indeed seeds in Confucius's thought that may be interpreted in such a way that they are thoroughly consistent with the views of Neo-Confucian philosophers. For example, it was reported in *The Analects*: "Confucius said, 'Shen, there is one thread that runs through my doctrines.' Tseng Tzu said, 'Yes.' After Confucius had left, the disciples asked him, 'What did he mean?' Tseng Tzu replied, 'The Way of our Master is none other than conscientiousness (*chung*) and altruism (*shu*).' "[26] Wing-tsit Chan's comment is as follows: "All agree . . . on the meanings of *chung* and *shu*, which are best expressed by Chu Hsi, namely, *chung* means the full development of one's [originally good] mind and *shu* means the extension of that mind to others."[27] Although Confucius never specified the one thread that ran through his doctrines, it is not difficult to figure out what it is by looking for cross-references in *The Analects*. For example, he said, "A man of humanity [*jen*], wishing to establish his own character, also establishes the character of others, and wishing to be prominent himself, also helps others to be prominent."[28] Wing-tsit Chan pointed out that "Liu Pao-nan [1791–1855] is correct in equating *chung* with Confucius' saying, 'Establish one's own character,' and *shu* with 'Also establish the character of others.' "[29] If such interpretation is not incorrect, then *chung* and *shu* must be the two sides of the same coin, for they are manifestations of *jen*. And *jen* is without any doubt Confucius's ultimate concern. As he says, "If a man is not humane (*jen*), what has he to do with ceremonies (*li*)? If he is not humane, what has he to do with music?"[30] Ceremonies and music are the two most important means that Confucius relies on to educate people, and *jen* is clearly the spirit under the practice of ceremonies and music. Again, he says:

Wealth and honor are what every man desires. But if they have been obtained in violation of moral principles, they must not be kept. Poverty and humble station are what every man dislikes. But if they can be avoided only in violation of moral principles, they must not be avoided. If a superior man departs from humanity, how can he fulfil that name? A superior man never abandons humanity even for the lapse of a single meal. In

moments of haste, he acts according to it. In times of difficulty or confusion, he acts according to it.[31]

From such evidence we cannot but conclude that *jen* is Confucius's ultimate
commitment as well as that one thread that runs through all his doctrines.
Therefore, even though Confucius never quite said that human nature is good,
he does believe that there is great potentiality in man and that the primary goal
of a man is to develop the great potentiality within himself and to help others
to develop their potentiality. Confucius was the first Chinese philosopher to give
jen a new meaning and make it the primary virtue, the foundation of all other
virtues. The Neo-Confucian philosophers showed the same commitment to and
faith in *jen*. Here it is clear that they were indeed the followers of Confucius—
only they attempted to add new dimensions in the understanding of *jen* and tried
to describe *jen* in more precise terms.

Now we shall examine Confucius's attitude toward Heaven. It seems naive
for Neo-Confucian scholars to believe uncritically that the so-called "Ten
Wings" (*Commentaries*) of the *Book of Changes* were Confucius's own writings
and then consider all the views expressed therein to represent Confucius's own
position. It is better for us to stick to the most reliable source to study Confucius—*The Analects*. On the surface, it seems that Confucius still believed in the
traditional concept of Heaven as a personal God, as he said, "Heaven produced
the virtue that is in me; what can Huan T'ui do to me?"[32] And when his beloved
student Yen Yüan died, he complained bitterly: "Alas, Heaven is destroying
me! Heaven is destroying me!"[33] But we must become skeptical when we find
that he also said, "He who commits a sin against Heaven has no god to pray
to."[34] It was also reported that "Confucius never discussed strange phenomena,
physical exploits, disorder, or spiritual beings."[35] Heaven does not seem to
intervene in either human affairs or natural events. We find an extremely interesting conversation recorded in *The Analects*. "Confucius said, 'I do not wish
to say anything.' Tzu-kung said, 'If you do not say anything, what can we little
disciples ever learn to pass on to others?' Confucius said, 'Does Heaven (*T'ien*)
say anything? The four seasons run their course and all things are produced.
Does Heaven say anything?' "[36] It is clear that Confucius was taking Heaven
as his model, while Heaven seems to be the ultimate creative force working
incessantly but quietly in the universe. Heaven here shows an impersonal rather
than a personal character.

But it would go too far to interpret Confucius as taking a totally naturalistic
position in regard to understanding Heaven. He said, "The superior man stands
in awe of three things. He stands in awe of the Mandate of Heaven; he stands
in awe of great men; and he stands in awe of the words of the sages."[37] Again,
he described his own learning process throughout his life as follows: "At fifteen
my mind was set on learning. At thirty my character had been formed. At forty
I had no more perplexities. At fifty I knew the Mandate of Heaven (*T'ien-ming*).
At sixty I was at ease with whatever I heard. At seventy I could follow my

heart's desire without transgressing moral principles.''[38] Surely Confucius still regarded Heaven as a transcendent source. Confucius's originality lies in his belief that there is no need to depart from human ways in order to know the Mandate of Heaven. He put the emphasis on man himself, as he said, "It is man who can make the Way great, and not the Way that can make man great."[39] The following exchange was recorded in *The Analects*: "Chi-lu (Tzu-lu) asked about serving the spiritual beings. Confucius said, 'If we are not yet able to serve man, how can we serve spiritual beings?' 'I venture to ask about death.' Confucius said, 'If we do not yet know about life, how can we know about death?' "[40] Here we find a model for future generations of Confucian scholars to follow. Confucius taught a humanism without cutting off its ties with a transcendent creative source in Heaven. One reads messages from Heaven in order to find guidance for self-realization in life. Here again, Neo-Confucian philosophers followed the lead of the Master. They may be guilty of reading too many things into the texts of the Classics, but in spirit, they are surely the heirs of Confucius's teachings.

Contrary to current opinion, which holds that Confucian scholars followed traditions slavishly without showing creative sparks, great Confucian philosophers were never satisfied with what was handed down from the past. Each generation broke new ground and continually added new dimension to the tradition. For example, Mencius surely went beyond Confucius by stating explicitly that human nature is good. By *human nature* he meant the distinctly human nature that distinguishes man from other animals. He believed that everyone has the Four Beginnings of Humanity, Righteousness, Propriety, and Wisdom in his mind.[41] By fully developing his potentiality, man can then know Heaven. As Mencius says, "He who exerts his mind to the utmost knows his nature. He who knows his nature knows Heaven. To preserve one's mind and to nourish one's nature is the way to serve Heaven."[42] Mind (*hsin*), nature (*hsing*), Heaven (*T'ien*) now form an inseparable trio. *The Doctrine of the Mean* went even further by saying, "What Heaven imparts to man is called human nature. To follow our nature is called the Way. Cultivating the Way is called education."[43] The Mandate of Heaven now is completely internalized in human nature. There is the correlation between Heaven and man. "Sincerity is the Way of Heaven. To think how to be sincere is the way of man."[44] Man not only knows Heaven but acts after the model of Heaven. Thus,

[o]nly those who are absolutely sincere can fully develop their nature. If they can fully develop their nature, they can then fully develop the nature of others. If they can fully develop the nature of others, they can then fully develop the nature of things. If they can fully develop the nature of things, they can then assist in the transforming and nourishing process of Heaven and Earth. If they can assist in the transforming and nourishing process of Heaven and Earth, they can thus form a trinity with Heaven and Earth.[45]

The idea of Heaven as the ultimate creative ontological principle was further developed in the *Commentaries* of the *Book of Changes*. It is said that "the great characteristic of Heaven and Earth is creativity [*sheng*]."[46] Again, "The successive movement of yin and yang constitutes the Way (Tao). What issues from the Way is good, and that which realizes it is the individual nature."[47] From these sources we can trace the development of a creative metaphysics, which holds that through the realization of the self the creative message of Heaven can become manifest. But in the Han dynasty, scholars turned their attention to textual studies and institutional considerations. They were also interested in cosmological speculations that degenerated into astrological speculations or even superstitions. During the Wei (220–265) and Chin (265–420) dynasties, Neo-Taoism and then Buddhism became the main streams for the intellectuals. The innermost Confucian message was being forgotten. It was under such circumstances that we see the emergence of Neo-Confucianism in the Sung dynasty.

Because the Neo-Confucian movement arose as a Confucian response to Buddhism and Taoism, naturally the Neo-Confucian philosophers received certain stimuli from, and in some ways were profoundly influenced by, these two schools. But the messages they spread were different. The Neo-Confucianists believed that man is endowed with a good nature and that it is imparted from Heaven, which is none other than the ultimate creative principle that works incessantly in the universe. Such messages were indeed ones that we can find in the Classics; only the expressions of them were quite different. The Neo-Confucian philosophers were totally uninhibited in borrowing from Taoism and Buddhism, and they were vigorous in their drive to open up new vistas for Confucianism. This explains why Chou Tun-i borrowed the Diagram of the Great Ultimate from an unmistakable Taoist source and turned it to Confucian use.[48] The Ch'eng brothers might have borrowed the term *li* (principle) from the Hua-yen school of Buddhism,[49] but they gave a completely new meaning to it. What is most important for Neo-Confucian scholars is that the essential Confucian message must be fully realized in the self; textual studies or scholarly learning are of only secondary importance. For example, Lu Hsiang-shan said, "If in our study we know the fundamentals, then all the Six Classics are my footnotes."[50] The reason why Lu held such an attitude may be seen from the following quotation:

> The four directions plus upward and downward constitute the spatial continuum (*yü*). What has gone by in the past and what is to come in the future constitute the temporal continuum (*chou*). The universe (these continua) is my mind, and my mind is the universe. Sages appeared tens of thousands of generations ago. They shared this mind; they shared this principle. Sages will appear tens of thousands of generations to come. They will share this mind; they will share this principle. Over the four seas sages appear. They share this mind; they share this principle.[51]

Lu firmly believed that because we can find and grasp principles in our own mind, it was not that important for us to study the Classics. Surely Chu Hsi would not go as far as Lu. In fact, one of his criticisms against Lu was that Lu's attitude of completely neglecting Classical studies would have harmful consequences. But Chu Hsi's main concern was also "the study for one's self." Even though he spent a lot of time and energy writing commentaries for the Classics, it is by no means true to say that he held a slavish attitude toward the Classics. When he defended Chou Tun-i's essay "An Explanation of the Diagram of the Great Ultimate" against Lu's charges that the Diagram was taken from a Taoist source and did not have any foundation in the teachings of the sages, he said:

> When Fu Hsi invented the trigrams and King Wen developed the system, they never talked anything about the Great Ultimate (*T'ai-chi*) but Confucius talked about it. When Confucius gave interpretations to the *Book of Changes*, he never talked about the Ultimate of Nonbeing (*wu-chi*) but Master Chou talked about it. Is it not true that the ancient sages and the modern sages were following the same principles? If we can truly see the reality of the Great Ultimate, then we know that those who do not talk about it are not doing too little, while those who talk about it are not doing too much. Why should we have so many troubles concerning this issue?[52]

What is interesting here is that these words could have been said by Lu Hsiang-shan himself. True, Chu Hsi honored the Classics, but only because he believed that there were truths embodied in them. When he wrote the *Commentaries* for the Classics, he was trying to manifest the truths he saw as embodied in them. This was creative work, not just a meaningless paraphrasing of the texts themselves. But what are important are the messages carried by the texts. On this score Chu and Lu did not really differ much from each other. Even Lu never said that we need not study the Classics at all; he simply felt that the emphasis should not be laid on pedantic classical studies per se. But even Chu was merely using the Classics for pedagogical purposes, because he also firmly believed that the mind has the ability to get hold of principles. He was trying to relive the experiences of the sages through studying the Classics with a view to recovering the intended meanings in the texts. Although there are indeed significant differences between Chu and Lu, they agreed on interpreting the Classics in such a way that the Confucian message can be realized in one's life. On this score they were allies.

Now we can clearly define the relationship between classical Confucianism and Sung-Ming Neo-Confucianism. Neo-Confucian philosophers claimed that they were transmitting the Way of Confucius and Mencius, as Confucius claimed that he was transmitting the Way of sage-emperors in the past—Yao and Shun, King Wen and King Wu. The words may be different, but the spirit remains the same. In their studies of the Classics, Neo-Confucian scholars sometimes seemed to have done violence to the texts by giving new interpretations, new meanings not intended by the original authors, but they had reasons for so doing. They believed that in essence the sagely mind is not different from our minds and that the principles embodied in the words and deeds of sages in the past are not different from those to be realized in our own lives. And we do find that the Neo-Confucian understanding of men through *jen* and their understanding of *T'ien* (Heaven) have their seeds in the thought of Confucius as recorded in *The Analects*. True, they did break some new ground. For example, classical Confucianism never identified *jen* with *sheng-sheng* (creative creativity) as Neo-Confucian scholars did. But we find nothing in classical Confucianism that contradicts or precludes such development in Neo-Confucian thought. Therefore, we must agree with Neo-Confucian philosophers when they claim that there is continuity between classical Confucianism and Neo-Confucianism and that they teach something quite different from Buddhist and Taoist thoughts, as these two schools do not believe in the classical and Neo-Confucian views of Heaven as the ultimate creative ontological principle in the universe and man as being endowed with humanity in his mind and nature.

By using these two criteria, we can tell easily who are true Confucianists and who are not. A case in point would be Wang Yang-ming (1472–1529) in the Ming dynasty. Even though he said that "[i]n the original substance of the mind there is no distinction between good and evil,"[53] we cannot say that Wang was giving expression to a Buddhist view, as Wang clearly submitted to the Confucian views of Heaven and man. What he really meant was only that we cannot give adequate characterization of the Supreme Good, as it is beyond good and evil.[54] Once he wrote a famous poem:

> The soundless, oderless moment of solitary self-
>   knowledge
> Contains the ground of Heaven, Earth, and all beings.
> Foolish is he who leaves his inexhaustible treasure,
> With a bowl, moving from door to door, imitating the
>   beggar.[55]

We should never take Wang to be a Taoist or a Buddhist simply because he used such seemingly Taoist images as "soundless and odorless" and such Buddhist metaphors as "inexhaustible treasure"; the thrust of his thought is totally consistent with Mencius's thought that human nature is good, and he could have easily found his precedent in Confucius's teaching without words and the concluding remarks in *The Doctrine of the Mean*:

> *The Book of Odes* says, "I cherish your brilliant virtue, which makes no great display in sound or appearance." Confucius said, "In influencing people, the use of sound or appearance is of secondary importance." *The*

Book of Odes says, "His virtue is as light as hair." Still, a hair is comparable. "The operations of Heaven have neither sound nor smell."[56]

Of course, we can always argue that even *The Doctrine of the Mean* may have already been influenced by Taoist thought. But such arguments, even if they could be proved to be true, could only serve to confuse the issues. The crux of the matter lies in whether the document as a whole as transmitted to the posterity is essentially Confucian or Taoist in character. The fact is that no school of thought, unless it is dead, can afford to remain unchanged. In order to revitalize itself or to enlarge its perspective, it cannot but learn from competing movements with a view to adding new dimensions to its own tradition. Only if it has lost the essential character of its own school and adopted the basic outlook of another school may we conclude that a conversion has happened.

In fact, two schools of thought intertwining over a long time may share quite a few ideas that from an outside viewpoint may appear to teach the same thing. But if we probe somewhat deeper, we would find that they are actually spreading very different messages. For example, both the Taoists and the Confucianists taught *wu-wei* (taking no [artificial] action), but they each meant something quite different by the term. The Taoists saw nothing positive in human institutions, while the Confucianists believed that the system of rituals and music is so natural for man that it could function so smoothly that no other means would be needed for a sage-king to run state affairs. Let us look at the problem from still another angle. Professor Mou Tsung-san claims that all three major traditions in China—Confucianism, Taoism, and Buddhism—asserted the possibility of what he called "intellectual intuition."[57] It is quite possible that from an outsider's viewpoint these three traditions may be seen to have taught very similar ideas. But these similarities should not mislead us to conclude that the three traditions are really teaching exactly the same thing, or that there is no need to find essential differences among these traditions. My personal opinion is that we must see the development of ideas from a dynamic, historical point of view: Schools with vitality constantly enlarge themselves and absorb certain insights from rival schools, but this fact does not make the differences among the schools disappear.

In the above, I have shown that there is some justification for the Neo-Confucianists in Sung to claim that they inherited the line of transmission from the classical Confucianism of Confucius and Mencius. Naturally, I do not mean that there is not an alternative way to claim a different line of orthodoxy. In fact, after Confucius died, it is said that Confucianism was split into eight different branches, and in Hsün Tzu's (313–238 B.C.) days, he could have claimed the orthodoxy for himself against the rival school of Mencius; then in the early Ch'ing dynasty (1644–1912) people like Yen Yüan (1635–1704) claimed that the whole movement during the Sung and Ming dynasties went wide off the mark and gave a distorted picture of Confucian teachings. But if one were to go into the circle of faith of Sung-Ming Confucianism, one would see clearly that the program was definitely not just an arbitrary concoction without a rationale among its proponents.

When definite criteria have been established to distinguish Neo-Confucianism from Buddhism and Taoism, many controversies are seen to be unnecessary and avoidable. For example, during the famous debates between Chu Hsi and Lu Hsiang-shan, each side charged the other side with teaching Buddhist ideas.[58] These criticisms are unfounded. The differences are differences within the Neo-Confucian tradition, not those between Confucianism and Buddhism. Their charges against each other only showed their emotional dissatisfaction against a rival school within the same tradition, as they were really worried that their orthodoxy would be usurped by some impure doctrine mixed up with Buddhist and Taoist thoughts.

Our next problem is whether it was Chu Hsi or his rival Lu Hsiang-shan who really represented the orthodox teachings of Confucius and Mencius. On the surface, this was never a problem, as we have seen that as a matter of historical fact Chu Hsi almost single-handedly established the line of transmission of the orthodoxy that was unquestionably accepted by the posterity. Lu, on the other hand, was completely ignored by scholars until his thoughts were again recognized to some extent by Wang Yang-ming.[59] He never gained such a prominent position that he could be compared with Chu Hsi. But the problem was reopened by Professor Mou Tsung-san's monumental work on Neo-Confucian philosophy, *Hsin-t'i yü hsing-t'i*,[60] and we must reexamine the problem carefully before we can reach a conclusion.

Professor Mou pointed out that although Chu Hsi belonged in the general movement of Neo-Confucianism, what he succeeded and developed were Ch'eng I's ideas, which were quite different from what Mencius had taught. Ch'eng I maintained that "love is feeling whereas humanity is the nature."[61] Feeling (*ch'ing*) and nature (*hsing*) pertain to two different levels. Chu Hsi further developed Ch'eng I's ideas by identifying nature with principle (*li*) and feeling with material force (*ch'i*); the mind (*hsin*) for Chu Hsi is constituted of the most subtle kind of material force, and it has the ability to comprehend principles in things.[62] But when we go back to Mencius we find that Mencius never used the term *ch'ing* in the sense that Ch'eng I and Chu Hsi used it. *Ch'ing* for Mencius means only *ch'ing-shih* (what is the case). And Mencius himself never made the distinction between the feeling (*ch'ing*) of commiseration and the mind-heart of commiseration. What Mencius advocates is that if we can recover our lost mind, then our feelings of commiseration, righteousness, propriety, and wisdom will naturally develop into the virtues of *jen, i, li,* and *chih*. For Mencius, there is no distinction between the original mind and the essential nature of man. When we fail to follow the naturally good tendencies of our mind and nature because of bad influences from the environment, then evils will ensue. *Ch'i* for Mencius is "the strong, moving power."[63] According to him, "If nourished by uprightness and not injured, it will fill up all between heaven and earth."[64] From these statements, we may infer that Mencius did not seem to make a distinction between *ch'i* (material force) and *li* (principle); the material force that filled up heaven and earth is naturally embodied with principles until it is obstructed by adverse influences so that it will deviate from principles. Hence for Mencius, the mind, the nature, principle, and material force all go together when they can perform their proper function according to their essential character without obstructions. This philosophy was labeled by Professor Mou as teaching a straightforward system that implies a creative metaphysics that takes the ultimate ontological principle to be both active and existing.[65]

In contrast to this system, Chu Hsi sees *li* and *ch'i* as pertaining to two different levels. Principles, which belong in a metaphysical realm, are pure, clean, devoid of content, and vast in scope, while material force is that which makes things real and concrete. When this metaphysics is applied to the analysis of man, we get the tripartite structure of the mind, the nature, and feelings. Only the nature is principle; feelings are constituted of material force, but the mind is made of the most subtle kind of material force, and hence it has the ability to comprehend principles and is the key to bringing about the unity between the nature and feelings. The function of the mind is to appropriate principles and make them work in one's life. Therefore, Chu Hsi's philosophy presupposes a dualism that we cannot find in Mencius's thought. However, Chu Hsi did make it clear that even though *li* and *ch'i* must be kept distinct from each other, they cannot be separated from each other. It would be quite wrong to read a Platonic dualism into his thought. Still, there is no denial that his thought was quite different from Mencius's in spite of the fact that he wrote his commentary for *The Book of Mencius*. For Chu Hsi, it is futile for the mind to remain in itself; it must direct itself toward principles in order to find any guidance for behavior. Therefore, he condemned those who put their exclusive attention on the mind. And as he saw it, the Buddhists had made great contributions in controlling the mind. Hence, he identified all those who put emphasis on the mind with the Buddhists. This was why he thought Lu was spreading the message of Buddhist teachings. Thus, what Chu accomplished was a subject-object related system in which the vital force of the mind can relate itself to principles that only exist but do not act.[66]

It is obvious that Lu could not be taken as a Buddhist, as he firmly believed that there is intrinsic value in human life and that man is endowed with humanity in his mind-heart. Furthermore, it is simply not the case that Lu did not pay any attention to the concept of *li*, as he declared, "Principle is endowed in me by Heaven, not drilled into me from outside."[67] And he said:

> The mind is one and principle is one. Perfect truth is a unity; the essential principle is never a duality. The mind and principle can never be separated into two. That is why Confucius said, "There is one thread that runs through my doctrines,"[68] and Mencius said, "The Way is one and only one."[69] (Quoting Confucius), Mencius also said, "There are but two ways

to be pursued, that of humanity (*jen*) and that of inhumanity.''[70] To do in a certain way is humanity. Not to do in a certain way is the opposite of humanity. Humanity is the same as the mind and principle. ''Seek and you find it''[71] means to find this principle. ''Those who are the first to know'' know this principle, and ''those who are the first to understand'' understand this principle.[72] It is this principle that constitutes the love for parents, reverence for elders, and the sense of alarm and commiseration when one sees a child about to fall into a well. It is this principle that makes people ashamed of shameful things and hate what should be hated. It is this principle that enables people to know what is right to be right and what is wrong to be wrong. It is this principle that makes people deferential when deference is due and humble when humility is called for. Seriousness (*ching*) is this principle. Righteousness is also this principle. What is internal is this principle. What is external is also this principle. Therefore it is said, ''Straight, square, and great, (the superior man) works his operation, without repeated effort, (and is) in every respect advantageous.''[73] Mencius said, ''The ability possessed by men without their having acquired it by learning is innate ability, and the knowledge possessed by them without deliberation is innate knowledge.''[74] These are endowed in us by Heaven. ''We originally have them with us,'' and ''they are not drilled into us from outside.''[75] Therefore Mencius said, ''All things are already complete in oneself. There is no greater joy than to examine oneself and be sincere (or absolutely real).''[76,77]

Lu's ideas all came directly from Confucius and Mencius. How can we charge him with teaching Buddhist ideas? His views both of man and Heaven are totally consistent with the Confucian tradition as set down in *The Doctrine of the Mean* and the *Appended Remarks* to the *Book of Changes*. As he said, ''The Way fills the universe. It does not hide or escape from anything. With reference to Heaven, it is called yin and yang. With reference to Earth, it is called strength and weakness. With reference to man, it is called humanity and righteousness. Thus humanity and righteousness are the original mind of man.''[78]

Strangely enough, if we follow Chu Hsi and accept Mencius's thought as representing the orthodox line of Confucianism, then Lu stands much closer to Mencius than Chu Hsi. Lu believed that principles naturally flow out of the mind, and so he did not see the need to draw a sharp distinction between the mind and principle as Chu Hsi did. He said:

My learning is different from that of others in the fact that with me every word comes spontaneously. Although I have uttered tens of thousands of words, they all are expressions of what is within me, and nothing more has been added. Recently someone has commented of me that aside from [Mencius's] saying, ''First build up the nobler part of your nature,'' I had nothing clever. When I heard this, I said, ''Very true indeed.''[79]

Not only because many of Lu's quotations came directly from Mencius or because his spirit was very close to that of Mencius but also for important philosophical reasons, we must say that Lu's thought should be regarded as more representative of the orthodox Neo-Confucian position if we should accept the tenets of the school, as Chu Hsi's approach must presuppose what Lu Hsiang-shan taught, but not the other way around. Once Lu commented on his difference with Chu Hsi as follows:

> Chu Yüan-hui (Chu Hsi) once wrote to one of his students saying, "Lu Tzu-ching (Lu Hsiang-shan) taught people only the doctrine of 'honoring the moral nature.' Therefore those who have studied under him are mostly scholars who put their beliefs into practice. But he neglected to follow the path of study and inquiry. In my teaching is it not true that I have put somewhat more emphasis on 'following the path of study and inquiry?' As a consequence, my pupils often do not approach his in putting beliefs into practice.'' From this it is clear that Yüan-hui wanted to avoid two defects (failure to honor the moral nature and failure to practice) and combine the two merits (following the path of study and inquiry and practicing one's beliefs). I do not believe this to be possible. If one does not know how to honor his moral nature, how can he talk about following the path of study and inquiry?[80]

These criticisms would not be sound if Chu Hsi refused to accept the principle of "honoring the moral nature," but Chu Hsi in fact was pursuing the sagely ideal. For him, following the path of study and inquiry was only a means to approach the realization of such an ideal. In Chu Hsi's famous commentary on the fifth chapter of *The Great Learning*, he said:

> The above fifth chapter of commentary explains the meaning of the investigation of things and the extension of knowledge, which is now lost. I have ventured to take the view of Master Ch'eng I and supplement it as follows: The meaning of the expression "The perfection of knowledge depends on the investigation of things (*ko-wu*)" is this: If we wish to extend our knowledge to the utmost, we must investigate the principles of all things we come into contact with, for the intelligent mind of man is certainly formed to know, and there is not a single thing in which its principles do not inhere. It is only because all principles are not investigated that man's knowledge is incomplete. For this reason, the first step in the great education is to instruct the learner, in regard to all things in the world, to proceed from what knowledge he has of their principles, and investigate further until he reaches the limit. After exerting himself in this way for a long time, he will one day achieve a wide and far-reaching penetration. Then the qualities of all things, whether internal or external, the refined or the coarse, will all be apprehended, and the mind, in its

total substance and great functioning, will be perfectly intelligent. This is called the investigation of things. This is called the perfection of knowledge.[81]

It is a controversial matter whether anything has been lost from the text of *The Great Learning*, but it is clear that in the supplement Chu Hsi wrote he was expressing his own ideas based on the insight of Ch'eng I as he had understood it. It would be absurd to interpret Chu Hsi to mean that man can be omniscient after he has made a vigorous effort to investigate things and to extend knowledge. What Chu Hsi means is that one may realize the ontological principle that governs the operation of the universe within his own mind after a long search on the path of study and inquiry. But this can be achieved only by a leap of faith. By following an inductive approach we may build up certain empirical knowledge of the world or even formulate a unified theory of the physical universe, but these are not enough to establish a metaphysics of creativity.

By the same method we also may learn a great deal about actual moral practice in the society but not the realization of the moral principle within the self. Since Chang Tsai, Neo-Confucian philosophers had made a sharp distinction between informative knowledge and moral or ontological knowledge.[82] And the insight can be traced back to Mencius's distinction between the nobler and the smaller parts of man.[83] Only by the realization of the moral and creative nature within man can he truly grasp the profound message of the Way of Heaven. Lu Hsiang-shan's approach followed closely Mencius's approach both in form and in spirit, while Chu Hsi took a roundabout way. But if Chu Hsi did not have an intrinsic faith in the nobler part of man's nature, all the studies and inquiries in the world would not lead him to the kind of "wide and far-reaching penetration" that he praised in his remark.

It seems that Chu Hsi believes that one can learn about one's own mind only through its ability to reflect the principles in things, so he dismisses all those approaches that go directly to the mind as Ch'an (Zen) teachings. He does not seem to realize that his own approach would not work if it did not presuppose Lu's approach, which is essentially no different from Mencius's approach. Can Chu Hsi then dismiss Mencius's teachings as Ch'an teachings? It appears that Chu Hsi enjoys much more the softer light from the moon while refusing to acknowledge that the origin of such light is the sun itself. It is ironic that one who almost single-handedly established the orthodox line of transmission of the Way should teach only a feeble reflection of the Way, if we may be allowed to use the metaphor to characterize Chu Hsi's position within the Neo-Confucian movement.

To say, however, that Lu's position is closer to the orthodox line of transmission from Mencius does not entail the conclusion that there are not serious limitations and shortcomings in his thought. True, the realization of the moral nature is the primary concern for Neo-Confucian philosophers, but it is not their only concern. One must constantly enlarge his vision and sharpen his skills so that he can help the Way to prevail in the world, and he must also take good care of his physical nature. Mencius's righteousness does not exist only in a transcendent realm; it is realizable in this mundane world amidst the pursuit of profit.[84] Lu's merit lies in his firm grip of the essence, but his door and court are certainly too narrow. His relative neglect of the path of study and inquiry becomes his Achilles' heel. History showed that he was no competition for Chu Hsi, who accumulated so many riches in his formidable pursuit.

From an educational point of view, Chu Hsi's gradual approach also has its merit. One needs external help as well as hard work before he can even reach that point of enlightenment that was the only concern for Lu Hsiang-shan. And one must realize his moral nature amidst the entanglement of the physical nature. If one does not pay enough attention to his physical nature, then what he claims to be the manifestation of his moral nature may very well be only a reflection of his physical nature.

Although Chu Hsi's position deviated somewhat from the Mencian orthodoxy, he added valuable new dimensions to Confucianism. It was through his great scholarship, his indefatigable hard work, and his unquestionable integrity that Neo-Confucianism after his death was honored to be the orthodox line of Confucianism. The result was a most remarkable phenomenon in the development of Chinese intellectual history that Professor Mou Tsung-san characterizes as "the side branch [taking] the position of the orthodoxy."[85] Through a careful examination of the materials available and reflection on the problem of orthodoxy in Neo-Confucian philosophy, I cannot but agree with Professor Mou's observation. After all, Chu Hsi's philosophy has been honored as the unchallenged orthodoxy in Confucianism for more than 600 years since the early Yüan dynasty (1277–1368).

NOTES

1. Wing-tsit Chan, "Chu Hsi's Completion of Neo-Confucianism," in *Études Song-Sung Studies in Memoriam Étienne Balazs*, ed. Françoise Aubin, Ser. 2, no. 1 (Paris, 1973): 75. For a general review of the formation of the orthodox line of transmission, also see William Theodore de Bary, *Neo-Confucian Orthodoxy and the Learning of the Mind-and-Heart* (New York: Columbia University Press, 1981), pp. 2–13.

2. *Chu tzu wen-chi* (SPPY ed. entitled *Chu tzu ta-ch'üan* [Complete literary works of Master Chu]), 76:21–22b.

3. Chan, "Chu Hsi's Completion of Neo-Confucianism," p. 75.

4. Ibid.

5. Ibid., pp. 75–76.

6. "Letter to Chu Yüan-hui," *Hsiang-shan ch'üan-chi* (Complete works of Lu Hsiang-shan) (SPPY ed.), 2:5b–11a.

7. *The Book of History*, ch. 3, "Counsels of Great Yü."

8. Cf. Wang *Biography*, 1A:7–9, 11–13.

9. *Chu tzu yü-lei*, 8:10a, p. 225.

10. Ibid., 125:4b, p. 4792. The Sixth Patriarch of Ch'an (Zen) in China was Hui-neng (638–713). He was originally an illiterate fuel-wood peddler. The story of his achieving sudden enlightenment was told in *Liu-tsu t'an-ching* (The Platform Scripture of the Sixth Patriarch).

11. *Chu tzu yü-lei*, 126:29a, p. 4873.

12. "Preface to the *Chung-yung chang-chu* (Commentary to The Doctrine of the Mean)."

13. For example, Chu Hsi was certainly wrong when he charged that the Buddhists had plagiarized from the *Lieh Tzu* and the *Chuang Tzu*. See *Chu tzu yü-lei*, 126:3b, p. 4822.

14. Ibid., 126:7a, p. 4829; see Chan, *Source Book*, p. 646.

15. *Chu tzu yü-lei*, 126:8b–9a, pp. 4832–4833; see Chan, *Source Book*, pp. 647–648. The quotation about human nature is from *The Doctrine of the Mean*, ch. 1.

16. *Chu tzu yü-lei*, 126:7b, p. 4828; see Chan, *Source Book*, p. 648.

17. See Shu-hsien Liu, "The Religious Import of Confucian Philosophy: Its Traditional Outlook and Contemporary Significance," *Philosophy East and West* 21, no. 2 (April 1971): 157–175.

18. *The Book of Odes*, Ode no. 267, "The Mandate of Heaven"; see Chan, *Source Book*, p. 6.

19. *Analects*, 9:16; see Chan, *Source Book*, p. 36.

20. *Chu tzu yü-lei*, 36:21b, p. 1556.

21. Tillich, *Systematic Theology*, 1:135–137; 2:97–118.

22. Ibid., 2:105.

23. Confucius said, "I can describe the civilization of the Hsia dynasty, but the descendent state of Ch'i cannot render adequate corroboration. I can describe the civilization of the Yin dynasty, but the descendent state of Sung cannot render adequate corroboration. And all because of the deficiency of their records and wise men. Were these sufficient then I could corroborate my views." *Analects*, 3:9; quoted from Fung, *History*, 1:55.

24. This point was stressed by Mencius, *The Book of Mencius*, 6A:6. Cf. Chan, *Source Book*, pp. 53–54.

25. *Analects*, 5:11; see Chan, *Source Book*, p. 28.

26. *Analects*, 4:15; see Chan, *Source Book*, p. 27.

27. Chan, *Source Book*, p. 27.

28. *Analects*, 6:28; see Chan, *Source Book*, p. 31.

29. Chan, *Source Book*, p. 27.

30. *Analects*, 3:3; see Chan, *Source Book*, p. 24. Even from a statistical point of view, *jen* was without any doubt the most central and the most discussed virtue in *The Analects*.

31. *Analects*, 4:5; see Chan, *Source Book*, p. 26.

32. *Analects*, 7:22; see Chan, *Source Book*, p. 32.

33. *Analects*, 11:8; see Chan, *Source Book*, p. 36.

34. *Analects*, 3:13; see Chan, *Source Book*, p. 25.

35. *Analects*, 7:20; see Chan, *Source Book*, p. 32.

36. *Analects*, 17:19; see Chan, *Source Book*, p. 47, with slight modification.

37. *Analects*, 16:8; see Chan, *Source Book*, p. 45.

38. *Analects*, 2:4; see Chan, *Source Book*, p. 22.

39. *Analects*, 15:28; see Chan, *Source Book*, p. 44, with slight modification.

40. *Analects*, 11:11; see Chan, *Source Book*, p. 36.

41. *The Book of Mencius*, 2A:6; see Chan, *Source Book*, p. 65: "The feeling of commiseration is the beginning of humanity; the feeling of shame and dislike is the beginning of righteousness; the feeling of deference and compliance is the beginning of propriety; and the feeling of right and wrong is the beginning of wisdom. Men have these Four Beginnings just as they have their four limbs."

42. *The Book of Mencius*, 7A:1; see Chan, *Source Book*, p. 78.

43. *The Doctrine of the Mean*, ch. 1; see Chan, *Source Book*, p. 98, with slight modification.

44. *The Doctrine of the Mean*, ch. 20; see Chan, *Source Book*, p. 107.

45. *The Doctrine of the Mean*, ch. 22; see Chan, *Source Book*, pp. 107–108.

46. *Book of Changes, Appended Remarks*, pt. 2, ch. 1; see Chan, *Source Book*, p. 268, with slight modification.

47. *Book of Changes, Appended Remarks*, pt. 1, ch. 5; see Chan, *Source Book*, p. 266.

48. Cf. Fung, *History*, 2: 435–442. Chou Tun-i wrote the famous essay "T'ai-chi-t'u shou" (An explanation of the Diagram of the Great Ultimate). This explanation has provided the essential outline of Neo-Confucian metaphysics and cosmology. Few short Chinese treatises like this have exerted so much influence. This essay is found in the *Chou Tzu ch'üan-shu* (Complete works of Master Chou), ch. 1. For a translation of the text, see Chan, *Source Book*, pp. 463–464.

49. Cf. Wing-tsit Chan, "The Evolution of the Neo-Confucian Concept of *Li* as Principle," *Tsing-hua Journal of Chinese Studies*, n.s., 4, no. 2 (February 1964): 123–149.

50. *Hsiang-shan ch'üan-chi*, 34:1b; see Chan, *Source Book*, p. 580.

51. *Hsiang-shan ch'üan-chi*, 22:5a; see Chan, *Source Book*, pp. 579–580.

52. *Chu tzu wen-chi*, 36:8a.

53. Wang, *Instructions*, sec. 315, p. 243.

54. Ibid., sec. 101, pp. 63–64: "The Teacher said, 'The state of having neither good nor evil is that of principle in tranquillity. Good and evil appear when the vital force is perturbed. If the vital force is not perturbed, there is neither good nor evil, and this is called the highest good.' "

55. *Wang Wen-ch'eng Kung ch'üan-shu* (Complete works of Wang Yang-ming) (SPPY ed.), 20:629a–b, trans. Ching, *To Acquire Wisdom*, p. 242.

56. *The Doctrine of the Mean*, ch. 33; see Chan, *Source Book*, p. 113. The two quotations from *The Book of Odes* were taken from Ode no. 241 and no. 260, respectively.

57. Mou Tsung-san, *Chih ti chih-chiao yü Chung-kuo che-hsüeh* (Intellectual intuition and Chinese philosophy) (Taipei: Commercial Press, 1971), p. 346.

58. For a detailed discussion of the debates between Chu Hsi and Lu Hsiang-shan, see Ch'ien, *Chu-tzu*, 3:293–356. See also Mou, *Ts'ung Lu tao Liu*, pp. 81–212; and Liu, *Chu-tzu*, pp. 427–479.

59. *Wang Wen-ch'eng Kung ch'üan-shu*, 7:242b–243a, "Preface to the *Collected Writings of Lu Chiu-yüan* (Lu Hsiang-shan)," trans. Ching, *To Acquire Wisdom*, pp. 206–208.

60. Mou, *Hsin-t'i*. See also my review of the work in *Philosophy East and West* 20, no. 4 (October 1970): 419–422.

61. *I-shu* (Surviving works), 18:1a (Chan, *Source Book*, p. 559), in the *Erh-Ch'eng ch'üan-shu* (Complete works of the two Ch'engs) (SPPY ed.).

62. See Shu-hsien Liu, "The Function of the Mind in Chu Hsi's Philosophy," *Journal of Chinese Philosophy* 5 (1978): 195–208. Chu Hsi said, "The mind is constituted of the most subtle kind of the material force" (*Chu tzu yü-lei*, 5:3b, p. 198). He also said,

"The whole substance of the mind is clearly vacuous and bright; it comprises tens of thousands of principles" (ibid., 5:11a, p. 213).

63. *The Book of Mencius*, 2A:2; see Chan, *Source Book*, p. 63.

64. *The Book of Mencius*, 2A:2; see Chan, *Source Book*, p. 63.

65. Mou, *Hsin-t'i*, 1:70–74.

66. Ibid.

67. *Hsiang-shan ch'üan-chi*, 1:3a; see Chan, *Source Book*, p. 574.

68. *Analects*, 4:15.

69. *The Book of Mencius*, 3A:1.

70. Ibid., 4A:2.

71. Ibid., 6A:6.

72. Referring to ibid., 5a:7.

73. *Book of Changes*, commentary on second hexagram, *k'un* (earth).

74. *The Book of Mencius*, 7A:15.

75. Ibid., 6A:6.

76. Ibid., 7A:4.

77. *Hsiang-shan ch'üan-chi*, 1:3b–4a; see Chan, *Source Book*, p. 574.

78. *Hsiang-shan ch'üan-chi*, 1:6b; see Chan, *Source Book*, p. 575, with slight modification.

79. *Hsiang-shan ch'üan-chi*, 34:5a; see Chan, *Source Book*, p. 582.

80. *Hsiang-shan ch'üan-chi*, 34:4b–5a; see Chan, *Source Book*, p. 582.

81. Chan, *Source Book*, p. 89, with slight modification.

82. "Knowledge gained through enlightenment which is the result of sincerity is the innate knowledge of one's natural character. It is not the small knowledge of what is heard or what is seen." From *Cheng-meng* (Correcting youthful ignorance), ch. 6; see Chan, *Source Book*, p. 507.

83. *The Book of Mencius*, 6A:15; see Chan, *Source Book*, p. 59.

84. *The Book of Mencius*, 1b:5; see Chan, *Source Book*, p. 61.

85. Mou, *Hsin-t'i*, 1:41–60.

11

Sources and Proper Understanding of Wang Yang-ming's Philosophy

Wang Yang-ming's (1472–1529) name has constantly been associated with that of Lu Hsiang-shan (1139–1193). As there is indeed affinity of spirit between the two thinkers, it is by no means an accident that Lu-Wang has been regarded as a single school. However, it would be a grave mistake to simply identify Wang's position with Lu's, as the approaches of the two thinkers were very different from each other. The school of Lu-Wang has been understood to be in sharp contrast with the school of Ch'eng-Chu, named after Ch'eng I (1033–1107) and Chu Hsi (1130–1200). There is no question that Chu Hsi took Ch'eng I as his mentor, that Chu and Lu were rivals, and that Wang strongly criticized some of Chu's central ideas. But it would also be a serious mistake to presume that there was no common ground between Chu and Wang whatsoever. In fact, in the course of development of Wang's philosophy, he had been profoundly influenced by Chu. If it were not the case, certainly the formulation of his problematic would be totally different. The relation between Wang and Chu is a most complex and intriguing one that deserves careful study. My purpose in this chapter is to destroy the myth once and for all that there is no discrepancy between Lu and Wang and that there is not a close relationship between Wang and Chu.

In Wang Yang-ming's *Instructions for Practical Living*, we find a very interesting conversation on Lu:

> I [Ch'en Chiu-ch'uan] further asked, "What do you think of the teachings of Master Lu Hsiang-shan?"
> The teacher said, "Since the time of Lien-hsi [Chou Tun-i] and Ming-

tao [Ch'eng Hao], there has been only Lu Hsiang-shan. But he was still somewhat crude."

I said, "In his elucidations, every chapter reveals the innermost fundamentals [of what is right] and every sentence seems to attack the underlying causes [of what is wrong]. He does not seem to be crude."

The teacher said, "He had made some effort in his mind and was of course different from those who imitated others, depended on others, or sought only literary meanings. However, if you scrutinize his doctrines carefully, you will find there are crude spots. You will see if you continue your effort long enough."[1]

In this conversation, we find that Wang thought highly of Lu because of his personal commitment to the Way, but Lu was still not in the class of Chou and Ch'eng, as he was still somewhat crude. But Wang had never quite elaborated in what ways Lu was crude. We may only infer that although Wang felt that Lu had gleaned the essentials, too many details were missing from his much-too-broad outlines, and sophistications were not enough in his much-too-straightforward expressions. In the development of his own thought, Wang had gone through many zigzag paths, and the expressions of his mature thought were smooth and refined. This perhaps explains why Wang rarely quoted Lu. And surprisingly enough, Wang's sophistications seem to have derived from the fact that he took his point of departure from Chu, as he had tried very hard to formulate new answers to the questions raised by Chu because he was not satisfied with the answers suggested by Chu. In this regard, we cannot but say that Chu had served as an indispensable stimulant to Wang's thought and, in this sense, must also be regarded as an important source for the development of Wang's philosophy. A closer examination is in order.

During Wang's day, scholars had to study Chu Hsi's *Commentaries to the Four Books* beginning in childhood, and Wang was no exception. In fact, he almost accepted Chu's authority without question until he had serious doubt on Chu Hsi's interpretation of *ko-wu* in *The Great Learning* as "investigation of things" because it had not produced any useful effects as anticipated. The story about Wang's investigation of bamboos in the courtyard was very well known,[2] but the story told us only Wang's feeling of dissatisfaction and psychological reaction against Chu when Wang was still in his twenties; it did not undermine Chu's interpretation of *ko-wu*, as Wang's practice was based on a misunderstanding of Chu Hsi's intention. In a letter to Chen Chi-chung, Chu said:

On *ko-wu* [investigation of things] I-chuan [Ch'eng I] meant that even though before our eyes are all things, and yet there must be an order of investigation, certain things are less urgent, others more urgent; some should be studied first, others next; it would not do just to put your mind on a blade of grass or a plant, or an utencil, and then expect a sudden enlightenment! If someone intends to pursue sagely studies, but fails to study extensively the Principle of Heaven [*T'ien-li*], understand relationships of man, study words of sages, and have a grasp of worldly affairs, and cares only to put his mind on a blade of grass or a plant, or an utensil in an isolated fashion, what kind of studies are these? Following this course and hoping to achieve something may be compared to cooking sand and expecting rice to eat![3]

It was amazing that Chu Hsi almost anticipated the follies committed by young scholars like Wang Yang-ming in his twenties who thought they were following Chu Hsi's instruction of investigation of things, while in fact they had no proper understanding of his teachings. Although Yang-ming fell short of making a confession about his misunderstanding of Chu Hsi's doctrine of *ko-wu*, he had implicitly acknowledged that such was the case. What was important for us, however, was the fact that Yang-ming's misunderstanding of Chu propelled him to search for a new path, which led to his mature thinking.

There is no need for me to repeat the well-known story of Yang-ming's sudden enlightenment when he was in exile.[4] But it would be highly instructive for us to study in depth Chu Hsi's and Yang-ming's theories of knowledge and action. Chu Hsi's views were complex and are easily subject to misinterpretations. Here I can only propose to set forth what I consider to be the correct interpretation of Chu Hsi's understanding of the relation between knowledge and action.[5] It is true that Chu did maintain that knowledge must come before action, as he felt that if one does not even know what the right course of action to take is, how can he ever act properly? But this view must be understood in its right context. In his mature thought Chu Hsi followed closely Ch'eng I's instruction that "Self-cultivation requires seriousness, the pursuit of learning depends on the extension of knowledge."[6] It appears that although knowledge is prior to action, self-cultivation is still prior to knowledge. This is indeed the case, as Chu Hsi explained the situation in his letter to Lin Tse-chih:

I suspect that the ancient people started with self-cultivation in *Small Learning*; they had already accomplished much in advance. Therefore *Great Learning* may start from investigation of things. Today people have not made any effort on self-cultivation, they learn from the text of the *Great Learning* that one must start with investigation of things, then they simply pursue by way of thinking and accumulating knowledge, and fail to work on preserving [the mind]. Hence even though they appear to know a great deal, there is in fact no solid ground to rest on. In sum, only seriousness can penetrate what is above and what is below. Investigation of things and extension of knowledge are just the steps for us to make progress in an orderly way.[7]

From this quotation, it is clear that Chu Hsi believed that in the learning process practice of self-cultivation is prior to both knowledge and action. This view is very much consistent with the traditional Confucian viewpoint. Obviously for Chu Hsi, moral knowledge still takes precedence over natural knowledge. It is only that Chu Hsi did not make a clear distinction between the two kinds of knowledge; he believed that the whole universe is governed by the same set of principles. Besides, Chu also realized that there is unity between knowledge and action. It is only in principle that knowledge is considered to be prior to action; in actuality, the two cannot be separated from each other. Wang acknowledged that Chu's main emphasis was on moral knowledge and hence included Chu among those who had made significant contributions to Confucian studies with the realization of the sagely way as its aim. But he felt that Chu failed to make certain necessary distinctions and also failed to appreciate the intimate relation between knowledge and action in a subtle way. Yang-ming took much more seriously than Chu Hsi the distinction between moral knowledge and natural knowledge. He said, "The innate knowledge of our moral nature did not come from hearing and seeing."[8] In fact, there is a dialectical relationship between our intrinsic moral and ontological knowledge, on the one hand, and our empirical knowledge of the natural world based on our sense perceptions, on the other. He said, "Innate knowledge [*liang-chih*] does not come from hearing and seeing, and yet all seeing and hearing are functions of innate knowledge. Therefore innate knowledge is not impeded by seeing and hearing. Nor is it separated from seeing and hearing."[9] Elsewhere he had elaborated:

> That the sage is omniscient merely means that he knows the Principle of Heaven and that he is omnipotent merely means that he is able to practice the Principle of Heaven. The original substance of the mind of the sage is clear and therefore in all things he knows where the Principle of Heaven lies and forthwith carries it out to the utmost. It is not that after the original substance of his mind becomes clear he then knows all the things in the world and is able to carry all of them out. Things in the world, such as the names, varieties, and systems, and plants and animals, are innumerable. Although the original substance of the sage is very clear, how can he know everything? What is not necessary to know, he does not have to seek to know. What he should know, he naturally asks others, like Confucius, who, when he entered the grand temple, asked about everything. A former scholar said that the fact although Confucius knew he still asked shows he was perfectly serious and careful. Such an interpretation is absurd. A sage does not have to know all the names and varieties of ceremonies and music. But since he knows the Principle of Heaven, all measures, regulations, and details can be deduced from it. The fact that when he did not know he asked shows how the measure and pattern of the Principle of Heaven operates.[10]

The so-called Principle of Heaven here was the translation of the Chinese term *T'ien-li*, literally "the heavenly principle," which means the ultimate ontological principle endowed by Heaven in man. Only man has the ability to under-

stand the dynamic, creative operation of the Way of Heaven, and there is no
need to depart from the human way in order to know Heaven; this has been the
faith transmitted by the mainstream of Confucian thought since the time of
Mencius, as he believed, "He who knows his nature knows Heaven."[11]

Knowledge realized in this way is united with and inseparable from action.
Yang-ming said in his famous letter to Ku T'ung-chiao:

> Knowledge in its genuine and earnest aspect is action, and action in its
> intelligent and discriminating aspect is knowledge. At bottom the task of
> knowledge and action cannot be separated. Only because later scholars
> have broken their task into two sections and have lost sight of the original
> substance of knowledge and action have I advocated the idea of their unity
> and simultaneous advance . . . that true knowledge is what constitutes ac-
> tion and that unless it is acted on it cannot be called knowledge.[12]

Now we know why Yang-ming criticized Chu Hsi's interpretation of *ko-wu*.
He said:

> What Chu Hsi meant by the investigation of things is "to investigate the
> principle in things to the utmost as we come in contact with them." To
> investigate the principles in things to the utmost as we come in contact
> with them means to look in each individual thing for its so-called definite
> principles. This means to apply one's mind to each individual thing and
> look for principle in it. This is to divide the mind and principle into two.
> To seek for the principle in each individual thing is like looking for the
> principle of filial piety in parents. If the principle of filial piety is to be
> sought in parents, then is it actually in my own mind or is it in the person
> of my parents? If it is actually in the person of my parents, is it true that
> as soon as the parents pass away the mind will lack the principle of filial
> piety? When I see a child fall into a well [and have a feeling of commis-
> eration], there must be the principle of commiseration. Is this principle of
> commiseration actually in the person of the child or is it in the innate
> knowledge of my mind? Perhaps one cannot follow the child into the well
> to rescue it. Perhaps one can rescue it by seizing it with the hand. All this
> involves principle. Is it really in the person of the child or does it emanate
> from the innate knowledge of my mind? What is true here is true of all
> things and events. From this we know the mistake of dividing the mind
> and principle into two.[13]

Wang proposed to give a new interpretation of *ko-wu* and solved the problem
as follows:

> What I mean by the investigation of things and the extension of knowledge
> is to extend the innate knowledge of my mind to each and every thing.
> The innate knowledge of my mind is the same as the Principle of Nature.

When the Principle of Nature in the innate knowledge of my mind is extended to all things, all things will attain their principle. To extend the innate knowledge of my mind is the matter of the extension of knowledge, and for all things to attain their principle is the matter of the investigation of things. In these the mind and principle are combined into one. As the mind and principle are combined into one, then all my humble opinions which I have just expressed and my theory that Chu Hsi arrived at his final conclusions late in life can be understood without discussion.[14]

It is interesting to note that the substantial differences in thought coincided with their different interpretations of the text of *The Great Learning*: Chu Hsi thought that the present text of *The Great Learning* was incomplete, and he ventured to write a supplement for it.[15] He was using the gradual approach to understand the operation of the Way.[16] Wang did not believe that this approach would work, as the accumulation of empirical knowledge would not lead automatically to a moral or ontological enlightenment. Chu Hsi seemed to have presupposed a leap without being able to specify that such was the case; his approach was at best misleading. Thus, Wang urged scholars to go back to the original text of *The Great Learning*. In his letter in reply to Lo Cheng-an, he said:

Your letter says that I revived the old text of the *Great Learning* because I believe that in the task of learning people should seek learning only from within, whereas according to the doctrine of the investigation of things of Ch'eng I and Chu Hsi, they should seek it in external things, and that I therefore omitted Master Chu's division into chapters and deleted his commentary which was intended to supplement the text. I dare not do so. Is there any distinction between the internal and the external in the matter of learning? The old text of the *Great Learning* is the original text transmitted from generation to generation in the Confucian school. Master Chu, suspecting that parts have been lost and errors have crept in, corrected and mended it. To me, there has been neither loss nor error. I follow the old text entirely, as it originally was, that is all. It is possible that I am wrong in believing too much in Confucius, but I did not purposely omit Master Chu's chapter divisions or delete his commentary.[17]

Although Yang-ming found fault with Chu Hsi's views expressed in his popular writings, he nevertheless believed that Chu Hsi in his later years had been converted to a position very similar to his own. He compiled a book entitled *Chu Hsi's Final Conclusions Arrived at Late in Life* and wrote a preface for it in which he said:

Although I earnestly searched within myself and tried hard to be humble and made sure to detect and remove any flaw there might be, my thoughts turned out to be more refined, clearer, and surer, and there was absolutely no more doubt left in my mind. Only in Master Chu's doctrines did I find some disagreement, for which I felt sorry for a long time. I was wondering whether, with his wisdom and virtue, Master Chu could still have failed to understand. When I was an official in Nanking [1514] I got hold of his works and searched through them. Only then did I find that in his later years he clearly realized the mistakes of his earlier doctrines. He regretted them so deeply as to say that he "cannot be redeemed from the sin of having deceived others as well as himself." His *Chi-chu* (Collected commentaries) and *Huo-wen* (Questions and answers) that have been transmitted from generation to generation represent the tentative conclusions of his middle age. He blamed himself for not having been able to correct the mistakes of the old text [of his commentaries], much as he had wanted to. As to his *Yü-lei* (Classified conversations) and the like, since his disciples, each with the spirit of rivalry, had injected into them their subjective viewpoints, they contradict even more his usual doctrines. Because of their limited information, scholars of today have followed and studied only these works. They have heard nothing about Chu Hsi's ideas after his awakening. Is it any wonder, then, that my words are not accepted and that what Chu Hsi had in mind has not been able to reveal itself to later generations?[18]

By compiling the book, Yang-ming's intention was to make a compromise and to end disputes with the followers of Chu Hsi. Unfortunately, however, Yang-ming's scholarship was so bad that he mistook Chu Hsi's earlier works to be his later works. Wing-tsit Chan pointed out, "The matter created one of the most violent intellectual storms in Chinese history. Throughout the Ming and Ch'ing dynasties, Wang was severely criticized for intellectual dishonesty and for trying to deceive students by utilizing Chu Hsi's name and influence to promote his own doctrine."[19]

Even when Wang Yang-ming was still alive, he was challenged by scholars such as Lo Cheng-an. His answer to Lo was:

I wrote "Chu Hsi's Final Conclusions Arrived at Late in Life" because I could not help it. It is true that I have neglected to ascertain whether certain passages were written earlier or later in life. However, although not all of them were written late in his life, most of them were. At any rate, my chief idea was that it was important to compromise as much as possible so as to clarify this doctrine of the investigation of things. All my life Chu Hsi's doctrine has been a revelation to me, as though from the gods. In my heart I cannot bear suddenly to oppose him. Therefore it was because I could not help it that I did it. Those who know me say that my heart is grieved but those who do not know me say that I am after something. The fact is that in my own heart I cannot bear to contradict

Master Chu but I cannot help contradicting him because the Way is what it is and the Way will not be fully evident if I do not correct him. As to your Honor's contention that I purposely differ from Master Chu, do I dare deceive my own mind?[20]

I find no reason why we should not believe Yang-ming at his own words. His confession showed the basic weakness of his approach. Because of his great respect for Chu Hsi, he could not bear to see that Chu Hsi did not have the same kind of enlightenment as he had; hence, when he found Chu Hsi wrote something very similar to what he had taught all along, he was overjoyed and hastily concluded that these were the final conclusions Chu Hsi arrived at late in his life. Yang-ming simply made an honest mistake. And in all fairness to Yang-ming, scholars in the Ming dynasty were generally short in historical scholarship; what was valued at that time was insight rather than scholarship. Yang-ming had so much faith in his own teachings that he believed Chu Hsi had to arrive at the same conclusions, and he had shown great courage to challenge the dominant view of his day, which was based on what Yang-ming considered to be Chu Hsi's popular writings. There is no reason for us to doubt the integrity of Yang-ming, and it appeared that throughout his life he held on to his erroneous belief that Chu Hsi late in life changed his position and shared the same view Yang-ming realized through his personal experience.

Now we can see that Yang-ming was taking Chu Hsi as his point for departure and came up with something he considered to be deeper than what had been set forth in Chu Hsi's popular writings. This approach had to be different from that of Lu Hsiang-shan, who simply declared that "all the Six Classics are my footnotes."[21] For a man like Lu, the study of the Classics is only a secondary matter. It is interesting to note that in some ways Wang's attitude is actually closer to Chu's rather than to Lu's, as he also took his point of departure from *The Great Learning* by giving it a new interpretation. In chapter 27 of *The Doctrine of the Mean*, it is said that "the superior man honors the moral nature and follows the path of inquiry and study."[22] Chu was in a mode of compromise when he conceded that he put more emphasis on following the path of inquiry and study, while Lu put emphasis on honoring the moral nature, and a synthesis should be worked out to combine the two approaches.[23] But Lu refused to accept the compromise—surely not without reasons if one sees things from Lu's perspective. Lu simply did not believe that the gradual, inductive approach could establish the ultimate commitment to moral principle.[24] No doubt Wang also thought that Chu's approach was inadequate—that was why he had to advance his own teachings—but he certainly would not want to go so far as to say that Chu Hsi's approach was totally irrelevant. He did not care to side with Lu against Chu, or vice versa. He saw that these are indeed two approaches within the Confucian tradition that are complementary to each other. Commenting on the disputes between the followers of Chu and Lu, he said:

In discussing the qualities and defects of the ancients, one must never rely on the imagination and decide the case summarily. Now in speaking of Hsiang-shan, [Wang] Yü-an said, "Although he concentrated on the respect of the moral nature, he did not avoid falling into the emptiness of Ch'an Buddhism. However, his conduct and faith would still be adequate to allow him to be counted as a disciple of the sage. But Hui-an [Chu Hsi], on the other hand, insisted on study and inquiry, and became fragmentary and divided in his knowledge, teaching what was no longer the sincerity of thought and the rectification of the mind of the school of sages." And you [Hsü Ch'eng-chih], in speaking of Hui-an, said, "Although he insisted mainly on knowledge and inquiry, and did not avoid keeping to the conventions and becoming fragmentary in his learning, he followed the teaching of order and gradual improvement, without going against the instructions of the *Great Learning*. Hsiang-shan, however, in concentrating on respect for moral nature, became empty and abstract, and no longer taught the investigation of things and the extension of knowledge in the *Great Learning*."

However, if one speaks of the respect of moral nature, one cannot also speak of falling into the emptiness of Ch'an Buddhism. And when one speaks of falling into the emptiness of Ch'an Buddhism, one cannot also speak of respect of moral nature. Also, when one speaks of study and inquiry, one cannot speak of keeping to the conventions and becoming fragmentary in knowledge. While when one speaks of keeping to the conventions and becoming fragmentary in knowledge, one cannot also speak of study and inquiry. The distinction between the two is very minute indeed. Yet the discussion which you two have held was not free from imaginative judgments. Formerly, when Tzu-ssu discussed learning, in an essay not less than a thousand and several hundred words, he summarized these in the sentence concerning "Respecting moral nature yet studying through inquiry." In your argument, however, with one emphasizing respect for moral nature, and the other study and inquiry, you are each insisting too much on one respect, and so cannot decide who was right and who was wrong. But how can each of you take one thing to be right and the other wrong? I wish you would both keep your minds fair and broad, without any desire to win. How can the discussion of learning with the motive of winning be called respect of moral nature, or study and inquiry? It would seem that not only are your criticism of Hsiang-shan and Yü-an's criticism of Hui-an both wrong, but your approval of Hui-an and Yü-an's approval of Hsiang-shan are also not given in their right contexts.[25]

The important thing is, according to Yang-ming, both Chu and Lu were respected scholars within the Confucian tradition; Lu's criticism of Chu and Chu's criticism of Lu were equally unfounded. Later scholars were even worse: Being unable to grasp the spirit of Chu's and Lu's teachings, their criticisms and defenses were all wrong. Wang was guided by the spirit of compromise, not for the sake of ending a dispute but for the sake of following the right principle laid down by ancient sages and worthies in the Classics. In short, Wang inherited Lu's emphasis on personal experience and commitment to the Way and also Chu's broadness and synthesizing spirit.

Yang-ming's understanding of the transmission of the Way is as follows:

> The transmission of the teachings of Confucius terminated with Mencius. It was not until one thousand and five hundred years later that Lien-hsi [Chou Tun-i] and Ming-tao [Ch'eng Hao] began to search again for its clues. From then on the system was developed . . . and branched off more and more, at the same time gradually tending to become fragmented and torn apart, and finally was altogether dissipated. I have gone deeply into the reasons for this, and believe that for the most part the whole situation has been confused by the fact that famous but mediocre scholars talk too much.[26]

It was clear that only Confucius, Mencius, Chou Tun-i, and Ch'eng Hao occupied the highest place in Yang-ming's thought. Both Chu and Lu had their limitations and could not rank with the four masters mentioned above. There was an interesting exchange between Yang-ming and his disciple Chou Tao-t'ung in *Instructions for Practical Living*:

> Your letter says, "At present the debate between those supporting Chu Hsi and those supporting Lu Hsiang-shan has not stopped. I have often said to friends that now that the correct learning has been obscured for a long time, we must not waste our time and energy engaging in the controversy between Chu and Lu, but only enlighten people on the basis of your teaching of making up the mind. If they really understand what this mind is and are determined to learn the correct doctrine, then by and large they have already understood the doctrine. Even though the opposite doctrines of Chu and Lu are not debated and made clear, they can find out the truth for themselves. I have noticed that among my friends some are quick to be perturbed when they hear people criticize your theories. The reason why Master Chu and Master Lu aroused criticism in later generations is, I believe, that their own efforts were not entirely thorough and were clearly not free from being perturbed. Ming-tao [Ch'eng Hao], however, was free from such defects. From his discussion with Wu She-li on the doctrine of Wang Chieh-fu [Wang An-shih, 1021–1086], saying, 'Tell Chieh-fu all that I said about him. If it does him no good, it will do me good,' we know how much at ease his feelings and dispositions were. I

have noticed that you quoted these works in a letter to someone. I hope all my friends are as much at ease as this. What do you think?''

The ideas expressed in this paragraph are very, very sound. I hope you, Tao-t'ung, will tell all our friends to discuss wherein they themselves are right or wrong but not wherein Chu Hsi or Lu Hsiang-shan was right or wrong. To slander people with words is to slander lightly. But if one cannot personally and sincerely practice their teachings and merely listens to them and talks about them all day without stop, that is to slander them with one's own person and to slander heavily. If I can learn from all those in the world who criticize me and thereby improve myself, they will all be polishing and correcting me. In that case, everywhere is the opportunity for me to be alert, to cultivate and examine myself, and to advance in virtue. An ancient philosopher said, ''Those who attack my shortcomings are my teachers.'' Should we dislike teachers?[27]

Yang-ming had endorsed Chou Tao-t'ung's attitude to follow the example of Ming-tao, as Chu and Lu were both one-sided and could not match Ming-tao's achievement in self-cultivation. But this does not mean that we had nothing to learn from them or that they did not make significant contributions to the Confucian tradition. In another letter to Hsü Ch'eng-chih he said:

I used to think that while Hui-an and Hsiang-shan were different as scholars, they both remained followers of the sages. Today, however, the teaching of Hui-an is studied by every man and child in the world. It has penetrated deeply into the minds of men, and can hardly tolerate any questioning. The teaching of Hsiang-shan, however, on account of his disagreement with Hui-an, has been neglected. Actually if the two had been considered different as were Yu [Tzu-lu] and Tz'u [Tzu-kung] it would be more acceptable. Rather, Hsiang-shan has been criticized and rejected, as though the difference between the two was like that between an inferior agate and a precious gem. Is that not somewhat excessive? Hui-an synthesized the teachings of many scholars, in order to proclaim to the world the meaning of the *Six Classics*, of the *Analects* and of the *Book of Mencius*. The ensuing benefit to later students is indisputable. But Hsiang-shan also distinguished between righteousness and profit, established the great foundation [of learning], taught the recovery of the lost mind, and pointed out to later students the way towards a genuine and solid self-discovery. Can we forget his contributions and berate him entirely? However, the scholars of the world, out of motives of conformity to established patterns, and without studying the facts, all regard him as a teacher of Ch'an Buddhism. This was certainly undeserved. That was why I once used to wish to risk the ridicule of the world by explaining the teaching of Hsiang-shan. Were I to be condemned for it, I should have no regret. However, even towards Hui-an I remain greatly indebted. How could I want to take up his lance to enter his house? For since the teachings of Hui-an are illuminating the world as the sun and the stars, while Hsiang-shan alone is being unjustly berated, already for four hundred years, without anyone to proclaim his innocence, I would imagine that if Hui-an were conscious of the situation, he would certainly not enjoy for a day the position accorded him in the annex of the Confucian temple! This is my personal feeling, which I must finally reveal to you.[28]

Several things are to be noted. First, according to Yang-ming, both Chu and Lu were followers of the sages and made significant contributions to the promotion of the teachings of the sages. They were compared to Tzu-lu and Tzu-kung, two prominent disciples of Confucius. Second, concerning Lu, Wang strongly felt that Lu had nothing to do with Ch'an Buddhism and that his being criticized and rejected was undeserved; this explained why Yang-ming had to come out and defend Lu at his own expense. Third, concerning Chu, Wang freely acknowledged his great contribution to the promotion of the Way of the sages, he was personally indebted to Chu, and there was no way that he should be regarded as one who was opposed to Chu within his own territory. And fourth, it was by no means true that either Chu or Lu was beyond criticism. Admittedly, Lu had his shortcomings. Wang was convinced that Chu's attack on Lu was excessive. He said, "I fear that Hui-an's criticism of Hsiang-shan being influenced by Ch'an Buddhism shows a certain amount of injustice due to passion."[29] But this only showed that "the faults of Hui-an were those of a gentleman";[30] we should not gloss over them, as "Hui-an possessed the virtue of knowing how to rejoice when he heard of his faults. Why should we follow him vainly, and engage in making excuses for him?"[31] What Wang suggested was that we should follow what Chu Hsi ought to do rather than rationalize what he actually did concerning his disputes with Lu Hsiang-shan.

Today after we have examined available evidence from various perspectives, we cannot but agree with Wang Yang-ming's judgment that Chu's attack on Lu as a teacher of Ch'an Buddhism was unfounded.[32] But this does not mean that Wang should have any less respect for Chu, as Wang did not expect anybody to be completely free from faults, so long as they are the faults of a gentleman. He said:

Confucius was a great sage, and yet he said, "Give me a few more years to study the *Book of Changes*, and then I should be without faults." Chung-hui praised King T'ang, saying merely, "He was not slow in correcting his errors." How can the fact that these men were lacking in self-cultivation alter the fact of their being virtuous? This shows precisely why the perception of Hui-an and Hsiang-shan did not reach that of Yen-tzu and [Ch'eng] Ming-tao. It is precisely here that we ought to admire their unequal qualities, and reflect over their deficiencies, as a means to cultivation and self-correction.[33]

We learn from Chu's and Lu's virtues as well as from their deficiencies. Very consistently Yang-ming held an evenhanded attitude toward Chu and Lu; he had acknowledged indebtedness to both of them and also criticized both of them. Now, if we say that Lu was an important source for the development of Wang's philosophy, is there any valid reason for us not also to say that Chu was an important source for the development of Wang's philosophy?

Probably no one would deny that Chu Hsi's thought, especially his doctrine of investigation of things, had served as a stimulant to the development of Wang's thought. But very few scholars noticed that Wang had also developed a new interpretation of *chung-ho* (equilibrium and harmony) in contrast to Chu Hsi's understanding of *chung-ho* based on his interpretation of the text of *The Doctrine of the Mean*.[34] Surely Wang Yang-ming could not agree to Chu Hsi's interpretation of equilibrium and harmony, as he had a totally different understanding of the relation between principle, material force, and the function of the mind. For him, principle is none other than the principle of material force; we can find no principle apart from the material force. Again, mind and principle are one; it would be wrong to say that mind pertains to material force, while nature pertains to principle. The function of the mind is penetrating; there is no need to make an arbitrary distinction between the states before and after the feelings are aroused. Wang said:

The equilibrium before the feelings are aroused is innate knowledge. It is neither before nor after any state and is neither internal nor external but is one substance without differentiation. Activity and tranquillity may refer to the mind's engaging in something or nothing, but innate knowledge makes no distinction between doing something and doing nothing. Activity or tranquillity may also refer to the state of being absolutely quiet and that of being acted upon and penetrating things, but innate knowledge does not make any distinction between such states. Activity and tranquillity appertain to the time when the mind comes into contact with things, whereas in the original substance of the mind there is no distinction between activity and tranquillity. Principle involves no activity. When the mind is active [stirred, perturbed], this means that it has selfish desires. If it follows principle, it is not active [stirred] in spite of countless changes in its dealing with things. On the other hand, if it obeys selfish desires, then even if it is like dry wood and reduced to one single thought, it is not tranquil. Is there any doubt that there is activity in tranquillity and tranquillity in activity?

When the mind engages in something and is thereby acted upon and penetrates things, it can of course be said to be active. But nothing has been added to the state of absolute quietness. When the mind engages in nothing and remains quiet, it can of course be said to be tranquil, but nothing has been subtracted from the state of being acted upon and penetrating. Is there any doubt that the mind is active without activity and tranquil without tranquillity? As the mind is neither before nor after any state, is neither internal nor external, but is one substance without differentiation, the question of absolute sincerity's having any moment of rest requires no answer. The state before the feelings are aroused exists in the state in which feelings have been aroused. But in this state there is not a separate state which is before the feelings are aroused. The state after the feelings are aroused exists in the state before the feelings are aroused. But in this state there is not a separate state in which the feelings have been aroused. Both are without activity or tranquillity and cannot be separately characterized as active or tranquil.[35]

For Yang-ming, ontologically, mind is the same as principle, and as a matter of the discipline of the self, preservation of the mind can be conducted under any circumstances regardless of the state, whether it is before or after feelings are aroused.

It seems that we can almost discern a pattern here: That in, within the context of the pursuit of sagely studies, Chu Hsi followed the lead of Ch'eng I, raised some important questions, and tried to provide some of his own answers; Yang-ming was dissatisfied with these answers, and he strived hard to develop his own answers, in spirit much closer to that of Ch'eng Hao's or Lu Hsaing-shan's.

Recently, by accident, I came across the phrase *pa-pen-sai-yüan* (pulling up the root and stopping up the source) in a letter written by Chu Hsi to Lü Tze-yüeh.[36] As Yang-ming reprinted quite a few passages from Chu Hsi's other letters to Lü in his *Chu Hsi's Final Conclusions Arrived at Late in Life*, it was impossible that he was not familiar with the letter to Lü mentioned in the above; the only conclusion we can draw is that Yang-ming consciously or unconsciously took the phrase from Chu Hsi and made it famous in his letter to Ku Tung-chiao.[37]

From what has been discussed so far, there is little doubt that Chu Hsi must be regarded as an important source for the development of Wang's philosophy. But we must still go further to specify exactly in what sense we may say that such is the case in order to avoid future misunderstanding. The following five points summarize what has been discussed:

1. As had been pointed out by Wang Yang-ming himself, in his day, Chu Hsi's works were studied by all scholars beginning in childhood. It was only natural that Chu Hsi became an important source for the development of his thought.

2. Wang's intention was the same as Chu's, as his aim was the pursuit of sagely studies, not to pass the examination and look for an opportunity to serve in the court. He studied the Classics selected by Chu Hsi and formulated the problematic of his thought

along the lines suggested by Chu Hsi. In short, he took Chu Hsi as his point for departure in his pursuit of sagely studies.

3. However, he was dissatisfied with Chu Hsi's thought expressed in his popular writings. The meaning of the kind of thought Wang developed can only be truly appreciated when it is studied in contrast to Chu Hsi's and taken to be a further development or improvement on Chu Hsi, such as his new interpretation of *ko-wu* and *chung-ho*, as discussed above.

4. Although Wang Yang-ming was opposed to Chu Hsi's thought expressed in what he considered to be his popular writings, he was not opposed to Chu Hsi. On the contrary, precisely because of his great respect for Chu Hsi, he edited *Chu Hsi's Final Conclusions Arrived at Late in Life*; it became a source of scandal during and after his life. Evidence shows that he continued to study Chu Hsi in virtually every phase of his life. What was unfortunate or even tragic was that he studied Chu Hsi not from the perspective of historical scholarship but from that of insight or enlightenment, which drove him to form the erroneous belief that Chu Hsi late in life was converted to a view very close to his own teachings. This proved indirectly that Chu Hsi had always served as the background for Yang-ming to develop his own philosophy.

5. Finally, as Yang-ming had showed great courage to criticize Chu Hsi in the open and simultaneously showed great respect for Chu Hsi, the sincerity he expressed on both ends appeared to be beyond doubt. Wang seemed to have exhibited a love-hate attitude toward Chu. Confucius taught us how to learn from others: "When you see a worthy person, you must think how to emulate his achievement, when you see a worthless person, you must turn around and examine yourself."[38] Yang-ming must have learned a great deal from Chu Hsi's achievement as well as from his mistakes. On both accounts, however, Chu Hsi must be taken as an important source alongside Lu Hsiang-shan for the development of the philosophy of Wang Yang-ming.

With background understanding, now we are ready to study Wang's thought. It seems safe to say that he was an idealistic philosopher.[39] But what kind of idealistic philosophy did Yang-ming actually teach? Answers to the question suggested by scholars often leave much to be desired.

One prevalent misconception is to take Yang-ming to be a subjective idealist like George Berkeley.[40] Those who subscribe to such a view often quote the following two sections in *Instructions for Practical Living* to support their interpretations of Yang-ming's philosophical position.

The teacher was roaming in Nan-chen. A friend pointed to flowering trees on a cliff and said, "[You say] there is nothing under heaven external to the mind. These flowering trees on the high mountain blossom and drop their blossoms of themselves. What have they to do with my mind?"

The teacher said, "Before you look at these flowers, they and your mind are in the state of silent vacancy. As you come to look at them, their colors at once show up clearly. From this you can know that these flowers are not external to your mind.[41]

I said, "The human mind and things form the same body. In the case of one's body, blood and the vital force in fact circulate through it and therefore we can say they form the same body. In the case of other men, their bodies are different and those of animals and plants are even more so. How can they be said to form the same body?"

The teacher said, "Just look at the matter from the point of view of the subtle incipient activating force of their mutual influence and response. Not only animals and plants, but heaven and earth also, form the same body with me. Spiritual beings also form the same body with me."

I asked the teacher kindly to explain.

The teacher said, "Among the things under heaven and on earth, which do you consider to be the mind of Heaven and Earth?"

"I have heard that 'Man is the mind of Heaven and Earth.' "

"How does man become mind?"

"Clear intelligence and clear intelligence alone."

"We know, then, in all that fills heaven and earth there is but this clear intelligence. It is only because of their physical forms and bodies that men are separated. My clear intelligence is the master of heaven and earth and spiritual beings. If heaven is deprived of my clear intelligence, who is going to look into its height? If earth is deprived of my clear intelligence, who is going to look into its depth? If spiritual beings are deprived of my clear intelligence, who is going to distinguish their good and evil fortune or the calamities and blessings that they will bring? Separated from my clear intelligence, there will be no heaven, earth, spiritual beings, or myriad things, and separated from these, there will not be my clear intelligence. Thus they are all permeated with one material force. How can they be separated?"

I asked further, "Heaven, earth, spiritual beings, and the myriad things have existed from great antiquity. Why should it be that if my clear intelligence is gone, they will all cease to exist?"

"Consider the dead man. His spirit has drifted away and dispersed. Where are his heaven and earth and myriad things?"[42]

After quoting these two sections, Fung Yu-lan compared Yang-ming's ideas with Chu Hsi's:

We have seen that for Chu Hsi the nature is Principle whereas for Wang Shou-jen [Yang-ming] the mind is Principle. . . . Chu maintains that our mind holds within itself the Supreme Ultimate in its entirety, and that it therefore also contains all the various Principles of things. According to his system, however, it is only these Principles that are thus contained, and not the actual concrete things governed by these Principles. Wang, on the contrary, maintains that Heaven, Earth, and all things are themselves all actually present within our mind. Thus his philosophy represents an idealism with which Chu Hsi could never agree.[43]

It goes without saying that there are substantial differences between Chu's and Wang's views. But Fung Yu-lan did not specify what kind of idealism was held by Wang Yang-ming. Hou Wai-lu, a leftist writer,[44] simply identifies Wang's position as a Berkelian type of subjective idealism.[45] Commenting on the conversation when Yang-ming was in Nan-chen, he said:

Wang Yang-ming denies that there is objective existence independent of man's consciousness, he believes that everything exists within the mind. . . .

This is fabrication opposed to the actual state of affairs. We know that sense perceptions are only the result caused by objective existents working on man's sense organs. . . . However, Wang would like to start from perceptions, and he has so exaggerated man's subjective perceptions as to take it to be some sort of deified Absolute separate from matter and Nature. . . .

Such a theory would inevitably lead to solipsism, as Lenin has pointed out that if material bodies . . . are nothing but association of ideas as Berkeley claims, then inevitably the conclusion would be drawn that the whole world were nothing but the manifestation of the self. Starting from this premise, there would not be other human existents apart from the existence of the self. This is pure solipsism.[46]

Hou then quoted the other section to show exactly how Wang's idealism leads to the absurd conclusion of solipsism.

The starting point and the major premise for Wang's world view is that there is no matter apart from the mind, and that there is no principle apart from the mind: all are derived from the mind. This is a further development of Lu Hsiang-shan's view that the universe is my mind and my mind is the universe, and that the Way is not outside of my mind. This is also a replica of Ch'an's [Zen's] view that the mind is the Way, it is Principle, hence there is no principle apart from the mind and there is no mind apart from principle.[47]

This interpretation simply makes the assertion that Wang has taught something exactly the same as Ch'an and Berkeley's subjective idealism. Leaving aside the erroneous assertion that Wang teaches a philosophy of Ch'an,[48] I would like to show that it is groundless to identify Wang's position as the same as Berkeley's subjective idealism.

Berkeley's main problem is an epistemological one. As he believes that the only source of our knowledge is sense perceptions, he then draws the conclusion that "to be is to be perceived." If such is the case, naturally the objects we perceive are nothing but the result of association of ideas and cannot exist apart from the perceiving mind. Consequently, there would also be difficulties to assert the existence of other selves, and solipsism becomes a problem. But Yangming's problematic is a completely different one. He never for a moment believes that sense perceptions are the only source of knowledge. What he worries about is how to make the moral mind the master of our sense perceptions, and he never believes that any physical existents can be reduced to the association of ideas. Allow me to quote a different section from *Instructions for Practical Living* to substantiate my claims:

The teacher said, "Beautiful color causes one's eyes to be blind. Beautiful sound causes one's ears to be deaf. Good taste causes one's plate to be spoiled, and racing and hunting cause one to be mad. All these are harmful to your ears, eyes, mouth, nose, and four limbs. How can this be considered as doing something for them? If you are really doing something for them, you must reflect upon the manner in which the ears listen, the eyes look, the mouth speaks, and the four limbs move. If it is not in accord with the rules of propriety, you must not look, listen, speak, or move. Only then can you fully realize the function of eyes, ears, mouth, nose, and the four limbs, and only in this way can you do something for them. Now all day long you chase after external things and direct yourself to fame and profit. All this is for things external to the body. When you want to do something for your ear, eye, mouth, nose, and four limbs, and will not look, listen, speak, move out of accord with the rules of propriety, are your ears, eyes, mouth, nose, and four limbs themselves capable of not doing so? The ability must come from your mind. These activities of seeing, listening, speaking, and moving are all of your mind. The sight of your mind emanates through the channel of the eyes, the hearing of your mind through the channel of the ears, the speech of your mind through the channel of the mouth, and the movement of your mind through the channel of your four limbs. If there were no mind, there would be no ears, eyes, mouth, or nose. What is called your mind is not merely that lump of blood and flesh. If it were so, why is it that the dead man, whose lump of blood and flesh is still present, cannot see, listen, speak, or move? What is called your mind is that which makes seeing, listening, speaking, and moving possible. It is the nature of man and things; it is the Principle of Nature. . . . In its capacity as the master of the body, it is called the mind. Basically the original substance of the mind is none other than the Principle of Nature, and is never out of accord with propriety. This is your true self. This true self is the master of the body. If there is no true self, there will be no body. Truly, with the true self, one lives; without it, one dies. If you really want to do something for your bodily self, you must make use of this true self, always preserve its original substance, and be cautious over things not yet seen and apprehensive over things not yet heard of, for fear that the true self be injured, even slightly. Then whenever the least desire to act out of accord with the rules of propriety germinates and becomes active, you will feel as though cut with a knife and stuck with a needle; the feeling will be unbearable, and will not stop until the knife and the needle are removed. Only then may you be said to have the determination to do something for yourself. Only then can you master yourself. But now when you treat a thief as a son why do you say that you cannot master yourself even though you have the determination to do something for yourself?''[49]

From this paragraph, we can see that external things are real for Yang-ming, and they pose a threat to man if the mind cannot be the master of the senses as well as the body. Yang-ming never denies that there is still a lump of blood and flesh after a man dies—only that lump of blood and flesh should not be identified with the human mind (heart) anymore. And without the mind, there will not be the true self; and without the true self, a man though he lives physically is nevertheless a dead man. By the same token, if there were no mind, there would be no ears, eyes, mouth, or nose, as ears are no longer ears if they cannot perform the proper function of ears. This is nothing strange, as the result is but the natural consequences of the application of the commonly accepted doctrine of the rectification of names by Confucian scholars. Henceforth, there is a really close relationship between the true self and the body. In effect, if there is no true self, there will be no body in the proper sense of the word, as the body must be the body of the self.

If my understanding of Yang-ming's thought is correct, then it becomes a real puzzle how scholars could ever represent Yang-ming as a Berkeley type of subjective idealist. Yang-ming's problematic cannot be that of an epistemologist, and difficulties concerning solipsism are epistemological issues that cannot be more remote for Yang-ming to put his mind into. In fact, Yang-ming's worries are exactly in the opposite direction. He worries that man cannot open himself and thus allows himself to be confined to a narrow scope of his existence. In his famous essay ''Inquiry on the Great Learning,'' he said:

The great man regards Heaven, Earth, and the myriad things as one body. He regards the world as one family and the country as one person. As to those who make a cleavage between objects and distinguish between the self and others, they are small men. That the great man can regard Heaven, Earth, and the myriad things as one body is not because he deliberately wants to do so, but because it is natural to the humane nature of his mind that he do so. Forming one body with Heaven, Earth, and the myriad things is not only true of the great man. Even the mind of the small man is no different. Only he himself makes it small.[50]

A solipsist would exactly be such a small man who makes himself small. Ontologically, the world is one; it is made of the same material force, and it is governed by the same principle. Yang-ming said:

In the dynamic operation of the material force of the universe there is from the beginning not a moment of rest. But there is the master. Consequently the operation has its regular order and it goes on neither too fast nor too slowly. The master [that is, the wonderful functioning of creation] is always calm in spite of hundreds of changes and thousands of transformations. This process makes it possible for man to live. If, while the master remains calm, the mind is ceaseless as heavenly movements are ceaseless, it will always be at ease in spite of countless changes in its dealings with things. As it is said, "The original mind remains calm and serene, and all parts of the body obey its command." If there is no master, the vital force will simply run wild. How can the mind not be flustered?[51]

Man is endowed with the mind that can understand the heavenly mind as well as the heavenly principle; the finite is then united with the infinite. The creative principle works incessantly in the universe. It penetrates both activity and tranquillity. In a famous letter to his disciple Lu Yüan-ching, Yang-ming wrote:

The principle of creative creativity of the Great Ultimate is ceaseless in its wonderful functioning, but its eternal substance does not change. The creative creativity of the Great Ultimate are the same as those of yin and yang. Referring to its process of creative creativity and pointing to the ceaselessness of their wonderful functioning, we say that there is activity and that yang is engendered, but do not say that there is first activity and then yang is engendered. Referring to its process of creative creativity and pointing to the unchanging aspect of their eternal substance, we say that there is tranquillity and that yin is engendered, but do not say that there is first tranquillity and that yin is engendered. If it is really true that yin is engendered after there is tranquillity and yang is engendered after there is activity, then yin and yang and activity and tranquillity are each a separate and distinct thing. Yin and yang are both the same material force. It becomes yin or yang as it contracts or expands. Activity or tranquillity are the same principle. It becomes activity or tranquillity as it is manifested or remains hidden.[52]

Equipped with understanding of Yang-ming's thought, now we can go back to his conversation at Nan-chen and find that it appears under a totally new light. When the flowering trees are not seen, they are in a state of hidden tranquillity, but their colors become immediately manifest the moment they are seen. If it were not that tranquillity and activity are governed by the same principle, how can the state from hidden to manifest ever be explained? Both these states must be encompassed by the same heavenly principle or mind, while man's mind in its essence is no different from the mind of Heaven. Therefore, Yang-ming said:

> For at bottom Heaven, Earth, the myriad things, and man form one body. The point at which the unity is manifested in its most refined and excellent form is the clear intelligence of the human mind. Wind, rain, dew, thunder, sun and moon, stars, animals and plants, mountains and rivers, earth and stones are essentially of one body with man. It is for this reason that such things as grains and animals can nourish man and that such things as medicine and minerals can heal diseases. Since they share the same material force, they enter into one another.[53]

It is really amazing that more than 400 years before our own time Yang-ming could have developed thought with such rich ecological implications. And since the universe is a dynamic universe, our senses and the mind are forever open to new influences. Yang-ming said:

> The eye has no substance of its own. Its substance consists of the colors of all things. The ear has no substance of its own. Its substance consists of the sounds of all things. The nose has no substance of its own. Its substance consists of the smells of all things. The mouth has no substance of its own. Its substance consists of the tastes of all things. The mind has no substance of its own. Its substance consists of the right or wrong of the influences and responses of Heaven, Earth, and all things.[54]

It would be futile for the mind to resist all changes: the key to it is for the mind to remain calm and be its own master amidst all changes, that is, the influences and responses of Heaven, Earth, and all things.

It appears that Wang Yang-ming's thought has implied an ontological idealism of some sort. But he did not reach his conclusion through epistemological considerations or cosmological speculations. Unless we find its root in his moral philosophy and existential concerns, it is impossible for us to realize to the full the implications of his philosophical thought.

It is commonplace for us to say that Wang asserts that mind is principle and that his position is in contrast to Chu Hsi's position, which claims that mind comprises principles. Now we need to examine the implications of his philosophy further. For Yang-ming, the human mind is uniquely endowed with the ability to understand the operation of the Way, even though he flatly denied that the sage is either omniscient or omnipotent. What he knows is the essence and the function of the creative ontological principle so that he is able to respond to different situations. A conversation between Wang and a disciple was reported in *Instructions for Practical Living*:

I asked, ''Sir, according to your doctrine of the investigation of things and the extension of knowledge, one should investigate things at any time in order to extend knowledge. If so, the knowledge extended is only a part and not the entirety. How can it reach the state described as 'all embracing and extensive as heaven and deep and unceasingly springing as an abyss?' ''

The teacher said, ''The human mind is heaven and it is the abyss. The original substance of the mind contains everything. In reality it is the whole heaven. Only because it is hidden by selfish desires is the original substance of heaven lost. The principle of the mind is infinite. In reality it is the whole abyss. Only because it is obscructed by selfish desires is the original substance of the abyss lost. Now if one extends the innate knowledge in every thought and removes all these hindrances and obstacles, its original substance will be recovered and right then it will become both heaven and abyss.'' Thereupon he pointed to heaven, saying, ''For instance, we see heaven in front of us. It is bright and clear heaven. If we see heaven outside the house, it is the same bright and clear heaven. Only because it is obscured by these many walls of the building do we not see heaven in its entirety. If we tear down the walls, we will see only one heaven. We should not say that what is in front of us is the bright and clear heaven but what is outside the house is not. From this we know that the knowledge of a part is the same as the knowledge of the whole, and the knowledge of the whole is the same as knowledge of a part. All is but one original substance.''[55]

There should not be a separation between the internal and the external. Moreover, there should not be a separation between knowledge and action, when knowledge in this context means moral and ontological knowledge. From Yangming's perspective, the emphasis on the mind will not entail a neglect of things. In fact he has developed a totally new understanding of the concept of ''things.''

The master of the body is the mind. What emanates from the mind is the will. The original substance of the will is knowledge, and wherever the will is directed is a thing. For example, when the will is directed toward serving one's parents, then serving one's parents is a ''thing.'' When the will is directed toward serving one's ruler, then serving one's ruler is a ''thing.'' When the will is directed toward being humane to all people and feeling love toward things, then being humane to all people and feeling love toward things are ''things,'' and when the will is directed toward seeing, hearing, speaking, and acting, then each of these is a ''thing.'' Therefore I say that there are neither principles nor things outside the mind. The teaching in the *Doctrine of the Mean* that ''Without sincerity there would be nothing,'' and the effort to manifest one's clear character described in the *Great Learning* mean nothing more than the effort to make the will sincere. And the work of making the will sincere is none other than the investigation of things.[56]

Again, he said:

The mind is the master of the body, and the pure intelligence and clear consciousness of the mind are the innate or original knowledge. When this innate knowledge which is pure intelligence and clear consciousness is influenced by things and events and responds to them with activity, it is called the will. With knowledge, there will be the will. Without knowledge, there will be no will. Is knowledge not the substance of the will? For the will to function, there must be the thing in which it is to function, and the thing is an event. When the will functions in the service to parents, then serving parents is a thing. When the will functions in governing the people, then governing people is a thing. When the will functions in study, then study is a thing. When the will functions in hearing a law suit, then hearing a law suit is a thing. Wherever the will is applied, there cannot be nothing. Where there is a particular will, there is a particular thing corresponding to it, and where there is no particular will, there will be no particular thing corresponding to it. Is a thing, then, not the function of the will?[57]

When we follow Yang-ming to understand a thing as an event, many of his sayings would lose their paradoxical character and are not difficult to follow. Yang-ming would certainly reject a naive realism. He shows us that there must be a structure of intentionality and there is a noetic-noematic correlation. Hence, the *world* that Yang-ming talked about was not just the world around us—what the Germans call *die Umwelt*—it is a meaningful structure formed by a correlation between the subject and the object, and there can never be a schism between the two. In fact, what kind of world one lives in depends exactly on what his consciousness correlates to. Yang-ming said:

In a single day a person experiences the entire course of history. Only he does not realize it. At night when the air is pure and clear, with nothing to be seen or heard, and without any thought or activity, one's spirit is calm and his heart at peace. This is the world of Fu-hsi. At dawn one's spirit is bright and his vital power clear, and he is in harmony and at peace. This is the world of Emperors Yao and Shun. In the morning one meets people according to ceremonies, and one's disposition is in proper order. This is the world of the Three Dynasties. In the afternoon one's spirit and power gradually become dull and one is confused and troubled by things coming and going. This is the world of the Spring and Autumn and the Warring States periods. As it gradually gets dark, all things go to rest and sleep. The atmosphere becomes silent and desolate. This is the world in which all people disappear and all things come to an end. If a student has confidence in his innate knowledge and is not disturbed by the vital force, he can always remain a person in the world of Fu-hsi or even better.[58]

This is why it is so important for us to make our existential decisions, to acquire wisdom, and to discipline ourselves so that we can live in a better world. If this is the kind of "world" Yang-ming talked about, naturally for a dead man, "[h]is spirit has drifted away and dispersed. Where are his heaven and earth and myriad things?"[59] The world around us will never disappear after we die, but the "world" as a structure of meaning does cease to exist. Hence, the word *his* is a very significant term. Such expressions have nothing to do with solipsism. Instead, they tell us that one's "world" is not that much apart from the "world" of the sages, as long as he can raise the level of his consciousness and correlate it to a better world. Yang-ming said:

Now the mind of everybody is at first not different from that of the sage. Only because it is obstructed by selfishness and blocked by material desires, what was originally great becomes small and what was originally penetrating becomes obstructed. Everyone has his own selfish view, to the point where some regard their fathers, sons, and brothers as enemies. The Sage worried over this. He therefore extended his humanity which makes him form one body with Heaven, Earth, and all things, to teach the world, so as to enable the people to overcome their selfishness, remove their obstructions, and recover that which is common to the substance of the minds of all men.[60]

Yang-ming had used a metaphor to illustrate his point of view:

The reason the sage has become a sage is that his mind has become completely identified with the Principle of Nature and is no longer mixed with any impurity of selfish human desires. It is comparable to pure gold, which attains its purity because its golden quality is perfect and is no longer mixed with copper or lead. A man must have reached the state of being completely identified with the Principle of Nature before he becomes a sage, and gold must be perfect in quality before it becomes pure.[61]

We may never match the sage in his achievements, but we can surely find our own self-realization, as what is important is not the quantity but the quality. We should never set wrong goals for ourselves; when we do, we are led astray and head toward the opposite direction and injure our humanity. Yang-ming said:

What is called sagehood depends only on the refinement and singleness of mind and not on quantity. As long as people are equal in their complete identification with the Principle of Nature, they are equally sages. As to ability, power, and spiritual energy in handling affairs, how can all people be equal in them? Later scholars have confined their comparison to quantity and have therefore drifted into the doctrines of success and profit. If everybody gets rid of the idea of comparing quantity and devotes his energy and spirit entirely to the effect of becoming completely identified with the Principle of Nature, everyone will become self-contained and everyone will be perfectly realized. The great will become great and the small will become small, each being self-sufficient without depending on the pursuit of external things. This is the real and concrete task of manifesting the good and making the personal life sincere. Later scholars do not understand the doctrines of the Sage, they do not know how to realize their innate knowledge and innate ability directly through personal experience and extend them in their own minds, but instead seek to know what they cannot know and do what they cannot do. They hope single-mindedly only for exalted position and they admire greatness. They do not know they have the evil mind of the wicked kings Chieh and Chou and at every turn they attempt to undertake the task of the sage-emperors Yao and Shun. How could they succeed? They toil year in and year out until they die in old age, and I do not know what they will have accomplished. What a pity![62]

Since everybody is endowed with the same innate knowledge, the only problem is how to extend this innate knowlege to things. There is no way that we can deny that we have such innate knowledge except through bad faith. But we may not be conscious of the fact that we have such innate knowledge. Hence, we must try to understand such knowledge and manifest it on the conscious level. Yang-ming said:

This innate knowledge of the good is what Mencius meant when he said, "The sense of right and wrong is common to all men." The sense of right and wrong requires no deliberation to know, nor does it depend on learning to function. This is why it is called innate knowledge. It is my nature endowed by Heaven, the original substance of my mind, naturally intelligent, shining, clear, and understanding.[63]

But now we seem to run into the problem of translating Chinese into English: liang-chih certainly means the innate knowledge of the mind, but since it also means the original substance of the mind, it acquires an ontological meaning and status that cannot be shown in the translated term "innate knowledge." Yang-ming tried to clarify the situation in the following conversation:

Chi Wei-ch'ien asked, "How is it that knowledge is in the original substance of the mind?"

The teacher said, "Knowledge is principle made intelligent. In terms of its position as master [of the body], it is called the mind. In terms of its position as endowment, it is called our nature. All infants know how to love their parents and respect their elder brothers. The simple truth is that when the intelligent faculty is not obstructed by selfish desires, but is developed and extended to the limit, it is then completely the original substance of the mind and can identify its character with that of Heaven and Earth. From the sage downward, none can be without obstruction. Therefore all need to investigate things so as to extend their knowledge.[64]

This conversation tells us that *liang-chih* can function because of its ontological status. It is endowed in the individual as his mind as well as his nature. When one follows his essential nature as well as his original mind, he can follow his innate knowledge to act. It is in this sense that everyone of us can be a sage, and the sagely endeavor is possible only if each of us is endowed with the original substance of the mind. Yang-ming said:

Innate knowledge is the original substance of the mind. It is what I have just referred to as that which is always shining. The original substance of the mind neither rises nor does not rise. Even when erroneous thoughts arise, innate knowledge is present. Only because man does not know how to preserve it is the mind sometimes lost. Even when the mind is most darkened and obstructed, innate knowledge is clear. Only because man does not know how to examine it is the mind sometimes obscured. Although it is perhaps sometimes lost, its substance is always present. The thing to do is to preserve it. And although it is perhaps sometimes obscured, its substance is always clear. The thing to do is to examine it. To say that innate knowledge arises from somewhere is to say that sometimes it is not present. That would not be the original substance of the mind.[65]

When the original substance of the mind is realized, the dichotomy between substance and function, activity and tranquillity, is overcome. Yang-ming said:

The equilibrium before the feelings are aroused is innate knowledge. It is neither before nor after any state and is neither internal nor external but is one substance without differentiation. Activity and tranquillity may refer to the mind's engaging in something or nothing, but innate knowledge makes no distinction between doing something and doing nothing. Activity or tranquillity may also refer to the state of being absolutely quiet and that of being acted upon and penetrating things, but innate knowledge does not make any distinction between such states. Activity and tranquillity appertain to the time when the mind comes into contact with things, whereas in the original substance of the mind there is no distinction between activity and tranquillity. Principle involves no activity. When the mind is active [stirred, perturbed], this means that it has selfish desires. If it follows principle, it is not active [stirred] in spite of countless changes in its dealing with things. On the other hand, if it obeys selfish desires, then even if it is like dry wood and reduced to one single thought, it is not tranquil. Is there any doubt that there is activity in tranquillity and tranquillity in activity?[66]

For Yang-ming, there is an intrinsic relationship between what he calls the mind, the innate knowledge, and the principle of nature.

"The function of the mind is to think. If we think, we will get it." Can thinking be dispensed with? To sink into emptiness and maintain silence and to manipulate and ponder are precisely selfishness and the exercise of cunning. In their loss of innate knowledge, they are the same. Innate knowledge is where the Principle of Nature is clear and intelligent. Therefore innate knowledge is identical with the Principle of Nature. Thinking is the emanation and functioning of innate knowledge.[67]

Seen under this perspective, there is no need to make a distinction between *liang-chih* (the innate knowledge) and *T'ien-li* (the principle of nature). Yang-ming said, "The Principle of Nature is present in the human mind at all times, past and present, and has neither beginning nor end. It is identical with innate knowledge. In our thousands of thoughts and tens of thousands of deliberations, we must only extend innate knowledge."[68] If the content of the innate knowledge and the principle of nature are essentially the same, then Yang-ming can say:

Innate knowledge is the spirit of creation. This spirit produces heaven and earth, spiritual beings, and the Lord. They all come from it. Truly nothing can be equal to this. If people can recover it in its totality without the least deficiency, they will surely be gesticulating with hands and feet. I do not know if there is anything in the world happier than this.[69]

This line of thought should never be understood as anthropomorphism, as Yang-ming believed that the human mind is endowed with the principle of nature; there is an isomorphism, almost an identity relationship, between the two. Hence, he said:

Sincerity is a true principle. It is only innate knowledge. The true principle in its wonderful functioning and universal operation is spirit. The point at which it emerges and begins to act is incipient activating force. The sage is the one who is in the state of sincerity, spirit, and incipient activating force.[70]

Again, he said:

> The whole universe is very lively and dynamic because of the same principle. It is the unceasing universal operation of one's innate knowledge. To extend innate knowledge is the task of always doing something. Not only should this principle not be departed from, in reality it cannot be. The Way is everywhere, and so is our task.[71]

It is in such a way Yang-ming developed a metaphysics of *liang-chih*. He said, "Now, innate knowledge is one. In terms of its wonderful functioning, it is spirit; in terms of its universal operation, it is force; and in terms of its condensation and concentration, it is essence. How can it be understood in terms of shape and locations?"[72] The metaphysics he developed is a monism of principle as well as material force, which is in sharp contrast to Chu Hsi's dualistic view. He said:

> Principle is the order according to which material force operates, whereas material force is the functioning of principle. Without order it cannot function, and without functioning there will be nothing to reveal what is called order. Refinement is refinement. If one is refined, he will be intelligent, single-minded, spiritual, and sincere, and if he is single-minded, he will be refined, intelligent, spiritual, and sincere. There are not two different things.[73]

Liang-chih in itself is unity. When it functions, it encompasses all things in the world; only those who lose themselves in things fail to see the subtle functioning of *liang-chih*. Yang-ming said, "The highest good is the original substance of the mind. It is no other than manifesting one's clear character to the point of refinement and singleness of mind. And yet it is not separated from events and things."[74] Again, "Innate knowledge does not come from hearing and seeing, and yet all seeing and hearing are functions of innate knowledge. Therefore innate knowledge is not impeded by seeing and hearing. Nor is it separated from seeing and hearing."[75]

This world is a creative universe. Principle is one, and yet its manifestations are many. We should not ignore the differences, and yet in spite of these differences, we should not fail to see the same underlying creative principle that works incessantly in the universe. *Instructions for Practical Living* recorded the following conversation:

> I said, "The great man and things form one body. Why does the *Great Learning* say that there is a relative importance among things?"
>
> The teacher said, "It is because of principles that there necessarily is relative importance. Take for example the body, which is one. If we use the hands and the feet to protect the head, does that mean that we espe-

cially treat them as less important? Because of their principles this is what should be done. We love both plants and animals, and yet we can tolerate feeding animals with plants. We love both animals and men, and yet we can tolerate butchering animals to feed our parents, provide for religious sacrifices, and entertain guests. We love both parents and strangers. But suppose here are a small basket of rice and a platter of soup. With them one will survive and without them one will die. Since not both our parents and the stranger can be saved by this meager food, we will prefer to save our parents instead of the stranger. This we can tolerate. We can tolerate all these because by principle these should be done. As to the relationship between ourselves and our parents there cannot be any distinction of this or that or of greater or lesser importance. For being humane to all people and feeling love for all comes from this affection toward parents. If in this relationship we can tolerate any relative importance, then anything can be tolerated. What the *Great Learning* calls relative importance means that according to innate knowledge there is a natural order which should not be skipped over. This is called righteousness. To follow this order is called propriety. To understand this order is called wisdom. And to follow this order from beginning to end is called faithfulness.''[76]

Yang-ming believed that there is a natural order of things; without the obstructions of selfish desires the innate knowledge of our mind can naturally grasp the principles of nature. The relationship between our innate knowledge and Heaven, id est, the creative origin of the universe, has been understood by Yang-ming as follows:

The statement, ''The superior man may precede Heaven and Heaven will not act in opposition to him,'' means that Heaven is the same as innate knowledge. The statement, ''He may follow Heaven but will act only as Heaven at the time would do,'' means that innate knowledge is the same as Heaven.[77]

Yang-ming elaborated on his understanding of Heaven:

Take those people today who talk about Heaven. Do they actually understand it? It is incorrect to say that the sun, the moon, wind and thunder constitute Heaven. It is also incorrect to say that man, animals, and plants do not constitute it. Heaven is the Way. If we realize this, where is the Way not to be found? People merely look at it from one corner and conclude that the Way is nothing but this or that. Consequently they disagree. If one knows how to search for the Way inside the mind and to see the substance of one's own mind, then there is no place nor time where the Way is not to be found. It pervades the past and present and is without beginning or end. Where do similarity and difference come in?

The mind is the Way, and the Way is Heaven. If one knows the mind, he knows both the Way and Heaven.[78]

What he means is that by personal realization one understands the essential operation of the function of Heaven. The human mind can also understand the principles that flow from the dynamic process of the Way. We cannot identify the Way or Heaven as a thing, or even the present natural order, and yet we also cannot say that there is another reality that lies beyond the scope of the Way:

I asked, "Sir, you once said that good and evil are one thing. But good and evil are opposed to each other like ice and burning coals. How can they be said to be only one?"

The teacher said, "The highest good is the original substance of the mind. When one deviates a little from this original substance, there is evil. It is not that there is a good and there is also an evil to oppose it. Therefore good and evil are one thing."

Having heard our Teacher's explanation, I know that we can no longer doubt Ch'eng Hao's sayings, "Man's nature is of course good, but it cannot be said that evil is not his nature" and "Good and evil in the world are both the Principle of Nature. What is called evil is not originally evil. It becomes evil only because of deviation from the mean."[79]

Following the Neo-Confucian tradition, Yang-ming took a natural view of evils. The Way taken in itself cannot be evil, but when it manifests itself in the world, there are bound to be evils, as there is either too much or too little. Only the humans are conscious of how the Way works properly, and one must work hard in order to avoid evils that are the result of deviation from the Mean until one day he can naturally conform to the Way.

Now we are ready to answer the question, How idealistic is Wang Yang-ming?

First, from an epistemological point of view, Yang-ming could not have taught a subjective idealism, as had been argued in the above. The mind can know the principle and its manifestations as long as it can get rid of its selfish desires and is not obstructed by its malfunctions. Even though man's empirical knowledge is limited, he can achieve profound moral as well as ontological knowledge by way of personal realization.

Second, from a metaphysical point of view, there is a dynamic, creative, all-encompassing ontological principle that works incessantly in the universe, and it is called Heaven.

Third, ethically, Yang-ming believed that everyone is endowed with the same mind as that of the sages as well as the cosmic mind. His job was to urge each person to develop the great potentiality in himself. Only man can make the Way manifest on the conscious level in order to find his self-realization and form one body with Heaven, Earth, and a myriad things. The individual mind is merged with the heavenly mind or the cosmic mind.

In conclusion, we may say that Yang-ming is an objective idealist of some sort or even an absolute idealist. But the problematic of the Chinese philosophers is quite different from that of the Western philosophers. He reached his conclusion not by cosmic speculation but by personal realization. One may agree or disagree with his view, but certainly there is nothing naive about his view. That is why his ideas deserve reexamination and reappraisal.[80]

NOTES

1. Wang, *Instructions*, pp. 192–193.
2. Cf. Wei-ming Tu, *Neo-Confucian Thought in Action: Wang Yang-ming's Youth (1472–1509)* (Berkeley: University of California Press, 1976), pp. 49–50 (hereafter cited as Tu, *Wang Yang-ming's Youth*).
3. *Chu tzu wen-chi*, 39:23a–23b.
4. Cf. Tu, *Wang Yang-ming's Youth*, pp. 118–129.
5. For details, see Liu, *Chu-tzu*, pp. 118–137.
6. Chan, *Source Book*, p. 562.
7. *Chu tzu wen-chi*, 43:28a–28b.
8. Wang, *Instructions*, p. 150.
9. Ibid. *Liang-chih* has both epistemological and ontological implications. It cannot be adequately translated as "innate knowledge," as the term conveys only the epistemological aspect of *liang-chih*. See the discussion later in this chapter.
10. Ibid., pp. 201–202.
11. Chan, *Source Book*, p. 78.
12. Wang, *Instructions*, p. 93.
13. Ibid., pp. 98–99.
14. Ibid., p. 99.
15. Chu Hsi's supplement to *The Great Learning* was quoted in the last chapter.
16. Chu Hsi's gradual approach was discussed in the last chapter.
17. Wang, *Instructions*, p. 159.
18. Ibid., pp. 265–266, with slight modification.
19. Ibid., p. 263.
20. Ibid., p. 164.
21. Chan, *Source Book*, p. 580.
22. Ibid., p. 110.
23. Ibid., p. 582.
24. See the discussion of the issue in the last chapter.
25. Julia Ching, trans., *The Philosophical Letters of Wang Yang-ming* (Columbia: University of South Carolina Press, 1972), pp. 70–71, with slight modification (hereafter cited as Ching, *Philosophical Letters*).
26. Wang, *Instructions*, pp. 264–265.
27. Ibid., pp. 129–130.
28. Ching, *Philosophical Letters*, pp. 75–76.
29. Ibid., p. 76.
30. Ibid., p. 77.

31. Ibid.

32. For details, see Liu, *Chu-tzu*, pp. 427–479.

33. Ching, *Phlosophical Letters*, p. 76.

34. Chu Hsi's views have been carefully examined in Chapter 8.

35. Wang, *Instructions*, pp. 136–137.

36. *Chu tzu wen-chi*, 47:26b.

37. Wang, *Instructions*, pp. 117–124.

38. *Analects*, 4:17.

39. Ching, *To Acquire Wisdom*, p. 191.

40. Ibid., pp. 192–193. Julia Ching has pointed out the problem, but she has made no attempt to answer the questions involved here.

41. Wang, *Instructions*, p. 222.

42. Ibid., pp. 257–258, with slight modification.

43. Fung, *History*, 2:609–610.

44. See Ching, *To Acquire Wisdom*, p. 192.

45. Hou Wai-lu, *Chung-kuo ssu-hsiang t'ung-shih* (A general history of Chinese thought), 6 vols. (Beijing: Jen-min ch'u-pan she, 1957–1960), Vol. 4, pt. 2, pp. 882–905.

46. Ibid., pp. 884–885.

47. Ibid., p. 884.

48. Cf. Shu-hsien Liu, "A Review of Julia Ching's *To Acquire Wisdom: The Way of Wang Yang-ming* and *The Philosophical Letters of Wang Yang-ming*," *Journal of the Chinese Language Teachers Association* 12, no. 3 (October 1977): 263–266.

49. Wang, *Instructions*, pp. 80–81.

50. Ibid., p. 272.

51. Ibid., pp. 66–67.

52. Ibid., 137–138, with modification.

53. Ibid., pp. 221–222.

54. Ibid., p. 223.

55. Ibid., pp. 199–200.

56. Ibid., pp. 14–15.

57. Ibid., p. 104.

58. Ibid., p. 238.

59. Ibid., p. 258.

60. Ibid., pp. 118–119.

61. Ibid., p. 60.

62. Ibid., pp. 68–69.

63. Ibid., p. 278.

64. Ibid., p. 76.

65. Ibid., p. 132.

66. Ibid., pp. 136–137.

67. Ibid., p. 152.

68. Ibid., p. 226.

69. Ibid., p. 216.

70. Ibid., p. 225.

71. Ibid., p. 255.

72. Ibid., p. 133, with slight modification.

73. Ibid., pp. 132–133.

74. Ibid., p. 7.

75. Ibid., p. 150.

76. Ibid., pp. 222–223.

77. Ibid., p. 228.

78. Ibid., p. 47. Heaven may mean the ultimate ontological principle itself or just one of its manifestations.

79. Ibid., p. 202.

80. Cf. ibid., p. xxxiii. I published a Chinese article *"Yang-ming hsin-hsüeh chih tsai-shan-shih"* (A reexamination of Wang Yang-ming's philosophy of mind) *New Asia Academic Annual*, no. 14 (September 1972): 133–156, in which I had given a rebuttal of the view that attributed a Berkeley type of subjective idealism to Wang Yang-ming. After Professor Wing-tsit Chan read my article in Chinese, he wrote me and said that the article had an awakening effect. He urged me to rewrite the article in English. But at that time I had too many things in hand and could not comply with his wishes. After a decade elapsed, however, subsequent publications on Wang Yang-ming showed very little progress on this point. Many scholars still simply take for granted that Yang-ming was a subjective idealist without bothering to look further into the matter. So finally I made up my mind to rewrite the article in English, entitled "How Idealistic Is Wang Yang-ming?" *Journal of Chinese Philosophy* 10, no. 2 (June 1983): 147–168. This article is dedicated to Professor Chan in honor of his contribution to the promotion of understanding of Chinese philosophy in the West and is now incorporated in the second half of this chapter.

12

The Last Neo-Confucian Philosopher: Huang Tsung-hsi

Huang Tsung-hsi (Nan-lei, Li-chou, 1610–1695) has never been considered an original thinker but is commonly recognized as an outstanding intellectual historian, as he compiled *Ming-ju hsüeh-an* (*The Records of Ming Scholars*)[1] and laid the groundwork for *Sung-Yüan hsüeh-an* (*The Records of Sung-Yüan Scholars*), which are necessary references for any serious student of Sung-Ming Neo-Confucian philosophy. With the scholarship developed by contemporary Neo-Confucian philosophers, however, many of Huang's interpretations and judgments are called into question and appear to be incorrect and lacking in depth. For example, his record on Chu Hsi was badly written and full of misinformation and wrong judgments;[2] and his discussion of *t'i* (substance) left much to be desired.[3] Professor Mou Tsung-san did not consider him a philosopher of note. This is perhaps why he took Liu Tsung-chou (1578–1645), Huang's teacher, as the last Neo-Confucian philosopher.

When we see the problem from a different perspective, however, it appears under a totally new light. Granted, Huang Tsung-hsi was primarily an intellectual historian; this does not mean that he did not have his own philosophy—only that it found its expression through his reflection of others' philosophies. In fact, his philosophy was a further development of Liu Tsung-chou's thought,[4] as he still worked within the accepted paradigm that had both a transcendent perspective and an immanent perspective, even though Professor Mou Tsung-san believes that he had failed to grasp some of the important insights of the Neo-Confucian tradition. Although his intention was to promote this paradigm, his mission was a total failure. In addition, his many-sided interests inadvertently contributed to the new current of thought with a radically different paradigm that abandoned the transcendent perspective of the Neo-Confucian tradition.[5] This development was parallel to his failure to defend the Ming dynasty against the invasion of the Manchus. It is in this sense that there is something tragic about his life and work, and it is also from this perspective that I see Huang Tsung-hsi as the last in the Neo-Confucian tradition. I would like to develop my thesis in the following.

In order to understand Huang's thought, it is necessary for us to understand the nature of *Ming-ju hsüeh-an* (*The Records of Ming Scholars*), the most important work of the history of philosophy Huang compiled. Here we find where Huang stands through his extensive comments on various schools of the Ming philosophy. Liang Ch'i-ch'ao has said that it is a most objective study of Ming philosophy.[6] But he is wrong, as the book was compiled through a certain perspective—that of teacher Liu Tsung-chou. In the beginning of the book, there is a section entitled "Quotations from Liu Tsung-chou." The presence of this section shows that Huang Tsung-hsi clearly intended to use his teacher's ideas as guiding principles to compile the book, even though it is mistaken to see him as one who slavishly followed his teacher's opinions. Liang Ch'i-ch'ao also suggested that Huang Tsung-hsi succeeded Liu Tsung-chou and represented the true heir of Wang Yang-ming.[7] He was wrong again. But when he said that Liu was a revisionist in the Wang camp,[8] he was not far from the mark. The complicated relationship between Wang and Liu and Huang will be carefully studied and discussed later on. In fact, Huang was very explicit about his intention in the preface of this work:

As a youth, I, Huang Tsung-hsi, suffered a family tragedy. Fortunately my deceased master Liu Tsung-chou regarded me as a son. He supported my weakness and balanced my unsteadiness, while I had the opportunity to hear words of inspiration every day. But I was then too young and in shock. Only after his death did I begin to learn about his main doctrines from his surviving writings, while many of my fellow disciples had already sacrificed their lives through loyalty [to the Ming house]. In the year 1669, Yün Jih-ch'u of Pi-ling came to Shao-hsing (Chekiang) to work on the *Liu-tzu chieh-yao* (Essential Teachings of Liu Tsung-chou). Yün was a respected disciple of our deceased master. When he had completed the book, I saw him off to the river bank. He held my hand and urged me, saying, "Today, there are only the two of us, you and I, who know our deceased master's teachings. But discussions of these teachings should not be allowed to grow in more than one direction. Where it concerns his teachings on 'intention,' let us harmonize more." I replied, "It is precisely on this issue of 'intention' that our deceased master differs in his teaching from other scholars. How can we not allow this to be known?" Yün had wanted me to write the preface to his book; I never dared to accept. With regard to a teaching that allows different pathways to truth and a hundred ideas, Yün showed that he still held a rigid position and could not change.

In compiling these *Records of Ming Scholars*, I have made manifest the profundity and shallowness, the perfections and faults of the various gentlemen included. Only where they have given the best of their efforts and exhausted the myriad dimensions of their minds, without working fuzzily or falsely appropriating the chaff of other's learning, have they established schools of thought. I have distinguished between the sources and tributaries, as of the rivers, in order to make clear their essential doctrines and to show how these should be followed as if they were the ears and eyes of the sages. At times, I have made a special effort to discover where the foundations of learning are to be found but without daring to add or subtract from what I find. This can be likened to a water pot placed at the main thoroughfare. Later people need only use a bowl or a wooden ladle and take from it all the water they wish. None of them should go away unsatiated.[9]

The book was finished sometime after 1676, but the preface was written in 1693 when Huang was eighty-three years old; it surely reflects his last views.[10] We can see that he was still deadly serious about holding the banner to defend the teachings of his deceased master.[11] As Yün abandoned Liu's teachings on "intention," Huang became the only one to inherit Liu's ideas and tried hard to keep his insights intact. Even more important, what he inherited was Liu's spirit. He rejected the dogmatic approach of philosophy, which was why he compiled *The Records of Ming Scholars*. Different philosophies have their strengths and weaknesses, and all should be explored. Actually, Huang held a very high opinion of the Ming philosophies. He used to say, "In letters as well as in exterior accomplishments, the Ming dynasty was inferior to the earlier ones. Only in philosophy is it superior. Every nuance, be it fine as the ox's hair and the cocoon's silk, has been carefully discerned and analyzed. What former scholars did not develop has been done for them."[12] He was confident that after a review of these philosophies, one would be led to confirm Liu's insights. This was why he placed "The Chi-shan School: Liu Tsung-chou" as the last chapter of the book and summarized his teachings as follows:

Liu's teaching considers as its essential doctrine vigilance in solitude (*shen-tu*). The Confucians all speak of vigilence in solitude, but only Liu acquired its truth. What fills Heaven and Earth is *ch'i* [material force]. In the mind of man, the process of *ch'i* penetrates all things and returns to its beginnings, dividing naturally into joy, anger, sorrow, and pleasure. The names of benevolence, righteousness, propriety, and wisdom all issue from this. Without the ordering of character, one could naturally avoid transgressing their norms, which is the meaning of the harmony of the Mean. That is what one possesses at birth and is common to all. Hence it is also called the goodness of nature, which is without any excess or deficiency. Now nature-in-itself is naturally in process, without injuring the virtue of the harmony of the Mean. Students need only attest the distinctness of nature-in-itself, and adhere to it constantly, in order to practice what is called vigilance. The effort of vigilance consists only of [self]-mastery. Our consciousness has a master, which is called intention. To be one step removed from the root of intention is illusion and therefore not solitude. So the more one is recollected, the more one's [intention] is also extended. But mastery does not refer to resting in one place. It is always present in the process itself. That is why one says: ''How it passes, without the difference of night and day.'' For there is no *li* [principle] separate from *ch'i*, no nature separate from mind.[13]

This paragraph gives the gist of Liu's thought. The implications of his philosophy will be examined later. Then, after commenting on the difference between Confucianism and Buddhism, Huang wrote the concluding words for this chapter:

In pointing all this out, Liu Tsung-chou has traced out the differences between the southern carriages and the northern tracks quite clearly. Since the time of Sung, there has been nothing like this. Those who knew [how to read the skies] say that when the five planets gathered around the K'uei, Chou Tun-i, the Ch'eng brothers, Chang Tsai, and Chu Hsi had emerged. When the five planets gathered around Shih, the teachings of Wang Yang-ming became prominent. And when the five planets gathered around Chang, the master Liu's way penetrated the world. Has this not been the work of Heaven? Has this not been the work of Heaven?[14]

Very few scholars pay any attention to these words, perhaps because of the fact that Huang's high hopes for Liu's way to prevail in the world had never materialized. But these words revealed the innermost wishes he cherished in his heart. We must not ignore these clues; otherwise, it will be impossible for us to have a proper understanding of *Ming-ju hsüeh-an* as well as Huang's philosophy behind his work.

Now, we realize that it is impossible to grasp the spirit of Huang's thought and the meaning of his scholarly work without understanding the guiding principles of Liu Tsung-chou's thought as seen through his eyes. Fortunately, Huang wrote his teacher's biography, as requested by the Liu family, and in it he summarizes his teacher's thought in a way that really captures the spirit as well as the essentials of Liu Tsung-chou's teachings. In this biography, Huang said:

The Master's essential doctrine is *shen-tu* [vigilance in solitude]. In the early going, he entered the way through maintaining seriousness. In his middle age, he concentrated on discipline through vigilance in solitude, as vigilance leads to seriousness, and seriousness to sincerity. In the later years, he became even more subtle, and at the same time more down-to-earth. The so-called *pen-t'i* [substance] is just this, and the so-called *kung-fu* [function, or discipline] is just this. There is actually no distinction between substance and function, and there is nothing to point to, just merging with what is authentically thus without sound and smell. From what is severe and austere, emerges the gentle wind and the bright moon. No matter expansion or contraction, and activity or tranquillity, step by step [the Way] is truly revealed. He developed what had not been developed by earlier Confucianists. On the whole there are four important doctrines:

1. There is no examination in activity other than preservation in tranquillity. . . .

2. The will is what is preserved by the mind, not what is emanated from the mind. . . .

3. The relationship between what is manifested and what is not manifested should be understood as that between what is inward and what is outward, not what is before and what is afterward. . . .

4. *T'ai-chi* [the Great Ultimate] is the collective term of myriad things in the world.[15]

It is in this way that Huang made the most succinct summary statement of Liu's doctrines and offered his observation of the guiding spirit of Liu's philosophy:

In sum, Tao [the Way] and *Li* [Principle] are established in terms of *hsing* [physical form] and *ch'i* [material force]. Apart from physical form, there is no Way, and apart from material force, there is no principle. *T'ien* [Heaven] is the collective name of myriad things, it is not the king of things; Tao is the collective name of concrete existents, it is not the substance [*t'i*] of concrete existents; Nature [*hsing*] is the collective name of myriad physical forms, it is not the opposite side of physical forms. With such understanding, it would be realized that the mind of Tao is none other than the original mind of the human mind, and moral nature is none other than the physical nature.[16]

Finally, in his concluding remarks, Huang said:

For earlier Confucianists, there was the contrast between mind and nature, the teacher said, "Nature is the nature of the mind." There was the contrast between nature and feeling, the teacher said, "Feeling is the feeling of the nature." The mind was said to unite nature and feeling, the teacher said, "The mind is differentiated into nature and feeling." It was said that selfish desires reflect the human mind, Principle of Nature reflects the mind of Tao, the teacher said, "There is only the human mind, the so-called mind of Tao only shows why the human mind is to be identified as the mind.'' There was the distinction between the physical nature and the moral nature, the teacher said, ''Nature is always physical, moral only shows why physical nature is nature.'' It was said that what is not manifested is tranquillity and what is manifested is activity, the teacher said, ''Preservation and manifestation come from the same motivation, and activity and tranquillity follow the same principle, the same can be applied to the distinction between preservation of the mind and the extension of knowledge, and the empirical knowledge through hearing and seeing and the moral knowledge. All must be seen as one.'' Then were they all wrong? The teacher said, ''Confucius already said that there is one thread running through my doctrines, if substance and function are divided into two, then there would no longer be one.''[17]

There is no denial that there is a strong monistic tendency in Liu Tsung-chou's thought, and his doctrines are the guiding principles Huang Tsung-hsi relied heavily upon to organize the materials for his *Records of Ming Scholars*. Once this is understood, then many seemingly puzzling phenomena are explained. Now I will show how these doctrines were taken to heart by Huang Tsung-hsi and applied to form judgments on various schools of the Ming philosophy. One crucial issue was the division of schools among Wang Yang-ming's followers.

Huang Tsung-hsi listed six schools according to geographical region:[18]

1. Che-chung school (in Chekiang)
2. Chiang-yu school (in Kiangsi)
3. Nan-chung school (in Kiangsu)
4. Ch'u-chung school (in Hukuang)
5. Northern school
6. School of Yüeh and Min (in Kwantung and Fukien)

In addition to these, there is also T'ai-chou school (in Northern Kiangsu).[19] It is listed separately, perhaps because of its controversial nature. Its founder was Wang Ken (1483–1541), an eccentric popular orator who attracted a large number of followers with miscellaneous characters. Its emphasis was on practice rather than on theory.

This list is of course not exhaustive, but it is quite adequate for our purposes. Wang Yang-ming first taught near his native place in Chekiang, then in Chiang-yu (the right bank of the Yangtze River), exerting profound influence on scholars in these regions. His influence was further spread to Kiangsu and Hukuang but was less prominent in North China and the far South. He taught different things in different places, as his thought underwent changes in its various stages, as reported by his faithful disciple Ch'ien Te-hung (1497–1574), who was responsible for the compilation of his biography:

The Master's learning changed three times, and his teaching also changed three times. When he was young, he began with wide reading in prose and poetry, then he drifted in and out of Buddhism and Taoism, until he was in exile among the aborigines and trapped by difficulties, he was suddenly enlightened to the meaning of sages and worthies. Thus his learning changed three times before he realized the Way. When he lived in Kwei-yang, he first taught the students the doctrine of unity of knowledge and action. Then he moved to Ch'u-yang and frequently taught the students sitting in meditation. It was after he moved to Chiang-yu that he referred to *chih-liang-chih* [extension of innate knowledge] only, pointing directly to the substance, and induced the students to be enlightened right on the spot. Thus his teaching also changed three times.[20]

Precisely because Yang-ming taught different things in different places to different students, it is quite natural that there was the division of schools after he passed away. The controversial issue is, then, Which school carried on the authentic teachings of the Master? According to Huang Tsung-hsi:

The Chiang-yu (Kiangsi) school alone acquired the true transmission of Wang Yang-ming. Tsou Shou-yi, Lo Hung-hsien, Lo Lun, and Nieh Pao were its best representatives. . . . All of them were able to make explicit Yang-ming's intended meanings. At this time, the Shao-hsing (Chekiang) school had developed many errors, and the members appealed to their master's authority as support for their own opinions in the face of their critics. Only the Chiang-yu school could point that out, thus preventing the Way of Wang Yang-ming from decaying. After all, Yang-ming had spent his whole life and energy in Kiangsi. It was reasonable and natural that his influence should be most felt there.[21]

There is no doubt that there are a number of longtime Wang Yang-ming faithful followers in Chiang-yu; Tsou Shou-yi, for one, is beyond question. But Chiang-yu scholars did not show a consensus on interpretation of the master's teachings. It appears odd for Huang Tsung-hsi to have given such prominent places to Lo Hung-hsien and Nieh Pao until we know the criteria he used to make such choices. Lo Hung-hsien did not even get to see Wang Yang-ming in person. Nieh Pao received his own enlightenment while he was in prison, and he became Wang's disciple posthumously. He met Wang in person only once in his lifetime and never enjoyed a close relationship with the master. Nieh had a fierce debate with Wang Chi from Chekiang. Huang's sympathy was on Nieh's side, not only because Liu Tsung-chou denounced Wang Chi as an important factor in bringing about the downfall of the Wang school[22] but also because Nieh advocated returning to tranquillity—something similar to Liu's first doctrine that there is no examination in activity other than preservation in tranquillity. However, the resemblance could be quite superficial. At any rate,

Nieh's views represented an absolute minority among Wang's followers; the only ally he had was Lo Hung-hsien—other Chiang-yu scholars were not on his side. I shall comment further on this later on.

Liu's second doctrine as summarized by Huang put emphasis on *yi* (will, intention). It is here that we find the unique features of Liu's thought. No wonder Huang refused to compromise and insisted that this was the core of Master Liu's teachings. Liu made a crucial distinction between *yi* and *nien* (fleeting thoughts at the moment), which is very similar to Humean thought. The will is resolute; for Liu it is the original substance and the master of feelings and emotions, while the stream of consciousness flows on without a moment of stillness. During Liu's time, some of Wang's followers liked to refer to the so-called *hsien-ch'eng liang-chih* (innate knowledge already formed); some even went so far as to say that there were sages "all over the street." While it is correct to say that there is the seed of *liang-chih* in everyone, it is also correct to say that the manifestation of *liang-chih* does not depend on book learning. But it is definitely incorrect to say that everyone is a miniature sage. In order to combat such a corrupted form of Wang's teachings, Liu offered still another interpretation of *The Great Learning*. He sided with Wang to reject Chu Hsi's dualism. But he could not accept the doctrine of *liang-chih*, which seems to have put too much emphasis on what is manifest at the expense of strict discipline of the self hidden from observation. This is why he shifted his emphasis to *ch'eng-yi* (sincerity of the will) and put emphasis on *shen-tu* (vigilance in solitude), which happened to be important concepts in both *The Great Learning* and *The Doctrine of the Mean*.

The emphasis on sincerity of the will has important bearing on the interpretation of *The Great Learning* and the debate on the so-called *Four-sentence-teaching* within the Wang school. Two of Yang-ming's major disciples—Ch'ien Te-hung and Wang Chi—held a different understanding of *hsin* (mind), *yi* (will), *chih* (knowledge), and *wu* (things). They also differed on how to conduct self-discipline; Ch'ien Te-hung favored the gradual approach, while Wang Chi favored the sudden approach. Yang-ming gave his answer, representing his final views:

> You two gentlemen complement each other very well, and should not hold on to one side. Here I deal with two types of people. The man of sharp intelligence apprehends straight from the source. The original substance of the human mind is in fact crystal-clear without any impediment and is the equilibrium before the feelings are aroused. The man of sharp intelligence has accomplished his task as soon as he has apprehended the original substance, penetrating the self, other people, and things internal and things external all at the same time. On the other hand, there are inevitably those whose minds are dominated by habits so that the original substance of the mind is obstructed. I therefore teach them definitely and sincerely to do good and remove evil in their will and thoughts. When

they become expert at the task and the impurities of the mind are completely eliminated, the original substance of the mind will become wholly clear. Ju-chung's [Wang Chi] view is the one I use in dealing with the man of sharp intelligence. Te-hung's view is for the second type. If you two gentlemen use your views interchangeably, you will be able to lead all people—of the highest, average, and lowest intelligence—to the truth. If each of you holds on to one side, right here you will err in handling properly the different types of man and each in his own way will fail to understand fully the substance of the Way.[23]

Then he summarized his views:

From now on whenever you discuss learning with friends be sure not to lose sight of my basic purpose.

1. In the original substance of the mind there is no distinction of good and evil.
2. When the will becomes active, however, such distinction exists.
3. The faculty of innate knowledge is to know good and evil.
4. The investigation of things is to do good and remove evil.

Just keep to these words of mine and instruct people according to their types, and there will not be any defect. This is indeed a task that penetrates both the higher and the lower levels. It is not easy to find people of sharp intelligence in the world. Even Yen Hui and Ming-tao [Ch'eng Hao] dared not assume that they could fully realize the original substance of the mind as soon as they apprehended the task. How can we lightly expect this from people? People's minds are dominated by habits. If we do not teach them concretely and sincerely to devote themselves to the task of doing good and removing evil right in their innate knowledge rather than merely imagining an original substance in a vacuum, all that they do will not be genuine and they will do no more than cultivate a mind of vacuity and quietness. This defect is not a small matter and must be exposed as early as possible.[24]

Yang-ming died not very long after he gave his "Four-sentence-teaching." Ch'ien Te-hung was never a problem, as he always faithfully followed the master's instructions; but Wang Chi gradually deviated from Yang-ming's teachings. Huang Tsung-hsi comments on them:

Wang Chi starts with actual consciousness to reach enlightenment regarding the substance (t'i), which is changing and unstable, while Ch'ien polished his mind in affairs and things. That is why Ch'ien's enlightenment is not as penetrating as Wang Chi's, while Wang's cultivation is not as good as Ch'ien's. But Wang Chi eventually drifted into Ch'an Buddhism, while Ch'ien never departed from Confucian norms. Why is this so? For Wang Chi dared to go to the very brink of the cliffs and could not be restrained by his master's teachings, while Ch'ien's more cautious behavior resembled that of a man who held to the ropes while sailing his boat. And so, if his catch was not vast, neither were his losses.[25]

Wang Chi drifted away from Yang-ming's teachings, as he refused to take the *Four-sentence-teaching* as final. Huang Tsung-hsi reported:

Ch'ien Te-hung regarded this formula as representing a fixed teaching that could not be changed. Wang Chi called it an expedient doctrine. According to him, reality (*t'i*) and its manifestations (*yung*), however minute and subtle, derive fundamentally from one dynamic source (*ch'i*), and mind, intention, knowledge, and things are actually all one thing (*wu*). When a person awakes to the understanding that the mind is neither good nor evil, he also realizes that intention, knowledge, and things are also neither good nor evil. Together, the two disciples questioned Wang Yang-ming about it. Wang said, "I have actually two ways of teaching. The Four Negatives are for men of superior gifts of understanding. The Four Positives are for men of medium gifts or less. The superior gifts refer to the understanding that reality itself (*pen-t'i*) is nothing but its manifestation (*kung-fu*) or effort. This is the teaching of sudden enlightenment. Those with medium gifts or less should devote themselves to the effort of doing good and ridding themselves of evil, in order to recover gradually the original reality (*pen-t'i*) [within themselves]." This proves to us that Wang Chi's interpretations belong generally to the category of the Four Negatives.[26]

Note that this account of the *Four-sentence-teaching* was quite different from the account quoted earlier, which is similar to another version adopted by the *Chronology of Wang Yang-ming*. In that account, Yang-ming was holding an evenhanded attitude toward both the gradual and the sudden approaches, and he never said anything about the so-called Four Positives and the Four Negatives. The Four Positives (*ssu-yu*) refer to the being (*yu*) of mind, will (intention), knowledge, and things, even though the characteristics of the mind are neither good nor evil; and the Four Negatives (*ssu-wu*) refer to the nonbeing of these four. This version was supplied by Wang Chi to elevate his own views above those of his master's. Clearly, he went to an extreme against the cautions given by Wang Yang-ming. Huang Tsung-hsi gave his own refutation of Wang Chi's views:

If the mind in itself is neither good nor evil, then the evil of intention, knowledge, and the things is also delusion, and even good itself is delusion. If the effort and manifestation (*kung-fu*) is delusion, how can one speak of restoring the original reality (*pen-t'i*)? Such words cannot be found in Yang-ming's daily teachings. Wang Chi is the only person who gives them.[27]

If we use Wang Yang-ming's ideas as the criteria, then Huang Tsung-hsi's refutation is incorrect, as Yang-ming was the one who taught that the original substance of the mind is neither good nor evil. The reason why he held such a view is actually very simple, as can be seen from the following conversation:

I asked, "When the mind is free from evil thoughts, it is empty and vast. Should we then harbor a good thought?"
The Teacher said, "As evil thoughts are eliminated, the good thought is already there and the original substance of the mind is already restored. It is like the sunlight which is obscured by clouds. When the clouds are gone, the sunlight appears again. If after evil thoughts are gone one then harbors a good thought, it would be like adding a lamp to sunlight."[28]

From this conversation, we realize that for Yang-ming the Supreme Good is beyond good and evil. He also said, "The highest good is the original substance of the mind. When one deviates a little from this original substance, there is evil. It is not that there is a good and there is also an evil to oppose it. Therefore good and evil are one thing."[29] Another way to express the same line of thought is to say that it is neither good nor evil. Thus, Wang Chi was not wrong to extend the characterization of the mind as "neither good nor evil" to intention, knowledge, and things. His error lay in his one-sided emphasis on the metaphysical aspect at the expense of the functional aspect emphasized by Ch'ien Te-hung. Yang-ming's teaching included both aspects and was declared final by himself. He cautioned against going to either extreme. Unfortunately, however, Wang Chi neglected his advice and indulged in metaphysical talks that took people in the wrong direction. It was precisely this one-sided interpretation of Yang-ming's teaching of *liang-chih* (innate knowledge) that was condemned by Liu Tsung-chou. Following the lead of his teacher, Huang Tsung-hsi gave a rebuttal of Wang Chi's views:

Speaking from the point of view of the Four Negatives, the effort of rectifying the mind, as given in the *Great Learning*, begins with the sincerity of intention [will]. To say now that one should fix the roots in the mind is to say that one need not worry about the intention, and that to fix the roots in the intention is something meant for those of medium gifts or less. Has the *Great Learning* really two such teachings about the efforts of cultivation, or does it only offer a teaching for those of medium gifts or less? . . .
Since *liang-chih* flows from consciousness itself (*chih-chüeh*) with no determination of space or direction, doctrine or law, effort in cultivation cannot but be troublesome to the reality of emptiness and nothingness.

Such teaching is necessarily close to Ch'an Buddhism. Manifestation and process (*liu-hsing*) is nothing but the source and center of consciousness (*chu-tsai*). When one lets fall one's hands while climbing a precipitous cliff, one is without any hold on [solid reality]. To take the mutual interdependence of mind and breath (yoga) as contingent teaching is necessarily close to Taoism. Even though Wang Chi talks about the manifestation of true nature, which of itself reveals natural laws (*t'ien-tse*), his doctrines disclose certain divergences from the Confucian norms of practice.[30]

The problem concerning Wang Chi is an extremely complicated one.[31] On the one hand, his thought was indeed rooted in Wang Yang-ming's thought and was its further development; on the other hand, his one-sided interpretation of the teaching of *liang-chih* caused a lot of problems, and he had a tendency to fall into the empty talks of Buddhism and Taoism. Precisely because *liang-chih* as manifested in the followers of Wang Yang-ming did not seem to provide the much-needed guidance for behavior and action, Liu Tsung-chou then turned around and taught everything opposite from Wang Chi's teaching. He put the emphasis on self-discipline through sincerity of the will and vigilance in solitude, which is hidden and not subject to observation. He also revised the first sentence of Yang-ming's "Four-sentence-teaching" to read: "Absolutely good without evil characterizes the mind-in-itself"—by extension, intention, knowledge, and things are all good without evil.[32] One interesting development was that Liu Tsung-chou seemed to agree with Wang Chi to take Wang Yang-ming's teaching of *liang-chih* as an expedient doctrine; only he went to the other extreme and formulated what he took to be the authentic view of the Four Positives. It is here that his theory differed significantly from Hu Hung's, which advocated that the Supreme Good is beyond the characterization of good and evil.[33]

The third doctrine concerns the problem of what is manifested (*yi-fa*) and what is not manifested (*wei-fa*). Chu Hsi followed the lead of Ch'eng I and held a dualistic view;[34] Wang Yang-ming, on the other hand, held a monistic view.[35] There was no debate on the issue among the followers of Wang until the question was reopened by Nieh Pao, as Huang Tsung-hsi reports

Nieh Pao's learning developed in prison, where he had plenty of tranquillity and nothing to do, until he suddenly perceived the reality of the mind-in-itself, in its radiance and brightness, as that which contains all things. He said joyfully, "This is the equilibrium (or Mean) prior to the rise of emotions. Should I only be able to keep this and not lose it, I would possess the source of all the principles under Heaven." After his release from prison, he regulated a method of quiet-sitting that he taught those who studied with him, guiding them to return to stillness for the sake of attaining harmony with themselves and a composure that enabled them to respond perfectly to events and happenings, so that in practical life they might be in accord with their [minds]. At the time, those of his fellow students who also followed the teaching of *liang-chih* regarded the prior state [before rise of emotions] to be present in the posterior—[a moment at which] emotions were rising and yet not arisen, so that the effort of achieving such a prior state could be made manifest in the posterior state, and the effort of the natural (*hsien-t'ien*, literally, before Heaven, preconscious) could be made manifest in the conscious (*hou-t'ien*, literally, after Heaven).

Those who disagreed with Nieh expressed three kinds of doubts. First: if the Tao were that which should not be abandoned even for one instant, then to say that no effort need be applied to activity would be to abandon it. Second: if the Tao were beyond activity and tranquillity, then the effort of maintaining tranquillity would separate it into two modes. Third: if mind and affairs ought to be one, and mind ought to be present everywhere, in every affair, to say then that one might forgo efforts in one's conscious responses while these are in the flow of process (*liu-hsing*) would be to abandon affairs and to draw near to Ch'an Buddhist doctrines of enlightenment. Thus did Wang Chi, Huang Hung-kang, Ch'en Chiu-ch'uan, Tsou Shou-yi, and Liu Wen-ming each raise difficulties, as Nieh sought to resolve them one by one. Only Lo Hung-hsien agreed profoundly with him.[36]

Note that not only Wang Chi sided with the majority; prominent scholars in the Chiang-yu school such as Tsou Shou-yi also subscribed to the same monistic view. It is evident that this view was taught by Yang-ming and was accepted without question by his longtime faithful followers. The only dissenters were Nieh and Lo, who were really outsiders who did not enjoy a close personal relationship with Yang-ming. And yet Huang Tsung-hsi gave them high marks:

For the mind-in-itself is that which is always in an unending flow of process, moving from tranquillity to activity, activity to tranquillity. The "prior" state refers to tranquillity, the "posterior" state to activity. To apply effort to the posterior state is to follow activity, to apply effort to the prior state is to follow tranquillity. Each shows partiality. But the *Doctrine of the Mean* speaks of "the great root," referring to the prior state, because the mind-in-itself is also Heaven-in-itself. . . . Heaven does not cease revolving for an instant. Yet its cardinal axis is grounded in eternal stillness, a tranquillity to which it must always return. For this reason Chou Tun-i said that the Human Ultimate is established by concentrating on tranquillity, and Yang Shih's disciples regarded the experiences of the state [of consciousness] prior to the rise of joy, anger, sorrow, and pleasure as their secret transmission. . . .

Wang Yang-ming started to speak of *liang-chih* after moving to

Kiangsi. When he was still in Nanchung, he regarded quiet-sitting to purify the mind as the goal of learning and inner composure to control our dispersed self as necessary. Only with the equilibrium (or Mean) prior to the rise of emotions could there be the harmony of due proportions following the rise of emotions. After that, his students showed the mistake of preferring tranquillity to activity, so he taught the extension of *liang-chih* as a remedy. However, he still said that *liang-chih* was itself present in equilibrium prior to emotions, so actually he continued to teach as before. Nieh Pao did not really diverge from Yang-ming's teachings and should not have been criticized by so many people.[37]

Obviously, Nieh found his own way to enlightenment; that was why he disagreed with practically all the longtime followers of Yang-ming who adhered to the master's teachings. And Huang Tsung-hsi's defense of Nieh was based not on the criteria of Wang Yang-ming's philosophy but rather on his teacher Liu Tsung-chou's philosophy, as he took the teaching of *liang-chih* as an expedient doctrine. Now we go back to examine Huang Tsung-hsi's interpretation of Wang Yang-ming's thought and find a twist that seems to have escaped the notice of most scholars.

All the students of Wang Yang-ming are familiar with the three stages of development of his thought. I have already quoted the version given by Ch'ien Te-hung, which carries great authority, as Ch'ien was chosen by Yang-ming's disciples to undertake the compilation of the master's chronology. As there are no significant differences in the understanding of the earlier stages of Wang's thought, now let us see how Huang Tsung-hsi described the changes that took place in each of the three stages after his sudden enlightenment, which enabled him to discover the gate to wisdom:

From then on, he eliminated entirely the leaves and branches and focused his mind on the roots [of learning]. [First,] he concentrated on sitting in meditation and purifying his mind, believing that only after attaining the equilibrium of consciousness that exists before the rise of emotions could one acquire the harmony of due proportion accompanying the rise of emotions. Such cultivation consisted generally in keeping a disciplined watchfulness over seeing, hearing, speaking, and acting, and allowing oneself to become relaxed only when absolutely necessary.

But after his sojourn in Kiangsi, he only talked of the words "extending *liang-chih*"; one did not have to rely on meditation to acquire stillness nor did one's mind require purifying. Without exercise or reflection, one naturally behaved according to natural norms. This was because *liang-chih* was identical to the equilibrium [of consciousness] prior to the rise of emotions, since such a state could not precede *liang-chih*; it was identical to the harmony of consciousness posterior to the rise of emotions, since such harmony could not be subsequent to *liang-chih*. *Liang-chih* could exercise discipline (*shou-lien*) of itself and did not require that one attend to it. *Liang-chih* also could relax of itself and did not require that one attend to relaxation. The exercise of discipline was the very substance of response, the shift from tranquillity to activity. Relaxation was the manifestation of stillness, the shift from activity to tranquillity. Knowledge in its genuine and earnest aspect was action, as action in its intelligent and discerning aspect was knowledge. These were not two separate entities.

After Wang Yang-ming went to Chekiang, he redoubled his efforts and further transformed his achievements. At each moment he knew what was right and what was wrong and yet transcended both right and wrong. Whenever he opened his mouth, he spoke from his original mind. There was no need to borrow ideas from others and patch things together. All phenomena were illuminated as if by the red sun in the sky. This shows that after completing his learning, he further underwent three changes.[38]

There is no denial that Huang Tsung-hsi did try to have a sympathetic understanding of Yang-ming's thought and also recognized his great achievement in the pursuit of the Way. His portrayal of the further development of Wang's thought looks innocently similar to the picture given by Ch'ien Te-hung. In fact, however, the guiding spirit was radically different, as he surreptitiously changed the picture to suit the taste of Liu Tsung-chou. Note that for Ch'ien Te-hung, after his sudden enlightenment, Yang-ming's teaching changed from an emphasis on "the unity of knowledge and action" to an emphasis on "sitting in meditation," then to "extension of *liang-chih*," which represented the final stage of his thought. But for Huang Tsung-hsi, "sitting in meditation" was moved to the first stage; "extension of *liang-chih*" now became only the second stage, to be surpassed by the third and final stage on which Huang offered only a portrayal of Yang-ming's great achievement in self-cultivation without a doctrine for us to follow. This is consistent with Liu Tsung-chou's view that "extension of *liang-chih*" was merely an expedient doctrine, and his own teaching of "sincerity of the will" and "vigilance in solitude" is final in the process of the pursuit of the sagely Way. Liu started out having great faith in Yang-ming; then he had serious doubts on his approach; finally, he endorsed Yang-ming's spirit but developed his own teaching, which was believed to have surpassed all the expedient doctrines in the past including Yang-ming's teaching on extending *liang-chih*. Now we can clearly see that Huang Tsung-hsi could not have been the true heir of Yang-ming. He followed his teacher Liu Tsung-chou faithfully and was, at best, a revisionist of Wang's thought.

The fourth doctrine shows that Liu Tsung-chou moved even closer to the position of what I call "immanent monism." For him, *T'ai-chi* (Great Ultimate) is just the collective name of a myriad things in the world. The advantage is that it is stressed that there is not another metaphysical realm apart from the world of nature. But the price paid is high—perhaps a bit too high—as the formulation of the concept in such a way cannot deliver the message that the

Way is a creative one. The consequence is that the spiritual aspect of Neo-Confucian philosophy is further diminished in Liu Tsung-chou's thought.

From the above discussion, I think I have established the case that these four doctrines were the guiding principles that Huang Tsung-chi used to analyze the different schools of thought in *The Records of Ming Scholars*. But I have no intention of reducing Huang Tsung-hsi to being just a supplement to Liu Tsung-chou. The two men had totally different idiosyncrasies and characteristics. For example, Huang was a man of action who had organized a band of soldiers to fight against the Manchus, while Liu was famous for his moral integrity and practicing strict self-discipline. Wang was widely read, and his broad interests covered natural sciences, mathematics, literature, and philosophy; Liu concentrated on studies related to the actualization of the sagely Way. Huang was never a slavish follower of Liu, as he himself confessed that he had only a superficial understanding of his master's ideas until he was forced to retire from action, then devoted himself to seriously studying the works of his deceased teacher, finally being able to transmit the Way of Master Liu late in his career. In the introduction to *The Records of Ming Scholars*, Huang said:

> In learning, we regard as truth what each person has discovered himself and made prominent. Those who depend upon other schools and copy from other people are either vulgar scholars or professional students. Included in this book are partial opinions as well as their opposite views. Students should pay attention to the differences. This is the meaning of the same root dividing into myriad branches. To simply add water to water cannot be called learning.[39]

Huang Tsung-hsi certainly cannot be accused of adding water to water as far as the transmission of his teacher's way is concerned. Unless he had not appropriated his teacher's ideas as his own and applied so well the principles he learned from his teacher, it would have been impossible for him to have completed such a monumental work as *The Records of Ming Scholars*. His ideas should never be seen as confined to the scope of his teacher's ideas. Now we want to find out where he did advance beyond his teacher and what his own philosophy is like. It seems that virtually no scholars have raised these questions, let alone provided answers to these queries. I would venture to take up the challenge and suggest that the clues can be found in his preface to *The Records of Ming Scholars*:

> That which fills Heaven and Earth is Mind. Its transformations are unfathomable and cannot but assume myriad forms. The Mind has no original substance (*pen-t'i*) except what is achieved by its activity (*kung-fu*). To exhaust and comprehend principles (*li*) is to exhaust and comprehend Mind's myriad manifestations rather than the myriad manifestations of all things. That was why the gentlemen of old preferred to dig out a mountain

road themselves, as did the five laborers [of Ch'in], rather than rely on the wild horses of Han-tan, and the paths they took all had to be different. Unfortunately, the gentlemen of today insist upon everyone taking the same path, obliging those with excellent endowments to become dried up like scorched shoots or abandoned harbors. But the recorded dialogs of the former scholars show that each of them was different, although they all reflected the mind-in-itself (*hsin-t'i*), which is always changing and quite without rest. One's insistence upon fixing the situation will turn out to be quite futile and useless. There is no other reason for this. Only after cultivating virtue could learning be discussed. Today, learning is being discussed (*chiang-hsüeh*) without virtue being cultivated. No wonder people point only to one thing while neglecting one hundred. The times are getting worse.... The situation resembles more the inner divisions of Buddhism, with the five schools fighting one another. So this small Almond Terrace has been made into a noisy marketplace. How tragic![40]

A further clue was provided by the belated epitaph of Huang written by Ch'üan Tsu-wang, a great admirer of his who completed the project of *The Records of Sung-Yüan Scholars*, as he said: "If one does not read much, then it would be impossible for him to realize the transformation of the principle; if one reads a lot, but does not seek within the mind, then his learning is just vulgar learning."[41]

From these sources, I would like to select four statements that I believe best characterize Huang Tsung-hsi's thought:

1. "That which fills Heaven and Earth is Mind. Its transformations are unfathomable and cannot but assume myriad forms."

2. "The Mind has no original substance (*pen-t'i*) except what is achieved by its activity (*kung-fu*)."

3. "To exhaust and comprehend principles (*li*) is to exhaust and comprehend Mind's myriad manifestations rather than the myriad manifestations of all things."

4. "If one does not read much, then it would be impossible for him to realize the transformation of the principle; if one reads a lot, but does not seek within the mind, then his learning is just vulgar learning."

Let us further elaborate on these views. The opening statement of the preface—"That which fills Heaven and Earth is Mind"—was often quoted to show that Huang was an idealist, but very few scholars have bothered to figure out the exact implications of the statement; hence, its meaning has remained in the dark. In recent years, however, there has been a revival of interest in Huang Tsung-hsi. Because his *Collected Writings* have been published in Chekiang, Huang's native place, now we can use materials hitherto unavailable to study his thought. From a philosophical perspective, two works are important: *Meng-tzu shih-shuo* (My teacher's views on Mencius) and *Tzu-liu-tzu hsüeh-yen* (Master Liu's sayings on learning).[42] The former work is really Huang's own writings. In the preface, Huang said that because his teacher left writings on *The Analects, The Great Learning*, and *The Doctrine of the Mean* but none on *Mencius*, he wrote the book to fill the gap. The words are his, but the guiding thoughts come from Liu Tsung-chou. The latter work consists of notes taken from Master Liu's sayings. The work on *Mencius* is especially important, as it clearly shows that Huang Tsung-hsi's thought can be traced back to Liu Tsung-chou, to Wang Yang-ming, and finally to Mencius.

Elsewhere I have shown that Yang-ming's thought has nothing to do with a Berkelley type of subjective idealism.[43] In order to make the point, it will suffice to quote two passages from *Instructions for Practical Living*:

These activities of seeing, listening, speaking, and moving are all of your mind. . . . If there were no mind, there would be no ears, eyes, mouth, or nose. What is called your mind[-heart] is not merely that lump of blood and flesh. If it were so, why is it that the dead man, whose lump of blood and flesh is still present, cannot see, listen, speak, or move? What is called your mind is that which makes seeing, listening, speaking, and moving possible. It is the nature of man and things; it is the Principle of Nature.[44]

"[I]n all that fills heaven and earth there is but this clear intelligence. It is only because of their physical forms and bodies the men are separated. My clear intelligence is the master of heaven and earth and spiritual beings. . . . Separated from my clear intelligence, there will be no heaven, earth, spiritual beings, or myriad things, and separated from these, there will not be my clear intelligence. Thus they are all permeated with one material force. How can they be separated?"

I asked further, "Heaven, earth, spiritual beings, and the myriad things have existed from great antiquity. Why should it be that if my clear intelligence is gone, they will all cease to exist?"

"Consider the dead man. His spirit has drifted away and dispersed. Where are his heaven and earth and myriad things?"[45]

From these quotations we realize that Yang-ming never denied that there was that lump of blood and flesh after death, but if it cannot function as a mind-heart, then it can no longer be called a mind-heart. By the same token, the "world" is a structure of meaning; if its meaning is lost, it is no longer the "world." Huang Tsung-hsi followed the same line of thought. He gave his interpretation of Mencius's thought: "Mencius thinks that only if there is the self and then there are heaven, earth, and myriad things, as it is my mind which distinguishes them according to their principles. Thus if the mind is preserved, the Principle will be manifest, there is no need to beg for fire from door to door."[46] He further elaborated on this line of thought by giving his interpretation of the Mencian doctrine that "All things are complete within the self":

There are not the so-called myriad things that fill up heaven and earth, as they derive their names from the self. For example, the father means my father, the king also means my king, can they be taken to be something external to myself? There has to be the mind to be filial to the father, then the father becomes my father; and there has to be the mind to be loyal to the king, then the king becomes my king. Such is the implication of "return to the self and be sincere." From thus can be seen that myriad things are not just myriad things, and I am not merely I, all are of one body. My existence within the world does not lack anything. What joy can be greater than this![47]

Obviously, Huang's thought is in total agreement with Yang-ming, who declared, "The great man regards Heaven, Earth, and the myriad things as one body."[48] The underlying spirit is opposite the kind of solipsism derived from an epistemological subjective idealism. Liu Tsung-chou was reported to have said:

That which fills up Heaven and Earth is Tao, and what are appropriated by the human mind is most real. This was why T'su-hu [Yang Chien, died 1226] taught the doctrine of *hsin-i* [changing mind]. The Great Ultimate, yin and yang, the Four Images, the Eight Trigrams, the Sixty-four Hexagrams, they are all constructions of the mind. It is in the same way that the Sage learns from what is near at hand, far off from things, and from Heaven and Earth. Thus we can see that the Principle is evenly distributed, there cannot be a distinction between great and small. Such a vivid [universe] is indeed beyond one's comprehension![49]

From this passage it is not difficult to see where Huang finds his fountainhead. But this passage gives us only one side of the picture; there is still another side. Liu was also reported to have made the following statement: "That which fills Heaven and Earth is *ch'i* [material force], which is the same as *li* [principle]."[50] Such an assertion certainly does not make Liu Tsung-chou a materialist, as the statement only shows the other side of the same coin. Rejecting the dualism of Chu Hsi's thought, Wang Yang-ming took the first giant step toward monism; Liu Tsung-chou pushed it further toward a radical form of monism that identifies material force and principle; then Huang Tsung-hsi took the final step, synthesizing Liu and Wang, and made his bold declaration: "That which fills Heaven and Earth is Mind." Now we realize that for Huang not only material force (*ch'i*) and principle (*li*) are mind (*hsin*), but even things (*wu*) are also mind. It is only in this way that we find the proper understanding of Huang Tsung-hsi's metaphysical position.

When the fundamentals are captured, the rest is easy. The second statement concerns matters on self-discipline. Wang Chi took the transcendent metaphysical approach, put the emphasis on the realization of the original substance (*pen-t'i*), and said that apart from this there is no need of additional effort for discipline (*kung-fu*). Liu Tsung-chou turned around and took the immanent functional approach, putting emphasis on discipline within daily activities, and said that apart from discipline there is not another original substance. Then Huang took the final step and declared, "The Mind has no original substance (*pen-t'i*) except what is achieved by its activity (*kung-fu*)." Actually, the two approaches have both their merits and their shortcomings. As Liu Tsung-chou saw the defects of Wang Chi's approach, which could lead to the assertion of *hsien-ch'eng liang-chih* (innate knowledge already formed) in every man in the street, he tried to avoid empty metaphysical talk and put exclusive emphasis on discipline in daily activities. This approach could lead to the undesirable consequence of the diminution or even elimination of the transcendent metaphysical aspect altogether. Certainly this was not intended by Liu Tsung-chou and Huang Tsung-hsi. Huang's perspective was spelled out in his new interpretation of the Mencian doctrine of "recovering the lost mind":

There are no traces and images of *jen* [humanity]. Under such circumstances, however, Mencius did point out certain traces and images that everybody can comprehend. For example, he said, "Humanity, righteousness, propriety, and wisdom are rooted in the mind." "The mind of commiseration is the beginning of humanity." "Humanity is the human mind." etc. For a human being to be a human being, there is no other mind than that of commiseration, shame and dislike, deference and compliance, right and wrong. That which is coming and going without any certainty, rising and perishing amidst changes, is resulted from [the stimulation] of external things, and has nothing to do with the mind. Thus it is enough to say only "seeking the lost mind," there is no need to say "seeking the mind of principle and righteousness," likewise it is enough to say "losing the original mind," there is no need to say "losing the mind of propriety and righteousness," precisely because the mind is principle. The sayings of Mencius are very clear, I do not understand why later Confucian scholars would have the misunderstanding of taking the human mind and the mind of Tao as two different things? If the function of the mind is limited to the vacuous, intelligent perceiving and feeling only, and principles are attributed to myriad things under heaven and earth, then one has to exhaust and comprehend principles in order to realize the mind of Tao, while the vacuous, intelligent perceiving and feeling are only the function of the mind of man. This view fails to realize that what is embodied in the vacuous, intelligent perceiving and feeling is none other than the mind of Tao, which is the original mind of the human mind. Precisely because it is so subtle that it is in a precarious situation. . . .

This mind would practice commiseration, shame and dislike as it is called for. It is undifferentiated without distinguishing itself, as it is embodied in man as conscious knowledge realized in solitude, transforming *ch'ien* [yang] and *k'un* [yin], all according to the flow of the natural process. This is the mind that is preserved without being lost; if there are any artificial efforts, then the mind is already lost.[51]

The late Confucian scholars referred to were followers of Chu Hsi who took preservation of the mind and investigation of principles as two different things and compared them to the two wings of a bird or two wheels of a cart. Huang's criticism of this approach leads us to the third statement, which makes the assertion, "To exhaust and comprehend principles (*li*) is to exhaust and comprehend Mind's myriad manifestations rather than the myriad minifestations of all things."

Wang Yang-ming was the first to openly challenge the authority of Chu Hsi's dualism; Liu Tsung-chou pushed along this direction still further; then Huang Tsung-hsi synthesized Liu and Wang's ideas and offered his own understanding of *li-i-fen-shu* (one principle, many manifestations). He said:

From the perspective of differentiation, heaven and earth and myriad things have their respective principles; how very broad they are! From the perspective of unity, there is just one Principle for heaven, earth and myriad things; the Principle is not to be taken as a principle; how very simple it is! If one proceeds to exhaust and comprehend the principles of heaven, earth, and myriad things, it would be very difficult to return to what is simple. But what are scattered and different have only one foundation, i.e., my mind. Whatever observed from the above and below are but the vital functioning of the substance of my mind. This is the implication of "going back to talk about what is simple." If my mind always follows things, then this is tantamount to roaming in things as to lose the purpose.[52]

There is no doubt that Huang's philosophy was a further development of Wang Yang-ming and Liu Tsung-chou's thought. Although he moved even closer to the position of immanent monism, he still kept the transcendent, metaphysical perspective, as he had not an iota of doubt over the reality of the original substance of the mind. He still worked within the paradigm of Sung-Ming Neo-Confucian philosophy: There is one foundation (*i-pen*), and there are thousands of particulars (*wan-shu*).

Obviously, Huang Tsung-hsi had a tendency to put even greater emphasis on the immanent, particular aspect than his predecessors. There is not much to say about the foundation, which is in a way beyond words, but there is a great deal to say about functioning in manifestations. Huang Tsung-hsi was widely read, as he believed that through words we can get to the intention of thoughts. He was an expert on Classical studies and wrote a book on the *I Ching* (*Book of Changes*) to show that the diagrams are later fabrications. This made him a forerunner of the movement that put emphasis on documentary evidence and objective scholarship; this movement became the main stream of Confucian studies in the Ch'ing dynasty. He was not only an expert on intellectual history; he also had a comprehensive understanding of history in general. He refused to serve under the new dynasty, but it was under his direction that his disciple Wan Ssu-tung undertook the task to compile Ming history. He was very diligent, collecting all sorts of materials. He compiled a collection of literary works that in volume were much larger than *The Records of Ming Scholars*, a philosophy work. And he was a famous essayist in his own time; insatiable demands asked him to write pieces such as prefaces, eulogies, and epitaphs. But he did not get lost in the vast sea of particulars. As he said in his introduction to *The Records of Ming Scholars*:

> Every teaching usually has its main doctrine. This is where the thinker in question applied his most effective effort. It is also the student's starting point. The principles of the things in the universe are inexhaustible. Unless one is able to define them in a few words, how can they be summarized and identified as one's own? Thus, he who teaches without any main doctrine, even if he has some fine words to say, gives what resembles entangled silk having no beginning.[53]

Through his own reflection, he chose to further develop Liu Tsung-chou and Wang Yang-ming's ideas into a philosophy of his own. In this sense, he was the true heir of Liu Tsung-chou and still worked within the paradigm of Sung-Ming Neo-Confucian philosophy. This was not true of other disciples of Liu, however. One notable example was Chen Ch'üeh (Ch'ien-ch'u, 1604–1677), who said:

> There is just one nature. It is called endowment from Heaven [*T'ien-ming*] by tracing back to its foundation. And it is called Material force [*ch'i*], emotion [*ch'ing*], ability [*ts'ai*] by following its extensive function. How can there be two things? Emotion comes from the manifestation of the nature, ability from the function of the nature, and material force from the pervasiveness of the nature. They are all one.[54]

Obviously, this was derived from Liu Tsung-chou's monistic thought. But then Chen Ch'üeh went further to say:

Master Chou's [Tun-i] teaching of no desire taught Ch'an [Zen] without the name of Ch'an. We Confucianists only say that there should be few desires. The mind of the sage is not different from that of the common people who desire also what the sage desires, only the sage does not allow them to run wild. Eating, drinking and sex are originated from principles, and richness, high position, and official titles are resulted from the actualization of morality. The Buddhists could say that they are all empty and talk about nothingness (*wu*). How can the Confucianists follow their suit?

I have said that there is originally no Principle of Nature (*T'ien-li*) in the human mind, it has to be manifest through human desires. When human desires attain due measure and degree, they become Principle of Nature. If there were no human desires, there would not be any Principle of Nature.[55]

Chen Ch'üeh went to the extreme: He was arguing for the position of a radical immanent monism in which the transcendent perspective simply disappears. After reading Chen's essays, in correspondence, Huang gave a rebuttal to Chen's views:

You maintained that Chou's doctrine of no desire taught Ch'an without the name of Ch'an, such a view was derived from our teacher's assertion that "The mind of Tao is the original mind of the human mind," and also that "The moral nature is none other than physical nature, apart from the physical nature, there is no moral nature." When one refers to the human mind, it is all right to talk about physical endowment, but it is not correct to talk about human desires, as the endowment of the human mind pertains to the substance that circulates without differentiation, it is something public, while human desires are confined to definite locations, they pertain to one's selfishness. The Principle of Nature is the opposite of human desires, when it increases, then the other side decreases, and when human desires increase, then the Principle of Nature decreases. That is why the desires must be further reduced, fewer and still fewer, until there is no human [artificial] desire whatsoever, then one would act purely according to the Principle of Nature. But how can you talk about reducing one's physical endowment? . . . If you want to look for the Principle of Nature through the attainment of human desires in due measure and degree, then one would be troubled for the whole life, not able to transcend worldly concerns. I am afraid that the so-called Principle of Nature would become human desires with a different appearance. As you do not like to talk about what is not manifested, so you simply dismiss all the sayings by Sung Confucianists somewhat resembling that which is not manifested as obstacles from Ch'an. However, you do not denounce residing in seriousness or preserving and cultivating. When the practice of these is not based on what is not manifested, the emphasis is on manifestation in functioning only, then there is the lack of discipline of preserving and cultivating the original substance in its entirety.[56]

Huang's arguments show that he still jealously guarded the transcendent aspect of Neo-Confucian philosophy and refused to endorse the position of a radical immanent monism. But the *Zeitgeist* was not on his side. Tai Chen (Tung-yuan, 1723–1777), after Chen Ch'üeh, independently developed a radical immanent monism and openly challenged the authority of Sung-Ming Neo-Confucian philosophy by declaring that the transcendent *li* (principle) divorced from human desires had become a tool for killing people.[57] A new paradigm emerged to replace the old one commonly accepted by Neo-Confucian philosophers. This is why I refuse to apply the label *Neo-Confucianism* to Tai Chen and Chen Ch'üeh and instead designate Huang Tsung-hsi as the last Neo-Confucian philosopher.

True, Huang Tsung-hsi's understanding of Ch'eng Hao, Chu Hsi, and Wang Yang-ming left much to be desired, as pointed out by Professor Mou Tsung-san. But such misunderstanding was not based on Huang's superficial understanding of his teacher's thought, as alluded to by Professor Mou. My study shows that it was due to loyalty to his teacher that he twisted the thoughts of those philosophers to suit his purposes. But he still worked within the paradigm of Sung-Ming Neo-Confucian philosophy and had great hopes for the future. But what he intended did not materialize; and inadvertently he contributed a great deal to bring about the advent of a paradigm that rivaled his own intentions. This makes him a tragic figure. From the perspective of intellectual history, he stood as the last in the line of Sung-Ming Neo-Confucian philosophers, and this line was broken until it was revived by contemporary Neo-Confucian philosophers in the twentieth century.[58]

NOTES

1. Huang Tsung-hsi, *The Records of Ming Scholars: A Selected Translation*, ed. Julia Ching (Honolulu: University of Hawaii Press, 1987) (hereafter cited as Huang, *Ming Scholars*).

2. Julia Ching only said, "The section on Chu Hsi is reportedly mediocre." See ibid., p. 32. This is an understatement. I have pinpointed the misinformation and wrong judgments in this section elsewhere. See Shu-hsien Liu, *Huang Tsung-hsi hsin-hsüeh ti ting-wei* (A study of Huang Tsung-hsi's philosophy of mind), pp. 62–71 (hereafter cited as Liu, *Huang Tsung-hsi*).

3. Professor Mou Tsung-san wrote a section to show Huang Tsung-hsi's misunderstanding of *t'i* in his monumental work on Sung-Ming Neo-Confucian philosophy: *Hsin-t'i yü hsing-t'i*, 2:117–135. Professor Mou maintained that Huang Tsung-hsi held the position of a monism of *ch'i* (material force) and had only a superficial understanding of his teacher Liu Tsung-chou's ideas. Granted, Huang moved even closer to the position of what I call "immanent monism," but he did so not because of his misunderstanding of Liu Tsung-chou but rather because of his loyalty to his teacher. Here my interpretation of Huang Tsung-hsi's thought is different from Professor's Mou's interpretation of his thought, even though I am greatly indebted to Professor Mou for understanding the important insights of Neo-Confucian philosophy.

4. I argued for the case quite thoroughly in my book. See Liu, *Huang Tsung-hsi*, pp. 1–29. This is the first time I presented my case in English.

5. See ibid., pp. 159–199. I am using the term *paradigm* in a loose way; it means something radically new and different within the Confucian tradition, as most scholars in the field of Chinese intellectual history use the term in this way.

6. Liang Ch'i-Ch'ao, *Chung-kuo chin-san-pai-nien hsüeh-shu shih* (A history of Chi-

nese scholarship of the last three hundred years) (Shanghai: Chung-hua shu-chü, 1936; reprinted in Taipei), pp. 48–49.

7. Ibid., p. 44.

8. Ibid., p. 46.

9. Huang, *Ming Scholars*, pp. 41–42. Note that Ching's "intention" is her translation of the term *yi* or *i*, which is rendered into English by Chan as "will."

10. Ibid., pp. 42–43.

11. Professor Ch'ien Mu was of the opinion that Huang Tsung-hsi's thought underwent great changes in his later years, as he was influenced by a fellow disciple of Liu Tsung-chou: Chen Ch'üeh; the reason he offered was that Huang wrote four different epitaphs for his deceased friend. See Ch'ien Mu, *Chung-kuo chin-san-pai-nien hsüeh-shu shih* (A history of Chinese scholarship of the last three hundred years), 2 vols. (Shanghai: Commercial Press, 1937; reprinted in Taipei), 1:42–46. But Professor Ch'ien did not get to see *Chen Ch'üeh Chi* (Collected writings of Chen Ch'üeh), 2 vols. (Beijing: Chung-hua, 1979). The editor drew the conclusion from the four epitaphs he saw that Huang's position was even further from Chen's in his later years. I subscribed to this view in my book on Huang; see Liu, *Huang Tsung-hsi*, p. 169. However, there are still interpretative problems. Most recently, Cheng Tsung-yi made a thorough study and concluded that even though in his later years Huang was willing to allow Chen Ch'üeh to present his case more fully, and had a somewhat more sympathetic understanding of his perspective, Chen was still said to have learned less than three tenths of Liu Tsung-chou's teachings; and there is no evidence whatsoever to show that Huang had ever departed from his teacher's position. See Cheng Tsung-yi, "Huang Tsung-hsi yü Chen Ch'üeh ti ssu-hsiang yin-yüan chih fen-hsi" (A study of exchange of ideas between Huang Tsung-hsi and Chen Ch'üeh), *Han-hsüeh Yen-chiu* 14, no. 2 (December 1996): 59–74.

12. Huang, *Ming Scholars*, pp. 45–46.

13. Ibid., p. 262.

14. Ibid., pp. 262–263.

15. Huang Tsung-hsi, *Tzu-liu-tzu hsing-chuang* (Master Liu's biography), in *Huang Tsung-hsi chüan-chi* (Collected writings of Huang Tsung-hsi), 12 vols. (Hangchou: Chekiang ku-chieh chu-pan-che, 1985–1994), 1:250–252 (hereafter cited as Huang, *Chüan-chi*).

16. Ibid., 1:252.

17. Ibid., 1:260.

18. Huang, *Ming Scholars*, pp. 107–160.

19. Ibid., pp. 165–201.

20. Ch'ien Te-hung, "Ko wen-lu shü-shuo" (Introduction to printing of collection of essays), in *Wang Yang-ming chüan-shu* (Collective works of Wang Yang-ming), 4 vols. (Taipei: Cheng-chung shu-chü, 1970) 1:10.

21. Huang, *Ming Scholars*, p. 118.

22. Ibid., pp. 61–62, 165.

23. Wang, *Instructions*, p. 244.

24. Ibid., pp. 244–245.

25. Huang, *Ming Scholars*, p. 113.

26. Ibid., p. 115.

27. Ibid., p. 116.

28. Wang, *Instructions*, p. 206.

29. Ibid., p. 202.

30. Huang, *Ming Scholars*, pp. 116–117.

31. Professor Mou Tsung-san had high praise for Wang Chi, as he developed even further the metaphysical aspect of Wang Yang-ming's thought. See Mou, *Yüan-shang lun (On Summum Bonum)* (Taipei: Hsüeh-sheng shu chü, 1985). Granted, Wang Chi had made significant contributions to that aspect, but he also deviated from Yang-ming's teachings and went to an extreme that brought about harmful consequences, as Yang-ming had cautioned. Thus, my assessment is somewhat different from Professor Mou's. See Liu, *Huang Tsung-hsi*, pp. 54–60.

32. See my discussion of the problem in Liu, *Huang Tsung-hsi*, pp. 41–46.

33. Professor Mou suggested that Hu Hung and Liu Tsung-chou belong to the same type of thought that sees *hsin* (mind) as a manifestation of *hsing* (nature). Thus, he proposed that the Hu-Liu approach should be added to Ch'eng-Chu and Lu-Wang to form a third branch of Neo-Confucian philosophy. See Mou, *Hsin-t'i*, 1:42–60. Professor Mou's ideas are very original and provocative from a philosophical point of view. From the perspective of intellectual history, however, even Professor Mou conceded that Liu developed his thought independently of Hu, and I find that there are significant differences between the two approaches.

34. See Liu, *Huang Tsung-hsi*, pp. 61–90.

35. Ibid., pp. 31–60.

36. Huang, *Ming Scholars*, pp. 128–129.

37. Ibid., pp. 129–130.

38. Ibid., pp. 104–105.

39. Ibid., p. 46.

40. Ibid., p. 41.

41. See Ch'üan Tsu-wang, *Chieh-ch'i-t'ing chi* (Collected writings) (Taipei: Commercial Press, 1968), 1:131–141.

42. I could not have written my book on Huang Tsung-hsi until these important materials were published in the first volume of Huang's *Collected Writings*; see note 15.

43. See the last chapter.

44. Wang, *Instructions*, pp. 80–81.

45. Ibid., pp. 257–258.

46. Huang, *Chüan-chi*, 1:134.

47. Ibid., 1:149.

48. Wang, *Instructions*, p. 272.

49. Huang, *Chüan-chi*, 1:303.

50. Ibid., 1:304.

51. Ibid., 1:141.

52. Ibid., 1:110.

53. Huang, *Ming Scholars*, p. 45, with slight modification.

54. *Chen Ch'üeh Chi*, 2:451; see note 11.

55. Ibid., 2:461.

56. Huang, *Chüan-chi*, 10:152–154.

57. This is why I refuse to apply the term *Neo-Confucianism* to early Ch'ing philosophy such as Tai Chen's. When Derk Bodde translated Fung Yu-lan's *A History of Chinese Philosophy* into English, he rendered the term *Tao-hsüeh* into Neo-Confucianism, used it in chapter headings, and applied the term to early Ch'ing philosophy as if these philosophies still belonged in the same paradigm. See Fung, *History*,

Vol. 2, chs. 10, 15. I have argued against such usage elsewhere; see Shu-hsien Liu,
"Some Reflections on the Sung-Ming Understanding of Mind, Nature, and Reason,"
Journal of the Institute of Chinese Studies of the Chinese University of Hong Kong 21
(1990): 331–332.

   58. See Liu, *Huang Tsung-hsi*, pp. 189–199.

Epilogue

In writing this book I have presupposed a contemporary Neo-Confucian perspective. I have also subscribed to the view of Three Epochs in Confucian philosophy, which was first initiated by Professor Mou Tsung-san and was later spread to the world by Professor Tu Wei-ming, who had studied under Professor Mou as a college student.[1]

The First Epoch refers to the late Chou of the pre-Ch'in period (ended in 221 B.C.) when the Chou culture was in decline, and it is said that a hundred schools were in contention to find a way to solve the problems of the day. This was the first golden age for Chinese philosophy, and Confucianism was only one of the schools that suggested instilling new spirit into the Chou system of rituals and ceremonies to restore order and peace to the world. Confucius was the spiritual leader of the movement, followed by another major figure in the movement: Mencius. Although Confucianism was adopted as the state doctrine in 136 B.C. during the Han period, from a philosophical perspective the spirit of Confucianism was in decline, as the Neo-Confucian philosophers claimed that the line of transmission of the Way had been broken since the time of Mencius.

The Second Epoch refers to the age of Sung (Yüan)-Ming Neo-Confucian philosophy. Chou Tun-i was honored as the forerunner of the movement. Under the promotion of the Ch'eng brothers, it became the main stream of Chinese philosophy, which enjoyed another golden age with Ch'eng-Chu, Lu-Wang, and other schools contending with one another. The major challenge the Neo-Confucian philosophers had to face was Buddhism, which was imported into China from India. They successfully took up the challenge, developed sophisticated new ideas, and absorbed important insights from both Buddhism and

Neo-Taoism. By the late Ming, there was a strong eclectic tendency that unified the three major traditions that became the backbone of the Chinese civilization.

Now the Third Epoch enters the scene. The challenge it has to face is far more stringent than the challenges of the other two epochs. In the last 200 years it had appeared that the Chinese tradition simply could not withstand the onslaught of a superior modern Western civilization, and Confucianism was thought to be something dead, something only found in museums.[2] It is under such unlikely circumstances that the contemporary Neo-Confucian philosophy as a movement emerged. At least another book would be required to tell the story of contemporary Neo-Confucian philosophy. Here I can only provide some background clues that led to the emergence of the movement.[3]

Huang Tsung-hsi has been identified as the last Sung-Ming Neo-Confucian philosopher. For reasons not completely known to us, even though in the early Ch'ing period Ch'eng-Chu teachings were honored as the orthodoxy by the state, suddenly scholars all flocked to historical scholarship and virtually paid no attention to philosophy at all.[4] In the late Ch'ing period, K'ang Yu-wei (1858–1927) pushed for radical reform within the Confucian framework but failed miserably in his attempt. The last dynasty fell in 1912 and was replaced by the Republic of China. In the early twentieth century, it had been vogue to place all the blame on the Confucian tradition. During the May Fourth cultural movement, begun in 1919, the slogans were ''Down with the Confucian shop!'' and ''Throw the stitched volumes into the toilet!''[5] Western learning came to the fore. The intellectual leader in those days, Hu Shih (1891–1962), the famous disciple of John Dewey, at one time advocated wholesale Westernization or modernization. But even his ideas of gradual reform were cast aside, as China had to face both serious internal problems and foreign power domination, culminating in the Japanese invasion in 1937. To survive, the Chinese adopted more and more radical means.

Eventually, these events led to the establishment of the People's Republic of China in 1949 under the leadership of Chairman Mao Tse-tung (1893–1976) and a Marxist-Leninist-Maoist official ideology. Under the direction of Mao and the Gang of Four, the Anti-Confucius Campaign reached its climax during the disastrous Cultural Revolution from 1967 to 1977. It was only after the death of Mao that China returned to a more moderate policy, and Confucius's fortune has gradually changed in recent years. Now that China is much more open to the outside world, the future of Chinese philosophy will depend on the interaction between the Marxist, the liberal Western, and the Neo-Confucian traditions.

Clearly, we can see that Confucianism does not occupy a place in mainstream Chinese thought in the present century. But this does not mean that Confucianism has been uprooted entirely. Some of its ideas and practices have become long-trenched habits of the Chinese that have produced beneficial as well as harmful consequences. Thus, I have always maintained that both heritage and the burden of tradition come from the same source. Every individual is deeply embedded in a certain culture—one cannot escape it. Only if one profoundly understands its strengths as well as its limitations can one hope to reach out from a firm foundation in order to look for a broader horizon in the future. This certainly applies to our assessment of the Confucian tradition.

In fact, it was during the most difficult wartimes that the contemporary Neo-Confucian movement began to take shape. Fung Yu-lan (1895–1990) firmly believed that after the worst is over, there will be a new beginning. He started by looking at the past and published his famous history of Chinese philosophy in the early 1930s; then he attempted to reconstruct Neo-Confucian philosophy and published six books of his own philosophy, written from when World War II began until it was over. His thoughts are ingenious, and his style is lucid. At one time, he was the most famous contemporary Neo-Confucian philosopher in China. After the Communist takeover of the Chinese Mainland in 1949, however, he gave up his thought, devoid of followers.[6]

Strangely enough, the one who really started a return to the Confucian tradition was Hsiung Shih-li (1885–1968), an obscure figure in Chinese society. As a young man he engaged in revolutionary activities to overthrow the Manchu dynasty. He turned to philosophy in middle age, as he was deeply puzzled by the problems of life. He studied Buddhism, finally returning to the Confucian tradition and developing a philosophy of creativity based on the insights he had learned from the *Book of Changes*. He published probably the most original work of philosophy of his time, *Hsin wei-shih lun* (New consciousness-only doctrine), which caused a great deal of controversy because of its critique of Buddhist philosophy. However, it also attracted a great deal of attention in the scholarly world. According to Wing-tsit Chan, Hsiung Shih-li has influenced more young Chinese philosophers than any other contemporary Chinese philosopher; in 1956 he restated his entire philosophy in a book entitled *Yüan-ju* (An inquiry on Confucianism)—a book not widely circulated, devoid of Communist slogans.[7]

The main difference between Hsiung Shih-li and Fung Yu-lan lies in that Fung takes *liang-chih* (innate knowledge) only as a postulate, while Hsiung takes it to be a presence. Hsiung greatly inspired his disciples with his spirit, though none of them followed his doctrines and preferred to develop their own thoughts to answer the challenges from the West.

T'ang Chün-i (1909–1978), Mou Tsung-san (1909–1995), and Hsü Fu-kuan (1903–1982) fled to Hong Kong and Taiwan and became the mainstay of contemporary Neo-Confucianism. They, along with Carsun Chang (1887–1969), signed the famous document "A Manifesto for a Reappraisal of Sinology and Reconstruction of Chinese Culture" on New Year's day 1958, which marked the birthday of the overseas contemporary Neo-Confucian philosophy movement.[8] They refused to follow archaeological, missionary, or political approaches to studying Chinese culture; they urged Western intellectuals to seek understanding of it, with sympathy and respect, and to try to dig deeply into the spiritual roots of that culture by studying the learning of mind and nature (*hsin-hsing-*

chih-hsüeh). Even though they made introspective criticisms of the shortcomings and limitations of the Chinese culture, and maintained that the Chinese must learn science and democracy from the West to broaden their own horizons, they urged the West to learn these five things from Chinese thought:

1. The spirit to assert what is here and now and to let everything go [in order for nature to take its own course];
2. All-round and all-embracing understanding or wisdom;
3. A feeling of warmth and compassion;
4. The wisdom of how to perpetuate its culture;
5. The attitude that the whole world is like one family.[9]

It seemed audacious for a few refugee Chinese scholars to advise the rich and powerful West; so it is no wonder that at the time of its publication the document was totally ignored. However, after nearly forty years, the accumulated scholarship and insights developed by the Neo-Confucian scholars began receiving more recognition and appreciation than ever before. In recent years, contemporary Neo-Confucianism has become a popular subject for study both on Mainland China and in the scholarly world of Western sinology. Because of the success of Japan and the four minidragons that share a Confucian background, there is more incentive to study the Confucian tradition seriously.[10]

The counsels given appear to make a lot of sense, as we are now forced to live in a global village peacefully and harmoniously together if mankind and the earth are not to perish. Perhaps the Third Epoch cannot be compared to the First and the Second Epochs, but in an age where multiculturalism has become vogue, there is much to learn about the Chinese culture, and it certainly has much to contribute to the world. In a recent article on the contemporary significance of Chinese philosophy, I made the following observations:

> If I may be allowed to borrow a dialectical scheme from Hegel in a very loose sense, I would like to suggest that the development of Chinese thought since the middle of Ch'ing dynasty has gone through three stages which may be roughly described as follows:
>
> 1. The Chinese were shocked to find the superiority of Western science and technology. They tried to absorb such Western achievements into their own culture, but they still believed in the basic soundness of the foundation of their traditional culture.
>
> 2. The Chinese were fed up with their own tradition; they could not find anything valuable in it. Tradition only served as the stumbling block to obstruct any move toward future progress. Hope only lay in a quick Westernization process.
>
> 3. The Chinese came to realize that the West was not all good and their tradition was not all bad. The Western culture as well as the modernization process had its problems. Although many traditional things had to go, some traditional

insights should be reconstructed in such a way that they might make significant contributions in order for us to move toward the future. A synthesis based on the realistic understanding of the problems of man and his world had to be sought.[11]

As I have already told the story of classical and Sung-Ming Confucian philosophy in this book, I intend to write a sequel to this volume to tell the story of contemporary Neo-Confucian philosophy in great detail.

NOTES

1. Tu Wei-ming, "Confucianism," in *Our Religions*, ed. Arvind Sharma (New York: HarperCollins Publishers, 1993).

2. Joseph R. Levenson, *Confucian China and Its Modern Fate: A Trilogy*, Vol. 3 (Berkeley: University of California Press, 1968).

3. Shu-hsien Liu, "Postwar Neo-Confucian Philosophy: Its Development and Issues," in *Religious Issues and Interreligious Dialogues*, ed. Charles Wei-hsun Fu and Gerhard E. Spiegler (Westport, Conn.: Greenwood Press, 1989), pp. 277–302.

4. Benjamin A. Elman, *From Philosophy to Philology* (Cambridge: Harvard University Press, 1984).

5. Chow Tse-tsung, *The May-Fourth Movement: Intellectual Revolution in Modern China* (Cambridge: Harvard University Press, 1960).

6. Chan, *Source Book*, pp. 751–754.

7. Ibid., pp. 763–765.

8. "A Manifesto for a Reappraisal of Sinology and Reconstruction of Chinese Culture," in Carsun Chang, *The Development of Neo-Confucian Thought*, 2 vols. (New York: Bookman Associates, 1957–1962), 2:455–483.

9. Ibid., 2:461.

10. Tu Wei-ming, ed., *Confucian Tradition in East-Asia Modernity: Moral Education and Economic Culture in Japan and the Four Mini-Dragons* (Cambridge: Harvard University Press, 1996).

11. Shu-hsien Liu, "The Contemporary Significance of Chinese Philosophy," *Journal of Chinese Philosophy* 13, no. 2 (June 1986): 204.

Selected Bibliography

For traditional texts I used mostly the editions of ssu-pu pei-yao (Essentials of the Four Libraries) and ssu-pu ts'ung-k'an (Four Libraries Series), respectively abbreviated as SPPY and SPTK.

Cassirer, Ernst. *An Essay on Man.* New Haven, Conn.: Yale University Press, 1944.

Chan, Wing-tsit, trans. and comp. *A Source Book in Chinese Philosophy.* Princeton, N.J.: Princeton University Press, 1963.

———, ed. *Chu Hsi and Neo-Confucianism.* Honolulu: University of Hawaii Press, 1986.

Ch'ien, Mu. *Chu-tzu hsin-hsüeh-an* (A new study of Chu Hsi). 5 vols. Taipei: San-min-shu-chü, 1971.

Ching, Julia, trans. *The Philosophical Letters of Wang Yang-ming.* Columbia: University of South Carolina Press, 1972.

———. *To Acquire Wisdom: The Way of Wang Yang-ming.* New York: Columbia University Press, 1976.

de Bary, William Theodore. *Learning for One's Self: Essays on the Individual in Neo-Confucian Thought.* New York: Columbia University Press, 1991.

Fang, Thomé H. *The Chinese View of Life.* Hong Kong: The Union Press, 1957.

———. *Chinese Philosophy: Its Spirit and Its Development.* Taipei: Linking Pub. Co., 1981.

Fingarette, Herbert. *Confucius: The Secular as Sacred.* New York: Harper and Row, 1972.

Fung, Yu-lan. *A Short History of Chinese Philosophy.* New York: Free Press, 1948.

———. *A History of Chinese Philosophy.* Translated by Derk Bodde. 2 vols. Princeton, N.J.: Princeton University Press, 1952–1953.

Huang Tsung-hsi. *Tzu-liu-tzu hsing-chuang* (Master Liu's biography). In *Huang Tsung-*

hsi chüan-chi (Collected writings of Huang Tsung-hsi). 12 vols. Hangchou: Chekiang ku-chieh chu-pan-che, 1985–1994.

———. *The Records of Ming Scholars: A Selected Translation.* Edited by Julia Ching. Honolulu: University of Hawaii Press, 1987.

Lau, D. C., trans. *Confucius: The Analects.* Hong Kong: Chinese University Press, 1983.

Legge, James, trans. *The Four Books.* New York: Paragon Reprint Corp., 1966.

Liu, Shu-hsien. *Chu-tzu che-hsüeh ssu-hsiang ti fan-chen yü wan-ch'eng* (The development and completion of Chu Hsi's philosophical thought). Taipei: Hsüeh-sheng-shu-chü, 1982. Rev. and enlarg. 3rd ed., 1995.

———. *Huang Tsung-hsi hsin-hsüeh ti ting-wei* (A study of Huang Tsung-hsi's philosophy of mind). Taipei: Asian Culture Co., 1986.

Metzger, Thomas A. *Escape from Predicament.* New York: Columbia University Press, 1977.

Mou, Tsung-san. *Hsin-t'i yü hsing-t'i* (The metaphysical principle of the mind and nature). 3 vols. Taipei: Cheng-chung-shu-chü. 1968–1969.

———. *Ts'ung Lu Hsiang-shan tao Liu Ch'i-shan* (From Lu Hsiang-shan to Liu Ch'i-shan). Taipei: Hsüeh-sheng-shu-chü, 1979.

Needham, Joseph. *Science and Civilization in China.* Vol. 2. Cambridge: Cambridge University Press, 1956.

Northrop, F.S.C. *The Meeting of East and West.* New York: Macmillan Co., 1945.

Schwartz, Benjamin I. *The World of Thought in Ancient China.* Cambridge, Mass.: Harvard University Press, 1985.

Shun, Kwong-loi. *Mencius and Early Chinese Thought.* Stanford: Stanford University Press, 1997.

Tillich, Paul. *Systematic Theology.* 3 vols. Chicago: Chicago University Press, 1951, 1957, 1963.

Tu, Wei-ming. *Neo-Confucian Thought* in *Action: Wang Yang-ming's Youth (1472–1509).* Berkeley: University of California Press, 1976.

———. "Confucianism." In *Our Religions,* edited by Arvind Sharma. New York: HarperCollins Publishers, 1993.

Wang, Yang-ming. *Instructions for Practical Living and Other Neo-Confucian Writings.* Translated by Wing-tsit Chan. New York: Columbia University Press, 1963.

Wang, Mou-hung. *Chu-tzu nien-p'u* (Chronological biography of Master Chu). Taipei: Shih-chieh shu-chü, 1973.

Whitehead, A. N. *Science and the Modern World.* New York: Fress Press, 1967. First published by Macmillan Co., 1925.

———. *Process and Reality.* New York: Free Press, 1969.

Index

About the Author

SHU-HSIEN LIU is Chair Professor of Chinese Philosophy at the Chinese University of Hong Kong. He has published many articles and books both in English and in Chinese. He has been widely recognized as a representative of contemporary Neo-Confucianism.